IFLA Publications

Edited by
Janine Schmidt and Joseph Hafner

International Federation of Library Associations and Institutions
Fédération Internationale des Associations de Bibliothécaires et des Bibliothèques
Internationaler Verband der bibliothekarischen Vereine und Institutionen
Международная Федерация Библиотечных Ассоциаций и Учреждений
Federación Internacional de Asociaciones de Bibliotecarios y Bibliotecas
国际图书馆协会与机构联合会
الاتحاد الدولي لجمعيات ومؤسسات المكتبات

Volume 185

New Horizons in Artificial Intelligence in Libraries

Edited by
Edmund Balnaves, Leda Bultrini, Andrew Cox and
Raymond Uzwyshyn

DE GRUYTER
SAUR

ISBN 978-3-11-133571-1
e-ISBN (PDF) 978-3-11-133643-5
e-ISBN (EPUB) 978-3-11-133681-7
ISSN 0344-6891
DOI https://doi.org/10.1515/9783111336435

Library of Congress Control Number: 2024943605

Bibliographic information published by the Deutsche Nationalbibliothek
The Deutsche Nationalbibliothek lists this publication in the Deutsche Nationalbibliografie;
detailed bibliographic data is available on the Internet at http://dnb.dnb.de.

© 2025 with the author(s), editing © 2025 Edmund Balnaves, Leda Bultrini, Andrew Cox and Raymond
Uzwyshyn, published by Walter de Gruyter GmbH, Berlin/Boston. This book is published with open
access at www.degruyter.com.

Cover Image: Imaginima / iStock / Getty Images Plus
Typesetting: Dr Rainer Ostermann, München

www.degruyter.com

Questions about General Product Safety Regulation: productsafety@degruyterbrill.com

Contents

About IFLA

www.ifla.org

IFLA (The International Federation of Library Associations and Institutions) is the leading international body representing the interests of library and information services and their users. It is the global voice of the library and information profession. IFLA provides information specialists throughout the world with a forum for exchanging ideas and promoting international cooperation, research, and development in all fields of library activity and information service. IFLA is one of the means through which libraries, information centres, and information professionals worldwide can formulate their goals, exert their influence as a group, protect their interests, and find solutions to global problems.

IFLA's mission to inspire, engage, enable and connect the global library field can only be fulfilled with the co-operation and active involvement of its members and affiliates. Currently, approximately 1,600 associations, institutions and individuals, from widely divergent cultural backgrounds are working together to further this mission Through its formal membership, IFLA directly or indirectly represents some 500,000 library and information professionals worldwide.

IFLA pursues its vision of a strong and united library field powering literate, informed and participatory societies through a variety of channels, including the publication of a major journal, as well as guidelines, reports and monographs on a wide range of topics. IFLA organizes webinars and workshops around the world to enhance professional practice and increase awareness of the growing importance of libraries in the digital age. All this is done in collaboration with a number of other non-governmental organizations, funding bodies and international agencies such as UNESCO and WIPO. The Federation's website is the key source of information about IFLA, its policies and activities: www.ifla.org.

Library and information professionals gather annually at the IFLA World Library and Information Congress, held in August each year in cities around the world. IFLA was founded in Edinburgh, Scotland, in 1927 at an international conference of national library directors. IFLA was registered in the Netherlands in 1971. The National Library of the Netherlands (Koninklijke Bibliotheek) in The Hague, generously provides the facilities for our headquarters. Regional offices are located in Argentina, South Africa and Singapore.

Preface

This book distils the experiences from the International Federation of Library Associations and Institutions (IFLA) Information Technology Section conferences focussed on artificial intelligence (AI) which were held in Dublin and Galway, Ireland and Singapore in 2022 and 2023. It brings together working projects and observations on the ethics and practice of AI in the library field. It is a book that explores the implications for libraries of engaging with AI, and the current and potential applications of AI in libraries. It highlights both technology and ethics of AI in libraries, the governance and ethical considerations for engaging in AI and showcases various library IT projects, collaborations, and future uses of AI tools and techniques that can enhance the services, progress and competitive advantage of libraries.

Aspects of AI addressed within the book include:
- Machine and deep learning, content indexing, metadata, labelling and summation: AI can automate the process of indexing and summarising documents, images and audiovisual media, making them more accessible and discoverable across different disciplines and contexts
- Information retrieval and analysis: AI can help users find and analyse relevant information from large and complex data sources, using natural language processing, machine learning, neural nets, deep learning and semantic web technologies
- User engagement and personalisation: AI can improve user experience and satisfaction by providing personalised recommendations, feedback, and assistance, using chatbots, voice assistants, and sentiment analysis, and
- Library management and operations: AI offers the promise of optimising library workflows and processes by automating tasks, reducing errors, and saving time and resources, using robotics, computer vision, and predictive analytics. It can open possibilities for new service delivery options, including enhanced 24/7 support for library operations including summarising and annotating research and other user assistance.

The book is divided into four sections:
- Section 1: Current Directions in Artificial Intelligence for Libraries, which provides an overview of AI and its intersection with libraries and robotics
- Section 2: Implications for Use of Artificial Intelligence in Libraries and Education, which extends the discussion of AI into the domains of ethics, the policy implications for governance, usage in the educational and learning domains and the infrastructure implications of AI

- Section 3: Projects in Machine Learning and Natural Language Processing, which provides deep dives into projects demonstrating the use of AI across key technology applications for libraries in machine learning and natural language processing, and
- Section 4: Artificial Intelligence in Library Services, which explores practical case studies in engaging with AI in different library applications.

We present this book as a resource for librarians who want to learn more about the opportunities and challenges of AI in the library field, commend it to you, the reader, and look forward to an exciting future for the application and use of artificial intelligence in libraries.

An Artificial Intelligence Special Interest Group (AI SIG) is sponsored by the IFLA Information Technology Section. Projects undertaken by the Group are publicised on the IFLA website, with two of particular interest: Developing a Library Strategic Response to Artificial Intelligence and Generative AI for Library and Information Professionals.

The area of AI is fast moving. This publication provides the reader with an opportunity to survey the many aspects of the application of recent developments in AI in the library context. The book is the culmination of the real and human projects and efforts of the authors, editors and our publisher, De Gruyter. It is they who have made this publication possible and we thank all involved. We gratefully acknowledge the funding from IFLA that has enabled this publication to be released in open access, and the work of Janine Schmidt, the Series Editor, in the final editing of the publication.

Edmund Balnaves, Leda Bultrini, Andrew Cox and Raymond Uzwyshyn, Editors

Edmund Balnaves

1 Artificial Intelligence and Libraries: An Introduction

Abstract: Artificial Intelligence (AI) is the use of computer systems to achieve tasks that would normally require human interpretive intervention. AI is integrally associated with Big Data and the Internet of Things, with large data stores of text, images, and videos on an extensive and wide-ranging scale providing the learning base. While AI does not purport to replace human cognition, the use of AI is becoming pervasive throughout society. It is present in smart phones to understand speech, help navigation and improve usability of apps. It is used in internet searching, surveillance systems, social credit systems, classification, and annotation systems. AI is used in advertising to match customers to products, and in social media to ensure content is exposed in a tightly directed way. AI is increasingly available or already present in the systems used by libraries. This chapter provides the background and context for this book *New Horizons in Artificial Intelligence in Libraries* which focuses on the current uses of AI in libraries and explores ways to prepare for and optimise the use of AI in libraries.

Keywords: Artificial intelligence; Big data; Internet of things; Machine learning

What is Artificial Intelligence?

Artificial Intelligence (AI) is the use of computer systems to achieve tasks that would normally require human interpretive intervention and includes:
- Interpreting images for place, facial or object recognition
- Interpreting audio for language recognition and translation
- Analysing data in depth and breadth to discern patterns
- Controlling and managing movement of robotics in a real physical environment, and
- Conversational dialogue management that recognises, interprets and responds appropriately.

The concept of AI dates back to the early stages of computers and the philosophical examination of the implications of emerging computer technology, and in particular to a workshop in 1956 at Dartmouth College (McCarthy et al. 1995) that included the early greats of computer science John McCarthy and Marvin Minsky. The initial emphasis on expert systems gave way to the emergence of deep learning models.

The value of AI in classification when used with large image stores was explored in projects such as the ImageNet Large Scale Visual Recognition (Krizhevsky, Sutskever, and Hinton 2012). Core to advances in AI in the last decade has been leveraging large online resources coupled with large-scale AI computing architectures to build models that can give credible predictive insights.

Big Data and the Internet of Things can be combined to operate at scale and in the real world. The core elements of AI bring together Big Data, text and image pattern recognition, natural language processing (NLP), and importantly the underpinning hardware capability to crunch through large data sets. The computer capabilities of massive parallel processing needed for AI originated with their use in the graphics processing units (GPUs) that enabled the hyperreal games now available on the market. GPUs and field-programmable gate arrays (FPGAs) provided the grunt needed for very large-scale model development and exploration of inferencing engines needed for AI (VerWay 2022, 36). AI toolkits, many written in the Python programming language or C, distil a range of complex pattern recognition algorithm and data management tools into simple and elegant processing pipelines to develop and train patterns in a large body of data to create models and apply real life data against the models to discern matches. These toolkits have provided the core to a rapidly evolving ecosystem of software applications covering all aspects of national language processing, pattern recognition and image recognition.

None of the work on AI has achieved human cognition and progress to date has not yielded the moment of singularity where computers become self-aware or achieve a level of artificial consciousness (Floridi and Chiriatti 2022). Nevertheless, use of AI tools embedded in many systems is becoming pervasive and persuasive. AI apps have been present on smart phones for many years and take an increasingly important role in extending the utility of the device to understand speech, dynamically translate audio inputs, assist with navigation and improve usability of apps.

The addition of AI to society creates a very new socio-political dynamic. While a few writers in the past forecast significant impacts of computer science developments, socialist theorists of the 19th and 20th centuries did not in general anticipate the effect on both labour and the political process the influence that AI systems might have. Potentially a class-based society is being supplanted by an information-based society. In its very nature, the information society is the perfect context for the application of artificial intelligence systems. In social media AI can be used to ensure that content emerges in a tightly directed way, with the potential to shape social ideas by biassing the content from social media systems in a particular direction. The Social Credit System in China involving a record system which tracks and evaluates businesses, individuals and government institutions for trustworthiness and China's Skynet ubiquitous surveillance system intrinsically depend on the toolsets of AI to achieve normative social goals. AI raises the possibility of at-scale social and behavioural intervention by both governments and global commercial entities such as Facebook, Google and Microsoft.

In the context of libraries, Bourg (2017) raises the question: what does it mean to maximise our collections for humans and what does it mean to maximise them for machines and algorithms? The process of re-envisaging the nature of the library has been gathering pace since the first library applications in machine learning emerged (Coleman 2017; Cordell 2020; Johnson 2018) and is exemplified in the formation of the International Federation of Library Associations and Institutions (IFLA) Artificial Intelligence Special Interest Group in 2022.

Central to the discussion of AI in libraries is the algorithm used to train AI systems to provide useful responses. Algorithm is the term used to encompass the set of machine learning techniques that may be deployed to glean intelligence from data, and probably more accurately refers to the process of model creation. The difficulty with the term algorithm is that it lends itself to an anthropomorphic interpretation of AI that is not accurate. Machine learning uses a range of techniques to harness the speed of computers in image, textual, location and other data points to derive an interpretive model from the data. The model can then be used to suggest a range of things: a face matched to a name, an emotional state or reaction, a set of structured terms to describe a document or image, a location based on an image, and many other similar activities. The underlying dataset and algorithm used in AI can lead to bias in the results and can be particularly visible in the ways in which AI can skew search results based on biases in the underlying training data (Snow 2018).

In 2018 the use of AI for initial job candidate selection emerged with the Russian bot Vera (Palmer 2018). Recent innovations include ChatGPT from OpenAI. GPT stands for Generative Pretrained Transformer and constitutes a model that takes the foundation of large text corpus modelling and integrates it with a neural network to parse the query and structure a logical response. The first GPT model was made available in 2018. Continual updates have been made and the current generation of the GPT architecture impressively goes beyond national language responses to provide code-meaningful responses to programming questions and semantically meaningful conversations and question responses. The semantic interpretation implied by the transformer neural networks is a generational advance in the capabilities of AI and has potentially profound implications in many areas.

An extension of ChatGPT is DALL-E, an AI image generating neural network built on a twelve billion-parameter version of GPT-3. DALL-E was trained on a data set of text-image pairs and can generate images from user-submitted text prompts. ChatGPT and DALL-E were both developed by OpenAI. The company name Open AI implies but does not mean that its systems are open-source with content available for others to use freely. DALL-E can creatively respond with image content to queries based on requested text descriptions. For example, the following query: "Give me a logo for a search and discovery system that incorporates artificial intelligence recommendations" yielded the creative result (Figure 1.1).

Figure 1.1: Logo Created by AI for a Search and Discovery System

Microsoft made headlines in 2020 replacing journalists with machine-generated story selection rather than human-curated story selection for the MSN home page (Waterson 2020) and highlighted the risks of job displacement with the use of AI. The further advances represented by ChatGPT take the potential risks to another order. AI is capable of sophisticated responses across many disciplines. The answers provided to queries are well crafted and explanatory, even when they contain elements of factual errors.

Implications of Artificial Intelligence for Libraries

Public libraries have grown in importance as gateways to information resources in a world where internet access is a prerequisite for engagement in community and social endeavours. The library has both explanatory and access roles. The transition to electronic collections heralded by Breeding (2011) has seen dramatic changes in research-oriented libraries. The preference for digital content has become entrenched in research institutions and the availability of AI-enhanced discovery tools is transforming the discovery, use and reuse of research data. The full implications of ChatGPT for research and reference librarians are yet to be seen. Some librarians may fear the development of AI in the research context, but others will embrace the potential and establish new and innovative services to enhance services provided to researchers.

Library integrated automation or management systems might be viewed as the precursors to AI within libraries. They have fundamentally changed the activities conducted by librarians, particularly as far as cataloguing and lending functions are concerned. Cataloguers have become metadata experts and subject analysts.

Cataloguing and classification have become shared activities across the world optimising collaborative efforts to improve the effectiveness of libraries and yield higher quality and consistency in item descriptions, content analysis, and information resource discovery. The developments have come at the practical cost of jobs on the ground for some librarians who have transferred to alternative roles. For example, the traditional bibliographic cataloguer once the quintessential exemplar of the library profession, is now a rare species.

The cataloguing role has changed considerably facilitated by library automation and touches the lives of fewer members of the profession. Outsourcing of library functions related to acquisition and selection of library collections and inclusion of the purchase of records with information resources has also changed activities. AI will be added to this mix to automate classification recommendations While there may be concern over algorithmic bias in machine learning systems, the bias in historical traditional classification schemes may be no better. The first edition of the Dewey Decimal Classification scheme is replete with unconscious and conscious bias (Mai 2016).

There is enormous potential for machine learning to enhance the quality of the work of librarians and to enrich access to the content of library collections held locally or accessed remotely in ways that might otherwise be impossible. The role of the metadata librarian is alive and well as the adjudicator of semantic description and content along with enhanced roles for reference librarians who can interact in new ways with large data and information stores.

The momentum of AI innovation and adoption is perhaps beyond the capability of libraries to control or manage. A rearguard action to block AI in what may well be a new industrial revolution in the making is not likely to be fruitful. By engaging with AI technology and enhancing knowledge and expertise concerning AI, the library and information profession can come to grips with its limits, risks, and opportunities. Through understanding the limits and capabilities of AI systems, librarians will be able to influence developments and provide new services to enhance information access and use for their communities.

There are many opportunities for the application of AI in libraries with the potential for the extension of activities in ways not currently possible. For instance, 24 x 7 assistance service can be provided through chatbots or in-library robotic assistants for check-in and checkout functions. The improvement of discovery for large collections of resources through automated classification, organisation, and retrieval makes possible at scale access to wonderful resources worldwide.

The debate regarding algorithmic bias is relevant to the library profession and the best way to engage in the debate is to participate in the work in the area. Many libraries are already participating in the AI debates. The bias in machine learning design can come from the source data sets which might be ethnically or culturally homogeneous, or in machine learning rules or algorithms used. In social media and online news, the rules around story selection become all the more important where systematic bias may be an inadvertent or deliberate element in framing the information landscape presented to the user. AI systems may also have value in detecting and removing or rebalancing bias present in existing systems. AI systems could, for instance, assist with daunting task of correcting historical classification bias in historical bibliographic databases.

Governance of Artificial Intelligence

There has been considerable debate within the community about the control of the use of AI and its future governance both within institutions and internationally. Institutional governance rules may increasingly incorporate mandates around the use of AI in the institution. The library profession can play a role in encouraging transparency in the use of AI. The debate around algorithmic bias is a case in point. The debates itself can lead to an awareness of the concerns and the need for adaptation and change in legislation around the world. The moves within the European Union to provide legislation related to AI (European Parliament 2023) and to enhance privacy and choice on the internet are cases in point. Algorithmic disclosure is all about transparency and the ability to understand the rules and assumptions that feed decision making. Openness enables a health public discourse about algorithms and their use and application.

The effectiveness of the open-source community illustrates the value of publishing coding and programming for scrutiny (Balnaves 2008). While openness permits attackers to understand vulnerability, it also facilitates discovery and resolution of vulnerabilities. Visibility fits well with the criteria for explainable machine learning outlined by Psychoula and others:

> There are several important elements to consider, and be able to explain, when creating automated decision-making systems:
> (1) The rationale behind the decision should be easily accessible and understandable
> (2) The system should maximise the accuracy and reliability of the decision.
> (3) The underlying data and features that may lead to bias or unfair decisions
> (4) The context in which the AI is deployed and the impact the automated decision might have for an individual or society (Psychoula et al. 2021, 50)

While the designers of AI systems might, for proprietary reasons, look askance at visibility into their systems, it is arguable that an open approach promotes a virtual cycle of improvement. Lack of regard for these principles was precisely the failure exhibited in implementing the Robodebt scheme in Australia (Shah 2023). The government took an automated algorithmic approach to assessing social security debt using model-based approximations. The result was the creation of debt notices based on estimates rather than actual social security debt figures, and in some cases the results were wildly wrong. The errors made resulted in great trauma for the people involved, including several deaths by suicide. The whole approach was ultimately found to be illegal in a subsequent class action brought against the government and harrowing insights from a Royal Commission (Australia. Royal Commission into the Robodebt Scheme 2023). Appropriate levels of governance and development frameworks along with legislative control are acutely important where AI is making critical judgements and will become even more necessary as AI becomes indistinguishable from a human response.

AI systems, once implemented, have potential risks, including spoofing or poisoning, where falsified data is fed to the system to skew the AI models developed (Laplante and Amaba 2021, 20). Where judgements are being made on an algorithmic basis, the risk of false positives is also a significant factor. Mortati and Carmel explore the issue of false positives in the case of cheating detection systems, an issue made all the more complex with the recent advent of ChatGPT (Mortati and Carmel 2021, 92).

How can libraries engage in AI firsthand? Chatbots are an uncomplicated way in which librarians can engage in the machine learning process to gain exposure to both the strengths and limitations of AI. Many tools for chatbot development are readily available online and allow free use. Most include natural language processing capabilities and methods to integrate additional textual analysis tools. Even without deploying chatbots, experimenting with them is an excellent way to understand both the opportunities and limitations of AI. Most people have undoubtedly experienced the friendly but hopelessly incompetent chatbots thrown up on websites by banks and other corporate entities as replacements for human interaction. They are examples of AI systems in their infancy. There is a long way to go in this area, but they will become ubiquitous in online systems.

Many toolkits for AI are open-source. For the adventurous who are willing to venture into coding, there are guides and examples abounding on the web to assist in experimenting with recommender systems which could make suggestions to library users.

The challenges of appropriate deployment of AI combine technological and governance elements. It is typical of any technological advance that governance and control elements lag behind the rapid advances occurring. The International Federation of Library Associations and Institutions (IFLA) has released a statement on libraries and AI that provides a good framework for considering the issues for AI in libraries (IFLA 2020). The European Union's High Level Expert Group on Arti-

<u>ficial Intelligence</u> has defined concerns in relation to AI and developed ethics guide-
lines which lists <u>seven key requirements</u> for trustworthiness of AI systems:

1. Human agency and oversight
2. Technical robustness and safety
3. Privacy and data governance
4. Transparency
5. Diversity, non-discrimination, and fairness
6. Societal and environmental wellbeing
7. Accountability (European Commission 2019, 14)

Librarians can engage with the vendors of their library systems to open discussion
around the ways in which AI is used in their systems. There are many systems
used by libraries where AI has the potential to add value. Each has different ethical
dimensions some of which are explored by Jaillant and Caputo in the context of
digital libraries. They argue:

> Instead, a framework of AI governance informed by well-developed language and procedures
> of consent, power, inclusivity, transparency, and ethics and privacy, inspired by consolidated
> practices among archivists as well in social science, historians and anthropologists, should
> drive the adoption of AI. (Jaillant and Caputo 2022, 833).

There is a *realpolitik* in institutions around investment that may make taking new
directions difficult: an investment in major change like the implementation of AI
may require a proof of concept initially to provide to the institution the value of
the expenditure. Furthermore, the adoption of AI may come organically through
the inclusion of AI in the software used in different sections of the library. The
level of governance needs to be measured against the level of risk. More scrutiny
is required where decisions about people and their livelihoods are involved, and
less scrutiny perhaps where the AI implementation is targeted at an activity like
reshelving books.

Many aspects of AI are beyond the governance of the library. The library's
clients may be using agents such as ChatGPT and this use would be beyond the
reach of the library's approach to governance as would the AI instruments built
into the architecture of systems purchased for use by the library. The laws around
use of AI are only now emerging, and lag in development and adoption behind
implementation of AI. There is indeed a tension in national competition to stay
on top of advances in AI, and the regulatory and governance elements that are
emerging to protect against the potential and actual harms arising from use of AI.
The responses at the national level vary according to the importance accorded to AI

and its governance by particular countries and vary significantly in relation to the democratic orientation of the legislature.

Governance issues are not the only ones that come into play with AI. The design of AI is grounded in models created from exceptionally large data sources of images, text, and video. The early efforts in natural language processing chatbots by Microsoft demonstrated the problems that analysis of such deep resources can present. The architects of large-scale AI consequently invest enormous funds into data sanitisation (Oprea, Singhal, and Vassilev 2022). The source datasets used may be skewed toward a particular group or area.

Engagement by Libraries with Artificial Intelligence

Short of actions like Butlerian Jihad against computers found in Frank Herbert's science fiction novel *Dune*, there is little doubt that AI will become ever more entrenched in all systems. The choice is not rejection but engagement with the changes that will be wrought by the use of AI. The IFLA Information Technology Section has sponsored the creation of an Artificial Intelligence Special Interest Group within IFLA to foster debate and engagement around AI. The IT Section has held a series of conferences in Europe, Africa and Asia and South America as a means of strengthening the discussion on AI in the library field.

Going forward, there are many avenues for libraries to engage in AI. They include formulation of governance and ethical policies within libraries and any parent institutions. Activities taken by libraries may entail evaluation and scrutiny of library software that includes AI. Libraries can engage directly in the use of AI software through the many commercial and open-source tools now available. Libraries will be on the frontline for those asking about the implications of AI and will need to be well placed to assist with answers.

References

Australia. Royal Commission into the Robodebt Scheme. 2023. *Report*. Canberra, ACT. https://robodebt.royalcommission.gov.au/system/files/2023-09/rrc-accessible-full-report.PDF.

Balnaves, Edmund. 2008. "Open Source Library Management Systems: A Multidimensional Evaluation." *Australian Academic & Research Libraries* 39, no. 1: 1–13. https://doi.org/10.1080/00048623.2008.10721320. Available at https://www.academia.edu/99739844/Open_Source_Library_Management_Systems_A_Multidimensional_Evaluation?f_ri=7803.

Bourg, Chris. 2017. "What Happens to Libraries and Librarians When Machines Can Read All the Books." *Chris Bourg blog*, March 16, 2017. https://chrisbourg.wordpress.com/2017/03/16/what-happens-to-libraries-and-librarians-when-machines-can-read-all-the-books/#_blank.

Breeding, Marshall. 2011. "Preparing for the Long-Term Digital Future of Libraries," *Computers in Libraries* 31, no. 1 (Jan./Feb.): 24–26. https://librarytechnology.org/document/15595.

Coleman, Catherine Nicole. 2017. "Artificial Intelligence and the Library of the Future, Revisited." *Coffeehouse: A Collection of Data Blog Posts from Around the Web*, November 3, 2017. https://coffeehouse.dataone.org/2017/11/03/artificial-intelligence-and-the-library-of-the-future-revisted/.

Cordell, Ryan. 2020. *Machine Learning + Libraries: A Report on the State of the Field*. Commissioned by LC Labs, Library of Congress. Version published July 14, 2020. https://labs.loc.gov/static/labs/work/reports/Cordell-LOC-ML-report.pdf.

European Commission. 2019. *Ethics Guidelines for Trustworthy AI*. Prepared by the High-Level Expert Group on AI. https://ec.europa.eu/futurium/en/ai-alliance-consultation.1.html.

European Parliament. 2023. "EU AI Act: First Regulation on Artificial Intelligence." *News European Parliament,* June 14, 2023. https://www.europarl.europa.eu/news/en/headlines/society/20230601STO93804/eu-ai-act-first-regulation-on-artificial-intelligence.

Floridi, Luciano, and Massimo Chiriatti. 2020. "GPT-3: Its Nature, Scope, Limits, and Consequences." *Minds and Machines* 30, no. 4 (December): 681–94. https://doi.org/10.1007/s11023-020-09548-1.

International Federation of Library Associations and Institutions (IFLA). 2020. *IFLA Statement on Libraries and Artificial Intelligence.* [Prepared by] Committee on Freedom of Access to Information and Freedom of Expression (FAIFE). https://repository.ifla.org/handle/123456789/1646.

Jaillant, Lise, and Annalina Caputo. 2022. "Unlocking Digital Archives: Cross-Disciplinary Perspectives on AI and Born-Digital Data." *AI & Society* 37, no. 3 (September): 823–35. https://doi.org/10.1007/s00146-021-01367-x.

Johnson, Ben. 2018. "Libraries in the Age of Artificial Intelligence." *Computers in Libraries* 38, no.1 (January/February): 14–16. https://www.infotoday.com/cilmag/jan18/Johnson--Libraries-in-the-Age-of-Artificial-Intelligence.shtml#_blank.

Krizhevsky, Alex, Ilya Sutskever, and Geoffrey E. Hinton. 2012. "ImageNet Classification with Deep Convolution Neural Networks." *Advances in Neural Information Processing Systems* 25, 1106–1114. Available at https://proceedings.neurips.cc/paper_files/paper/2012/file/c399862d3b9d6b76c8436e924a68c45b-Paper.pdf.

Laplante, Phil, and Ben Amaba. 2021. "Artificial Intelligence in Critical Infrastructure Systems" *Computer* 54, no. 10: 14–24. doi: 10.1109/MC.2021.3055892. Available at https://ieeexplore.ieee.org/stamp/stamp.jsp?tp=&arnumber=9548022.

McCarthy, John, M.L. Minsky, N. Rochester, and C.E. Shannon. 1955. "A Proposal for the Dartmouth Summer Research Project on Artificial Intelligence, Dartmouth College." http://jmc.stanford.edu/articles/dartmouth/dartmouth.pdf

Mai, Jens-Erik. 2016. "Marginalization and Exclusion: Unraveling Systemic Bias in Classification." *Knowledge Organization* 43, no. 5; 324–330. Available at https://www.nomos-elibrary.de/10.5771/0943-7444-2016-5-324.pdf .

Mortati, Joseph, and Erran Carmel. 2021. "Can We Prevent a Technological Arms Race in University Student Cheating?" *Computer* 54, no. 10: 90–94. doi: 10.1109/MC.2021.3099043. Available at https://ieeexplore.ieee.org/stamp/stamp.jsp?arnumber=9548108.

Oprea, Alina, Anoop Singhal, and Apostol Vassilev. 2022. "Poisoning Attacks Against Machine Learning: Can Machine Learning Be Trustworthy?" *Computer* 55, no. 11 (November): 94–99.

doi: 10.1109/MC.2022.3190787. Available at https://ieeexplore.ieee.org/stamp/stamp. jsp?arnumber=9928202.

Palmer, Annie. 2018. "Meet 'Vera,' the Russian AI that Could Vet You for Your Next Job: Pepsi, Ikea, and Other Major Firms Turn to Bizarre Humanoid to Find Candidates and Conduct Interviews." *Daily Mail. Australia*, March 30, 2018. https://www.dailymail.co.uk/sciencetech/article-5560547/ Russian-AI-Vera-helping-companies-candidates-conduct-interviews.html.

Psychoula, Ismini, Andreas Gutmann, Pradip Mainali, Sharon H. Lee, Paul Dunphy, and Fabian A.P. Petitcolas. 2021. "Explainable Machine Learning for Fraud Detection." *Computer* 54, no. 10 (October): 49–59. doi: 10.1109/MC.2021.3081249. Available at https://arxiv.org/pdf/2105.06314. pdf?trk=public_post_comment-text.

Shah, Chiraag. 2023. "Australia's Robodebt Scheme: A Tragic Case of Public Policy Failure." *Voices: University of Oxford Blavatnik School of Government [Blog]*, July 26, 2023. https://www.bsg.ox.ac.uk/ blog/australias-robodebt-scheme-tragic-case-public-policy-failure#:~:text=Introduced%20in%20 2015%20as%20part,supposed%20overpayments%20to%20welfare%20recipients.

Snow, Jackie. 2018. "Bias Already Exists in Search Engine Results and It's Only Going to Get Worse." *MIT Technology Review*, February 26, 2018. https://www.technologyreview.com/2018/02/26/3299/ meet-the-woman-who-searches-out-search-engines-bias-against-women-and-minorities/.

VerWey, John. 2022. "The Other Artificial Intelligence Hardware Problem." *Computer* 55, no. 1 (January): 34–42. https://doi.org/10.1109/mc.2021.3113271. Available at https://www.osti.gov/ pages/servlets/purl/1847077.

Waterson, Jim. 2020. "Microsoft Sacks Journalists to Replace Them with Robots." *The Guardian*, May 30, 2020. https://www.theguardian.com/technology/2020/may/30/microsoft-sacks-journalists-to-replace-them-with-robots.

Part I: Current Directions in Artificial Intelligence for Libraries

Leda Bultrini

2 Current Directions for Artificial Intelligence in Libraries: An Introductory Overview

"Is AI already in our libraries?" is the question posed by JuJa Chakarova in the first chapter of this section on current directions in AI for libraries. And what is the answer? In February 2024, a Google search using the keywords "artificial intelligence" AND libraries yielded 400 million results. The numbers provide an unequivocal answer: absolutely. However, the picture is multifaceted and complex, and not without uncertainties.

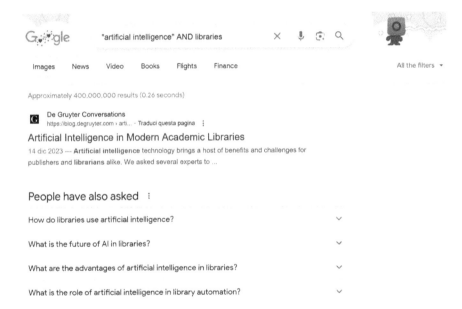

Figure 2.1: Screen shot of Google Search on Artificial Intelligence and Libraries, February 2024

The Impact of Artificial Intelligence on Libraries: Challenges and Opportunities

The recent whirlwind in the field of AI and its pervasive evolution seem to have ended, once and for all, the alternating springs and winters of AI developments witnessed over the past 70 years. The ongoing rapid advances by no means exclude libraries. Are libraries perceived as isolated paradises that will remain unaffected by the rise of AI? Or are libraries remnants of the past doomed to decline and disappear, unable to enjoy the benefits of AI? It depends on whether one wishes to highlight the many risks or the enormous opportunities of AI.

A journey has certainly begun, but to understand and explore the potential for AI in libraries, one must first focus on the overall scenario of AI and the scope of the AI revolution and its impact on the world and society. Where is AI headed and how should it be directed? The various domains of AI and the applications that can significantly enhance available knowledge and access to it impact on the founding purpose of libraries. It is necessary however to appreciate the vast changes occurring not only in the technology but in the world at large before examining the import for libraries of AI. Engaging with the structural turning point caused by the ubiquity of AI exposes libraries to risks that are fundamentally similar to those faced by society as a whole. But the perceived risks of using AI in libraries might include the potential undermining of the essential defining characteristics and fundamental values of libraries which emphasise the absence of discrimination in knowledge access, the prevention of bias in access tools and knowledge content, respect for privacy, and due regard for intellectual property rights. AI might endanger the basis of the very existence of libraries.

Libraries have never been exempt from deficiencies and inadequacies in relation to implementing their declared values. For example, bibliographic classifications and subject headings in catalogues and databases bear witness to widespread bias. However, the compounding capacity of AI can lead to an exponential amplification of any bias already present in knowledge content when constructing responses to information searching. AI, through its unparalleled capacity for penetrating multiple layers of knowledge, has a greater potential to encroach on the right to privacy than in the past. AI can also engender intellectual production of new content in a manner that makes it difficult, if not impossible, to understand or trace improperly used sources. Simultaneously, AI presents itself as a fertile wide-ranging means of enhancing in previously unimaginable ways the core functions that define the *raison d'être* of libraries through augmenting discovery, access to, and use of available knowledge, the creation of user-friendly dialogue tools, the provision of personalised response to enquiries, and delivery of uninterrupted service availability.

Navigating the Future of Librarians: Adapting to the Age of Artificial Intelligence

The inexhaustible and as yet unknown potential of AI brings forth another spectre: that of the redundancy of the librarian, whose role as an intermediary between the user and knowledge might be better fulfilled by artificial intelligent agents. However, the proactive presence of library professionals is crucial to ensuring that AI developments remain aligned with the basic principles and values of libraries and guaranteeing the quality of AI-generated outcomes. On the one hand, librarians must work for useful applications of AI in the library even though there might be a lack of sense of any opposition to the penetration of AI in the library. Opposing the integration of AI into the work of librarians to avoid the risk of librarians becoming superfluous would be futile. History demonstrates that no profession has survived when its necessity or utility has waned with the emergence of new ways of meeting service needs. Paradoxically, if the adoption of artificial intelligence were to lead to the extinction of the librarian profession, the librarians themselves should make every effort to ensure that what replaces them outperforms their own performance.

The mere preservation of the species is not a worthy aspiration for a profession in the service of the community. But the disappearance of librarians is not currently on the horizon.

The work of libraries and librarians remains essential, not only to ensure the development of AI applications that uphold the library's core values but also to provide the sustenance and innovative directions required by libraries. Libraries continue to be custodians of an enormous wealth of knowledge not all of which has been digitised and libraries must emphasise the need of transferring knowledge to new formats to fuel AI processes. The creation of the digital body of knowledge is an ongoing task, which has its roots in the past, is far from complete and must continue. The AI "methods... promise enormous potential for the (semi-)automated curation of digitized cultural heritage in libraries, archives, and museums, as well as for the computational analysis of cultural heritage data" (Neudecker 2022) and provide new and diverse opportunities for responsible and effective curation and stewardship of cultural data which will reveal additional content and ensure quality service delivery.

Unlocking New Directions for Established Functions and Skills

AI offers enhanced opportunities for adding value to the information produced by libraries in the course of their functions. Existing data available on collections and their use, inquiries, consultations, loans, requests for materials not held, user evaluations, along with the metadata in catalogues and databases, and the development of collections, to name just some of the areas. The availability of vast quantities of data of this kind, on a large scale, with due respect for privacy, could potentially serve as valuable material for AI applications. As noted futurist David Weinberger has observed in an interview with Zaccuri, manipulation and analysis of such data using AI would benefit not only the libraries themselves and their interactions with users, but also contribute to a broader spectrum of knowledge about communities (Zaccuri 2021).

With regard to reading skills and digital literacy, libraries have both the responsibility and the capacity to play a crucial role in narrowing the knowledge gap in society concerning the tools, applications, opportunities, and challenges associated with the pervasive influence of AI in people's lives (Ylipulli and Luusua 2019). Many lack awareness of AI developments and their impact, while AI is shaping people's lives in an ontological way and changing the very nature of being (Escobar 2018).

An open arena for the involvement of libraries and librarians lies in their interaction with commercial producers of AI. Libraries and librarians can take the lead in shaping market trends in AI applications, steering vendors in the right direction by providing standards and guidelines and focusing on applications that are not only effective but also ensure transparency, scalability and accessibility (Cordell 2020, 63–64). Libraries through taking proactive stances in relation to AI developments can safeguard equal opportunities for smaller institutions and peripheral communities. Ensuring equity is even more critical than the development of specialised implementations. It is easier for large, academic, national entities to make appropriate and useful AI projects and the examples presented in the book prove this. The difficulties are mainly for small or marginal libraries. The successful interventions in AI and case studies within large libraries and well-endowed institutions explored within this book nonetheless provide models for others to follow.

Resource Challenges in the Age of Artificial Intelligence: Expertise, Funding, and Competition

The availability of resources and their allocation are critical to the successful development and implementation of AI in libraries. Resources encompass the requisite expertise, which is not always available in libraries, particularly in smaller institutions. Training programmes, both within libraries and in academic institutions responsible for training or educating new professionals, can address this need but are not effective solutions when staff numbers are limited, and/or when an information technology (IT) team presence is minimal or absent.

Resources also include the funds required to execute specialised projects tailored to specific contextual needs. AI application projects are often intricate, long-term, subject to technological evolution, and therefore expensive and challenging. Securing approval from decision-makers, even within well-funded institutions, can be difficult. For simpler implementations like chatbots, the availability of numerous open-source resources facilitates the process but does not replace the work of specialists who may not be available locally.

Another issue is the highly competitive market for specialised expertise. Libraries and their parent institutions play in the AI space at a disadvantage, due not only to limited financial resources but also to the regulatory constraints they face. They may not be able to recruit appropriate staff because the governance regimes may result in longer decision-making timelines compared to private companies. Recruiting appropriate staff can be difficult with long lead times because of bureaucratic obstacles.

But libraries have at their disposal a traditional and well-established tool that has proven indispensable and successful in addressing various challenges: cooperation. Collaborating on specific projects maximises the resources available, pools expertise and knowledge, provides opportunities for multiple implementation, extends outcomes and benefits many libraries and their communities. Presenting a united front in interactions with the marketplace provides greater strength and credibility to libraries as potential buyers who prioritise innovation while being mindful of product quality and user rights. Converging on common positions in dialogue with the political institutions responsible for shaping AI regulations ensures, in the midst of competing interests, an additional voice for advocates of AI developments that do not result in rights violations and increased inequity (Bradley 2022).

The Contributions in this Section

This section undertakes an examination of AI adoption levels within libraries, identifies associated challenges, and proposes possible approaches. Delving into ethical and regulatory dimensions alongside organisational and economic facets, it offers insights into navigating the complexities inherent in AI integration. Juja Chakarova explores the historical progression of technical development across industrial revolutions, highlighting the current advancements in communication and computing that have led to ubiquitous computing, robotics, and AI, with a focus on major subfields of AI and its potential impact on traditional professions like librarianship, emphasising the need for investment in new skills and ethical standards. Mojca Rupar Korošec addresses the importance of establishing open ethical and legal frameworks for AI, particularly in library environments, to tackles issues such as user privacy, transparency, and bias, with a particular focus on developments in the European Union. She also refers to international initiatives like the International Research Centre on Artificial Intelligence under the auspices of UNESCO (IRCAI) in Slovenia and the Global Partnership on Artificial Intelligence (GPAI) promoting responsible AI development globally. Bohyun Kim provides examples of AI applications in libraries and discusses the slow adoption of AI and machine learning in libraries and archives due to experimental use and limited deployment of machine learning applications, highlighting the challenges such as cost implications and the need for specific expertise and infrastructure.

References

Bradley, Fiona. 2022. "Representation of Libraries in Artificial Intelligence Regulations and Implications for Ethics and Practice." *Journal of the Australian Library and Information Association* 71: 189–200. https://doi.org/10.1080/24750158.2022.2101911. Available at https://api.research-repository.uwa.edu.au/ws/portalfiles/portal/192841824/JALIA_fbradley_accepted.pdf.

Cordell, Ryan. 2020. *Machine Learning + Libraries: A Report on the State of the Field*. Commissioned by LC Labs Library of Congress. Version published July 14, 2020. https://labs.loc.gov/static/labs/work/reports/Cordell-LOC-ML-report.pdf.

Escobar, Arturo. 2018. *Designs for the Pluriverse: Radical Interdependence, Autonomy, and the Making of Worlds*. Durham NC: Duke University Press.

Neudecker, Clemens. 2022. "Cultural Heritage as Data: Digital Curation and Artificial Intelligence in Libraries." in *Qurator 2022: Proceedings of the 3rd Conference on Digital Curation Technologies, Berlin, Germany, Sept. 19th–23rd, 2022,* edited by Adrian Paschke, Georg Rehm, Clemens Neudecker, and Lydia Pintscher. CEUR Workshop Proceedings. https://ceur-ws.org/Vol-3234/paper2.pdf.

Ylipulli, Johanna, and Aale Luusua. 2019. "Without Libraries What Have We? Public Libraries as
      Nodes for Technological Empowerment in the Era of Smart Cities, AI and Big Data." in *C&T '19:
      Proceedings of the 9th International Conference on Communities & Technologies – Transforming
      Communities*, 92–101. New York: Association for Computing Machinery. https://doi.
      org/10.1145/3328320.3328387.
Zaccuri, Alessandro. 2021. "Lo Studioso Usa. Weinberger: 'L'Intelligenza Artificiale Entra in Biblioteca'."
      Avvenire, February 25. https://www.avvenire.it/agora/pagine/conoscere-collaborare.

Juja Chakarova

3 Artificial Intelligence: Already in Libraries?

Abstract: This chapter explores ideas of technical development through four industrial revolutions. Current innovations in communication and computing have led to ubiquitous computing, robots and artificial intelligence (AI). While the term AI was introduced in the mid-20th century, its ideas build on the developments in logic, mathematics, engineering and philosophy from antiquity to the present. Major subfields of AI include machine learning (ML), neural networks, computer vision, speech recognition, and natural language processing (NLP). AI is expected to disrupt the traditional professions as they are currently known. Fears are raised regarding job insecurity, along with AI biases and risks. Governments and international organisations are seeking to assist the progress of a human-centric AI by developing ethical standards. What are the current uses of AI and robots in libraries? How will they impact the profession of librarianship? Libraries promote innovation in their services because they are traditionally user-oriented but must share the risk and cost of AI projects to be effective. Most importantly, libraries must invest in new skills and knowledge to ensure competent librarians for the future.

Keywords: Robots; Artificial intelligence – Library applications; Fourth industrial revolution

Four Industrial Revolutions

Human development has striven to understand nature's forces and increase its chances for survival and consequently involved itself in scientific research and the application and implementation of technological results to ensure ongoing adaptation to new circumstances. The term Industrial Revolution (IR) was first used by Arnold Toynbee (1852–1883) to describe Britain's economic development from 1760 to 1840, but later applied more broadly to describe the process of economic transformation (Britannica 2023). The last two and a half centuries have witnessed four industrial revolutions. The first IR was powered by steam and water and transformed society from an agrarian society to an industrial one. The steam engine developed by James Watt was introduced commercially in 1776 and succeeded in the early 1800s by the steam-powered locomotive of Richard Trevithick. Steam-powered ships began to transport freight across the Atlantic and locomotives connected Britain's industrial hubs.

The second IR (1870–1914) was powered by oil and steel and witnessed the invention of the telephone, light bulb and internal combustion engines by Nicolaus Otto in 1864 and Rudolf Diesel in 1892. Electrical power was also introduced leading to industrialisation, standardisation and mass production.

The third IR or digital revolution began in the latter part of the 20th century, was, and continues to be, marked by the developments in electronics, and information and communication technologies (ICT). Society has witnessed the development of ubiquitous computing as predicted by the now famous Moore's law stating that the number of transistors on a microchip doubles about every two years. This so-called exponential growth enables the computer power to also double and allows the miniaturisation of computing devices. Some famous predictions about the future of computing have failed to eventuate, like the one by IBM's early President, Thomas J. Watson, who allegedly said in 1943: "I think there is a world market for maybe five computers".

The fourth IR combines the physical, digital and biological worlds, enabled by quantum computing, genetic engineering, robots, cyber-physical systems and artificial intelligence (AI) (Schwab 2016). Is society on the verge of the 4IR or has it already started?

What is Artificial Intelligence?

Although the term artificial intelligence (AI) was introduced in the mid-20th century, the pillars of the concept were erected throughout many earlier centuries. Out of the *pléiade* of philosophers and scientists over time, one whose earlier contributions were crucial, was the Greek philosopher Aristotle (384–322 BC) who developed in his *Analytica Priora* the first principles of reaching a conclusion from a set of premises, guided by rules known as syllogisms (Aristotle 350BC). A syllogism is a logical argument based on two propositions or premises which if assumed to be true lead to a conclusion. A familiar example of a syllogism is:
– All humans are mortal
– All Greeks are humans
– Therefore all Greeks are mortal.

To be mortal belongs to all human beings; to be a human being belongs to all Greeks; therefore, to be mortal belongs to all Greeks. Aristotle was the founder of formal logic, which is widely used in academic discourse, IT and AI. The If-Then principle, is the core of computer programming and loops.

Key scientists related to developing AI include Alan Turing, John McCarthy and Douglas Hofstadter. Alan Turing (1912 – 1954) was an English mathematician and computer scientist, widely considered the father of theoretical computer science and AI. As a cryptologist he broke the code of the German Nazi Enigma machine in 1939. In 1950 Turing addressed the differences between human and machine intelligence and developed a standard test for a machine to be called intelligent. A computer could be said to think if a human interrogator asked questions of both a computer and a human and could not differentiate between the answers provided.

John McCarthy (1927 – 2011) was an American computer and cognitive scientist. In 1955 McCarthy along with Marvin Minsky, Nathaniel Rochester, and Claude Shannon drew up the Dartmouth Workshop proposal to the Rockefeller Foundation. For the workshop he envisioned "a 2-month, 10-man study of artificial intelligence" (McCarthy et al. 1955, 2). The six-week workshop took place at Dartmouth College in Hanover, New Hampshire in 1956 and became a seminal event. The most remarkable result of the Dartmouth proposal was the successful adaptation of the term "artificial intelligence" with its origins in an engineering discipline whose relationship to biological organisms is mostly metaphorical and inspirational. Even now, there is an ongoing debate about whether machines can think or just simulate thinking.

Douglas Hofstadter (1945–) is an American cognitive scientist. In 1977 at Indiana University, he launched a program called "artificial intelligence research", but later renamed it to "cognitive science research". Even though Hofstadter stated that he had no interest in computers, his extraordinary work inspired many students to start careers in AI (Hofstadter 1979, 2007).

Definitions of Artificial Intelligence

Numerous definitions exist to capture the meaning of AI. According to McCarthy and his colleagues in the Dartmouth proposal "…the artificial intelligence problem is taken to be that of making a machine behave in ways that would be called intelligent if a human were so behaving" (McCarthy et al.1955, 11). Half a century later, McCarthy defined AI as "the science and engineering of making intelligent machines, especially intelligent computer programs. It is related to the similar task of using computers to understand human intelligence, but AI does not have to confine itself to methods that are biologically observable" (McCarthy 2007).

But how can intelligence be defined? McCarthy added to his definition of AI "Intelligence is the computational part of the ability to achieve goals in the world. Varying kinds and degrees of intelligence occur in people, many animals and some

machines" (McCarthy 2007). Debates are ongoing about the most appropriate definition of human intelligence. Highly advanced machines like Deep Blue and others
beat humans in chess, and games like Jeopardy or Go. Are the machines intelligent,
or just fast processors? Such machines possess enormous datasets and simulate
mental activity but are they really thinking?

Some writers like Ray Kurzweil and Nick Bostrom have predicted that computers will surpass human intelligence before the end of this century. Kurzweil uses the
term "singularity" (Kurzweil 2005), while Bostrom calls the phenomenon "superintelligence" (Bostrom 2014). Other researchers are more sceptical. Hubert Dreyfus
ridicules the claims of "progress" in human cognitive processes as a "displacement
toward the ultimate goal" saying: "According to this definition the first man to
climb a tree could claim tangible progress toward reaching the moon" (Dreyfus
1972, 12). Jerry Kaplan argues that the term artificial intelligence itself is misleading and creates unfounded expectations and misconceptions. Kaplan provocatively
asks what would have happened if airplanes were called "artificial birds" (Kaplan
2016, 16). Such a nomenclature would "spark philosophical debates as to whether
airplanes can really be said 'to fly' as birds do, or merely simulate flying". Inter-
estingly, a great scientist and a great innovator of the 21st century voiced caution
towards artificial intelligence exceeding human intelligence. Stephen Hawking
said at the Web Summit conference in Lisbon in 2017: "Success in creating effective
AI, could be the biggest event in the history of our civilization, or the worst" (Molina
2017). Elon Musk said in 2014 that AI is probably our biggest existential threat and
with it "we are summoning the demon" (McFarland 2014).

Subfields of Artificial Intelligence

Dreyfus defined the following four areas of AI: game playing, language translating, problem solving and pattern recognition (Dreyfus 1972, xxxiii). Over fifty years
after this segmentation of AI, numerous subfields have emerged. One researcher
listed 87 of them. The following list is much shorter but contains the main subfields:
machine learning (ML) and its branch artificial neural networks (ANN), computer
vision (CV), speech recognition, natural language processing (NLP), and robotics.

ML is the science of training a device or software to perform tasks. Its capabilities may be fine-tuned by feeding in more data, so that it can learn over time. ML is
used in libraries for automated indexing of documents against a controlled vocabulary or a thesaurus. The process can involve the use of ANN and deep learning. ANN
is a computer program inspired by principles of a real neural network, such as the
human brain. ANN consists of nodes connected by edges, which model the neurons

and synapses in a brain. Signals travel through the layers of the nodes and produce an output prediction. Deep learning is used in areas ranging from autonomous cars to robotics.

Computer vision (CV) is the process of analysing visual images, so that computers can read the imagery and see. When a Google search for images is conducted, the search engine algorithms search the metadata associated with the images, but the development of CV changes the process. The computer can process, for example, flat two-dimensional images of a scene from different angles and reconstruct a three-dimensional model. CV can be used to analyse sound because the sound chart is also a visual image.

Speech recognition or speech-to-text is a "capability which enables a program to process human speech into a written format" (IBM n.d.). Analysing and transcribing speech faces different problems, like separating signal from noise. As many discover when learning a new language and listening to native speakers, there is no obvious break between words. The flow or signal is continuous, and the intonation of the speaker can change the meaning completely. The tools performing speech recognition need a period of training to adjust to the voice of the user before becoming operative.

An early approach characteristic of NLP focused on codifying word categories and syntax. It was not fully successful because many exceptions exist in any language. NLP moved on to the use of statistical machine learning methods. For example, Google Translate, Trados and DeepL Translator build on big data files containing the official translations of documents which codify and confirm existing rules and practices combined with maintaining flexibility for learning. Translating is but one example of the use of NLP. NLP is used for indexing, creating summaries and answering questions. Chat GPT provides all these services and can even create a presentation with one's own voice. Time is the most expensive commodity and saving it creates a niche for NLP.

Robotics is a large subfield of AI. Multiple types of robots have been developed ranging from pre-programmed to humanoid to autonomous, teleoperated and augmented. Pre-programmed robots operate based on a predetermined set of instructions or programming. They follow a specific sequence of actions and are suitable for repetitive tasks, for example, on manufacturing assembly lines. Autonomous robots have the ability to operate and make decisions without continuous human intervention. They use sensors, algorithms, and artificial intelligence to navigate and perform tasks independently. Examples include self-driving cars, drones, robotic vacuum cleaners, and radio frequency identification (RFID) inventory robots. Humanoid robots are designed to resemble and mimic human movements and characteristics. They typically have a human-like appearance with arms, legs, and a head. Humanoid robots are developed for various purposes, including research, assistance to elderly people, and even companionship.

Teleoperated robots are controlled by a human operator from a remote location. These robots receive commands from a human, usually through a controller or a computer interface, and perform tasks in environments that may be hazardous or difficult for humans to access directly. This type of robot is commonly used in fields such as bomb disposal, space exploration, and underwater exploration. Augmented robots are equipped with additional technologies or capabilities to enhance their performance. The additions might include sensors, cameras, or other tools to improve their perception abilities, decision-making processes, or overall functionality.

The integration of AI into the field of art has led to innovative and intriguing creations with many questioning the results. Many services are now available for the creation of music (McFarland 2024), but when a song for Luxembourg's National Day in 2017 was composed by AI , it was novel but provoked serious discontent among the composers (Huberty 2017). AI algorithms on systems like DALL-E2 can be used to create visually stunning and abstract artworks although many ask what it means for creativity (Clarke 2022).

The Future of the Professions

Machines have made human life more secure and comfortable throughout the various industrial revolutions. The changes and improvements have however also seen a parallel trend of creating fear and job insecurity. The beginning of the 19th century saw for example the emergence of the Luddites in England, a group of textile workers who sought to destroy the machines in their industry which they perceived were replacing skilled workers. With the vast implementation of robots and AI, fears of loss and change are revived on a new scale. Richard Susskind (1961–), a British author and professor specialising in legal technology, predicts in a book, co-authored with his son, Daniel, *The Future of the Professions*, the decline of the professions as they are currently known (Susskind and Susskind 2015). The book refers to an article of Julian Baggini on the changes wrought by new technology on the role of the barista in Italy. The traditional skilled task of blending and serving coffee was fundamentally altered with the introduction of coffee machines and capsules containing special coffee blends. "Baristas were talented artisans in a richly human process...baristas themselves also lament the loss of their craft" (Susskind and Susskind 2015, 324). While the introduction of coffee capsules was an innovative technology, it brought a disruption in the task of the barista.

"Disruptive innovation", a term introduced in the early 1990 by Clayton Christensen (1952–2020), is an innovation that makes products and services more accessible and affordable, however displacing established competitors (Clayton Christensen Institute n.d.). Disruptive technologies and services lead to the decline of some professions and create the need for new ones. The Susskinds reflected in 2015 on the professions of lawyers, teachers, tax advisors and consultants and argued that the traditional knowledge gatekeepers would gradually delegate some of their tasks to intelligent systems, first the repetitive tasks, but later more sophisticated ones. The prediction was that:

> ... Increasingly capable systems will transform the work of professionals , giving birth to new ways of sharing practical expertise. In the long run... our professions will be dismantled incrementally (Susskind and Susskind 2015, 271).

While the book does not refer specifically to the profession of librarianship, a magnifying glass can be applied to reflect on the possibilities. Robots and AI will in the future be able to take decisions, even in a courtroom. Legal technologists are asking: "Is court a service or a place?" (Susskind 2019, 93) questioning whether people in dispute really need to congregate in physical court rooms to settle their differences. As libraries increasingly offer their resources and services online, the same question can be asked: Are libraries services or places? With the introduction of AI and robots, another reasonable question to put is whether the robot will assist the librarian or replace her. Asked that question in 2018, 89.47% of an international survey's respondents declared that they did not have such fears (Chakarova 2018, 100–104). Would a different answer emerge six years later in 2024?

Robots in Libraries

The International Federation of Robotics (IFR) distinguishes industrial and service robots and refers to the International Organization for Standardization (ISO) definitions:

> "Industrial robot" is an "automatically controlled, reprogrammable multipurpose manipulator, programmable in three or more axes, which can be either fixed in place or fixed to a mobile platform for use in automation applications in an industrial environment" (ISO 8373:2021).
> "Service robot" is a "robot in personal use or professional use that performs useful tasks for humans or equipment" (ISO 8373-2021).

ISO has recently added a third category, "medical robot," which is also defined by ISO 8373:2021. The World Robotics Reports issued by IFR in 2023 stated that the stock of operational robots around the globe exceeded 3.9 million units in 2022 (IFR 2023a; IFR 2023b). However, sales of professional service robots marked an impressive 48% growth in 2022. Robots can perform the functions conducted by doctors, policemen, composers (Huberty 2017), people who care for the elderly, and can even build a museum of robotics (Archello 2022).

It is certain that AI and robotics will affect the profession of librarians as traditional custodians of knowledge. There are already numerous AI implementations in libraries, archives, and museums, namely in computer vision, NLP, robots that make RFID inventories, item delivery and storage, machine learning, search engines, indexing and many other areas. A new framework called STEP, Segmentation, Transition, Education and Performance, has been developed by a three-year research project to help staff make effective use of new technologies like AI. Once implemented, STEP assists leaders to segment tasks suitable for AI, transition tasks among work roles, educate staff about AI and evaluate performance to reflect learning and use of AI (Leonardi 2023).

Why do libraries delegate some tasks to machines or systems? Since the introduction of online catalogues, library holdings are discoverable 24/7. With the implementation of RFID based self-check lending systems, libraries can be open to users 24/7 with no need for librarians to be present. The readiness to delegate tasks to machines is motivated by professional dedication to serve users and constituencies better and to deliver continuous and seamless services. Is there a limit to this trend, or will librarians contribute to the annihilation of their own profession? Will librarians contribute to the disruptive process or allow libraries to be disrupted? Will librarians lead the process, contribute actively to developments, or be part of the collateral damage?

Artificial Intelligence and Ethics

AI raises concerns not only regarding the loss of jobs, but also concerns about biases and other ethical issues. International organisations, as well as national bodies, have defined the framework of AI development and ethical standards. In April 2019, the European Commission's High-Level Expert Group on AI presented *Ethics Guidelines for Trustworthy Artificial Intelligence*. According to the *Guidelines*, trustworthy AI should be:

(1)   lawful – respecting all applicable laws and regulations
(2)   ethical – respecting ethical principles and values

(3)   robust – both from a technical perspective while taking into account its social environ-
        ment (European Commission 2019).

To ensure a human-centric and ethical development of AI in Europe, the European
Commission further submitted in April 2021 a proposal for AI regulation or the
so-called *Artificial Intelligence Act* (European Commission 2021). The rules establish different levels of risk and prohibit AI systems which might have an unaccept-
able level of risk to people's safety. While the Council of the European Union (EU)
approved a compromise version of the Act, discussion continued with various dis-
agreements on the definitions of AI systems and autonomy. The EU Parliament and
the EU Council finally agreed on a draft Regulation, or the so-called AI Act in late
2023 (Council of the European Union 2023). The AI Act, published in the Official
Journal of the EU on June 13, 2024, builds on the high-risk classification, to ensure
that AI systems on the European market are not likely to cause serious fundamental
rights violations or other significant risks (European Union 2024).

UNESCO adopted a Recommendation on the Ethics of AI in November 2021
to contribute to the international regulatory framework seeking to achieve
human-centred AI (UNESCO 2021). Italy launched in November 2021 its strategic
programme on AI for 2022–2024, aiming to develop a global hub of AI research and
innovation within Italy (Italian Government 2021).

Conclusion

The last few years have witnessed a number of AI implementations in libraries.
However, the process is not only costly, but also involves many iterations in project
development accompanied by the risk of error and failure. It is necessary to work
with others, combine efforts and share the risk and the cost of library AI projects.
Adopting the long view on the library and the profession and ensuring the library
meets its mission in serving the information needs of its community require significant investment. The investment is not only in AI infrastructure and technology,
but firstly and most importantly in the education and development of library staff
to ensure successful implementation of AI. Librarians must begin to plant seeds in
a field where they may never live to harvest the crop.

References

Archello. 2022. "Robot Science Museum. Melike Altinisik Architects. Seoul, South Korea." https://archello.com/project/robot-science-museum.

Aristotle. 350 BC. *Prior Analytics*. Translated by A. J. Jenkinson. *The Internet Classics Archive.* Massachusetts Institute of Technology. http://classics.mit.edu/Aristotle/prior.html.

Bostrom, Nick. 2014. *Superintelligence: Paths, Dangers, Strategies*. Oxford: Oxford University Press.

Britannica. 2023. "Industrial Revolution." https://www.britannica.com/money/topic/Industrial-Revolution.

Chakarova, Juja. 2018. "Ich, der Roboter, helfe dir, dem Bibliothekar: Die Bibliothek des MPI Luxemburg als Wegbereiter." *BuB: Forum Bibliothek und Information* 02–03: 100–104. https://www.b-u-b.de/roboter-tory/. Available at https://bibliotheksportal.de/wp-content/uploads/2023/04/bub_2018_02_100_104.pdf.

Clayton Christensen Institute. n.d. "Disruptive Innovation."https://www.christenseninstitute.org/disruptive-innovations/.

Clarke, Laurie. 2022. "When AI Can Make Art – What Does It Mean for Creativity?" *The Guardian. The Observer Artificial Intelligence (AI),* November 13, 2022. https://www.theguardian.com/technology/2022/nov/12/when-ai-can-make-art-what-does-it-mean-for-creativity-dall-e-midjourney.

Council of the European Union. 2023. "Artificial Intelligence Act: Council and Parliament Strike a Deal on the First Rules for AI in the World." *Press Release,* December 9, 2023. Updated February 2, 2024. https://www.consilium.europa.eu/en/press/press-releases/2023/12/09/artificial-intelligence-act-council-and-parliament-strike-a-deal-on-the-first-worldwide-rules-for-ai/.

Dreyfus, Hubert. 1972. *What Computers Can't Do: A Critique of Artificial Reason*. New York: Harper & Row Publishers.

European Commission. 2021. "Proposal for a Regulation of the European Parliament and of the Council Laying Down Harmonised Rules on Artificial Intelligence (Artificial Intelligence Act) and Amending Certain Union Legislative Acts." *EUR-Lex*. https://eur-lex.europa.eu/legal-content/EN/TXT/?uri=celex%3A52021PC0206.

European Commission. Independent High-Level Expert Group on Artificial Intelligence. 2019. "Ethics Guidelines for Trustworthy AI." Directorate-General for Communications Networks, Content and Technology. https://digital-strategy.ec.europa.eu/en/library/ethics-guidelines-trustworthy-ai. Also available at https://data.europa.eu/doi/10.2759/346720.

European Union. 2024. "Regulation (EU) 2024/1689 of the European Parliament and of the Council of 13 June 2024 laying down harmonised rules on artificial intelligence and amending Regulations (EC) No 300/2008, (EU) No 167/201 3, (EU) No 168/2013, (EU) 2018/858, (EU) 2018/1139 and (EU) 2019/2144 and Directives 2014/90/EU, (EU) 2016/797 and (EU) 2020/1828 (Artificial Intelligence Act) (Text with EEA relevance)." *EUR-Lex*. PE/24/2024/REV/1. http://data.europa.eu/eli/reg/2024/1689/oj.

Hofstadter, Douglas.1979. *Gödel, Escher, Bach: An Eternal Golden Braid*. New York: Basic Books.

Hofstadter, Douglas. 2007. *I Am a Strange Loop*. New York: Basic Books.

Huberty, Martine. 2017. "An Artificial Intelligence Song for National Day?" *Delano*, May 15, 2017. https://delano.lu/article/delano_an-artificial-intelligence-song-national-day.

IBM. n.d. "What Is Speech Recognition?" https://www.ibm.com/cloud/learn/speech-recognition.

International Federation of Robotics (IFR). 2023a. "World Robotics. Industrial Robots: Statistics, Market Analysis, Forecasts and Case Studies." IFR Statistical Department. https://ifr.org/img/worldrobotics/Executive_Summary_WR_Industrial_Robots_2023.pdf.

International Federation of Robotics (IFR). 2023b. "World Robotics Service Robots: Statistics, Market Analysis and Case Studies." IR Statistical Department. https://ifr.org/img/worldrobotics/Executive_Summary_WR_Service_Robots_2023.pdf.

Italian Government. 2021. "Strategic Program on Artificial Intelligence 2022–2024." Jointly developed by the Ministry of Education, University and Research, the Ministry of Economic Development, and the Minister of Technological Innovation and Digital Transition. https://assets.innovazione.gov.it/1637777513-strategic-program-aiweb.pdf.

Kaplan, Jerry. 2016. *Artificial Intelligence: What Everybody Needs to Know*. Oxford: Oxford University Press.

Kurzweil, Ray. 2005. *The Singularity is Near: When Humans Transcend Biology*. New York: Viking Penguin.

Leonardi, Paul. 2023. "Helping Employees Succeed with Generative AI." *Harvard Business Review*, Nov.–Dec. 2023: 49–53. https://hbr.org/2023/11/helping-employees-succeed-with-generative-ai.

McCarthy, John, M.L. Minsky, N. Rochester and C.E. Shannon. 1955. *A Proposal for the Dartmouth Summer Research Project on Artificial Intelligence*. http://jmc.stanford.edu/articles/dartmouth/dartmouth.pdf.

McCarthy, John. 2007. "What is AI?/ Basic Questions." http://jmc.stanford.edu/artificial-intelligence/what-is-ai/index.html.

McFarland, Alex. 2024. "9 Best AI Music Generators (March 2024)." *Unite.AI*, Updated March 1, 2024. https://www.unite.ai/best-ai-music-generators/.

McFarland, Matt. 2014. "Elon Musk: 'With Artificial Intelligence We Are Summoning the Demon'." *Washington Post*, October 24, 2014. https://www.washingtonpost.com/news/innovations/wp/2014/10/24/elon-musk-with-artificial-intelligence-we-are-summoning-the-demon/.

Molina, Brett. 2017. "Hawking: AI Could Be 'Worst Event in the History of Our Civilization'." *USA Today*, November 7, 2017. https://www.usatoday.com/story/tech/talkingtech/2017/11/07/hawking-ai-could-worst-event-history-our-civilization/839298001/.

Schwab, Klaus. 2016. *The Fourth Industrial Revolution: What It Means, How to Respond.* Geneva: World Economic Forum. https://www.weforum.org/agenda/2016/01/the-fourth-industrial-revolution-what-it-means-and-how-to-respond/.

Susskind, Richard, and Daniel Susskind. 2015. *The Future of the Professions: How Technology will Transform the Work of Human Experts*. Oxford: Oxford University Press.

Susskind, Richard. 2019. *Online Courts and the Future of Justice*. Oxford: Oxford University Press.

UNESCO. 2021. "Recommendation on the Ethics of AI." SHS/BIO/REC-AIETHICS/2021. https://unesdoc.unesco.org/ark:/48223/pf0000380455.

Mojca Rupar Korošec

4 Developing Artificial Intelligence in an Ethical Way in European Libraries

Abstract: Artificial intelligence (AI) is already playing a role in people's everyday lives and its proper evaluation is increasingly important. This chapter explains the priority of AI in the context of the European Union (EU) as the technology is central to the digital transformation of the economy and society. The trends in the legal framework proposed by the EU are laid out and the strategies followed by institutions dealing with the issues are explored. Appropriate handling of data is the most important aspect in the library ecosystem and the links between the use of AU in an ethical way and libraries are discussed. Various documents produced by the EU on AI are identified and their implications explored. The implications of a report on the use of AI in the fields of education, culture and audiovisual fields are particularly noteworthy for libraries. The impact of work by the World Commission on the Ethics of Scientific Knowledge and Technology (COMEST) established by UNESCO is also highlighted. An important document on artificial intelligence and libraries published in 2020 by the International Federation of Library Associations and Institutions (IFLA) inspired this chapter (IFLA 2020).

Keywords: European Union; Data protection; Artificial intelligence – moral and ethical aspects; Intellectual property

Introduction

This chapter presents a review of the guidelines on data handling that the European Union (EU) is setting due to the growing role of artificial intelligence (AI) in everyday lives. There are many dimensions related to the use of AI, but whatever the application, a top priority must be ethical considerations. Today, data is the most valuable of assets, and libraries need to be aware of its value and treat it accordingly. This chapter seeks to show that libraries can be a model to demonstrate to others how data can be treated ethically. Special attention is given to the library ecosystem and how data is managed within it. The appropriate governance of data in the library environment shows how data can be managed and demonstrates what ethical data governance means. Finally, the Slovenian approach to AI development and governance is presented.

A definition of data ethics is provided from the handbook *Dataethics: Principles and Guidelines for Companies, Authorities & Organisations* as context for what follows in this chapter:

> Data ethics is about the responsible and sustainable use of data. It is about doing the right thing for people and society. Data processes should be designed as sustainable solutions benefitting first and foremost humans (Tranberg et al 2018, 7).

Given that current AI is data driven, it follows that data ethics underlie AI developments. But it is now well understood that AI poses fundamental ethical challenges. For example, the guide *Understanding Artificial Intelligence Ethics, and Safety* identifies the potential harms caused by AI systems and proposes concrete, operational measures to counteract them (Leslie 2019). Those harms are the misuse, abuse, poor design, or negative unintended consequences. The public sector or organisations such as libraries can anticipate and prevent potential harm by developing and stewarding a culture of responsible implementation of ethical, fair, and safe AI systems including data.

> Fostering the development and applications of data science while ensuring the respect of human rights and the values shaping open, pluralistic and tolerant information societies is a great opportunity of which we can and must take advantage (Floridi and Tadeo 2016, 2)

Developing such checks will be supported in the EU because of its approach to the regulation of AI. Therefore, much of this chapter points the reader to some of the key documents that set out the EU vision.

The European Union's Emerging Position on Artificial Intelligence

AI is a priority for the EU, because the technology is predicted to play a key role in the digital transformation of the economy and society. The European Parliament has adopted as a priority a European regulatory framework for AI, which seeks to provide a safe, stable, and competitive environment for the research and development of AI applications that can stimulate innovation and economic growth in Europe. The EU has prepared many studies and proposals.

The study by the European Parliament entitled *The Ethics of Artificial Intelligence: Issues and Initiatives* released in March 2020, presented the requirements for transparency, accountability, and equity in data collection and data ethics with their ethical implications. The study proposed guidelines and raised ethical issues

regarding mechanisms for the fair sharing of benefits and the allocation of responsibilities in light of all the changes being witnessed (European Parliament 2020).
The path to implementing appropriate regulations in the EU on artificial intelligence has been complex and a useful library guide on the topic has been provided
by the European Commission (European Commission 2024a).

The legal basis for the use of AI by the EU was put forward in early 2021 in a
proposal from the European Commission: "Proposal for a Regulation of the European Parliament and of the Council Laying Down Harmonised Rules on Artificial
Intelligence (Artificial Intelligence Act) and Amending Certain Union Legislative
Acts" (hereinafter referred to as Proposal) for a regulation of the European Parliament and Council which would lay down harmonised rules applying to the
use of AI and recommending the adoption of an Artificial Intelligence Act. The
European Commission set out a strategic vision to promote the internal development and use of legal, secure and trustworthy artificial intelligence systems and
prepared to implement the world's first comprehensive law on artificial intelligence. The Proposal included concrete actions on how the Commission would
build institutional and operational capacity to ensure the safe, transparent and
human-centred use of AI in its work. It set the objectives to be achieved within
the EU:

- ensure that AI systems placed on the Union market and used are safe and respect existing law on fundamental rights and Union values;
- ensure legal certainty to facilitate investment and innovation in AI;
- enhance governance and effective enforcement of existing law on fundamental rights
  and safety requirements applicable to AI systems;
- facilitate the development of a single market for lawful, safe and trustworthy AI applications and prevent market fragmentation (European Commission 2021).

The document highlighted the areas to be covered by the *Artificial Intelligence
Act*. The rules proposed by the European Commission three years ago aimed to set
global standards and parameters for the use of AI in a wide range of industries.
Much of the attention of experts focused on the safety of using generative AI, which,
with its algorithms, can obscure facts and introduce fiction into public life.

In December 2023, the European Parliament and Council reached a provisional
agreement on the Act "to ensure that fundamental rights, democracy, the rule of law
and environmental sustainability are protected from high-risk AI, while boosting
innovation and making Europe a leader in the field" (European Parliament 2023).
France finally signed up to the agreement after ensuring strict conditions that balanced transparency and commercial confidentiality and reduced the administrative burden of high-risk AI systems.

In January 2024, the Commission adopted the _AI@EC Communication_, which underlines the importance of safe, transparent and human-centred use of AI technologies. The guidelines call for internal adaptation, innovation and early adoption of AI to set an example of best practice (European Commission 2024b).

Artificial Intelligence in Education and Cultural Areas

Given the importance of the particularly significant issues associated with the use of AI in education and cultural areas, the European Parliament adopted a _Report on the Use of Artificial Intelligence in the Fields of Education and Culture and Audiovisual_ (European Parliament 2021a), calling for AI technologies to be designed in a way that would avoid bias based on gender, social status or culture and protect diversity. This report is currently the most appropriate starting point for consideration of the issues in a library environment. An ethical framework for data and the algorithms applied to the data is necessary because the use of AI technologies in education, culture, and the audiovisual sectors has the capacity to affect the very foundations of t society's rights and values. The report makes many important General Observations, including:

1. Underlines the strategic importance of AI and related technologies for the Union; stresses that the approach to AI and its related technologies must be human-centred and anchored in human rights and ethics, so that AI genuinely becomes an instrument that serves people, the common good and the general interest of citizens;
2. Underlines that the development, deployment and use of AI in education, culture and the audiovisual sector must fully respect fundamental rights, freedoms and values, including human dignity, privacy, the protection of personal data, non-discrimination and freedom of expression and information, as well as cultural diversity and intellectual property rights, as enshrined in the Union Treaties and the Charter of Fundamental Rights;
3. Asserts that education, culture and the audiovisual sector are sensitive areas as far as the use of AI and related technologies is concerned, as they have the potential to impact on the cornerstones of the fundamental rights and values of our society; stresses, therefore, that ethical principles should be observed in the development, deployment and use of AI and related technologies in these sectors, including the software, algorithms and data used and produced by them (European Parliament 2021a)

Specific indicators for measuring diversity and inclusive ethical datasets must be developed and humans must always take responsibility.

Trustworthy Artificial Intelligence

The European Commission proposed new rules and actions for trustworthy AI in its 2021 Proposal. The Commission presented regulations on AI as one of the key technologies for future innovation, nothing that the ethical implications needed to be considered for any specific use case.

> This proposal aims to implement the second objective for the development of an ecosystem of trust by proposing a legal framework for trustworthy AI. The proposal is based on EU values and fundamental rights and aims to give people and other users the confidence to embrace AI-based solutions, while encouraging businesses to develop them. AI should be a tool for people and be a force for good in society with the ultimate aim of increasing human well-being (European Commission 2021).

Decisions made by AI systems only come with a certain, measurable accuracy, and rarely reach 100%. The accuracy of human oversight should be used as a benchmark for assessing the quality of an AI system. Section 2.3 of the Proposal notes:

> For high-risk AI systems, the requirements of high quality data, documentation and traceability, transparency, human oversight, accuracy and robustness, are strictly necessary to mitigate the risks to fundamental rights and safety posed by AI and that are not covered by other existing legal frameworks (European Commission 2021).

The Proposal indicates in Article 15, Accuracy, robustness and cybersecurity:

1. High-risk AI systems shall be designed and developed in such a way that they achieve, in the light of their intended purpose, an appropriate level of accuracy, robustness and cybersecurity, and perform consistently in those respects throughout their lifecycle.
2. The levels of accuracy and the relevant accuracy metrics of high-risk AI systems shall be declared in the accompanying instructions of use.
3. High-risk AI systems shall be resilient as regards errors, faults or inconsistencies that may occur within the system or the environment in which the system operates, in particular due to their interaction with natural persons or other systems (European Commission 2021).

The Work of Other Organisations

It is important to take note of the work around AI of the World Commission on the Ethics of Scientific Knowledge and Technology (COMEST) as an advisory body and forum established by UNESCO in 1998. The Commission is composed of leading scholars from scientific, legal, philosophical, cultural and political disciplines from various regions of the world and is mandated to formulate ethical principles for decision-makers. The COMEST Extended Working Group on Ethics of Artificial Intelligence developed a *Preliminary Study on the Ethics of Artificial Intelligence* in 2019 (UNESCO COMEST 2019)). The Bureau of COMEST was mandated to develop ethical principles that would provide decisionmakers with criteria that go beyond purely economic considerations. It works in several areas of ethics in science and technology. In March 2022 the Bureau of COMEST included in its work programme for 2022–2023:

> The Commission will address the Ethics of Science in Society, in light of recent lessons learnt from the pandemic of COVID-19.
> The Commission will also address the topic of the Ethics of Climate Engineering, including its importance for the sustainable development agenda.
> The Commission will remain open to addressing other emerging challenges related to the ethics of science and technology during the 2022–2023 biennium (UNESCO COMEST n.d.).

Related European Union Activity

In addition to the *Artificial Intelligence Act* which is specifically designed to regulate the development, deployment, and use of artificial intelligence (AI) systems across the European Union focusing primarily on safety, fairness, transparency, and accountability in all aspects of AI, is the *Digital Services Act* which seeks to create a safer and fairer online environment by establishing rules for online platforms and intermediaries operating in the EU. EU Member States and the European Parliament have also agreed on new rules for future data sharing, embodied in the so-called *Data Governance Act*. "These new rules set the foundation for trust in the data economy. Only if trust and fairness are guaranteed, can data sharing flourish to its fullest potential" noted Angelika Niebler, MEP, the European Parliament chief negotiator on new rules for future data sharing (EPP Group 2021; European Parliament 2021b). The new rules emphasised that more trustworthy data is needed to unlock the potential of AI:

> – Scheme aims to boost data sharing through trust, giving more control to citizens and companies
> – MEPs secured specific provisions to ensure fair access and stimulate voluntary data sharing
> – …
> – "Our goal with the DGA was to set the foundation for a data economy in which people and businesses can trust. Data sharing can only flourish if trust and fairness are guaranteed, stimulating new business models and social innovation. Experience has shown that trust – be it trust in privacy or in the confidentiality of valuable business data – is a paramount issue. The Parliament insisted on a clear scope, making sure that the credo of trust is

inscribed in the future of Europe's data economy", said lead MEP Angelika Niebler (EPP, DE). "We are at the beginning of the age of AI and Europe will require more and more data. This legislation should make it easy and safe to tap into the rich data silos spread all over the EU. The data revolution will not wait for Europe. We need to act now if European digital companies want to have a place among the world's top digital innovators", she said (European Parliament 2021b).

The new rules were approved in 2022 (European Parliament 2022b).

In the continuing story of EU developments, in 2022, the Special Committee on Artificial Intelligence in the Digital Age (AIDA) presented reporting on artificial intelligence in the digital age which complemented ongoing legislative work in the area (European Parliament 2022a). The report indicated that a more favourable regulatory environment, including flexible lawmaking and modern governance, should be encouraged, as current European and national legislation was fragmented, slow, and lacked legal certainty. Only high-risk uses of Ai should be strictly regulated to enable innovation and minimise the bureaucratic burden. As AI technologies are based on accessible data, data sharing in the EU needed to be modernised and scaled up. Full integration would help cross-border exchanges and innovation. The work of the Special Committee concluded in 2022 (European Parliament 2024).

Various actors within the EU are helping to shape the ethical use of AI. For example, DataEthics.eu is an independent non-profit organisation with a global reach, founded in 2015 by a group of female leaders in data and AI ethics. Based in Denmark, its purpose is to ensure individual control over data based on the European legal and values framework. The organisation focuses on collecting, generating, and disseminating knowledge on data ethics in close collaboration with international institutions, organisations, and academia. The range of information they supply is carefully selected and useful for many.

Developments in the EU around intellectual property rights are important. Various documents have been prepared under the auspices of the EU which address various aspects of the topic for different groups of users. One such document aimed at researchers, a Toolkit for Researchers on Legal Issues, was issued in 2019 under the auspices of OpenAIRE (OpenAIRE 2019). Usefully in respect of intellectual property matters, the European Union Intellectual Property Office (EUIPO) which is the EU agency responsible for managing EU trade marks and registered designs at EU level is focusing on clarifying the position in relation to intellectual property. It provides a transparency portal (EUIPO n.d.) and a variety of support materials on legal issues related to the re-use of research data, privacy, copyright and access to the Data Protection Register.

The Library Context: Handling Data Ethically

The library ecosystem is facing challenges with the use of AI in libraries. Libraries have always adapted to the use of new technology and must continue to do so. One of the areas concerning AI in libraries relates to the processing and analysis of copyrighted text. Intellectual property for digital content in the context of libraries often refers to copyright, which protects literary, scientific, and artistic content. Libraries must obtain appropriate permission or licences to use copyrighted content in their AI systems and it is crucial that libraries and librarians work with rightsholders to ensure copyright compliance and respect for intellectual property.

The International Federation of Library Associations and Institutions (IFLA) has developed a statement on AI for use by libraries. "The use of AI technologies in libraries should be subject to clear ethical standards, such as those spelled out in the IFLA Code of Ethics for Librarians and other Information Workers" (IFLA 2012; IFLA 2020, 1). "Libraries and library associations can, for example, interact with AI researchers and developers to create applications specifically for library use and/ or in response to user needs, including by creating accessible services which have not been possible before" (IFLA 2020, 1). But IFLA's guidelines consistently warn that libraries should consider ethical aspects and respect user privacy when using AI systems. When undertaking procurement for the purchase of AI technologies, libraries should choose providers that respect ethical standards of privacy and inclusion. Europe has effective legal protections in place. The guarantee of privacy is one of the library's fundamental values, and the concept of intellectual freedom remains one of the most important values of libraries in the 21st century.

What can libraries contribute to the development and implementation of AI, and how are changes reflected in the field of library and information science? AI is already being implemented in libraries in the field of applied ontology, in applications of natural language processing, in machine translation and in knowledge systematisation. The requirements for software to manage, for example, thesauri are relevant, as are uses for databases used directly in search or indexing applications. The results of automatic metadata generation depend heavily on the quality of the bibliographic metadata, which means that efforts should be focused on clarifying, interpreting, and classifying the semantic differences between library-assigned metadata and machine-generated metadata. Many libraries are considering using language technologies to combine library metadata with the possibility of machine-generated classification.

Librarians as trained information management professionals can make a major contribution to the development of data management services in their institutions and work directly with researchers in the field to support data management and publication. There are opportunities to learn about the management and cleaning of large databases to understand how bibliographic data from library catalogues can be better used. There are differences between data sources, with implications for metrics and classification at the institutional level. There are significant differences between databases. The differences put data users in an unequal position. Librarians must consider the effect of the choice of data sources and choose approaches where data from multiple sources is integrated to provide a more robust dataset. Issues must be addressed at the institutional level and at other levels involving collaborative activities.

Data Ethics Practices in Libraries

Open ethical and legal frameworks must be put in place to build consensus around values and norms that can be accepted by the community. AI shapes individuals, societies, and their environments in a way that has ethical implications and open debate must be undertaken on issues of social acceptability. The ethics of AI is a sub-field of applied ethics and is part of the ethics of technology, specific to artificially intelligent entities. How should planners act to mitigate the ethical risks that may arise from the use of AI in society, whether through design, inappropriate use, or deliberate misuse of the technology?

The cultural heritage of the future is based on today's digital information. The ethical use of AI requires that digital skills in the library environment support a more open and transparent lifecycle of data, making it more findable, accessible, interoperable, and reusable (GOFAIR 2020). Openness of data must be achieved in such a way that data can be consulted and used for a variety of purposes by other users. Open access to data means, in principle, equal conditions of access within each category of interested users, such as researchers, educators, students, and others.

There are several important aspects to consider when dealing with data ethics in libraries.

- User privacy: Protecting user privacy is crucial. Libraries must ensure that users' personal data is secure and that it is used in only legal ways
- Legal and ethical handling of data: Libraries must comply with applicable laws and ethical guidelines regarding the collection, storage, and use of data. This includes respect for copyright, protection of personal data, compliance with GDPR, and other similar regulations
- Transparency: Libraries must be transparent about their data collection practices. Users must be regularly informed of privacy policies and given control over their data

- Data protection: Libraries must ensure that appropriate security measures are in place to protect data from unauthorized access, loss, or misuse, and
- Data retention and deletion: Libraries must have clear policies on data retention and the period after which data is deleted.

AI has changed the ethical landscape, forcing a rethink and reanalysis of the ethical basis of library activities. In thinking about AI and its societal implications, the ethics of AI must come first. Consideration is needed for all frameworks to review codes of ethics for data-driven algorithmic systems.

AI and Open Access, Open Source and Open Science are important areas in libraries and their integration can bring many benefits. The benefits include:

- Improved information retrieval and access to information enhance the user experience
- Personal recommendations increase the efficiency of recommendation systems and allow users to discover new works of interest
- Process automation and access to open-source software can be supported by AI to support research based on principles of transparency, collaboration, and knowledge sharing, and
- Greater transparency and collaboration between libraries, and
- Enhanced reliability and adaptability of systems.

Openness in Libraries

Bibliographic data is proving to be an important asset for libraries and becoming increasingly exposed with the dominance of AI in the library environment. Libraries must examine and re-evaluate the institutional value of their bibliographic tools and resources. The data created by libraries in describing and making available information resources held and created by their institutions has considerable value for reuse in various ways. Databases permit manipulation of bibliographic citations. Bibliometric statistics are used by libraries to examine and determine their own performance and the performance of their institutions. There are various differences across data sources used with implications for metrics and rankings at the institutional scale. The results of the evaluations can in turn affect the mandate, funding and other functional aspects of the library, any governing board and the institution as a whole. There is an obsession with excellence in undertaking the valuations which can lead to various negative influences on both academic behaviour and research bias. "Any institutional evaluation framework that is serious about coverage should consider incorporating multiple bibliographic sources. The challenge is in concatenating unstandardized data infrastructures that do not necessarily agree with each other" (Huang et al. 2020).

Developments in Slovenia

Before closing this chapter, some reflections are offered on AI developments in Slovenia. The International Research Centre on AI (IRCAI) was established in Slovenia in 2019 under the auspices of UNESCO (IRCAI 2023). The UNESCO General Conference in Paris confirmed that the first UNESCO-sponsored international centre for AI would be based in Slovenia. The centre represents the result of close cooperation between the Slovenian government and UNESCO, particularly in the area of open-access educational resources. IRCAI offers insights and examines impact via an open and transparent dialogue on research specifically addressing the United Nations Sustainable Development Goals (SDGs). The purpose of the centre is to provide an open, transparent environment extending public and political support to stakeholders around the world for the drafting of policies and action plans in the field of AI. The focus is on the use of AI and assistive technologies to improve the performance of digital libraries and digital humanities. It develops technological solutions and provides expertise and advice for libraries and researchers in the digital environment and aims to improve the accessibility, usability, and efficiency of digital libraries and to support open research in the digital humanities. Specifically, IRCAI conducts activities for libraries: AI development and use, process automation, user interface development, and decision support. IRCAI aims to bring together researchers, practitioners, and users of digital libraries and the digital humanities.

Slovenia is also one of the founding members of the Global Partnership on Artificial Intelligence (GPAI 2023). All GPAI activities are based on a shared commitment to the OECD Recommendation on Artificial Intelligence, which aims to bridge the gap between theory and practice on AI by supporting cutting-edge research and applied activities on AI-related priorities. GPAI aims to promote the responsible development of AI based on the principles of human rights, inclusion, diversity, innovation, and economic growth.

Conclusion

This chapter has focused on the European library environment, defined by its legal basis in EU policies and documents which shape the everyday life of librarians and users. The various approaches taken by the EU have been invaluable in shaping the responses made by libraries and others in implementing AI solutions. There is an awareness that EU's approach to AI is only one of the many facets of our new changed reality and that librarians and researchers need to be aware of many other aspects. The implementation of AI systems must be carefully undertaken to ensure measurable accuracy with equivalent human performance used as a benchmark to assess the quality of an AI system. Various ethical frameworks are available to prevent bias based on gender, social position or culture, and diversity must be protected through the development of appropriate performance indicators. Librarians must step up and take responsibility. Human beings are ultimately responsible for ensuring that society's mistakes are not passed on to machines.

To manage AI effectively, libraries know that they must be prepared to continuously learn and keep abreast of developments in the industry. The world of AI is changing rapidly, and libraries and librarians must be willing to continuously improve their knowledge. AI can have a profound impact on the experience of library users in the way they access information. The ethical aspect of using AI in libraries is extremely important in ensuring user privacy, transparency of algorithms, and the avoidance of potential biases in automated decisions. Libraries' practices and services must be responsible and socially inclusive. It is important to comply with guidelines, standards, and legislation regarding data protection and the ethical use of AI in library environments. A permanent network of experts who can provide support and guidance to libraries in the introduction of AI technologies into their services is required. AI is changing the world and affecting the way libraries operate as service providers to their users. Libraries must have excellent knowledge of the potential of concrete application of AI in libraries, the willingness to introduce AI projects, and the ability to implement them. A better understanding of AI means better use of AI, which libraries can gain by promoting the exchange of good practices, collaboration, and standardisation of AI between institutions.

References

EPP Group. 2021. " New Data Sharing Rules Will Be Catalysts for New Business Models." [Newsroom blog], November 30, 2021. https://www.eppgroup.eu/newsroom/new-data-sharing-rules-are-catalysts-for-new-business-models.

EUIPO. n.d. "Transparency Portal: EU Intellectual Property Office." https://euipo.europa.eu/ohimportal/en/transparency-portal.

European Commission. 2021. "Regulation of the European Parliament and of the Council Laying Down Harmonised Rules on Artificial Intelligence (Artificial Intelligence Act) and Amending Certain

Union Legislative Acts." COM/2021/206 final. 21.04.2021. Brussels: EUR-Lex. https://eur-lex. europa.eu/legal-content/EN/TXT/?uri=celex%3A52021PC0206.

European Commission. 2024a. "EC Library Guide on Artificial Intelligence, New Technologies and Democracy: Introduction: A Selection of Information Resources Relevant to the Work of the European Commission." Last updated October 25, 2024. https://ec-europa-eu.libguides.com/ ai-and-democracy.

European Commission. 2024b. "Artificial Intelligence in the European Commission (AI@EC) Communication Strategic Plan." https://commission.europa.eu/publications/artificial-intelli- gence-european-commission-aiec-communication_en.

European Parliament. 2020. "The Ethics of Artificial Intelligence: Issues and Initiatives." EPRS European Parliamentary Research Service. Scientific Foresight Unit (STOA) PE 634.452. https:// www.europarl.europa.eu/RegData/etudes/STUD/2020/634452/EPRS_STU(2020)634452_EN.pdf.

European Parliament. 2021a. "Report on Artificial Intelligence in Education, Culture, and the Audiovisual Sector." Report A9-0127/2021. https://www.europarl.europa.eu/doceo/document/a- 9-2021-0127_en.html.

European Parliament. 2021b. "Data Governance: Deal on New Rules to Boost Data Sharing Across the EU." *News. Press Releases.* November 30, 2021. https://www.europarl.europa.eu/news/en/ press-room/20211129IPR18316/data-governance-deal-on-new-rules-to-boost-data-sharing- across-the-eu.

European Parliament. 2022a. "Report on Artificial Intelligence in a Digital Age. (2020/2266(INI))" Report – A9-0088/2022. Special Committee on Artificial Intelligence in a Digital Age. https:// www.europarl.europa.eu/doceo/document/A-9-2022-0088_EN.html

European Parliament. 2022b. "Data Governance: Parliament Approves New Rules Boosting Intra-EU Data Sharing." *News. Press Releases.* April 6, 2022. https://www.europarl.europa.eu/news/en/ press-room/20220401IPR26534/data-governance-parliament-approves-new-rules-boosting-in- tra-eu-data-sharing.

European Parliament. 2023. "Artificial Intelligence Act: Deal on Comprehensive Rules for Trustworthy AI." *News. Press Releases.* December 9, 2023. https://www.europarl.europa.eu/news/en/ press-room/20231206IPR15699/artificial-intelligence-act-deal-on-comprehensive-rules-for-trust- worthy-ai.

European Parliament. Multimedia Centre. 2024. "AIDA – Special Committee on Artificial Intelligence in a Digital Age." Updated January 13, 2024. https://multimedia.europarl.europa.eu/en/topic/ aida-special-committee-on-artificial-intelligence-in-digital-age_16506.

Floridi, Luciano, and Mariarosaria Taddeo. 2016. "What is Data Ethics?" *Philosophical Transactions of the Royal Society: Mathematical, Physical and Engineering Sciences. A* 374:20160360. https://doi. org/10.1098/rsta.2016.0360.

The Global Partnership on Artificial Intelligence (GPAI). n.d. https://gpai.ai/.

GOFAIR. n.d. "FAIR Principles." https://www.go-fair.org/fair-principles/.

Huang, Chun-Kai (Karl), Cameron Neylon, Chloe Brookes-Kenworthy, Richard Hosking, Lucy Montgomery, Katie Wilson, and Alkim Ozaygen. 2020. "Comparison of Bibliographic Data Sources: Implications for the Robustness of University Rankings." *Quantitative Science Studies* 1, no.2: 445–478. https://doi.org/10.1162/qss_a_00031.

International Federation of Library Associations and Institutions (IFLA). 2012. "IFLA Code of Ethics for Librarians and other Information Workers (full version)." https://www.ifla.org/publications/ ifla-code-of-ethics-for-librarians-and-other-information-workers-full-version/.

International Federation of Library Associations and Institutions (IFLA). 2020. "IFLA Statement on Libraries and Artificial Intelligence." https://repository.ifla.org/bitstream/123456789/1646/1/ifla_statement_on_libraries_and_artificial_intelligence-full-text.pdf.

International Research Centre on Artificial Intelligence Under the Auspices of UNESCO (IRCAI). n.d. https://ircai.org/.

Leslie, David. 2019. *Understanding Artificial Intelligence Ethics and Safety: A Guide for the Responsible Design and Implementation of AI Systems in the Public Sector*. Zenodo. London: The Alan Turing Institute. https://doi.org/10.5281/zenodo.3240529.

OpenAIRE. 2019. "Toolkit for Researchers on Legal Issues: Advancing Open Scholarship. D3.2. https://www.openaire.eu/d3-2-toolkit-for-researchers-on-legal-issues.

Tranberg, Pernille, Gry Hasselbalch, Birgitte Kofod Olsen and Catrine Søndergaard Byrne. 2018. *Dataethics: Principles and Guidelines for Companies, Authorities & Organisations.* Copenhagen: DataEthics.eu The Independent Thinkdotank. https://dataethics.eu/wp-content/uploads/Dataethics-uk.pdf.

UNESCO. World Commission on the Ethics of Scientific Knowledge and Technology (COMEST). n.d. "Work Programme for 2022–2023." https://www.unesco.org/en/ethics-science-technology/comest.

UNESCO. World Commission on the Ethics of Scientific Knowledge and Technology (COMEST). 2019. "Preliminary Study on the Ethics of Artificial Intelligence." *UNESCO Digital Library*. SHS/COMEST/EXTWG-ETHICS-AI/2019/1. https://unesdoc.unesco.org/ark:/48223/pf0000367823.

Bohyun Kim

5 Investing in Artificial Intelligence: Considerations for Libraries and Archives

Abstract: This chapter highlights the relevance of artificial intelligence (AI) and machine learning (ML) to library and archive work through various pilot projects conducted in libraries and archives. It describes several projects that leveraged machine learning (ML) technologies, including computer vision, speech-to-text, named entity recognition, natural language processing NLP), and an AI chatbot powered by a large language model (LLM). This chapter presents examples of libraries' and archives' adopting and applying AI and ML to provide engaging and efficient information services and to generate richer metadata at scale, which allows users to discover, identify, access, navigate, cluster, analyze, and use materials more easily and effectively. Also discussed are where and how libraries and archives should invest in AI and ML to reap the most benefit and the implications of such investments in costs and prospects.

Keywords: Artificial intelligence – Economic aspects; Machine learning; Artificial intelligence – Library applications

Introduction

With the emergence of ChatGPT, artificial intelligence (AI) and machine learning (ML) have become popular topics in mass media. Although chatbots are not new and ChatGPT is not the only generative AI tool available, ChatGPT's much-improved performance as a chatbot surprised many and quickly captured people's imagination. AI and ML have been topics of interest among librarians and archivists well before ChatGPT. But the adoption and implementation of AI and ML in libraries and archives has been slow. Given that most libraries and archives do not have existing expertise in AI and ML, this slow adoption may be partly attributed to uncertainty about which ML technologies are relevant to the work of libraries and archives and unfamiliarity with a range of compelling use cases that apply ML technologies to library and archive-related tasks. To address such uncertainty and unfamiliarity, this chapter discusses several pilot projects that make use of specific ML technologies, highlights the relevance of AI and ML to library and archive work, and explores ways in which libraries and archives can invest in AI and ML and the costs and prospects associated with those potential investments.

Machine Learning Technologies Relevant to Libraries

In adopting AI and ML, the goal of libraries and archives is to enhance and improve their services and operations. If newly developed AI and ML capabilities can add value in that manner, that is a good reason for a library or an archive to investigate and invest in AI and ML. However, many libraries experience difficulties in determining where and how they should begin. Fortunately, previous ML pilots conducted in the library and archive setting can serve as good starting points for those libraries that are looking to build capacity and invest in AI and ML. The rest of this section summarizes some pilot projects and highlights the ML technologies that are likely to be most relevant to libraries and archives.

Computer Vision

With the Project AIDA (Image Analysis for Archival Discovery), the University of Nebraska-Lincoln and the Library of Congress in the United States explored the use of ML in the library and archive context, in particular computer vision. Computer vision is an ML technology that enables computers to identify objects and people in digital images and videos and to derive meaningful information from them. Computer vision applications process a large volume of digital images and video data to perform tasks such as object identification, facial recognition, and image classification (IBM n.d.a). The AIDA project included several ML experiments that applied computer vision technology to archival images, such as developing an ML algorithm that identifies the region of graphical content in historical newspaper page images, determining whether an item is handwritten, printed, or a mix of both and classifying manuscript collection images as digitized from the original format or a microform reproduction (Lorang et al. 2020, 3–18). This pilot showed the potential of ML technology, specifically computer vision, to expedite image processing in archival materials.

Another ML pilot was run by the Frick Art Reference Library in New York in collaboration with researchers at Stanford University, Cornell University, and the University of Toronto. Also using computer vision, the research team developed an image classifier algorithm for the library's digitized Photoarchive. Based on visual elements, the image classifier algorithm applied a local hierarchical classification system and automatically assigned metadata to the digitized images of portrait paintings (Prokop et al. 2021, 15). The image classifier showed that an AI tool can help the library staff assign metadata to digitized images more quickly, thereby improving the ability of users to access and retrieve those images.

Natural Language Processing

The AMPPD (Audiovisual Metadata Platform Pilot Development) project was run jointly by Indiana University (IU) Libraries, the University of Texas at Austin School of Information, the New York Public Library (NYPL), and AVP, an information innovation company. The goal of the project was to improve metadata workflows using ML technology. Using both proprietary and open-source ML tools, the AMPPD project team developed automated metadata generation mechanisms (MGMs) and integrated them with the human metadata generation process (Dunn et al. 2021, 5).

Various ML techniques such as optical character recognition (OCR), speech recognition also known as speech-to-text, and named entity recognition were used in the project to automate metadata work. OCR software converts an image of text in a printed format into a machine-readable text format for searching and further manipulation (AWS 2024c). Speech-to-text software enables computers to process human speech into a written format, thereby producing the text transcription of human speech in audio files (IBM, n.d.c). Named entity recognition (NER) is a component of a well-known ML technology, natural language processing (NLP). NLP techniques enable computers to recognize, interpret, generate, and respond to human language in voice and text data and are used for tasks such as translation, summarization sentiment analysis (IBM n.d.b). NER takes in a string of text and identifies and classifies entities that belong to specific categories, such as names of individuals, locations, organizations, and expressions of times.

The AMPPD project built a fully functioning platform with twenty-four MGMs that could be used to analyze, describe, and document the audiovisual materials in IU and NYPL's collections (Dunn et al. 2021, 13). The ML technologies mentioned above were used for detecting silence, speech, and music; speech-to-text and speaker diarization; named entity recognition for people, geographic locations, and topics; video and structured data OCR; and music genre detection. The experiment demonstrated how a library's traditional metadata creation workflow for audio and moving image materials can be augmented and improved by ML technologies.

The University of Notre Dame Libraries applied NLP to enhance metadata for its Catholic Pamphlets collection, which consisted of over 5,500 PDFs. MARC summary fields had been assigned to half of the collection, but most of the summaries were a few words at most, lacking sufficient metadata. The team used NLP automated summarization techniques to create more robust summaries by combining the summaries with Library of Congress subject headings (Flannery 2020, 23–24). The work undertaken provides another example of how libraries can make use of ML to enhance existing metadata for their collections.

Chatbot

Another ML pilot project using NLP is a custom chatbot developed by Zayed University Library in the United Arab Emirates. The library chatbot named Aisha was created with Python programming language and OpenAI's ChatGPT application programming interface (API) to provide reference and support services when students and faculty need help outside the library's operating hours (Lappalainen and Narayanan 2023, 38, 51). A chatbot is an ML computer program that simulates human conversation in text or voice (OCI 2024). A sophisticated AI chatbot such as ChatGPT utilizes NLP, one of the AI/ML technologies, to generate conversational responses to a user's input to mimic a human dialogue. Large language models (LLMs) underpin ChatGPT's NLP capability. ChatGPT API supports the creation of a customized version of ChatGPT chatbot powered by gpt-3.5-turbo and gpt-4, which are OpenAI's LLMs, with data specific to the purpose of the custom chatbot. An LLM is a type of mathematical ML model, which is a set of parameters and structure that allows a system to make predictions. It is built with neural networks, which consist of an encoder and a decoder, which extract meanings from a sequence of text and understand the relationships between words and phrases in it (Elastic 2024.). A neural network refers to an ML model that teaches computers to process data and makes decisions in a manner similar to the way interconnected biological neurons work together in a layered structure in the human brain weighing options and learning and improving by trial and error (AWS 2024b). Pre-trained on vast amounts of data and with hundreds of billions of parameters, an LLM processes a user's input given in human language and predicts and generates plausible language as a response (AWS 2024a).

Zayed University Library's chatbot, Aisha, was customized with the content of over 100 library guides and information in the library website and a list of 100 typical questions and answers regarding academic libraries generated by ChatGPT, which were further revised and updated with Zayed University-specific information found in previously asked questions and answers from LibAnswers (Lappalainen and Narayanan 2023, 45). Aisha suggests ways in which libraries can provide users with more personalized and engaging information services by adopting and experimenting with AI/ML chatbot technology.

Promising Artificial Intelligence and Machine Learning Technologies

Although there are many other AI/ML pilots, the five examples described in this chapter point to areas of ML technologies that are likely to be relevant and promising for libraries and archives to explore and in which to invest. Computer vision is pertinent to libraries and archives as it can create, enhance, and augment item-level metadata with efficiency and accuracy. It is particularly useful for still or moving image materials as shown in pilot projects described earlier. Another area of ML technologies that holds great potential for libraries and archives is NLP, the most sophisticated example of which is a chatbot powered by an LLM. NLP techniques can be used to analyze and summarize text, assign subjects, generate summaries, and extract main claims from text materials held in libraries and archives. The work of creating and enhancing metadata for materials can significantly benefit from the tasks NLP techniques enable such as named entity recognition for people, geographic locations, and topics that appear in library materials, as the AMPPD project and the Notre Dame University Libraries project both demonstrated.

AI/ML technologies make it possible for libraries and archives to not only extract content residing in their collections as machine-readable and interpretable data but also create new or enhance existing metadata with more detailed and accurate information. By adopting and leveraging AI/ML technologies, libraries and archives can generate richer metadata at scale to be verified and further augmented by human catalogers if necessary to improve search options and to make it easier for users to discover, identify, access, navigate, cluster, analyze, and use library and archive materials. Breakthroughs in chatbot technology with LLMs point to innovative and engaging ways in which libraries and archives can provide their information and reference services tailored to their own users.

Where and How to Invest in Artificial Intelligence and Machine Learning

The previous section of this chapter highlighted areas of library and archive work that appear to be a good match for AI/ML technologies. Based on the specific areas chosen and local needs, individual libraries can determine which type of ML use would make most sense. The library's respective collections, services, current strengths, and future directions should also be taken into consideration.

Libraries and archives will also benefit by directing their efforts to address problems that emerged in previous ML pilot projects. For example, several projects discovered limitations in custom-built ML models due to available training data being too small in amount or poor in quality (Flannery 2020, 26; Lorang et al. 2020, 32–34). The greater the amount of data fed into an ML model, the better it performs. For this reason, libraries and archives can take full advantage of ML only when a sufficiently large volume of data is amassed. To ensure that an ML model performs as expected, it is also critical for libraries and archives to build reliable ground truth sets, which serve as the expected result against which the performance of an ML model is measured. Without reliable ground truth data sets, it is difficult to estimate how well an ML model meets its intended purpose. If libraries and archives decide to build more custom ML models, they should also make efforts to collaborate across institutions to create a sufficiently large training data and ground truth sets to support the creation of ML algorithms appropriate for libraries and archives to use.

Libraries and archives can also more actively explore the use of pre-trained off-the-shelf ML models. Pre-trained ML models, such as AWS Rekognition and Google Cloud Vision AI, can be useful for text recognition, face and object detection, and image labeling. It is to be noted that the pre-trained ML models have some limitations. For example, the generic ML models trained mostly with color images are likely to perform poorly with historic black-and-white photographs. For this reason, their usefulness varies depending on the type, age, and other conditions of library materials, to which those generic models are applied. If the models are applied indiscriminately, pre-trained off-the-shelf ML models may impose social and historical biases and harmful assumptions to library and archive materials due to their opaqueness. However, pre-trained off-the-shelf ML models can successfully tackle certain tasks, presenting fewer barriers for adoption, and libraries and archives can also work on better informing users regarding the use of ML models in the description of materials (Craig 2021, 203–205).

Growing generative AI cloud platforms and also something for libraries and archives to explore further. Amazon, Google, and Microsoft all offer various generative AI services and products through their cloud platforms, called Amazon Bedrock, Vertex AI, and Azure Open AI respectively. These platforms and services make it easier for AI/ML developers to access, customize, fine-tune, and deploy ML models, including many foundational models. Foundational models are large neural networks trained on massive amounts of unlabeled broad data. They are designed to produce a variety of outputs and can perform a wide range of general tasks, such as understanding languages, generating text and images, and mimicking human conversations (Jones 2023). Foundational models such as GPT-4, Imagen, and PaLM can serve as standalone systems or foundations on which other AI/ML applications with more specific purposes are built.

Lastly, libraries and archives interested in AI and ML must continue digitization. Digitization has been taking place for many years and has lost the allure of being new and exciting. However, vast numbers of physical items held within libraries and archives are still waiting to be properly digitized. Only when more of them are converted into digital objects can libraries and archives take full advantage of ML, which relies on a large amount of data rather than a set of rules to train and build an intelligent system.

Considerations for Libraries and Archives

Although interest in AI and MI has grown steadily in recent years, the use of AI and ML in libraries and archives remains experimental. Few ML applications have been developed and deployed in production by libraries and archives and led to significant improvement in their services. The situation is not vastly different in commercial library products. As indicated in Elsevier's Scopus AI, however, vendors are in the process of developing new AI products or adding new AI features to existing products by applying ML technologies. AI-enhanced products driven by ML that are marketed to libraries are increasing in number. For example, Consensus is an AI-powered search tool that answers research questions by extracting findings from scientific research papers in the Semantic Scholar database. Elicit is an AI research assistance tool that aims to expedite the literature review process by providing a list of relevant articles for a user's query in addition to summaries of content and syntheses of findings. Scite is a chatbot that allows users to find answers from the full texts of research articles with 1.2 billion citation statements extracted and analyzed from 187 million articles, book chapters, preprints, and datasets. Scopus AI offers expanded and enhanced summaries of academic articles and more refined search capabilities. Talpa Search provides users with a way to ask about and find books in a library catalog in natural language. The pace of the adoption of AL and ML by library vendors is likely to quicken, and more AI-powered products that aim to either enhance or replace the library's existing services and systems will follow.

Before the rise of generative AI, libraries and archives have taken a boutique-like approach to AI and ML. They have been experimenting more with building highly customized ML models than with testing and using generic off-the-shelf ML models. Libraries and archives have been primarily interested in training ML models with their unique and relatively small datasets and developing ML applications with functionalities related to highly specialized work ML models and tech-

niques are most powerful when trained and applied at scale. Given that, a boutique-like approach may become a limitation to successful future applications of
AI and ML in libraries and archives. It remains to be seen whether libraries and
archives will begin to use more generic ML models and applications made available
through growing AI cloud platforms and services.

Experimenting with AI and ML requires the preparation and assembly of large
data sets. It also means that libraries and archives need new staff expertise. Cleaning up data and preparing data sets for ML work is time-consuming and labor-in-
tensive. Building staff expertise in AI and ML can be tricky and may require hiring
staff with new skills and expertise. AI and ML projects will also require additional
funding to obtain appropriate ML tools and set up a robust computing environment
and a necessary digital infrastructure. While it is natural for any novel endeavor
to incur additional cost, the cost implications of adopting AI and ML must be given
careful consideration because many libraries and archives face flat budgets or
budget cuts year after year.

While investing in AI and ML may pose some logistical challenges, such investments can allow libraries and archives to promote specific areas of their services
and operations where AI and ML can make significant improvements. By directing
AI/ML-related work towards the areas where the impact will be high, libraries and
archives can also signal to the vendors the problems that they deem most critical
to be addressed in developing AI/ML applications for enhanced user experience.
However, ML models and techniques are most powerful when trained and applied
at scale. This will allow libraries and archives to influence the future directions of
commercially available products, particularly when vendors are actively looking
for new product ideas or features using AI. However, if libraries and archives
miss the narrow window of time and opportunity currently open, the prospects
of enhancing the activities of libraries and archives through the effective use of AI
and ML may not be realized. System vendors may fail to leverage and integrate AI
and ML to add value to existing products that will meet the rising expectations of
both libraries and library users. Libraries and archives may end up as dissatisfied
consumers of inadequate commercial ML products. And users may find libraries
and archives less useful and relevant in meeting their needs.

Conclusion

This chapter has highlighted aspects of library and archive work that appear to be a
good match for AI/ML technologies, described specific AI/ML technologies that are
particularly relevant, and suggested areas in which libraries and archives looking

to build capacity in AI and ML may invest efforts to maximize their impact. When a library or an archive decides to make an investment in AI and ML, administrators and decision-makers should carefully consider whether the project ideas connect AI/ML with significant needs in their organization, how the needed data for the project is to be obtained and prepared, whether the existing staffing and the digital infrastructure can sufficiently support the new ML project work, and whether the project team has the right mix of skills and knowledge in areas relevant to the project, including knowledge of specific library workflows, metadata, information and communications technology, data science, and software development.

Investing extensively in AI and ML may not be realistic or appropriate for all libraries and archives. But for most, AI and ML present opportunities to improve their services in new and creative ways. To seize the opportunities, library and archives staff must become familiar with how AI and ML models and techniques can be used in the library and archive context. They will also need to develop the ability to determine which library and archive tasks may most benefit from ML and to evaluate ML applications in a meaningful way. Library administrators and decision-makers must tackle the problem of how libraries and archives can develop new knowledge and skills to build long-term capacity in AI and ML to achieve desired outcomes and benefits with limited resources. They will also have to develop a compelling vision, acquire the resources needed, gain support from all levels of the organization, and build necessary staff buy-in, skills, expertise, and participation.

References

Amazon Web Services (AWS). 2024a. "What Are Large Language Models (LLM)?" https://aws.amazon.com/what-is/large-language-model/.

Amazon Web Services (AWS). 2024b. "What Is a Neural Network?" https://aws.amazon.com/what-is/neural-network/.

Amazon Web Services (AWS). 2024c. "What Is OCR?" https://aws.amazon.com/what-is/ocr/.

Craig, Jessica. 2021. "Computer Vision for Visual Arts Collections: Looking at Algorithmic Bias, Transparency, and Labor." *Art Documentation: Journal of the Art Libraries Society of North America* 40, no.2: 198–208. https://doi.org/10.1086/716730.

Dunn, Jon W., Ying Feng, Juliet L. Hardesty, Brian Wheeler, Maria Whitaker, Thomas Whittaker, Shawn Averkamp, et al. 2021. "Audiovisual Metadata Platform Pilot Development (AMPPD) Final Project Report." Indiana University. https://scholarworks.iu.edu/dspace/handle/2022/26989.

Elastic. 2024. "What Is a Large Language Model (LLM)?" https://www.elastic.co/what-is/large-language-models.

Flannery, Jeremiah. 2020. "Using NLP to Generate MARC Summary Fields for Notre Dame's Catholic Pamphlets." *International Journal of Librarianship* 5, no. 1: 20–35. https://doi.org/10.23974/ijol.2020.vol5.1.158.

IBM. n.d.a. "What Is Computer Vision?" https://www.ibm.com/topics/computer-vision.

IBM. n.d.b. "What Is Natural Language Processing (NLP)?" https://www.ibm.com/topics/natural-language-processing.

IBM. n.d.c. "What Is Speech Recognition?" https://www.ibm.com/topics/speech-recognition.

Jones, Elliot. 2023. "Explainer: What Is a Foundation Model?" Ada Lovelace Institute. July 17, 2023. https://www.adalovelaceinstitute.org/resource/foundation-models-explainer/.

Lappalainen, Yrjo, and Nikesh Narayanan. 2023. "Aisha: A Custom AI Library Chatbot Using the ChatGPT API." *Journal of Web Librarianship* 17, no. 3: 37–58. https://doi.org/10.1080/19322909.2023.2221477.

Lorang, Elizabeth, Leen-Kiat Soh, Yi Liu, and Chulwoo Pack. 2020. "Digital Libraries, Intelligent Data Analytics, and Augmented Description: A Demonstration Project." *University of Nebraska-Lincoln.* https://digitalcommons.unl.edu/libraryscience/396.

Oracle Cloud Infrastructure (OCI). 2024. "What Is a Chatbot?" https://www.oracle.com/chatbots/what-is-a-chatbot/.

Prokop, Ellen, X. Y. Han, Vardan Papyan, David L. Donoho, and C. Richard Johnson jr. 2021. "AI and the Digitized Photoarchive: Promoting Access and Discoverability." *Art Documentation: Journal of the Art Libraries Society of North America* 40, no. 1: 1–20. https://doi.org/10.1086/714604.

Part II: **The Implications for Use of Artificial Intelligence in Libraries and Education**

Andrew Cox

6 The Implications for Use of Artificial Intelligence in Libraries and Education: An Introductory Overview

Introduction

Artificial Intelligence (AI) is not solely about technologies, standards and practical applications, though these topics are of great interest and rightly make up much of this book. This section explores some of the wider issues that shape library responses to the opportunities created by the current wave of AI. The issues and the influences on them operate at different levels, including national, organisational, institutional and individual levels and relate to policy and strategic areas. There is an overarching concern with AI ethics.

National Policies and Strategies for Artificial Intelligence

Library use of AI occurs in the context of government policy and existing and emerging legal frameworks. Since around 2019, many countries have recognised AI as a strategic priority. National policies are varied, but according to an analysis by Papyshev and Yarime (2023), some strong common themes emerge, including the need to:

- Develop human capital
- Apply AI ethically
- Develop a research base
- Regulate, and
- Develop data infrastructure and policy.

One can immediately understand the importance of information professionals playing some role in realising many of these priorities, such as by educating citizens in the skills for an AI literate society; by advocating for their unique perspective on the ethics of AI; by supporting researchers to develop the research base for AI; and by inputting on the design and use of appropriate data infrastructures. If AI is a national priority, it seems that libraries have a significant role to play alongside other actors.

While there are common themes across national policies, the emphasis in individual policies varies. Papyshev and Yarime (2023) suggest that the approaches taken fall into three groups, focusing on:

- Development, where the state steers development of AI towards national goals. This kind of policy is found in China and Japan, and in Russia and some of the former communist bloc in Eastern Europe
- Control, where the focus is on state regulation and protecting society from the risks of AI. It is the approach taken by countries in the European Union (EU), for example and
- Promotion, where the emphasis is on innovation, especially led by the private sector, and the state plays only a facilitating role. Promotion is the emphasis in the United States, United Kingdom, and other countries including Australia, Ireland and India.

The three categories seem to reflect persistent patterns related to the political culture in these different countries and one would expect to see them similarly reflected in the way that libraries approach AI too.

It can be speculated that there has been a shift towards regulation internationally because of the controversy around ChatGPT. Existing legal frameworks are also still relevant, such as that for the protection of intellectual property rights. Generative AI has been pushing the boundaries of intellectual property. There is an emerging appetite for regulation beyond the EU. This could have radical implications for how AI is developed and used in the library sector.

Institutional Strategy

The wider strategies of the institutions in which libraries are embedded, such as academic libraries within universities, are of direct relevance to the implementation of AI in libraries. Several studies seem to show limited mentions of AI in university strategies (Huang, A.M. Cox, and J. Cox 2023; Wheatley and Hervieux 2019), but there may be hooks in institutional strategies that can help libraries proactively sell the benefits of AI to their institutions, for example, around research excellence and student experience (Cox 2023).

But rather than expecting AI to be mentioned specifically in institutional strategies, arguably it could be seen as simply the latest strand in technological triggers for digital transformation. If so, it would follow that adoption of AI is likely to be linked to the wider commitments around digital transformation.

> Digital transformation is the profound and accelerating transformation of business activities, processes, competencies, and models to fully leverage the changes and opportunities brought by digital technologies and their impact across society in a strategic and prioritized way (Demirkan, Spohrer and Welser 2016, 14).

The proposition here is that social + mobile + analytics + cloud + Internet of Things (SMACIT) technologies initiate and make possible organisational changes in a way quite unlike the IT driven changes within organisations which have been seen in the past. Digital transformation is not solely about implementing a new technology. SMACIT technologies are generative, malleable and with impacts beyond "automation" of existing processes. Integrating SMACIT into organisational life is about reinventing what organisations do. Critically they are being used not just within organisation but have widespread usage in society. This creates the need for more customer driven strategies. Digital transformation potentially creates new business models, and even new industries, and it happens in stages. AI is very much this kind of technology. For Educause, digital transformation is

> ...a series of deep and coordinated culture, workforce, and technology shifts that enable new educational and operating models and transform an institution's business model, strategic directions, and value proposition (Brown, Reinitz, and Wetzel 2020).

From a strategic perspective, it is important to think about how AI technologies and their implementation interact with other technologies such as SMACIT and augmented or virtual reality in reinventing what libraries and the institutions they serve do.

Organisational Capability

Moving from organisational strategy to capacity requires consideration of whether libraries have the ability to develop and implement AI solutions. This is partly about competencies that library staff need to develop and competencies are often the focus. But using AI effectively makes wider demands on libraries' financial and more intangible resources. Collectively these resources could be called AI capability: the ability of an organisation "to select, orchestrate, and leverage its AI-specific resources" (Mikalef and Gupta 2021, 2).

A convincing model of organisational capability for AI has been developed by Mikalef and Gupta (2021). Rooted in the resource-based theory of the firm their approach differentiates three types of resource that make up AI capability: Tangible resources, human resources and intangible resources (Table 6.1).

Table 6.1: Resources Required for AI Capability (Adapted from Mikalef and Gupta 2021)

Tangible resources	
	Data
	Technology
	Basic resources
Human resources	
	Technical skills
	Business skills
Intangible resources	
	Inter-departmental coordination
	Organisational change capacity
	Risk proclivity

Tangible resources comprise not only data resources including user data and collection data and a suitable technical infrastructure, but also access to basic resources such as money and time to invest in AI. Many libraries do have data in the form of both collections and user data. They may also have access to the necessary technical infrastructure to support AI. Funding is always a challenge, but the exciting potential of AI may make it possible to construct a business case to obtain funding.

Human resources combine both the technical skills to develop AI applications, and, equally importantly, the business skills to plan and deliver AI projects and implement AI as a service. Libraries may well have significant technical skills in their teams. They are used to delivering on technical projects, which experimenting with AI involves. Given the changing technical landscape of the last few decades, there is a huge amount of experience in libraries in implementing and promoting new systems. It is increasingly recognised that AI should be developed in participatory ways with stakeholders, which is very much in tune with previous developments within libraries.

Mikalef and Gupta's (2021) intangible resources include the ability to coordinate activities between departments, the ability to manage organisational change, and the willingness to take risks, all of which might be regarded as leadership challenges. Delivering them may also imply structural reorganisation. Again, libraries frequently have the capabilities required, especially in terms of coordination. So much organisational change has happened in libraries in the last few years, that the ability to adapt with agility has increased. Risk-taking may require further organisational change.

Mikalef and Gupta's (2021) model can be used as a framework to evaluate whether a library and its host organisation) have the capacity or the readiness to develop and implement AI systems, especially descriptive AI. Readiness is likely to vary across library sectors. A strengths, weaknesses, opportunities and threats (SWOT) analysis for academic libraries can be found in Cox (2023). National libraries, and some research libraries, have a proven track record of development in descriptive AI, as chapters in this book show. Critically they have vast bodies of collection data that need advanced techniques to enable improved access. Given the benefits, libraries may be able to obtain the funds to support such projects. Libraries and librarians can develop technical skills through proof of concept projects and acquire the business skills through turning projects to services.

The case is less clear for smaller, less resourced libraries, particularly if they do not have unique collections requiring special treatment. Smaller libraries are more likely to buy in systems. Licensing systems does not diminish the possibilities of using descriptive AI, but smaller libraries are more likely to make successful implementations of AI through collaboration. There might need to be longer term processes of capacity building through staff training and proof of concept projects. Defining the AI capabilities and competencies needed for the wide range of institutions in the library sector is an important but complex task.

Artificial Intelligence Literacy and Competencies

Returning to the question of technical skills, it may be useful to say something about what knowledge and skills are relevant to applying AI in the library context, from the policy and organisational level to what skills and knowledge are needed at the level of the individual professional.

Given the range of AI applications relevant to libraries, from descriptive AI used to improve access to collections through chatbots to the improvement of backend systems, it may not be possible to come to a general conclusion about what AI competencies are needed. But there is a starting point in definitions of AI literacy, " a set of competencies that enables individuals to critically evaluate AI technologies; communicate and collaborate effectively with AI; and use AI as a tool online, at home, and in the workplace" (Long and Magerko 2020, 2). The extended definition implies knowing:
– What AI is, the ability to recognise AI when it is encountered and understand distinctions between general and narrow AI

- What AI can do, the skill of differentiating the tasks AI is good at doing from those it is not good at, and imagining future uses, reflecting the evolving nature of AI
- How AI works, including how computers represent the world in models, with an emphasis on data literacy
- How AI should be used, emphasising ethical considerations, and
- How people perceive AI.

Long and Magerko's approach defines general knowledge about AI needed by every citizen and therefore what all librarians involved in AI literacy training need to know, not least if they are seeking to train users in AI literacy. Applying AI to library services requires deeper knowledge. For example, to use AI in describing library collections, the technical requirements would involve knowledge of:
- Collections as data (Padila et al. 2023)
- Relevant algorithms, and
- Ethics and governance.

Lee (2022) summarizes key points to form a generic guideline of key questions that need to be answered to develop an AI project around a collection. Other types of AI application less collection-centric would require a different skill set. There is a need for more work around defining relevant competencies for AI literacy. What does emerge is that since AI today is data driven, high level data skills are necessary, and the pre-existing knowledge and competencies of librarians and information professionals are of immense value, including knowledge of library-specific data for library projects or contributions to data governance and stewardship in wider institutional applications of AI. All of the following aspects of data use and governance might be areas where librarians can contribute:
- Skills in finding data in a complex information landscape
- Advocacy for the value of sharing, openness and interoperability, but along with awareness of the legitimate reasons for protecting confidentiality and privacy
- Knowledge of the copyright and licensing requirements for the appropriate uses of data
- Awareness of the provenance, validity and quality of data relevant to its use
- Knowledge of how to attach descriptions (metadata) to data, and a commitment to metadata standards
- Development of criteria for selection of tools for undertaking data analysis, and
- Approaches to the storage, preservation, or destruction, of data.

Of particular importance are the issues around provenance and validity. Knowing the origins of any data, such as the creator and the purpose, helps understand how it can be used, and the limits on its interpretation. Validity is about whether the data measures what is cared about. It is always a danger that AI is applied to data without understanding the limits of the data available, arising from how it was created. For data-driven AI, the value of the data-related skills of librarians has great importance. Librarians' focus on understanding user needs is another area where the knowledge of information professionals is highly relevant to AI projects.

The Ethics of Artificial Intelligence

AI promises so much and has great potential in many domains. AI can help clinicians identify patients at risk through scanning and analysis of health data; provide people with disabilities with a voice assistant and improve customer service through 24/7 chatbots. It has the ability to automate routine tasks. AI also offers to support the prime objectives of the library profession in supporting the creation of knowledge through new research methods, the promotion of better and more equitable access to knowledge, the improvement of descriptions of different types of material, as well as through techniques such as translation, transcription, summarisation, and recommendation.

The potential benefits of AI are immense. Yet its emergence and adoption are surrounded by considerable controversy, particularly because it is being developed by the dominant powerful Big Tech companies for commercial ends, and with deep societal and geopolitical implications. As already noted, national policies frequently mention ethics and the need for responsible and trustworthy AI.

Thus, one important dimension of AI are issues of ethics, thinking about how to ensure long-term benefits to society and minimise the risks. Long and Magerko list eight ethical issues:

- Privacy
- Employment
- Misinformation
- The singularity
- Ethical decision making
- Diversity
- Bias, and
- Transparency and accountability (Long and Magerko 2020).

The singularity, the idea that at some point AI gets out of control in an irreversible way, is perhaps not of immediate concern; the current era involves narrow AI with systems designed to perform a specific task or a set of closely related tasks. But the other issues listed are all genuine areas of concern and require potential response and action. The issues highlighted are ones where the library world has always had a strong stance, enshrined in ethics and values statements, like those issued by IFLA. The library and information profession has an important role to play in speaking out about the ethical risks of AI, which are often a secondary consideration for Big Tech. Ensuring that the risks and issues are addressed is inherent to any AI project. It is not a separate consideration, but embedded and ongoing from the design of the project through into the future, as AI systems are implemented and maintained.

Promoting AI literacy in society is an important task for libraries including enabling citizens and workers to understand how to protect their privacy, and their employment. Complementing this, there could be a role for information professionals in ensuring that AI is less opaque(Ridley and Pawlick-Potts 2021).

Bias in AI is of particular importance. Algorithms trained on biased data will produce biased outcomes. There are many cases where AI tools have shown gross and discriminatory bias (AIAAIC 2023). For example, a request for generative AI to produce an image of a doctor will probably produce an image of a white man. Of course, library collections themselves are not unbiased. Work over the last few years on the decolonisation of library collections has alerted the profession to such biases in library collections. What the library and information profession has learned about resolving bias in collections can be applied to reducing bias in AI. The impact of bias in AI is critical, especially where AI operates autonomously in decision making. And the issue of bias in AI is not accidental. At the root of the problem are structural issues. The core AI workforce remains predominately white and male (Collett, Neff and Gomes 2022). Barriers for women and people from ethnic minorities or disabilities to enter work in computing and engineering are well known and has been a problem from the early days of computing. Librarianship with its strong value propositions around issues such as bias and a female majority profession may be in a position to help address such structural issues. Experiences in seeking to diversify the library and information profession further may be helpful in developing approaches to equality, diversity and inclusion in AI.

The wider societal impacts of AI are not mentioned directly by Long and Magerko (2020) in their list of ethical issues, but everyone in the profession should be concerned about the impact on social equity of an AI industry driven primarily by commercial motives. Exemplary AI projects led by libraries will not only reap the benefits of implementing AI but also demonstrate that a deep concern for ethics is one-way libraries can promote responsible AI.

Conclusion

This section of the book in exploring the wider issues of AI in libraries opens with a chapter by Fiona Bradley on the policy context. She addresses the issues and concerns in ensuring that AI applications are deployed for successful and safe use by the community and outlines progress in several parts of the world on developing such policies. Josette Riep and Annu Prabhakar report on a pilot study conducted to assess potential bias when leveraging AIML in recruitment and retention of students in higher education in the US. There have been consistent reports on race and equity issues in American education and ongoing persistent and painful gaps in educational outcomes (Collins 2021). Leveraging AIML in higher education opens up great benefits for measuring and impacting equality in education. Raymond Uzwyshyn focuses on building AI skills and infrastructure with particular reference to research data repositories and digital scholarly ecosystems and provides a list of educational resources which can be used to construct expertise for both library staff and researchers within the community. Neli Tshabalala describes a project involving the implementation of a robotic solution at the North-West University in South Africa which reviewed the potential of available AI applications and tracked their progress. Andrew Cox concludes the section with reflections on the value of ethics scenarios in clarifying the myriad of ethical issues faced by library and information professionals in implementing and using AI applications in their libraries and ensuring that users understand the limitations of new services like ChatGPT.

References

AI, Algorithmic, and Automation Incidents and Controversies (AIAAIC). n.d. "AIAAIC Repository." https://www.aiaaic.org/aiaaic-repository.

Brooks, D. Christopher, and Mark McCormack. 2020. *Driving Digital Transformation in Higher Education*. ECAR Research Report, June 15. Boulder, CO: EDUCAUSE. https://www.educause.edu/ecar/research-publications/driving-digital-transformation-in-higher-education/2020/introduction-and-key-findings.

Brown, Malcolm, Betsy Reinitz, and Karen Wetzel. 2019. "Digital Transformation Signals: Is Your Institution on the Journey?" *EDUCAUSE Review, Enterprise Connections Blog*, October 9. https://er.educause.edu/blogs/2019/10/digital-transformation-signals-is-your-institution-on-the-journey

Collett, Clementine, Gina Neff, and Livia Gouvea Gomes. 2022. *The Effects of AI on the Working Lives of Women*. Paris: United Nations Educational, Scientific and Cultural Organization, InterAmerican Development Bank, Organisation for Economic Co-operation and Development. https://unesdoc.unesco.org/ark:/48223/pf0000380861.

Collins, Michael. 2021. "Opinion: Why College Majors Are Another Form of Implicit Bias in Higher Education: Instead of Being a Great Equalizer, Higher Education is Leaving Too Many Students

Behind..” *The Hechinger Report*, December 20, 2021. https://hechingerreport.org/opinion-why-college-majors-are-another-form-of-implicit-bias-in-higher-education/r.

Cox, Andrew M. 2023. “Developing a Library Strategic Response to Artificial Intelligence.” *Jisc. National Centre for AI. Understanding AI in Education*, June 5. https://nationalcentreforai.jiscinvolve.org/wp/2023/06/05/library-strategy-and-artificial-intelligence/.

Demirkan, Haluk, James C. Spohrer, and Jeffrey J. Welser. 2016. “Digital Innovation and Strategic Transformation.” *IT Professional* 18, no.6: 14–18. DOI: 10.1109/MITP.2016.115

Huang, Yingshen, Andrew M. Cox, and John Cox. 2023. “Artificial Intelligence in Academic Library Strategy in the United Kingdom and the Mainland of China.” *The Journal of Academic Librarianship* 49, no. 6: 102772. https://doi.org/10.1016/j.acalib.2023.102772.

Lee, Benjamin Charles Germain. 2023. “The ‘Collections as ML Data’ Checklist for Machine Learning and Cultural Heritage.” *Journal of the Association for Information Science and Technology*. Early view. https://doi.org/10.1002/asi.24765. Available at https://arxiv.org/pdf/2207.02960.pdf.

Long, Duri, and Brian Magerko. 2020. “What is AI literacy? Competencies and Design Considerations.” in *CHI ’20: Proceedings of the 2020 CHI Conference on Human Factors in Computing Systems*, 1–16. New York: Association for Computing. https://doi.org/10.1145/3313831.3376727. Available at https://static1.squarespace.com/static/53c69580e4b08011fc2337bf/t/5e2893e4a9d342214836e832/1579717605435/CHI+2020+AI+Literacy+Paper-Camera+Ready.pdf.

Mikalef, Patrick, and Manjul Gupta. 2021. “Artificial Intelligence Capability: Conceptualization, Measurement Calibration, and Empirical Study on Its Impact on Organizational Creativity and Firm Performance.” *Information & Management* 58, no. 3: 103434. https://doi.org/10.1016/j.im.2021.103434.

Padila, Thomas, Hannah Scates Kettler, Stewart Varner, and Yasmeen Shorish. 2023. “Vancouver Statement on Collections as Data.” V.3 *Zenodo*, September 13. https://zenodo.org/records/8342171.

Papyshev, Gleb, and Masaru Yarime. 2023. “The State’s Role in Governing Artificial Intelligence: Development, Control, and Promotion through National Strategies.” *Policy Design and Practice* 6, no. 1: 79–102. https://doi.org/10.1080/25741292.2022.2162252.

Ridley, Michael, and Danica Pawlick-Potts. 2021. “Algorithmic Literacy and the Role for Libraries.” *Information Technology and Libraries* 40, no. 2. https://doi.org/10.6017/ital.v40i2.12963. Available at https://ital.corejournals.org/index.php/ital/article/view/12963/10391.

Wheatley, Amanda, and Sandy Hervieux. 2019. “Artificial Intelligence in Academic Libraries: An Environmental Scan.” *Information Services & Use* 39, no. 4: 347–356. DOI: 10.3233/ISU-190065. https://content.iospress.com/articles/information-services-and-use/isu190065.

Fiona Bradley

7 The Policy Context of Artificial Intelligence

Abstract: Policies, rules and laws have a direct impact on technologies including artificial intelligence (AI), and the companies, organisations, and researchers that develop these technologies. Despite rapid developments in AI policy, further effort is required by governments and industry to ensure that policy at all levels from laws to industry self-regulation addresses human rights, risks, and ethical concerns. As organisations committed to freedom of access to information and literacies, libraries are both important stakeholders in AI policy development, and users of AI tools and methods. The library sector's contribution to AI policies in Canada, Europe, and Australia demonstrate the sector's impact to date and potential for further influence. The chapter concludes by observing that while the heightened media attention paid to AI could be short-lived, opportunities to safeguard the free flow of information and rights must be sought to ensure that AI lives up to aspirations of being trustworthy, responsible, and people-centred.

Keywords: Library policies; Artificial intelligence – library applications; Artificial intelligence – political aspects

The Context

The policy context of AI is complex and rapidly changing. Policy is developed by government at the intergovernmental, international, national, and regional levels. It can also be designed to regulate specific sectors, often in collaboration with the industries and companies that are the subject of policy. In addition to formal policies, regulations, and laws, there are voluntary, industry-led agreements, standards, and other instruments. These agreements support self-regulation by industry. At another level, institutions such as universities and schools, library associations, and individual libraries may also set policies that define their obligations under relevant legislation and policies and outline how they will provide services. This chapter focuses on how government, industry, and institutional policies are shaping the changing landscape of AI regulation. Government, industry, and institutional policies matter for libraries because they impact the free flow of information, influence funding, shape how libraries provide their services, inform legal and reporting obligations, and provide for remedies if something goes wrong.

Government Policy Frameworks

Government AI policies often include a mix of research agenda-setting objectives, investment in research and development, standards, and broader geopolitical issues (Smuha 2021). In turn, AI itself has numerous applications and sub-fields that have influenced diverse policy developments. The use of natural language processing (NLP), machine learning (ML) and algorithms in information processing, recommender systems, and generative AI are prominent topics in AI policy. At the same time, harms and errors that result from mishandling data, data breaches, and bias have been documented by researchers and reporters in relation to the use of AI in applications including facial recognition, automated job candidate screening, and welfare payments (Bender et al. 2021; Henriques-Gomes 2021; Krafft et al. 2020). These errors have led to greater scrutiny and policy focus on the harms that these new technologies can cause. Policymakers have recognised both the opportunities and risks associated with AI in policies with concepts centred on trustworthy AI in Europe (European Commission 2024a) and responsible use of AI in Canada (Canada Treasury Board of Canada Secretariat 2019; Smuha 2021). At the intergovernmental level, UNESCO has adopted in 2021 recommendations on AI with a focus on people-centred AI (UNESCO 2022). UNESCO's recommendations aim to set a global standard to ensure AI systems work for the benefit of humanity and the environment and avoid harms through principles in line with international laws and agreements, respect for human rights, and practical action. Commitments to privacy, sustainability, awareness and AI literacy, transparency, and explainability are among the key principles. Further work has been undertaken by UNESCO at the second Global Forum on the Ethics of AI in February 2024.

At the same time, as governments consider responsible use of AI and its impact on people, awareness of AI is now rising across other portfolios which is likely to lead to further waves of policy development with implications for information management, data sharing, and privacy. At the intergovernmental level, the United Nations (UN) has raised numerous concerns about AI and risks to human rights (UN 2021). The European Space Agency (ESA) has been exploring the implications of AI in space, including applications spanning surveillance to satellite operations in space (ESA 2023). In the United States, the intelligence community has indicated that the rapid development of AI could have consequences across all aspects of research with impacts on security and stability (USODNI 2023). These examples highlight that there is no policy area that AI will not impact. While some of the policy areas are much further away from the interests of libraries than others, some of the policies being developed for the future may potentially have unanticipated impacts on the free flow of information and rights of individuals and will require consistent monitoring and potential action.

The Policy Challenges

With so many policy areas and stakeholders involved, a key challenge is to bridge the gap between researchers, industry, and policy to ensure policy options are effective. Furthermore, despite the rapid growth in AI policy across a range of government portfolios, there remain many gaps. Some of the gaps arise due to the multiple definitions of AI that have arisen over time, that take different perspectives on how AI systems think like humans, act like humans, think rationally, and act rationally (Russell and Norvig 2021). In the policy space, it is perceived that there is a gap between the way researchers conceptualise and define AI, and the way policymakers define AI. AI policies to date reflect a tendency of policymakers to focus on how AI systems compare to human thought or behaviour, while researchers tend to put systems and technical elements at the centre (Krafft et al. 2020). Some policy gaps provide the opportunity for further engagement by libraries, civil society, and industry alike to shape future policy (Bradley 2022). Yet, how and when these opportunities are likely to arise can be challenging to determine. Policy studies identify numerous factors that can influence when policy is likely to emerge. The factors include competition between topics for space on the political agenda, the role of interest groups in influencing policymakers, and a tendency towards incrementalism in policymaking that can be punctuated by crises (Baumgartner and Jones 2012; John 2012; Sabatier 1988). The specific political context in each country and opportunities to participate are other critical factors (John 2012). Policymakers are further challenged by the complexity of determining when to develop policies and regulations. Intervene too early and innovation may be stifled; take action too late and governments must play catch up (Guston 2014). Analysis of major AI policies to date concludes that there is no single approach that will work in all countries. The context is key (O'Shaughnessy and Sheehan 2023).

A vital area that policymakers must now play catch up in is to ensure that AI policies more fully consider human rights impacts and the interests and rights of consumers. The intersection between AI, privacy, and other human rights is still emerging (Rodrigues 2020). Since 2022 and the launch of a wave of public-facing generative AI tools for text, images, and audio, there has been a sharp growth in awareness about the impact of AI on consent, data protection, and copyright. Large language models (LLMs) rely on extremely large corpora of text and images for training (Bender et al. 2021). There is little transparency about exactly what content such models are able to access leading to speculation that any open content on the web may be ingested without the knowledge or consent of the creators (Mims 2023). In response, some media organisations have called for a licensing scheme to compensate organisations for traffic and revenue lost to chatbots, with a passing resemblance to Australia's News Media Bargaining Code that compensates large media organisations for revenue lost to social media and search platforms (Bossio et al. 2022; Di Stefano 2023). These responses are important to monitor because the interests of large rightsholders and the rights of individuals in consent and data sharing must be balanced. Despite growing awareness of the issues, the opportunity for full engagement with the human rights impacts of AI has not yet come to pass.

Several countries and regions have begun to pursue algorithmic transparency as one way to begin to address questions about fairness, consent, and data rights. An Australian report on human rights and technology recommended the development of accountability mechanisms for government and corporations, and compliance with anti-discrimination laws to promote algorithmic fairness (Australian Human Rights Commission 2021). In Europe, the *Digital Services Act* requires social media and e-commerce platforms to be transparent about their recommender systems and content moderation decisions (European Commission 2022). The introduction of the *Digital Services Act* aims to update existing regulations and harmonise legislation across the European Union's member countries that deal with illegal content and advertising online. "The Digital Services Act and Digital Markets Act aim to create a safer digital space where the fundamental rights of users are protected and to establish a level playing field for businesses" (European Commission 2024a).

The European *Digital Services Act* has designated social media and e-commerce platforms which must comply with stringent regulations.

> The DSA classifies platforms or search engines that have more than 45 million users per month in the EU as very large online platforms (VLOPs) or very large online search engines (VLOSEs). The Commission has begun to designate VLOPs or VLOSEs based on user numbers provided by platforms and search engines (European Commission 2024b)

The very large online platforms and search engines include US-based platforms provided by Facebook, Apple, and Google along with Chinese platforms including Alibaba and Bytedance's TikTok, and European e-commerce sites Zalando and booking.com, among others (European Commission 2024b). Many of the platforms are actively investing in developing and launching generative AI tools and chatbots, and multi-modal AI that can generate sound and images from text prompts. Europe's approach to regulating companies and platforms through the *Digital Services Act* will be closely watched. Europe's approach taps into the region's longstanding orientation as a regulatory leader (Smuha 2021). As of late 2023, the EU reached agreement on laws on AI that would consider different applications and risks, however the proposed laws are not due for implementation until 2025 (European Parliament 2023).

Beyond Europe, amid a flurry of regulations designed to clean up the internet and data protection, China introduced regulations on algorithmic transparency in mid-2021 (Deutsche Welle 2021). Early reviews of the policy suggest that while regulation has helped to push for some transparency, algorithms created by platforms are extremely complex to understand and companies can be vague in their reporting (Sheehan and Du 2022). Likewise, when Twitter voluntarily released part of its algorithm in 2023, the effort was criticised for doing little to increase transparency (Bell 2023). The latest version of OpenAI's ChatGPT-4 was released without details about the training model and size, unlike earlier versions (OpenAI 2023). It remains uncertain what policy and self-regulation aimed at algorithmic transparency can achieve in practice, particularly if disclosures are selective and policymakers lack technical capacity to interpret them.

The Current State and Limitations of Voluntary Industry Self-Regulation

Turning from government to industry, voluntary codes and standards are intended to address the need for self-regulation either instead of government policy or in addition to it. A prominent example in March 2023 of concern for regulation of AI was an open letter penned by prominent US tech names that called for a voluntary pause in developing LLMs for six months (Future of Life Institute 2023). However, the letter was criticised by AI researchers for ignoring real harms to people that already exist due to AI, and for being inaccurate in indicating how the letter cited the researchers' earlier work on LLMs (Bender et al. 2021; Coldewey 2023). Some companies have been accused of restricting freedom of expression by pre-emptively facilitating censorship by not allowing some prompts to be actioned, such as images of politicians (Stanley-Becker and Harwell 2023). Ethics, bias, and accuracy are some of the key concerns raised concerning AI, but technology is fast outpacing industry standards and government policy. The consequences of bias in training data sets, unethical labour practices, and the predatory role of data brokers are widely documented in the literature (Krafft et al. 2020; Noble 2018; Smuha 2021). When industries fail to self-regulate effectively, policymakers may step in. In Australia, for example, the government has welcomed the development of industry-focused responsible AI networks while foreshadowing that government regulation may become necessary if self-regulation efforts are not sufficiently effective (Tonkin 2023).

Library Engagement in Artificial Intelligence Policy Development

Having introduced the broader policy context for AI, this chapter seeks now to highlight where the library sector has engaged with governmental and industry policy before turning to the work libraries are doing in their institutions to develop and implement policies. Libraries have engaged in different jurisdictions and across portfolios to ensure that policies safeguard research, culture, and the rights of creators. Library associations working with their member libraries and staff have a particular role in leading advocacy campaigns and policy engagement. Many AI applications are reliant on related policies such as data protection and copyright reforms to operate. These policies have in turn influenced the development of AI policy and how different platforms and industries are treated. For example, libraries advocated to the European Commission on copyright policy reforms to argue that new neighbouring rights in favour of publishers would impact the ability of libraries to make use of text of data mining or existing copyright exceptions in support of research, culture, and preservation activities (European Commission 2016). More recently, an analysis of national AI plans registered in the OECD AI Policy Observatory identified that libraries were included in plans in Switzerland, Germany, Norway, the Netherlands, Ireland, and Bulgaria (Bradley 2022).

Another example of engagement in policy development by libraries includes a response by the Canadian Association of Research Libraries (CARL-ABRC) to the consultation on AI regulation and its relation to Canadian personal information protection laws (CARL-ABRC 2020). Several Australian library organisations made a joint submission to a federal inquiry on the use of generative AI in education (Australia. Parliament. House Standing Committee on Employment, Education and Training 2023; ALIA 2023). As more policies are developed at international and local levels, the library sector will undoubtedly continue to identify opportunities to engage to make the case for access to information, maintenance of the cultural record, and user rights.

At the institutional or library level, there is a small but growing number of policies developed by libraries as more challenging and risky AI applications become available. Some AI methods and tools have been embedded in library systems and services for some time. Recommender systems, optical character recognition (OCR), and some elements of Natural Language Processing (NLP) that underpin collections as data work are familiar to many libraries. These somewhat prosaic uses of AI and ML have been joined by an explosion of media coverage around generative AI, consumer-facing robots, self-driving vehicles, and facial recognition.

While the recent developments have increased consciousness, enthusiasm, and concern about AI among the public, they have also raised questions from the library sector about the library's role in explaining the technologies responsibly such as by developing algorithmic literacy (Ridley and Pawlick-Potts 2021). Library associations have a key role in outlining the issues and policy considerations. While a statement rather than a policy, IFLA's statement on AI and libraries highlighted a range of ethical and technical issues for libraries to consider (IFLA FAIFE 2020) and IFLA has indicated that AI policy remains on its agenda in ten things to look out for in 2024 (IFLA 2024). In the United States, the American Library Association adopted a resolution on opposition to facial recognition in libraries in 2021 (ALA 2021).

At the institutional level, research, academic and school libraries have implemented guidance regarding the use of generative AI in assignments and research articles. Some guidance may be in response to government policy, for example in Western Australia students were briefly banned from using Chat-GPT in the classroom (Davis 2023). A framework for the use of generative AI in schools was subsequently released by the Australian federal Department of Education in late 2023 (Australia. Department of Education 2023). Educational institutions may set policies about the use of AI tools and other technologies, which libraries interpret through guidance about the responsible use of research materials, accurate referencing, privacy obligations, and managing digital well-being. These activities are ones with which libraries have long been involved. Consequently, these approaches can be viewed largely as an update to existing roles and practices.

Future of Artificial Intelligence Policy

AI policy is developing rapidly across multiple issue areas, regions, and sectors. Further engagement is required to prioritise access to information and to preserve individual rights at different levels. Emergent policy has a direct and indirect impact on access to information, the rights of creators and users of information, and the human rights of individuals and society as a whole. The breadth and speed of policy development mean that those monitoring the issues and opportunities for engagement must prioritise the aspects most likely to impact the library sector and the interests of library users. While many aspects of AI have received significant media attention recently, the period of deliberation and consideration will likely be short-lived as AI tools are further embedded into everyday applications, search, and other basic computing and information processing tasks. The challenge for the library sector will be to continue to find opportunities to make the case for the free flow of information and to safeguard individual rights to ensure future AI policy lives up to aspirations of being trustworthy, responsible, and people-centred.

References

American Library Association (ALA). 2021. "Resolution in Opposition to Facial Recognition Software in Libraries." https://www.ala.org/advocacy/intfreedom/facialrecognitionresolution.

Australia. Department of Education. 2023. "The Australian Framework for Generative Artificial Intelligence (AI) in Schools." *Announcements*, December 1, 2023. https://www.education.gov.au/schooling/announcements/australian-framework-generative-artificial-intelligence-ai-schools. The Framework itself is available at https://www.education.gov.au/schooling/resources/australian-framework-generative-artificial-intelligence-ai-schools.

Australia. Parliament. House Standing Committee on Employment, Education and Training. 2023. "Inquiry into the Use of Generative Artificial Intelligence in the Australian Education System." https://www.aph.gov.au/Parliamentary_Business/Committees/House/Employment_Education_and_Training/AIineducation.

Australian Human Rights Commission. 2021. "Human Rights and Technology: Final Report." Canberra: Australian Human Rights Commission. https://web.archive.org/web/20230322213034/https://tech.humanrights.gov.au/sites/default/files/2021-05/AHRC_RightsTech_2021_Final_Report.pdf

Australian Library and Information Association (ALIA). 2023. "Joint Submission from Library and Information Related Organisations to the Inquiry into Generative Artificial Intelligence in the Australian Education System." Submission 51. CAVAL, CAUL, AI4LAM, Open access Australia, Australian Library and Information Association, National and State Libraries Australasia. https://www.aph.gov.au/DocumentStore.ashx?id=e8ba1ba1-c42b-415c-b3a6-b0e-d43a52644&subId=745310.

Baumgartner, Frank R., and Bryan D. Jones. 2012. *The Politics of Information: Problem Search and Public Policy in Post-War America*. Chicago, ILL: University of Chicago Press.

Bell, Karissa. 2023. "What Did Twitter's 'Open Source' Algorithm Actually Reveal? Not a Lot." *Engadget*, November 7, 2023. https://www.engadget.com/what-did-twitters-open-source-algorithm-actually-reveal-not-a-lot-194652809.html.

Bender, Emily M., Timnit Gebru, Angelina McMillan-Major, and Shmargaret Shmitchell. 2021. "On the Dangers of Stochastic Parrots: Can Language Models Be Too Big?." In *Proceedings of the 2021 ACM Conference on Fairness, Accountability, and Transparency*, 610–23. FAccT '21. New York NY: Association for Computing Machinery. https://doi.org/10.1145/3442188.3445922.

Bossio, Diana, Terry Flew, James Meese, Tama Leaver, and Belinda Barnet. 2022. "Australia's News Media Bargaining Code and the Global Turn Towards Platform Regulation." *Policy & Internet* 14, no.1: 136–50. https://doi.org/10.1002/poi3.284.

Bradley, Fiona. 2022. "Representation of Libraries in Artificial Intelligence Regulations and Implications for Ethics and Practice." *Journal of the Australian Library and Information Association* 71, no.3: 189–200. https://doi.org/10.1080/24750158.2022.2101911. Available at https://research-repository.uwa.edu.au/en/publications/representation-of-libraries-in-artificial-intelligence-regulation.

Canada. Treasury Board of Canada Secretariat. 2019. "Ensuring Responsible Use of Artificial Intelligence to Improve Government Services for Canadians." *News Release*, March 4, 2019.

https://www.canada.ca/en/treasury-board-secretariat/news/2019/03/ensuring-responsi-ble-use-of-artificial-intelligence-to-improve-government-services-for-canadians.html.

Canadian Association of Research Libraries (CARL-ABRC). 2020. "Canadian Association of Research Libraries Submission on the Office of the Privacy Commissioner of Canada's Proposals for Ensuring Appropriate Regulation of Artificial Intelligence." March 13, 2020. https://www.carl-abrc.ca/wp-content/uploads/2020/03/CARL_Submission_AI_and_PIPEDA.pdf.

Coldewey, Devin. 2023. "Ethicists Fire Back at 'AI Pause' Letter They Say 'Ignores the Actual Harms'." *TechCrunch*, April 1, 2023. https://techcrunch.com/2023/03/31/ethicists-fire-back-at-ai-pause-let-ter-they-say-ignores-the-actual-harms/.

Davis, Ashleigh. 2023. "ChatGPT Banned in WA Public Schools in Time for Start of School Year." *ABC News*, January 30, 2023. https://www.abc.net.au/news/2023-01-30/chatgpt-to-be-banned-from-wa-public-schools-amid-cheating-fears/101905616.

Deutsche Welle. 2021. "China Sets New Rules for Internet Algorithms." *Deutsche Welle*, August 27, 2021. https://www.dw.com/en/china-sets-new-rules-for-internet-algorithms/a-58999473.

Di Stefano, Mark. 2023. "News Corp in Talks with AI Firm about Compensation." *Australian Financial Review*, March 8, 2023. https://www.afr.com/companies/media-and-marketing/news-corp-in-talks-with-ai-firm-about-compensation-20230308-p5cqcp.

European Commission. 2016. "Synopsis Report on the Results of the Public Consultation on the Role of Publishers in the Copyright Value Chain." https://ec.europa.eu/information_society/newsroom/image/document/2016-37/synopsis_report_-_publishers_-_final_17048.pdf.

European Commission. 2022. "Digital Services Act: Commission Welcomes Political Agreement on Rules Ensuring a Safe and Accountable Online Environment." *Press Release*, April 23, 2022. https://ec.europa.eu/commission/presscorner/detail/en/ip_22_2545.

European Commission. 2024a. "The Digital Services Act Package." https://digital-strategy.ec.europa.eu/en/policies/digital-services-act-package.

European Commission. 2024b. "Shaping Europe's Digital Future: DSA: Very Large Online Platforms and Search Engines." Last updated February 21, 2024. https://digital-strategy.ec.europa.eu/en/policies/dsa-vlops.

European Parliament. 2023, "AI Act: A Step Closer to the First Rules on Artificial Intelligence." *Press Releases.* May 11. 2023, https://www.europarl.europa.eu/news/en/press-room/20230505IPR84904/ai-act-a-step-closer-to-the-first-rules-on-artificial-intelligence.

European Space Agency. 2023. "Artificial Intelligence in Space." *[News]*. Last updated August 3, 2023. https://www.esa.int/Enabling_Support/Preparing_for_the_Future/Discovery_and_Preparation/Artificial_intelligence_in_space.

Future of Life Institute. 2023. "Pause Giant AI Experiments: An Open Letter." *Future of Life Institute*, March 22, 2023. https://futureoflife.org/open-letter/pause-giant-ai-experiments/.

Guston, David H. 2014. "Understanding 'Anticipatory Governance'." *Social Studies of Science* 44 , no.2: 218–42. https://doi.org/10.1177/0306312713508669.

Henriques-Gomes, Luke. 2021. "Robodebt: Court Approves $1.8bn Settlement for Victims of Government's 'Shameful' Failure." *The Guardian*, June 11, 2021. http://www.theguardian.com/australia-news/2021/jun/11/robodebt-court-approves-18bn-settlement-for-victims-of-gov-ernments-shameful-failure.

International Federation of Library Associations and Institutions (IFLA). 2024. "Libraries, Advocacy & Digital affairs – 10 Things to Look Out For in 2024." *News*, January 12, 2024. https://www.ifla.org/news/libraries-advocacy-digital-affairs-10-things-to-look-out-for-in-2024/.

International Federation of Library Associations and Institutions (IFLA). Committee on Freedom of Access to Information and Freedom of Expression (FAIFE). 2020. "IFLA Statement on Libraries and Artificial Intelligence." https://repository.ifla.org/handle/123456789/1646.

John, Peter. 2012. *Analyzing Public Policy*. 2nd ed. Abingdon, Oxon.: Routledge.

Krafft, P. M., Meg Young, Michael Katell, Karen Huang, and Ghislain Bugingo. 2020. "Defining AI in Policy Versus Practice." In *Proceedings of the AAAI/ACM Conference on AI, Ethics, and Society*, 72–78. New York NY: Association for Computing Machinery. https://doi.org/10.1145/3375627.3375835.

Mims, Christopher. 2023. "Chatbots Are Digesting the Internet. The Internet Wants to Get Paid." *Wall Street Journal*, April 29, 2023. https://www.wsj.com/articles/chatgpt-ai-artificial-intelligence-ope-nai-personal-writing-5328339a.

Noble, Safiya Umoja. 2018. *Algorithms of Oppression: How Search Engines Reinforce Racism*. New York: New York University Press. Introduction available at https://safiyaunoble.com/wp-content/uploads/2020/09/Algorithms_Oppression_Introduction_Intro.pdf.

O'Shaughnessy, Matt, and Matt Sheehan. 2023. "Lessons from the World's Two Experiments in AI Governance." *Carnegie Endowment for International Peace*. Commentary, February 14, 2023. https://carnegieendowment.org/2023/02/14/lessons-from-world-s-two-experiments-in-ai-gover-nance-pub-89035.

OpenAI. 2023. "GPT-4 Technical Report." *arXiv*. https://doi.org/10.48550/arXiv.2303.08774.

Ridley, Michael, and Danica Pawlick-Potts. 2021. "Algorithmic Literacy and the Role for Libraries." *Information Technology and Libraries* 40, no. 2: 1–15. https://doi.org/10.6017/ital.v40i2.12963.

Rodrigues, Rowena. 2020. "Legal and Human Rights Issues of AI: Gaps, Challenges and Vulnera-bilities." *Journal of Responsible Technology* 4, 100005. https://doi.org/10.1016/j.jrt.2020.100005.

Russell, Stuart J., and Peter Norvig. 2021. *Artificial Intelligence: A Modern Approach*. 4th ed. Hoboken NJ: Pearson.

Sabatier, Paul A. 1988. "An Advocacy Coalition Framework of Policy Change and the Role of Policy-Oriented Learning Therein." *Policy Sciences* 21, no. 22–3: 129–68. https://doi.org/10.1007/BF00136406.

Sheehan, Matt, and Sharon Du. 2022. "What China's Algorithm Registry Reveals about AI Governance." *Carnegie Endowment for International Peace*, December 9, 2022. https://carnegieendowment.org/2022/12/09/what-china-s-algorithm-registry-reveals-about-ai-gover-nance-pub-88606.

Smuha, Nathalie A. 2021. "From a 'Race to AI' to a 'Race to AI Regulation': Regulatory Competition for Artificial Intelligence." *Law, Innovation and Technology* 13, no.1: 57–84. https://doi.org/10.1080/17579961.2021.1898300.

Stanley-Becker, Isaac, and Drew Harwell. 2023. "How a Tiny Company with Few Rules Is Making Fake Images Go Mainstream." *Washington Post*, March 30, 2023. https://www.washingtonpost.com/technology/2023/03/30/midjourney-ai-image-generation-rules/.

Tonkin, Casey. 2023. "Government Prepared to Step in with AI Regulation." *ACS Information Age*, March 23, 2023. https://ia.acs.org.au/article/2023/govt-prepared-to-step-in-with-ai-regulation.html.

UNESCO. 2022. "Recommendation on the Ethics of Artificial Intelligence: Adopted on 23 November 2021." Paris: UNESCO. https://unesdoc.unesco.org/ark:/48223/pf0000381137/PDF/381137eng.pdf.multi. [Submitted on 15 Mar 2023 (v1), last revised 4 Mar 2024 (this version, v6)].

UNESCO. n.d. "Ethics of Artificial Intelligence." https://www.unesco.org/en/artificial-intelligence/recommendation-ethics.

United Nations (UN). 2021. "Urgent Action Needed over Artificial Intelligence Risks to Human Rights." *UN News*, September 15, 2021. https://news.un.org/en/story/2021/09/1099972.

United States (US) Office of the Director of National Intelligence (ODNI). 2023. "Annual Threat Assessment. Intelligence Community Assessment." March 8, 2023. Washington, DC: Office of the Director of National Intelligence. https://www.dni.gov/index.php/newsroom/reports-publications/reports-publications-2023/3676-2023-annual-threat-assessment-of-the-u-s-intelligence-community

Josette Riep and Annu Prabhakar

8 Toward Bias-free Artificial Intelligence for Student Success in Higher Education

Abstract: Artificial Intelligence (AI) has continued to increase its footprint in (HCI). Systems that span every aspect of daily life have become increasingly reliant on algorithms to identify products, promote opportunities, and guide strategy and operations. The field of higher education has seen a dramatic increase in the use of AI to drive recruitment and retention decisions. Persistence predictors and risk factors for example have garnered broad use across institutions in some cases without a thorough assessment of the impact on underrepresented groups in areas such as science technology, engineering, and mathematics (STEM). Tangible examples of bias that exist within algorithms are too often developed by teams that lack inclusive representation or an inclusive approach through training and design. The study reported on in this chapter analysed US educational data and focused on leveraging AI to remove bias and inform the design of meaningful solutions to facilitate innovative pathways towards STEM graduation attainment for an increasingly diverse student body. The background and details of the study are outlined in the chapter, together with explanations of the methods chosen and an evaluation of the models chosen to minimize bias.

Keywords: Artificial intelligence; Big data; Machine learning; Neural networks (computer science); Bias-free language; Cultural pluralism; STEM

Introduction

Artificial intelligence (AI) and deep learning are transforming the way everyone engages, interacts and makes decisions. By executing system driven intelligent tasks, AI has a growing impact in multiple sectors including entertainment, marketing, the world of work, healthcare, and education.

The importance of science, technology, engineering and medicine (STEM) in society and education has been emphasized by many, including the Smithsonian Science Education Center.

> Four billion people on the planet use a mobile phone, while 3.5 billion people use a toothbrush. In the past two years, 90% of all of the world's data has been generated. NASA plans to set foot on Mars in the next 20 years, and driverless cars are already being tested in Europe. The future is here, and it requires a citizenry fluent in science, technology, engineering, and math (STEM) (Smithsonian Science Education Center 2024).

Yet in the years 2011 to 2017 there was an alarming overall decline in enrolments in STEM by multiple groups, with particularly stark declines for Blacks and African Americans (National Center for Educational Statistics 2023). The gap is real but nuanced by the complexity of today's environment. An increasing demand for professionals in technology and engineering is surpassed only by an inability to fill the demand. Companies are in dire need of professionals in fields like data science, software development and cybersecurity (Goupil et al. 2022). The pipeline challenge is real and spans many demographic areas. Data from the US National Center for Educational Statistics (NCES) longitudinal study from 2011 – 2017 provided in Table 8.1 shows that almost half of all students (48.99%) who pursued a degree in science, engineering and math attained the degree (Bryan et al. 2019). The numbers are significantly worse for Black/African Americans where only 30.53% attained the degree. Furthermore, 36.27% of Black/African American students left with no degree compared to 22.57% across all races. The gap highlights the need to determine the factors contributing to the disparity and to explore ways in which bias and AI might impact student success.

Table 8.1: NCES STEM Degree Attainment Longitudinal Study Data (Bryan et al. 2019)

	Attained bachelor, degree	Attained associate degree	Attained certificate	No degree Still enrolled	No degree l Left without return	Total
	(%)	(%)	(%)	(%)	(%)	%
Science, engineering, and math (all)	48.9958	10.4094	4.1211	13.8993	22.5743	100
Science, engineering, and math (Black / African American)	30.5329	8.8300	5.9101	18.4473	36.2797	100

In addition to challenges demonstrated by the large number of students who fail to graduate with a STEM degree, there is a surprising trend in the overall year to year growth across most demographic areas. Figure 8.1 plots the growth from 2013 to 2021 in STEM related programs by race and ethnicity. There are only two demographics, Hispanic and Asian, that are seeing sustained growth in degree attainment. African Americans show overall low numbers. Perhaps most shocking is the dramatic drop in STEM degree attainment by whites, perhaps partially explained by Covid. In examining how outcomes for underrepresented groups in STEM are improved, the broader question should be asked about how to improve outcomes in STEM generally.

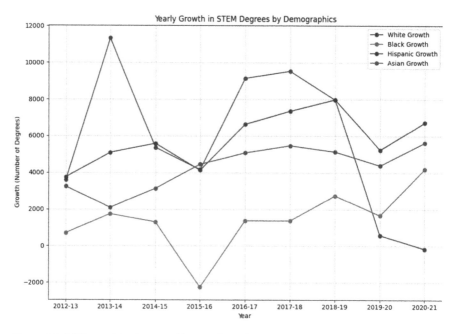

Figure 8.1: STEM growth by demographic (Data drawn from NCES 2023)

In addition, the track record on the use of AI and machine learning with African Americans has not been good. There have been many documented cases of AI bias. AI engines have disproportionately identified African Americans as animals or criminals. Incredibly, examples include an AI driven folder named gorillas being used to organize photos of Black people, which makes the disgraceful reality of inbuilt bias abundantly clear (Metz 2021).

This chapter reports on a pilot study conducted to assess potential bias when leveraging AI to support student success. Recruitment and retention are two factors but not the only evaluated in higher education in the US. By conducting the study on the use of AI and machine learning and the identification of impact factors, it was hoped to identify the potential ways and methods that bias is introduced and subsequently what can be done to raise awareness of the issues and provide solutions so that everyone can benefit from the great potential AI in higher education promises to deliver. The study was conducted leveraging available longitudinal data from the National Center for Education Statistics (NCES) within the Department of Education in the US. The research undertaken relied heavily on the ability to create a predictive model or set of models derived from the processing and analysis of data spanning multiple years. Given the vast amount of information available through NCES, it served as a foundational source for data analysis and training.

The Use of Artificial Intelligence in Higher Education

Enhanced personalization, dynamic content delivery, gaming, and predictive analytics are all driven by increased adoption of AI and machine learning (ML). AI and machine learning have transformed higher education through a wide range of applications. Student recruitment and retention initiatives in particular have garnered increased attention as educational institutions work to leverage new technologies including AI to improve student success. Systems such as Civitas Learning tout the ability to leverage machine learning to impact student attainment. Scientists and experts who work at Civitas Data and elsewhere have highlighted specifically the need to transition student success from risk factor assessment to impact factor analysis. They emphasize the need to conduct data mining and analysis within an ecosystem that encompasses the full student life cycle and promote what they describe as a caring culture that leverages a rich knowledge base of information that ties success to institutional activities (Kil, Baldasare, and Milliron 2020).

Researchers undertaking a systematic review of artificial intelligence in education in 2019 highlighted hundreds of higher education-focused AI implementations that spanned several core areas including intelligent tutoring systems (ITS); adaptive group formations for collaboration; intelligent virtual reality; and recruitment and retention strategies (Zawacki-Richter et al. 2019). The following content highlights some AI applications in higher education and refers to research undertaken into their effectiveness.

Intelligent Tutoring Systems

The systematic literature review by Zawacki-Richter et al. identified twenty-nine studies focused on intelligent tutoring systems including gap diagnosis, strength identification, learning material curation and collaboration (Zawacki-Richter et al. 2019). There are several examples of implementations in the area of STEM including tools such as ALEKS and Metatutor. ALEKS is used in multiple institutions to provide personalized online dynamic learning in the areas of mathematics and science. A 2021 study highlighted the effectiveness of ALEKS by studying 9,238 students from more than 50 institutions. The study found that ALEKS was most effective as a supplement to traditional instruction. The results of this study emphasized the ability to leverage ITS as a supplemental tool and not a replacement for instructor led courses. Stratification by populations based on race, gender or ethnicity were not the primary focus.

Additional research leveraging ALEKS has focused on analyzing drop-out and graduation rates and the impact of procrastination. The research attempted to make a correlation between time spent on a task and successful completion by analyzing student cohorts from 2014-2019 who were required to complete bridge course material in ALEKS. By analyzing student activity and comparing the amount of activity along with the timeliness of participation, the research sought to apply an empirical assessment that derived poor academic performance as a function of procrastination (Harati et al 2021). The approach provided an example of where bias might play a key role in the categorization applied to students with very little inclusion of other variables that could be contributing factors.

Student Success

The use of predictive analytics and systems that focus on data driven success models have continued to expand in use. Tools like Civitas Learning are used in multiple institutions in an effort to drive student success across a broad and diverse population of students. Since 2017 Civitas has participated in a collaborative initiative focused on promoting equity and degree completion. *Driving Toward a Degree* is a research collaborative for increasing student success across the higher education landscape. Data is collected and analyzed to offer insights to institutions for enhancing student support and success, retention, and completion. The survey responses shed light on perceptions across multiple institutions who have acknowledged the same challenges since 2017. The 2021 study evaluated responses from 2800 respondents over 1300 institutions (Shaw 2021). Questions on racial equity help gauge strategic direction and institutional priorities across institutions although there is no detail on the role that predictive analytics play in achieving equity and enhancing student success. Many companies offer proprietary algorithms that on the surface seem promising but lack detail to determine if the results are effective. Some highlight the importance of analyzing student success programs by effectively measuring impact factors (Carmean, Baer, and Kil 2021). The challenge and opportunity reside in ensuring that the impact factors being examined are holistic and representative for all groups. How for example are underrepresented groups impacted when the algorithms used are based on training data sets that lack representation? Is it an accurate predictor for all or does unintended bias play a key role?

Use of Intelligent Virtual Assistants

Neural networks or the practice of automating and processing data regarding pathways to support everything from autonomous vehicles to automated photo tagging to medical diagnoses has become one of the world's fastest growing industries. In the US alone, it was projected in 2019 that revenues would increase from 9.5 billion in 2018 to 118.6 billion in 2025 (Heinonen 2019). Page and Gelbach undertook a progressive experiment in 2016 at Georgia State University (GSU) to determine whether AI was capable of replacing human decision-making processes in addressing an individual's personal needs. They delved into the use of neural networks to facilitate student pathways to college by applying the analogy of autonomous cars to facilitate active learning and machine-driven response to external inputs. The student journey from high school to college over the summer was investigated in an effort to reduce summer melt or failure to proceed by implementing a new AI system between April and August of 2016 to determine if machine-oriented activities could automate human decision-making activities. Conversational technologies and AI were used to support students as they worked through the pre-enrollment, enrollment and orientation phases required for successful matriculation and university entrance.

Key matriculation and entrance activities including the financial aid application process, submission of transcripts, required health records, loans and tuition were included, and a virtual assistant focused on three key areas: required pre-enrolment tasks; reliable data regarding student accomplishments; and initial responses to frequently asked questions from students related to those tasks. The overall findings of the research study were encouraging. GSU was able to maintain a high level of engagement with only 6.6% of students opting out of the program Through the use of artificially intelligent virtual assistants, The hypothesis that AI driven intervention would increase successful matriculation was proven as students who participated in the program had an increased enrolment of 3.3 percent over the group that did not participate in the program resulting in a 21% reduction in failed summer matriculation. The project provided a glimpse into the new possibilities that AI could bring as well as the potential for improved outcomes and expanded impact (Page and Gelbach 2017).The student outreach program continues to operate at GSU through the Panther Experience which:

> is designed to maximize your success both inside and outside the classroom. Being a truly engaged Panther means having a diverse holistic experience built upon the POUNCE Pillars… the foundation upon which Georgia State Panthers build the necessary skills and talents to achieve all of your personal and professional life goals. Each pillar aligns with

specific programs, activities, and services available to all students: Promote Panther Pride; Own Your Academic Journey; Understand Ethics and Integrity; Nurture Healthy Habits; Connect College to Career; Embrace Campus, Cultures and Community (Georgia State University n.d.)

Bias Associated with Artificial Intelligence

Damaging examples of machine learning bias or algorithm bias have been well publicized (IBM 2023). Beyond the obvious are the subtler examples that go undetected. There are situations where the impact of AI models on staff and student recruitment, promotion, retention, educational opportunities, and educational support to name a few is not immediately known or identifiable. What happens when AI is used to identify students likely to fail particular programs or those more likely to succeed? Do models disproportionately steer African American students towards vocational opportunities and away from advanced technology fields such as cybersecurity? There are very real challenges that must be understood and addressed.

There are some leaders in this space who are working to remove bias from AI. Timnit Gebru is one. An AI expert and leader for more inclusive AI practices, Gebru has been an advocate for a strong ethical approach to AI that includes fairness, transparency, and accountability. Through a rich focus on ethics, Gebru has highlighted the lack of diversity in AI and the need to increase the number of African Americans and other underrepresented groups developing AI models (Metz 2021). Gebru and others postulate that models are in part biased because the creators of the models tend to be a monolithic group of primarily Caucasian men. Although including people of different experiences and backgrounds may help, there is also an acknowledgement that standards and guidelines must be established (Schiffer 2021). In addition, there is an acknowledgement that goes beyond the model creators, to the data used to generate the models. Models trained by data that is not also analyzed by subpopulations, for example, African Americans, may present outcomes that are not reflective of the needs of identified subgroups.

The AI industry has many opportunities for improvement. And although some glimmers of desire for improved eradication of bias have come from companies such as Microsoft and Google, there is undeniably the reality that those who speak out against bias are at risk as evidenced by the treatment of champions such as Timnit Gebru and Margaret Mitchell. Gebru and Mitchell were fired from Google after highlighting biases within Google's search engine (Schiffer 2021). Since being fired, Gebru has been subjected to accusations and racist comments with some saying that the efforts to oust prejudice were self-aggrandizing and others stating that Gebru, a Stanford computer science graduate, had no business in the AI field. Comments telling Gebru to "go back to Africa" highlight both indirect and overt forms of oppression that plague the technology space.

The Study of Bias in Artificial Intelligence through Analysis of Data from the National Center for Education Statistics

This study, reported in this chapter, was conducted against the backdrop of growing developments in the use of AI in higher education – particularly in student recruitment and retention – and the evident biases associated with these applications. The study is based on an analysis of data from the National Center for Education Statistics in the US.

The Data Available from the National Center for Education Statistics

NCES has at least two longitudinal studies pertinent to the research undertaken. Beginning Post-secondary Students and Baccalaureate and Beyond both look at data that spans multiple years

> The Beginning Postsecondary Students Longitudinal Study (BPS) currently surveys cohorts of first-time, beginning students at three points in time: at the end of their first year, and then three and six years after first starting in postsecondary education (NCES n.d.a)

> The Baccalaureate and Beyond Longitudinal Study (B&B) examines students' education and work experiences after they complete a bachelor's degree, with a special emphasis on the experiences of new elementary and secondary teachers (NCES n.d.b)

In the case of Beginning Post-secondary, the data was collected between 2011 and 2017. With approximately 22,500 respondents, the repository contains a wealth of information on students spanning their acceptance into college to the closure of their collegiate career either through degree completion, or an egress from post-secondary education.

The data analyzed includes both traditional and non-traditional students, covering over 80 categories of information. While it encompasses traditional measures such as financial status, first-generation status, and grade point average (GPA), the NCES data also captures elements that have historically been considered intangible, such as peer support, faculty-student relationships, campus climate, confidence, and other factors impacting student success. These elements provide a broader understanding of the challenges students face, including those stemming from an unfriendly or non-inclusive campus environment. Beyond measuring academic participation, the data offers insights into social interactions, experiences with faculty, and the support structures provided by peers or family. While this data alone helps narrate a comprehensive story, the application of AI could reveal success patterns that remain hidden with traditional analytical methods. Additionally, this approach could open new avenues for research into previously unexplored pathways.

The Methodology

The study used quantitative analysis to examine the educational data provided by NCES from 2011–2017. Data was first prepared, then explored, visualized, classified, and analyzed (Figure 8.2).

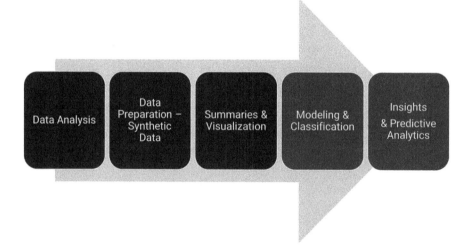

Figure 8.2: Research methodology

Data Preparation

The data was reviewed, scrubbed, prepared, and processed through multiple machine learning algorithms. Analysis for validity included the assessment of statistical pattern recognition over large data sets following three fundamental components:

– Training, using representative data from NCES's beginning post-secondary data
– Validation, using model analysis and fine tuning, and
– Testing to confirm of output accuracy.

NCES provides a detailed dictionary that summarizes available data elements along with source details including category, subject, description, source, time of collection and descriptive statistics for simple to complex data sets. The first step in data preparation included a review of all available data elements to determine which elements would be most beneficial to the development of the model. Part of the challenge in determining which elements to include was the fundamental acknowledgement that any decision to **e**xclude data may as a matter of practice introduce a certain level of bias in the form of assumptions. To alleviate any concerns, the study included most available data elements with the exception of elements that were identified to have a high level of correlation with other existing data. The following steps were taken to initially prepare the NCES data:

– High level review of beginning post-secondary (BPS) categories of data via the NCES codebook
– Creation of NCES DataLab reports filtered by STEM categories and stratified by degree attainment, race, and gender
– Execution of percentage distribution reports spanning 40 categories by subject leveraging the NCES DataLab
– Export of generated reports for post review and processing
– Generation of synthetic data, and
– Import of data into a relational database for further processing.

Although NCES provides institutions with access to raw data for analysis, raw data was not leveraged for this study. In order to address any concerns, synthetic data generation was adopted to reverse engineer aggregate report data into individual unidentifiable records.

High Level Analysis

Although the data available from NCES is not solely focused on technology and engineering, a deeper look at the data available from the <u>Baccalaureate and Beyond</u> longitudinal study identifies many factors that may be beneficial to understanding the higher education landscape for students pursuing a career in engineering and technology. Before delving into these high-level assessments, it is important to understand the foundation upon which the <u>Beginning Post-Secondary</u> repository rests.

Dataset Overview

The beginning post-secondary longitudinal study (NCES n.d.a) consists of a series of survey assessments spanning 6 years. The comprehensive study includes:
– Over 22,500 US participants
– Participants interviewed biannually over the 6-year period, and.
– Data results spanning over 1900 institutions across the United States.

In addition to survey data, NCES collected institutional data including transcripts, financial aid information and pre-enrollment data including first generation status. A demographic breakdown of assessments for the largest populations by race is contained in Figures 8.3 and 8.4.

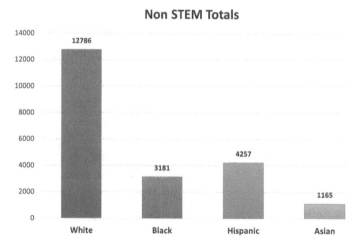

Figure 8.3: Breakdown by race

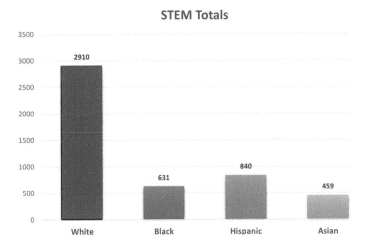

Figure 8.4: STEM Breakdown by race

Synthetic Data

Synthetic data is data generated for use in various forms of analysis including predictive analytics. There are multiple reasons researchers use synthetic data including:
– Anonymity or maintaining the privacy of study participants
– Lack of available data, and
– Algorithm training.

Synthetic data is useful only if the generated data mimics the characteristics of real data sets. The process used to generate synthetic data is key to a successful implementation. Synthetic data can be generated by different techniques (Dilmegani 2024):
– Distribution which is useful when the data is restricted or unavailable as individual records but the distribution of the data is well known across key criteria
– Variational autoencoder, which is an unsupervised model, and
– Generative adversarial network based on iterative model training.

Whether the distribution model is adopted using the Monte Carlo algorithm for example or a form of deep learning adopted for data generation, the use of synthetic data is still somewhat controversial. Concerns and debate over the validity of generated data persist. There are however many examples of proven uses for synthetic data.

Examples of Synthetic Data Use

Several tangible examples of synthetic data use in multiple areas exist including marketing, finance, systems development, quality assurance, security, clinical trials, and other forms of research (Chen et al 2019). Fraud detection methods for example is a growing area within synthetic data use. The ability to create data that provides testing and effectiveness evaluation prior to the implementation of new security measures can prove to be invaluable as it provides a means of validating controls without waiting for real data in the form of fraudulent activities to occur.

As the use of synthetic data continues to expand the processes to generate synthetic data and its overall effectiveness continue to grow. In a 2020 study, Tucker, Wang, Rotalinti and Myles set out to create more predictable outcomes and by using resampling, latent variable identification and outlier analysis, the researchers produced results that more closely tracked real world data (Tucker et al. 2020). A final example demonstrates the capabilities of synthetic data generation by introducing dependency modeling. SynC was created by researchers to move beyond the reconstruction of data from aggregate source information to modeling of dependencies across available parameters. Researchers used Canadian census data from 65,000 respondents to conduct two experiments. The process followed several key steps including synthetic reconstruction, outlier removal, dependency analysis, and predictive modeling. In addition, data sets used for analysis included variables such as personal and family history, which may have some level of impact when predicting outcomes. Researchers found that they were able to closely model results found in original data with a high level of accuracy (Li, Zhao, and Fu 2020).

Process for Synthetic Data Analysis

Although rich and plentiful access to aggregate data existed from NCES, the lack of access to the raw data warranted a novel approach that provided a means of taking the research forward. A considerable amount of time was committed to the analysis and creation of synthetic data leveraging aggregate data from NCES as the primary source. Key steps included data review and core dependency analysis, aggregate report generation, aggregate translation, and data generation.

NCES provides data tools in its DataLab for online review and analysis of source information. Powerstats in particular provides the ability to generate reports across all available subject areas. Because this study focused on predicting outcomes related to degree attainment, a foundational set of control and outcome variables was identified and included highest degree attained, race and gender and major field of study. Other data elements were reviewed and identified for detailed analysis. The list included elements that spanned institutional character-istics, education, social experiences, financial background, faculty and student interactions, confidence factors and other criteria that might have had indirect or indirect impact on the desired outcome. Ninety-seven different characteristics with multiple permutations were sourced. Each of the 97 characteristics was ana-lyzed and a report generated from NCES DataLab. Each report was restricted to National Science Foundation STEM programs in the areas of computers, engineer-ing technologies, mathematics, medicine, health, and science. Behavioral sciences were excluded for the purpose of this study. Each report provided a breakdown in percentages for a given characteristic stratified by a combination of race and gender.

To translate the individually generated reports from percentages into raw values or student counts, calculations were used to convert base percentages to overall counts first by the overall characteristics breakdown by race followed by conversions by both race and degree attainment type. Floor values were used for data analysis and model generation. Generating synthetic records for all param-eters within each of the 97 characteristics was completed using a cursor driven implementation. Due to the nature of the data and variations of the parameters within each characteristic, cursors provided an effective means of ensuring that the accurate number of person records was created. Approximately 22,500 records were generated with counts per characteristic adhering to the identified values and boundaries by race and degree attainment. Once all data was imported into a small relational database, a simple query of the more than 90 elements as a flat file with 22,500 rows was used to create a data file or efficient importing and analysis against multiple model types.

Model Analysis

As part of the process to identify the model(s) best suited for the study, research was conducted on the most prevalent predictive modeling practices. Some form of supervised learning was the best approach for what was a classification problem, although there least one study argues that supervised learning intro-duces bias into the process (Andaur Navarro et al. 2021). Research had indicated that logistic regression, gradient boosting, and random forest might be strong candidates for the predictive modelling required. The criteria used for assess-ment were:

- Type of outcome expected
- Method for identifying and excluding characteristics with a high correlation
- Process for identifying and excluding outliers
- Model complexity with this study involving a large number of characteristics and parameters
- Accuracy both overall and by one of the three key groups: Black, Black, and White, All Races, and
- Weight analysis.

Figures 8.5 and 8.6 show the results of an initial run of models to determine the best candidates, with Figure 8.5 examining error rates and Figure 8.6 indicating weight comparisons. When examining accuracy alone, many of the models appear to be ideal candidates. Fast Large Margin for example appeared to be ideal in relation to both accuracy and classification errors (Figure 8.5). However, Fast Large Margin seemed to be the most unpredictable when making small and large changes to the weighting of characteristics in the data set. Changes in race, GPA, and other key characteristics had no impact or significantly opposite impacts when comparing its output to the output of other models. Random Forest on the other hand seemed to present more predictable and consistent outputs based on the weighting of selected parameters (Figure 8.6).

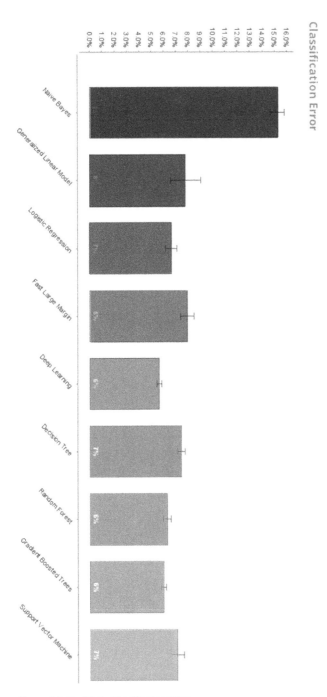

Figure 8.5: Models by Classification Error

Deep Learning		Logistic Regression		Random Forest		Gradient Boost	
Attribute	Weight	Attribute2	Weight3	Attribute4	Weight5	Attribute6	Weight7
LikelihoodExpectedEdu	0.264	LikelihoodExpectedEdu	0.2689	ProgramLastEnrolled17	0.170	LikelihoodExpectedEdu	0.2620
ProgramLastEnrolled17	0.164	Jobintensity1112	0.1133	healthservices12	0.166	intensity1314	0.1753
Jobintensity1314	0.133	Jobintensity1213	0.1007	HighestDegreeExpected14	0.135	ProgramLastEnrolled17	0.1355
HighestDegreeExpected	0.106	NumberHSScienceCourses	0.0812	UndergradProgram1112	0.128	healthservices12	0.1181
health14	0.100	HighestDegreeExpected14	0.0761	LikelihoodExpectedEdu	0.126	intensity1112	0.0954
Jobintensity1415	0.093	Jobintensity1314	0.0747	intensity1112	0.122	LikelihoodEverExpected14	0.0899
NumberofHonors	0.085	StudentInteractions12	0.0736	LikelihoodEverExpected14	0.100	SocialSatisfaction14	0.0795
NumberHSScienceCours	0.084	UndergradProgram1112	0.0632	NumberofHonors	0.096	FacultyInteractions14	0.0752
intensity1112	0.071	finaid14	0.0615	StopsThrough17	0.096	Jobintensity1314	0.0710
FamilyandFriendsSuppo	0.069	noservicesused12	0.0596	jobsoncampus17	0.095	NumberHSScienceCourses	0.0676
RaceGender	0.068	intensity1112	0.0588	jobintensity1415	0.094	intensity2017	0.0673
intensity1516	0.066	intensity1617	0.058	FacultyInteractions14	0.088	FamilyandFriendsSupport	0.0643
FacultyInteractions14	0.064	finaid12	0.0569	intensity1314	0.085	academicsupport14	0.0596
LikelihoodEverExpected	0.064	LikelihoodEverExpected14	0.0567	Jobintensity1112	0.084	StudiesSatisfaction12	0.0556
Jobintensity1516	0.063	collegecreditsHS	0.0559	intensity1415	0.083	finaid12	0.0546
				health14	0.077		

Figure 8.6: Weight comparison across models

Modeling and Bias

Understanding the role that bias has in modelling can be examined from multiple perspectives. For the purpose of this study, bias was examined from two points of view: dominance of one population over another, and inherent bias introduced in modeling algorithms. A high-level view of the generated study data identified key factors to consider in recognizing and eradicating bias. The first was simply the breakdown of the population size by a core factor of race and gender. Figure 8.7 shows that the majority of college participants are white. Given the prevalence of white participants, it is highly likely that weights will be skewed and not fully consider characteristics that may vary based on multiple factors including race and gender.

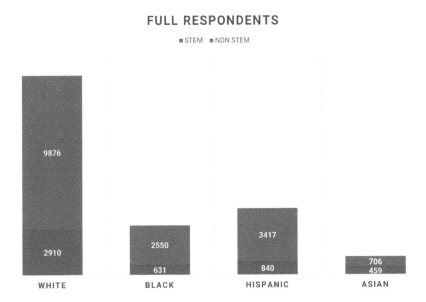

Figure 8.7: Beginning post secondary population breakdown by race

Determining the best method of addressing the challenges associated with dominance may not be as obvious as, for example, excluding the dominant race from the modeling analysis. Hanna, Denton, Smart and Smith-Loud rightfully argue that an examination of racial categories for algorithmic fairness must acknowledge that race is multifaceted and consists of both institutional and social constructs that are hard to quantify with a single attribute (Hanna et al. 2020).

Inherent Bias in Modeling

Benthall and Haynes argue that the use of supervised learning modeling intro-
duces bias by falling toward a dependence on a single variable to quantify race.
They recommend an adoption of unsupervised learning and a reliance on clustering to identify groupings based on multidimensional characteristics (Benthall and
Haynes 2019). Although unsupervised learning provides for grouping based on
multiple characteristics, it appears to be a first step that still includes some supervised learning modeling against clusters if not race. If it is a first step; questions
regarding validity must be considered to ensure that the replacement of generated
clusters does not supplant the importance of race and its potential value as part of
the overall analysis (Benthall and Haynes 2019).

In this study, a model that focused on existing identifiable data by race and also
addressed the need to consider the dimensions related to historical, institutional,
and social constructs of race was deemed desirable and was part of the evaluation process. Based on an analysis of existing supervised learning models and a
set of determining criteria including classification error, accuracy, weighting and
identified key factors, the list of potential models was reduced to three for a final
comparative analysis:

- Logistic Regression
- Gradient Boosting, and
- Random Forest.

Performance of the Models under Consideration

Logistic Regression

Although Logistic Regression is best used when the dependent variables are binary,
it warranted inclusion in the top three models to be considered for multiple reasons:

- The overall performance of the model was one of best in the algorithms
  tested against bachelor's degree attainment
- The accuracy of assigned weightings in comparison to other models was statistically significant
- The identified factors that help improve the likelihood of obtaining a bachelor's degree meshed well with other high scoring models, and
- There appeared to be a reasonable amount of weight sensitivity and ability
  to adjust weights for multiple scenarios and identify outcome changes.

The overall performance of Logistic Regression is presented in Figure 8.8.

Performances

Criterion	Value	Standard Deviation
Accuracy	98.2%	± 0.1%
Classification Error	1.8%	± 0.1%

Confusion Matrix

	true Associates	true Bachelors	true Certificate	true NoDegree	class precision
pred. Associates	551	12	4	54	88.73%
pred. Bachelors	1	1787	1	0	99.89%
pred. Certificate	1	1	348	10	96.67%
pred. NoDegree	0	0	0	1791	100.00%
class recall	99.64%	99.28%	98.58%	96.55%	

Figure 8.8: Overall performance of the Logistic Regression model

Although the class precision was not as accurate for associate degrees and certificates, the model rightly predicted bachelor's degree attainment 99.8% of the time. The model appeared to work best when running the analysis against a population of Black and White Only (Figure 8.9) or Black Only. Although more visible in decision tree models, one can see that a lack of intensity or students who attend less than full time, students who lack confidence and students who are not living on campus tend to face greater challenges with degree attainment. Conversely, students whose parents have at least a high school degree and students who are well versed and know requirements for their desired degree tend to excel. Although the results seem plausible, they are not surprising and similar to other model results.

An interesting difference in use of the model emerged when run against a Black only population (Figure 8.10). Clear changes in important factors and weights were present. In particular, the model identified two additional criteria, mental health, and the number of breaks during college, which might positively impact degree attainment. African American students whose mental health remains constant are more likely to succeed in college. The area warrants additional study as it may reflect challenges related to race faced by African American students on and off campus.

Most Likely: Bachelors

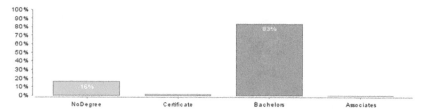

Important Factors for Bachelors

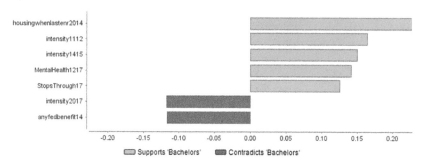

Figure 8.9: Logistic regression model key factors: Black and White

Most Likely: Bachelors

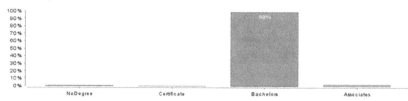

Important Factors for Bachelors

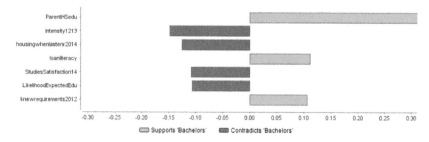

Figure 8.10: Logistic regression model key factors: Black only

Gradient Boosting

Gradient boosting is one of two decision tree models analyzed against the study data. Gradient boosting strengthens the accuracy of decision trees by creating a series of weaker decision trees that build upon one another with the goal being that each successive tree becomes a stronger predictor of outcomes (Chong 2021). From a strictly performance perspective, Gradient Boosting trees performed exception-ally well against the study data. The model accurately predicted bachelor's degree attainment with 100% accuracy (Figure 8.11).

Performances

Criterion	Value	Standard Deviation
Accuracy	99.9%	± 0.1%
Classification Error	0.1%	± 0.1%

Confusion Matrix

	true Associates	true Bachelors	true Certificate	true NoDegree	class precision
pred. Associates	555	2	1	1	99.28%
pred. Bachelors	0	1795	0	0	100.00%
pred. Certificate	0	1	354	1	99.44%
pred. NoDegree	0	0	0	1852	100.00%
class recall	100.00%	99.83%	99.72%	99.89%	

Figure 8.11: Gradient Boosting accuracy and classification

The key to Gradient Boosting trees is identifying the number of successive trees required to obtain optimization. In this study, 90 trees were created with a depth of four.

Gradient Boosted Trees - Optimal Parameters

Optimal Parameters   **Error Rates for Parameters**
Number Of Trees: 90
Maximal Depth: 4
Learning Rate: 0.100

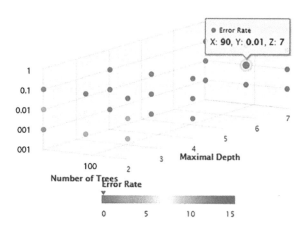

Figure 8.12: Error rate parameters

In addition to the low error rate short learning rate and optimized tree depth (Figure 8.12), the Gradient Boosting tree model also identified key factors that mirrored factors found in both the logistic regression model and random forest model. The gradient model added additional factors of health and faculty interactions (Figure 8.13).

Most Likely: Bachelors

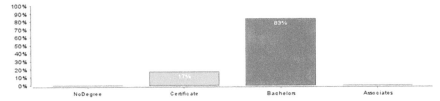

Important Factors for Bachelors

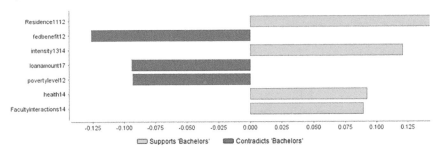

Figure 8.13: Gradient Boosting trees key factors: Black and White

Gradient boosting trees were a strong candidate as the optimal model for the study although the actual tree definitions appeared limited for practical application. As an example, one of the generated trees (Figure 8.14) depicts groupings that appear to work better for binary decisions, that is, in a group or not. The multiple dimensions of the actual study data might not fit well within this dynamic.

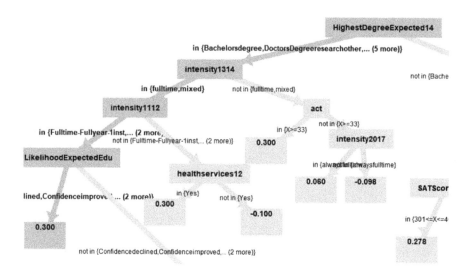

Figure 8.14: Gradient Tree: Black and White

Random Forest

Random Forest is like Gradient Boosting in the sense that both comprise an ensemble of trees. One of the main differences between the two is bagging. In Random Forest trees, a collection of independent trees is created using varying subsets of training data (Yiu 2019). The independence of trees is key as they have no knowledge of each other and therefore the outcomes of each are not influenced by one another. Random Forest in this case might provide additional flexibility in analyzing parameters that are not simply binary. The overall performance of Random Forest was comparable to Gradient Boosting trees. The Random Forest model was able to predict bachelor's degree attainment 100% of the time (Figure 8.15). In addition, the Random Forest model's optimal tree generation is less than Gradient Boosting with 60 trees 7 levels deep (Figure 8.16).

Performances

Criterion	Value	Standard Deviation
Accuracy	99.8%	± 0.1%
Classification Error	0.2%	± 0.1%

Confusion Matrix

	true Associates	true Bachelors	true Certificate	true NoDegree	class precision
pred. Associates	550	1	0	1	99.64%
pred. Bachelors	0	1797	0	0	100.00%
pred. Certificate	3	1	354	2	98.33%
pred. NoDegree	0	0	0	1852	100.00%
class recall	99.46%	99.89%	100.00%	99.84%	

Figure 8.15: Random Forest model key factors: Black only

Random Forest - Optimal Parameters

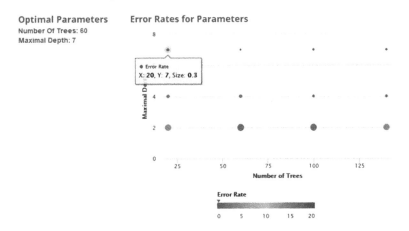

Figure 8.16: Random Forest Tree: Black only

Like Logistic Regression and Gradient Boosting tree models, Random Forest was also able to identify comparable key factors for successful completion of a bachelor's degree (Figure 8.17).

Most Likely: Bachelors

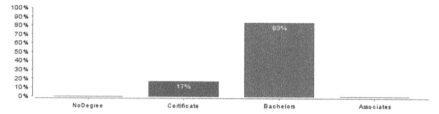

Important Factors for Bachelors

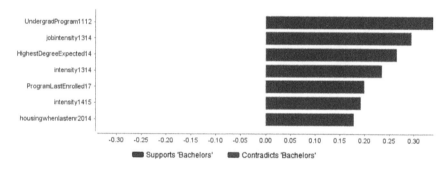

Figure 8.17: Random Forest key factors: Black only

The strength of the Random Forest model appears when examining the independent trees. As an example, the tree in Figure 8.18 shows pathways for attainment related to housing and other key factors. The tree shows multiple pathways toward successful attainment of a bachelor's degree while clearly identifying additional pathways with some probability of success.

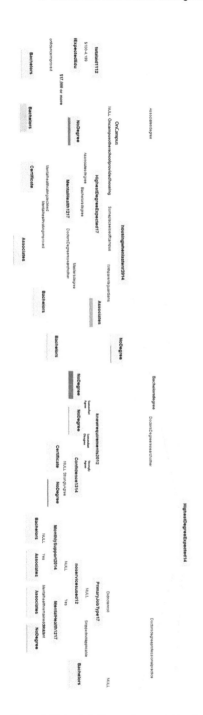

Figure 8.18: Logistic Regression model key factors: Black only

Selected Model: Supervised Learning Random Forest

Although each of the models had advantages and disadvantages, Random Forest was deemed to be the best for the study for the following reasons:
- Good balance between bias and variance with minimal difference between the expected and actual values
- Lack of dependence on other trees, unlike Gradient Boosting's dependence on pathways defined in previous trees
- Majority voting provides a means of returning optimal results as a prediction from the parallel and independently processed trees
- Overall performance, and
- Ease of analysis.

Some of the results from the survey are shown in the sample trees below generated from the Random Forest model.

The Results of the Survey

Faculty Interactions and Campus Climate

Across most models, faculty interaction was heavily weighted. Student experiences with faculty appeared to be a core factor in determining success. Both positive and negative experiences with faculty can either improve or diminish a student's ability to attain a bachelor's degree. The Random Forest tree (Figure 8.19) points out the importance of interactions with students and support from parents, family, and friends.

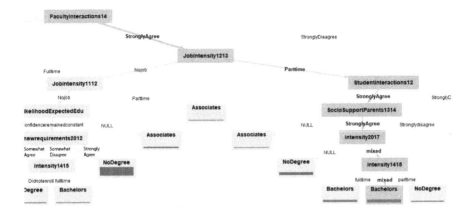

Figure 8.19: Faculty interaction, job intensity and student interactions

Financial Aid and Confidence

Overall and not surprisingly financial aid is a key factor for many African American students. However, even for those who receive financial aid it is not the only factor. A student's confidence level as well as the time spent on campus contributes significantly to success. For example, students who take breaks in their collegiate career or who are not able to attend classes full time are less likely to graduate (Figure 8.20).

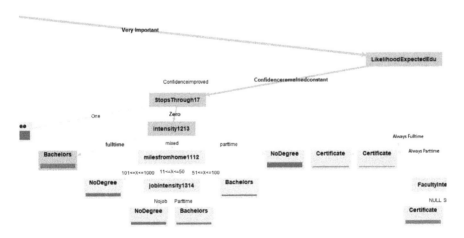

Figure 8.20: Financial aid, confidence, and the number of breaks

Intensity, Confidence, and Belonging

The advantages of full-time attendance are identified repeatedly over multiple models and multiple trees within the decision tree models. Intensity alone however is not enough. Figure 8.21 shows the importance of confidence and the importance of feeling a sense of belonging. Students who feel part of the institution or have a high level of confidence are more likely to succeed.

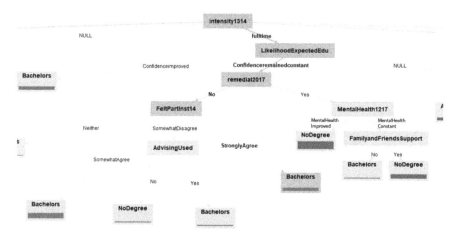

Figure 8.21: Academic intensity, confidence, remediation, and belonging

Parental Support, Positive Campus Climate and Housing

Students to whom parents have provided support from a socialization perspective are more likely to reach degree attainment. But parental support alone is not sufficient. Figure 8.22 indicates that a positive campus climate along with on-campus housing helps to increase the likelihood of graduating.

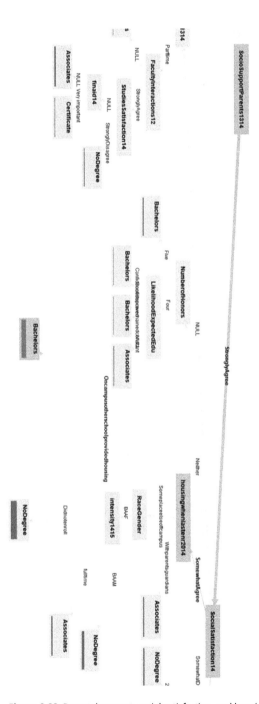

Figure 8.22: Parental support, social satisfaction, and housing

Confidence, Housing, and Intensity

Student confidence is critical to overall success. In addition, campus climate and campus living seem to be dominant factors as well (Figure 8.23).

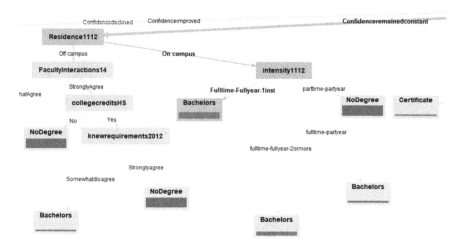

Figure 8.23: Housing

Years of Mathematics and Number of Breaks from Study

Data has historically demonstrated the importance of a strong mathematics background for students in STEM. Additional research in this study provides further validation of that experience. However, the study also emphasized that a strong mathematical background is not sufficient. The number of breaks during a student's collegiate career has significant impact. Figure 8.24 shows that students who took at least one break were much less likely to graduate regardless of their mathematical background.

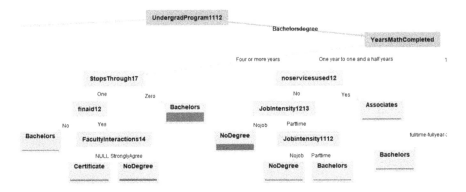

Figure 8.24: Years of mathematics and breaks from study

Mathematics, Support, and Social Satisfaction

Another example that shows the weight of a strong mathematics background along with underlying dependencies is found in Figure 8.25. One can see the impact campus climate can have on degree attainment. Students who experienced strong social satisfaction or satisfaction with relationships spanning fellow students, friends, and faculty were more likely to succeed than students with negative campus experiences.

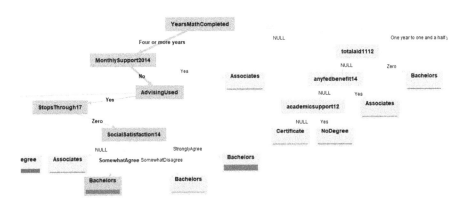

Figure 8.25: Years of advising, support, and social satisfaction

The Random Forest trees presented are but a few examples from 60 independent parallel trees within the model. Random Forest encapsulates the complexity and inter-dependency of a multitude of variables that have some level of impact on student success and present the results in a clear way.

Key Findings

The data was not only analyzed using multiple models but also through two key perspectives. Each model was run initially using four key groups by race: White, African American, Hispanic, and Asian. The data was then run through the various models using African Americans only. Consistently across models the results showed that factors identified as success or failure factors for African Americans differed when focusing on African Americans only as opposed to the entire group. The differing outcomes reinforced the potential for bias when one population is overshadowed by the dominant group.

Confidence

Across multiple models, confidence became a dominant factor for African Americans in higher education. Factors such as high school GPA continued to play a key role; however, in many cases confidence alone was a key differentiator between students who drop out and students who successfully complete a bachelor's degree.

Faculty Interactions

Faculty interactions regardless of race appeared to play a key role as well. African American students who documented poor faculty interactions more frequently than not failed to graduate. White peers however had significantly fewer poor faculty interactions. Furthermore, white peers who had negative interactions were still more likely to complete their degree.

Mental Health

Mental health was a key success factor for all race groups. Students challenged with mental health concerns were at a significant disadvantage. In all groups students who measured their mental health as good or higher were more successful. The data also appears to show that many students in this study experienced a decline in their mental health. This area warrants more research.

Advising

Surprisingly for both White and African American students the use of Advising in the first year was seen as a detractor to successful graduation. More analysis is needed to understand the implications of the finding in this area.

General Findings

The project highlighted several instances where institutions leveraged AIML with varying degrees of success and exemplified common traits in terms of both successes and continued challenges. One challenge in particular is the continued lack of student success for underrepresented groups in areas such as STEM. "Black and Hispanic workers remain underrepresented in the science, technology, engineering and math (STEM) workforce compared with their share of all workers, including in computing jobs, which have seen considerable growth in recent years" (Fry, Kennedy, and Funk 2021). Even with the advent of AI and machine learning and the wide adoption of tools like Civitas Learning the overall numbers in areas like engineering have not improved. The Hechinger Report consistently reports on race and equity issues in American education and has drawn attention to the ongoing persistent and painful gaps in educational outcomes. The problems continue and the number of African American engineering and mathematics graduates declined in 2021 (Collins 2021; Newsome 2022).

Conclusion

The use of AI and machine learning in higher education opens up a world of possibilities. The thorough analysis of existing data collected over multiple years provides a glimpse into what is possible. By running analytical models for both the collective population and subpopulations by race, a glimpse of the significant outcome differences can be gained. The differences highlight the importance of ensuring subpopulations are adequately represented and weighted during the training and modelling phase. If done correctly, there is an opportunity to improve outcomes for not only African Americans but all students (Riep and Prabhakar 2021). If done incorrectly, Artificial intelligence and machine learning have the power to perpetuate existing bias and stereotypes that make it difficult for students to succeed. Although this study focused primarily on STEM there is every reason to believe that the same process could be used across multiple subject areas.

References

Andaur Navarro, Constanza L., Johanna A. A. Damen, Toshihiko Takada, Steven W. J. Nijman, Paula Dhiman, Jie Ma, Gary S. Collins et al. 2021. "Risk of Bias in Studies on Prediction Models Developed Using Supervised Machine Learning Techniques: Systematic Review." *BMJ*: 375 n2281. https://doi.org/10.1136/bmj.n2281.

Benthall, Sebastian, and Bruce D. Haynes. 2019. "Racial Categories in Machine Learning." In *FAT* '19: Proceedings of the Conference on Fairness, Accountability, and Transparency, January 2019*, 289–298. New York: Association for Computing Machinery. https://doi.org/10.1145/3287560.3287575. Available at https://arxiv.org/abs/1811.11668v1.

Bryan, Michael, Darryl Cooney, Barbara Elliott, and David Richards. 2019. *2012/17 Beginning Postsecondary Students Longitudinal Study (BPS: 12/17); Data File Documentation*. US National Center for Education Statistics. Institute of Education Sciences. https://nces.ed.gov/pubs2020/2020522.pdf.

Carmean, Colleen, David Kil, and Linda Baer. 2021. "Why Data Matters for Student Success in a Post-Pandemic World." *Educause Review*, August 10, 2021. https://er.educause.edu/articles/2021/8/why-data-matters-for-student-success-in-a-post-pandemic-world. An adapted version is available on the Civitas Learning website at https://www.civitaslearning.com/blog/sustainable-outcomes/why-data-matter-for-student-success-post-pandemic/.

Chen, Junqiao, David Chun, Milesh Patel, Epson Chiang, and Jesse James. 2019. "The Validity of Synthetic Clinical Data: A Validation Study of a Leading Synthetic Data Generator (Synthea) Using Clinical Quality Measures." *BMC Medical Informatics and Decision Making* 19: 44, https://doi.org/10.1186/s12911-019-0793-0.

Chong, Jason. 2021. "Battle of the Ensemble-Random Forest Vs Gradient Boosting: Two of the Most Popular Algorithms in the World of Machine Learning, Who Will Win?" *Medium*, June 2, 2021. Published in *Towards Data Science*. https://towardsdatascience.com/battle-of-the-ensemble-random-forest-vs-gradient-boosting-6fbfed14cb7.

Collins, Michael. 2021. "Opinion: Why College Majors Are Another Form of Implicit Bias in Higher Education: Instead of Being a Great Equalizer, Higher Education is Leaving Too Many Students Behind." *The Hechinger Report*, December 20, 2021. https://hechingerreport.org/opinion-why-college-majors-are-another-form-of-implicit-bias-in-higher-education/

Dilmegani, Cem. 2024. "Synthetic Data in 2024: Techniques & Best Practices." *AIMultiple Research*, February 14, 2024. https://research.aimultiple.com/synthetic-data-generation/#what-are-the-techniques-of-synthetic-data-generation.

Edu.gov. "Federal Role in Education." (Jun, 2021). https://www2.ed.gov/about/overview/fed/role.html.

Franklin, Jeremy. 2016. "Racial Microaggressions, Racial Battle Fatigue, and Racism-Related Stress in Higher Education." *Journal of Student Affairs of the University of New York* 12, no. 1: 44–55. Available at https://static1.squarespace.com/static/50ccaa7ee4b00e9e60845daa/t/5768045be58c628d3598f632/1466434651823/Franklin.+J.+-+Racial+Microaggressions%2C+Racial+Battle+Fatigue%2C+and+Racism-Related+Stress+in+Higher+Education.pdf.

Fry, Richard, Brian Kennedy, and Cary Funk. 2021. "Stem Jobs See Uneven Progress in Increasing Gender, Racial and Ethnic Diversity." *Pew Research Center. Report,* April 1, 2021. https://www.pewresearch.org/science/2021/04/01/stem-jobs-see-uneven-progress-in-increasing-gender-racial-and-ethnic-diversity/.

Georgia State University. n.d. "The Panther Experience." Explore Student Life. Student Engagement. https://engagement.gsu.edu/the-panther-experience#pride.

Goupil, Francois, Pavel Laskov, Irdin Pekaric, Michael Felderer, Alexander Dürr, and Frederic Thiesse. 2022. "Towards Understanding the Skill Gap in Cybersecurity." In *ITiCSE '22: Proceedings of the 27th ACM Conference on Innovation and Technology in Computer Science Education*, vol. 1 July 2022, 477–483. https://doi.org/10.1145/3502718.3524807.

Hanna, Alex, Emily Denton, Andrew Smart, and Jamila Smith-Loud. 2020. "Towards a Critical Race Methodology in Algorithmic Fairness." In *FAT* '20: Proceedings of the 2020 Conference on Fairness, Accountability, and Transparency, Barcelona, January 2020*, 501–512. https://doi.org/10.1145/3351095.3372826.

Harati, Hoda, Laura Sujo-Montes, Chih-Hsiung Tu, Shadow Armfield, and Cherng-Jyh Yen. 2021. "Assessment and Learning in Knowledge Spaces (ALEKS) Adaptive System Impact on Students' Perception and Self-Regulated Learning Skills." *Education Sciences* 11, no. 10: 603. https://doi.org/10.3390/educsci11100603.

Heinonen, Henri. 2019. "Artificial Intelligence AI — Over 100 Billion in Revenues by 2025." *Medium*, December 3, 2019. Published in *Towards Data Science*. https://towardsdatascience.com/artificial-intelligence-ai-over-100-billion-in-revenues-by-2025-e737459a345e.

IBM. 2023. "Shedding Light on AI Bias with Real World Examples." by IBM Data and AI Team." *[Blog]*, October 16, 2023. https://www.ibm.com/blog/shedding-light-on-ai-bias-with-real-world-examples/.

Kil, David, Angela Baldasare, and Mark Milliron. 2021. "Catalyzing a Culture of Care and Innovation Through Prescriptive and Impact Analytics to Create Full-Cycle Learning." *Current Issues in Education* 22, no. 1 Special Issue. https://cie.asu.edu/ojs/index.php/cieatasu/article/view/1903/887.

Li, Zheng, Yue Zhao, and Jialin Fu. 2020. "SynC: A Copula Based Framework for Generating Synthetic Data from Aggregated Sources." In *International Conference on Data Mining Workshops (ICDMW), 17–20 November 2020. Proceedings*, 571–8. New York: IEEE. https://doi.org/10.1109/ICDMW51313.2020.00082. Available at https://www.andrew.cmu.edu/user/yuezhao2/papers/20-icdmw-sync.pdf

Metz, Cade. 2021. "Who is Making Sure the A.I. Machines Aren't Racist?" *The New York Times*, March 15, 2021, updated June 23, 2023. https://www.nytimes.com/2021/03/15/technology/artificial-intelligence-google-bias.html.

National Center for Education Statistics (US) (NCES). n.d.a. "Beginning Postsecondary Students (BPS)." https://nces.ed.gov/surveys/bps/.

National Center for Education Statistics (US) (NCES). n.d. "Baccalaureate and Beyond Longitudinal Study (B&B)." https://nces.ed.gov/surveys/b&b/.

National Center for Education Statistics (US) (NCES). 2019. "Status and Trends in the Education of Racial and Ethnic Groups 2018." NCES 2019-038. Washington DC: NCES Institute of Education Research. https://nces.ed.gov/pubs2019/2019038.pdf.

National Center for Education Statistics (US) (NCES). 2023. "Table 318.45.Number and Percentage Distribution of Science, Technology, Engineering, and Mathematics (STEM) Degrees/Certificates Conferred by Postsecondary Institutions, by Race/Ethnicity, Level of Degree/Certificate, and Sex of Student: Academic years 2012–13 through 2021–22". *Digest of Education Statistics*. https://nces.ed.gov/programs/digest/d23/tables/dt23_318.45.asp.

National Center for Science and Engineering Statistics (US). 2023. "Diversity and STEM: Women, Minorities and Persons with Disabilities." Alexandria, VA.: National Science Foundation. https://ncses.nsf.gov/pubs/nsf23315/.

Newsome, Melba. 2022. "Computer Science has a Racism Problem: These Researchers Want to Fix It." *Nature. News Feature,* October 19, 2022. https://www.nature.com/articles/d41586-022-03251-0

Riep, Josette, and Annu Prabhakar. 2021. "Leveraging Artificial Intelligence to Increase STEM Graduates among Underrepresented Populations." In SIGITE '21: Proceedings of the 22nd Annual Conference on Information Technology Education October 2021, 73–74 https://doi.org/10.1145/3450329.3476848.

Schiffer, Zoe. 2021. "Timnit Gebru was Fired from Google – Then the Harassers Arrived." *The Verge*, March 6, 2021. https://www.theverge.com/22309962/timnit-gebru-google-harassment-campaign-jeff-dean.

Shaw, Catherine. 2021. *Driving Toward a degree 2021: Caseload, Coordination, Student Engagement, and Equity*. Tyton Partners. https://tytonpartners.com/driving-toward-a-degree-2021-caseload-coordination-student-engagement-and-equity./

Smithsonian Science Education Center. 2024. "The STEM Imperative." https://ssec.si.edu/stem-imperative.

Tucker, Alan, Zhenchen Wang, Ylenia Rotalinti, and Puja Myles. 2020. "Generating High-Fidelity Synthetic Patient Data for Assessing Machine Learning Healthcare Software" *npj Digital Medicine* 3: 147. https://doi.org/10.1038/s41746-020-00353-9.

Yiu, Tony. 2019. "Understanding Random Forest: How the Algorithm Works and Why It Is So Effective." *Medium*, June 12, 2019. Published in *Towards Data Science*. https://towardsdatascience.com/understanding-random-forest-58381e0602d2.

Zawacki-Richter, Olaf, Victoria I. Marín, Melissa Bond, and Franziska Gouverneur. 2019. "Systematic Review of Research on Artificial Intelligence Applications in Higher Education – Where are the Educators?" *International Journal of Educational Technology in Higher Education* 16: Article no.39. https://doi.org/10.1186/s41239-019-0171-0.

Raymond Uzwyshyn

9 Building Library Artificial Intelligence Capacity: Research Data Repositories and Scholarly Ecosystems

Abstract: Artificial intelligence (AI) possibilities for deep learning, machine learning and natural language processing present fascinating new library service areas. These areas are being integrated into traditional academic library activities, digital literacy, and university research environments. Most university faculty, graduate students and library staff work outside of computer science disciplines and require help in discovering, accessing and using data. This chapter overviews methodologies, infrastructure, and skills needed for building AI capacity and new AI services within academic libraries suggesting steps that may be taken by way of training to establish a sound foundation for future implementation. The role of AI in the digital scholarly ecosystem is discussed. Library AI scholarly pathways are clarified and focused steps are suggested to move library staff, researchers, and students towards new AI possibilities.

Keywords: Artificial intelligence – Training; Deep learning, Data storage and retrieval systems; Academic libraries; Research libraries

Introduction

Deep learning, machine learning and natural language processing are fascinating new areas of artificial intelligence (AI). This chapter overviews pragmatic steps which can be taken to establish sound foundations for optimizing AI possibilities. Topics outlined include research data repository foundations, digital scholarly research ecosystems and relevant tools and services to set the groundwork for new emerging AI possibilities. The ideas presented draw on the pragmatic work of the author in two universities and over nine years of AI related projects, 2014–2024. Developing AI-related library scholarly services for research faculty, graduate students and library staff begins with education and training. This chapter provides a list of learning resources in the Appendix, along with background material references.

Educational Steps and Scaffolding

To build any successful library AI program, educational steps and scaffolding are needed (Figure 9.1). The learning curve for AI is steep and staff education and training must be seriously considered by library managers and administrators. AI implementation combines areas of computer and information science, programming, and information technology project management. The objective of any AI educational program is to develop a more sophisticated vocabulary towards AI programmatic literacy enabling larger conversations. The university's learning community must become familiar with the language of AI to facilitate subsequent conversations on project possibilities and work effectively with AI engineers and experts for successful implementation of projects.

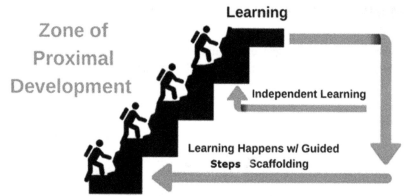

Figure 9.1: Educational Scaffolding and Steps Towards Learning (Warren 2021)

Artificial Intelligence Paradigms and Origins

AI has many origins, each with unique algorithmic paradigms (Table 9.1). Some paradigms are better suited than others for particular problem areas and it is best for any algorithmic literacy program to begin generally. There are many good introductory texts, documentaries, online courses, and *YouTube* videos to inspire learners before engaging with more complex aspects like deep learning's back propagation, matrix math and calculus cribs needed to understand processes. Learning materials are listed in Appendix 1 of this chapter, with two parts A and B. Part A lists introductory materials and Part B provides a list of learning materials in specific aspects of AI. Carnegie Mellon's Tom Mitchell and independent scientist from Vienna University of Technology Károly Zsolnai-Fehér through his *Two Minute Papers YouTube* videos (Appendix 1A Mitchell 2022; Zsolnai-Fehér 2022) provide inspiring overviews of recent AI development and progress. Pedro Domingos' book *The Master Algorithm,* provides an excellent categorization of the different AI schools, origins, algorithms and best solutions for various problem areas or tasks (Domingos 2015). Video interviews with Domingos provide additional useful information (Appendix 1A Domingos 2016, 2020, 2022).

The goal of building awareness of AI in the larger university community and library staff is to inspire and create the desire for further knowledge to build new skill sets. Present AI attention is largely focused on deep learning, machine learning (Hart and Recht 2022) and neural nets or networks (Carnes 2019; Appendix 1A ColdFusion 2020, LeCun 2022, Mitchell 2022; Appendix 1B Fridman 2022). While there are other important areas, beginning with deep learning and moving on to machine learning present useful approaches for an initial focus on AI which can be used as the basis for extending to a wider program.

Table 9.1: AI Paradigms, Origins and Algorithms (Based on Domingos 2015)

AI Paradigm	Origin	Algorithm	Problem	Solution
Deep Learning Machine Learning	Neuroscience (Neural Nets)	Back Propagation Neural Nets	Complex Tasks, Hidden Patterns	Back propagation
Symbolic AI	Logic, Philosophy	Inverse Deduction	Knowledge Composition	Inverse Deduction
Bayesian Inference	Statistics, Probability Theory	Probabilistic Inference	Uncertainty	Probabilistic Inference
Evolutionary Computation	Evolutionary Biology (Complexity Theory)	Genetic Algorithms	Structure Discovery	Genetic Programming
Reasoning by Analogy	Psychology	Kernel Machines (Support Vector Machines)	Similarity	Kernel Machines

The last ten years of developments in deep learning or neural net algorithms have shown incredible progress. There have been significant results in natural language processing, conversational chatbots, cybersecurity and strategic reasoning with sophisticated AI programs like AlphaGo that plays the board game Go, computer vision and object recognition (Appendix 1A Mitchell 2022). In initially exploring AI, it is best to overview the field briefly and set scalable limits. Progress can be made incrementally with both algorithmic paradigms and pragmatic applications for library staff, research faculty and graduate students so that projects may be achieved, and core research and data analysis enabled. Once a level of awareness of the subject area has been attained, along with inspiration about potential uses, learners can gain skills which lead to mastery (Figure 9.3). Deeper knowledge and skills enable library projects and ensure that faculty and graduate student research moves to new levels.

Levels of Learning

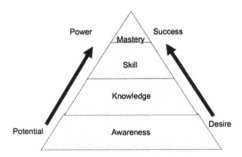

Figure 9.2: Levels of Learning

Online Research Data Repositories

There is a clear trajectory in academic libraries from data and data collection to data science, analytics, visualization, and AI. Everything begins with the data and its organization. A good online research data repository will allow a university library to consolidate and share online faculty and graduate student research. A data repository organizes university research data and provides important online data archiving and publishing strategies. Constructing and using a data repository provide library staff, faculty, researchers, and students foundational skills surrounding important tasks of data organization, cleaning and creating structured data, data citation and building metadata schemas. The skills acquired will be important building blocks for forging AI's larger pathways.

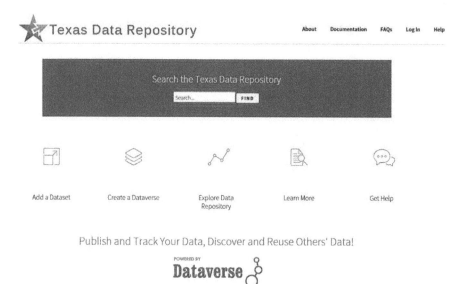

Figure 9.3: Original Homepage for Texas Data Repository (Uzwyshyn 2016, 2022b)

The Texas Data Repository (Figure 9.3) is an example of a research data repository which reconfigures the open source Harvard Dataverse as a consortial, environmental, aggregating data from various Texas universities. Establishing such an open-source software application on an individual, institutional or consortial configuration builds staff human resource infrastructure skills contributing to understanding and implementing AI. Building a data repository for an institution encourages scholars and library staff to use and understand basic data cleaning tools such as OpenRefine which is a powerful tool for working with messy data and transforming it to a suitable state for use by an AI algorithm for later training and processing.

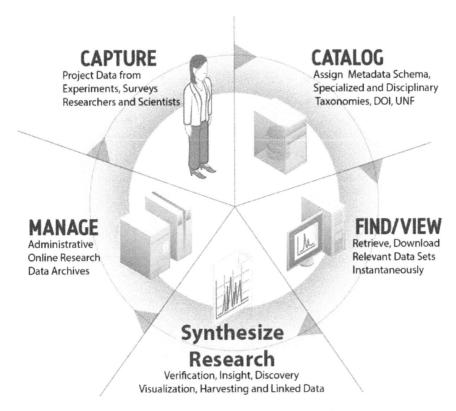

Figure 9.4: The Online Research Data Repository Lifecycle (Uzwyshyn 2022b)

Gaining fundamental data literacy through experience with the online research data repository lifecycle (Figure 9.4) will serve the university community and library staff well for building AI projects.

Digital Scholarship Ecosystems

A digital scholarship ecosystem (Figure 9.5) should be pursued following the development of an online research data repository. While a data repository will always be central, an online institutional collections repository should also not be overlooked, especially for the ability to store and house metadata, core data and textual files. The well-known open-source software, dSPACE, can be used for the university's digital collections repository. There are four tertiary communication components to the Texas repository: an online electronic theses and dissertation management system (ETD) using VIREO software; an identity management system using ORCID; an open academic journal system using OJS3; and user interface content management software based on OMEKA. The combination of the content and communication components make up the digital scholarly ecosystem which can be used as the foundation to enable future larger AI pathways.

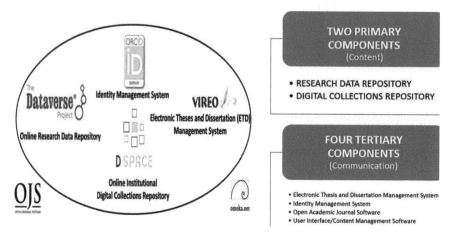

Figure 9.5: Digital Scholarship Research Ecosystem, (Uzwyshyn 2022a).

Capitalizing on Digital Scholarship Ecosystems through Artificial Intelligence

Innovative open science and AI possibilities can be used to extend the use and value of a DSE. The following exemplifies what can be achieved. Harvard's Dataverse allows for the uploading of datasets from other universities to a specific research data repository for later sharing or use by anyone globally. The HAM10000 image dataset is a large collection of multi-source dermatoscopic images of cancerous skin lesions uploaded to Dataverse by Viennese dermatologist, Dr. Philipp Tschandl (Tschandl 2018). The data was subsequently used by Islam, Khan, and Chowdhury (2021) at BRAC University in Bangladesh for an undergraduate thesis. The students downloaded and used the image data to train a deep learning neural net algorithm to recognize cancer growths with efficiency greater than, or equal to, board certified dermatologists. BRAC University library provides an institutional repository to house theses and dissertations and the student work has been further opened globally by this means. The example demonstrates the power of open science combined with AI operating on global levels through the enabling power of digital scholarship ecosystems and data repositories. Content and data that would otherwise be unavailable can be brought together with new machine learning algorithmic techniques (Esteva et al. 2017). New research is enabled; students can produce quality theses; and geographically dispersed content and knowledge from different continents can be aggregated to advance the pursuit of knowledge and science.

Artificial Intelligence and Human Resources

In creating an appropriate AI staffing infrastructure, hiring a whole new department is not feasible for most libraries. Most research and academic libraries have in place operational digital collections and/or data repositories and some have DSEs. Previous experience with such systems will shorten the AI learning curve and facilitate the training process. A staff member already in place working on repositories can initially take up a data-centered function with a new AI-focused research data repository. Other skills related to cataloguing digital metadata creation can be transferred. Use of existing staff skills will serve upcoming AI functions well, especially with regards to machine learning.

One particular skill required for AI implementation relates to data labeling which is a key step in neural net training and machine learning (Kudan 2023). Various other data cleaning and metadata skills are also useful. As a tiered gateway towards AI, hiring a data visualization specialist is useful for expanding skills and knowledge for more complex AI initiatives. A data visualization specialist can initially provide support through the creation of dashboards (Figure 9.6), visual representations for analytical projects and data-driven decision making. Visual techniques can be applied to faculty and graduate student research data. Library staff working with researchers can introduce the potential of expanded data repositories and create bridges toward upcoming AI pathways.

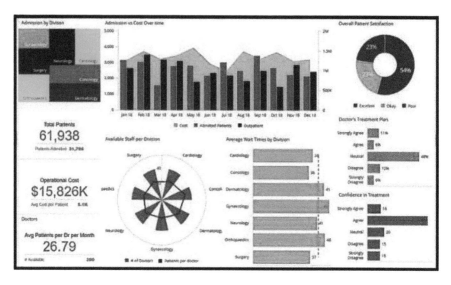

Figure 9.6: Library Data Driven Dashboards as Operational Gateways Towards AI

Artificial Intelligence Learning Paths from Data to Carpentries

As the algorithmic literacy needs of both library staff and the surrounding university research community are recognized and understood, researchers and library staff alike will require more pragmatically oriented foundational coding and data science skills to optimize research data through higher level insights. Education and training for librarians, researchers and faculty should include development of strategies to clean and normalize data along with the use of programming languages like Python.

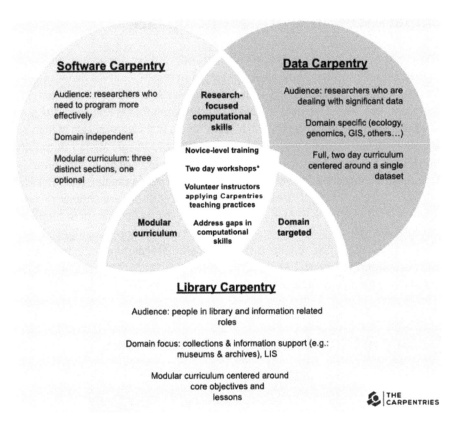

Figure 9.7: Data, Software and Library Carpentries. (Appendix 1A Carpentries n.d.)

The Carpentries is a global community project based in California, US, which provides foundational computational and data science educational programs. The Carpentries' workshops (Appendix 1A The Carpentries n.d.) combine pragmatic programmatic knowledge needed by university researchers and graduate students with algorithmic literacy needs of library staff (Figure 9.7). Collaborative work may begin between research faculty working on learning how to empower their research through effective data organization and programming and library staff who are taking up new methodologies towards enhanced library algorithmic literacy AI infrastructures and programs.

Conferences on Artificial Intelligence

It is important to keep staff both motivated and inspired through understanding benchmarks and milestones being achieved in society in areas like medicine, natural language processing, and games. New library AI conferences are emerging along with specialized sessions at general library conferences and serve the purposes of informing and inspiring. Early conferences included Carnegie Mellon on Artificial Intelligence for Data Discovery) 2019, 2020 (Carnegie Mellon University 2023). The annual Fantastic Futures International Conference on AI for Libraries, Archives, and Museums has been held in various locations ranging from Norway with the 2018 Conference to Canberra, Australia in 2024. AI presentations are now regularly held at library technology conferences such as Computers in Libraries scheduled for March 2024, and events sponsored by the US based Coalition for Networked Information. The activities of the International Federation of Library Associations and Institutions (IFLA) Artificial Intelligence Special Interest Group have sponsored conferences on topics like New Horizons for AI in Libraries in 2022.

Library Artificial Intelligence Prototypes

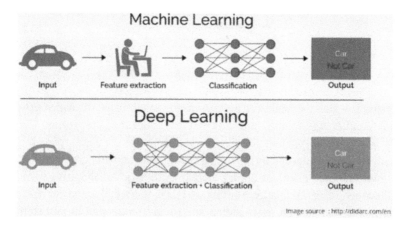

Figure 9.8: Convolutional Neural Net (Uzwyshyn 2022a)

Figure 9.9: Image Extraction Classification (Uzwyshyn 2022a)

Encouraging library staff to pursue AI beta projects allows them to gain initial understandings of the various models for use in machine learning and deep learning (Figure 9.8) and to become familiar with various pieces of the puzzle needed for working on machine learning projects. Involvement in visual AI projects will require knowledge of new tools like NVIDIA graphic cards and skills in image extraction (Figure 9.9). What is important in conducting AI experiments is encouraging staff to think about new possibilities. Understanding processes and possibilities is more important than achieving results at the early stages. Experimenting with protypes provides opportunities for library staff to learn and gain expertise in the various applications of AI to research and development.

Other Artificial Intelligence Training Programs and Experiences

AI library specific institutes and workshops are being offered by organizations like the Institute of Museum and Library Services (IMLS). The IDEA (Innovation Disruption Enquiry Access) Institute on Artificial Intelligence (Table 9.2) is a one-week professional development program for library and information professionals. Initially funded by the IMLS Laura Bush 21st Century Librarian Program (2020–23), it now operates under the banner of the Association for Information Science and Technology. It has provided a wide range of content related to AI, with the 2020 program held at the University of Tennessee and the 2021 program at the University of Texas at Austin. Some information and library schools are extending their offerings into AI-related areas and offering doctoral programs in specialized areas including AI, which will bring new skillsets into libraries. Organizations like the Council for Library and Information Resources (CLIR) promote and provide programs on both US and global levels (CLIR n.d.).

It is important for library leaders to encourage attendance by library staff at such programs, to write recommendation letters and to ensure motivated employees apply for and attend training programs available. Workshops and institutes motivate staff, provide curriculum content, facilitate sharing of ideas and create new networks for attendees.

Table 9.2: IDEA Institute on Artificial Intelligence

INSTITUTE of Museum and Library SERVICES	IDEA INSTITUTE ON ARTIFICIAL INTELLIGENCE
• Weeklong Fellows Program at University of Texas, Austin (20 Fellows)	■ AI challenges and opportunities ■ Ethical considerations and guidelines ■ UX-Human/AI Interaction Lifecycle
• Onboarding, • AI Institute • Library Centered AI • Programming Workshops • Final Project • AI Specialist Support	■ Existing library, archive, and museum projects ■ AI project planning o Project Design o Data collection, classification, and transformation o Roles and implementation ■ Python Basics, Python for Machine Learning ■ APIs and bibliometrics ■ AI in search and discovery
• Networking with National Library AI Experts • Other Fellows	■ Machine learning and coding ■ Harvesting, evaluating, and training data sets for use in AI ■ Conversational AI – Theoretical Foundations ■ Conversational AI – applications ■ Linked Open Data Machine Learning for text with topic modeling and clustering

Library staff attendance at such programs is essential. Attendees can be offered leadership opportunities through sharing curricula content with others and planning infrastructure development at the local level to meet emerging needs.

Library Collaboration

As libraries retool for the paradigm shift caused by the emergence of AI, so too must parent institutions and associated information technology infrastructures. Adopting new processes and implementing new hardware and software provide unexpected opportunities for collaboration, participation, and partnerships. Many universities are adopting new AI ChatGPT-like (Open AI 2024) infrastructures for students and faculty campus-wide. The use of chatbots presents opportunities for libraries and librarians to utilize old skills in different ways and to develop new skills for improved services to users.

Subject librarians may retrain to gain new skills for AI projects, Previous research skills can be retooled towards new AI research software possibilities or deeper understanding of AI natural language processing models ranging from Open AI's GPT4 to Google DeepMind and other upcoming models. The previous research and instruction librarian can be newly minted in the role of Chatbot Administrator or Prompt Engineer (Cohere 2023; Go 2023; Woodie 2023).

Libraries as Complex Adaptive Systems

Universities are complex adaptive systems (Bryant, Dortmund, and Lavoie 2020) and libraries are dynamic systems within them (Figure 9.10). Patterns emerge from complex interdependencies (Human Dynamics Systems Institute 2024). As patterns emerge from relationships between faculty, librarians, and others, it is helpful to formalize activity through some kind of mechanism such as an AI Working Group. Ideally, the membership of such a group will begin through informal partnerships and collaborations of interested library staff and others within the university or organization. As work ramps up on specific projects, the group should be formalized to continue conversations. Membership of the group can be extended to include university faculty, researchers, and graduate students. Formal structuring of activity will help guide future directions and lead to the development of strategic paths adding innovation and vision to new activities and optimizing the potential use of AI within the university.

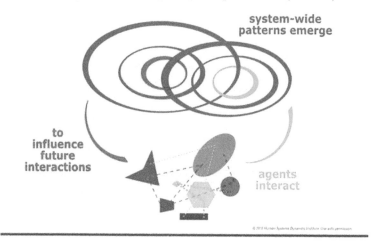

Figure 9.10: Libraries as Complex Adaptive Systems (Human Dynamics Systems Institute 2024)

Conclusion

The new road to library success in AI is largely open (Cordell 2020) and there are further trailblazing opportunities. AI adds value through deriving insight from the vast arrays of data which make up the 21st century academic research library research content areas (Hervieux and Wheatley 2022; Kleinveldt 2022; Nogales, García, and Medina 2022). The prospects of using AI for advances towards the next levels of human knowledge seeking and discovery are huge. The potential for exploration of new connections between ideas from disparate disciplinary sets and making new discoveries with fresh insights is incredible. It is vitally important that libraries and librarians develop knowledge and expertise in AI and its applications. Libraries should be currently taking planned steps along the AI path to begin exploring possibilities and implementing projects which will allow them to deliver new leading edge information services to the communities they serve.

References

Bryant, Rebecca, Annette Dortmund, and Brian Lavoie. 2020. *Social Interoperability in Research Support: Cross-campus Partnerships and the University Research Enterprise.* Dublin, OH: OCLC Research. https://www.oclc.org/content/dam/research/publications/2020/oclcresearch-social-interopera-bility-research-support-a4.pdf.

Carnegie Mellon University. 2023. *"Artificial Intelligence for Data Discovery and Reuse (AIDR) Symposium, Carnegie Mellon University, October 19, 2020."* Contributors: Huajin Wang, Melanie Gainey, Katie Behrman, Neelam Bharti, Hannah C. Gunderman, Ann Marie Mesco, and Sarah Young. Materials from the virtual symposium held by Carnegie Mellon University to discuss innovations in the dissemination and reuse of scientific data. Data created May 11, 2020, and last updated September 1, 2023. https://osf.io/tchdq/. Conference report: Artificial Intelligence for Data Discovery and Reuse (AIDR) and Open Science Symposium (OSS) 2020, by Huajin Wang. https://doi.org/10.1184/R1/12092193.

Carnes, Beau. 2019. *Grokking Deep Learning in Motion.* New York: Manning Publications.

The Carpentries. n.d. "Teaching with the Carpentries." https://carpentries.org/teach/.

Cohere docs. 2023. "Prompt Engineering." https://docs.cohere.ai/docs/prompt-engineering.

Cordell, Ryan. 2020. *Machine Learning + Libraries: A Report on the State of the Field.* Washington DC: LC Labs Library of Congress. https://labs.loc.gov/static/labs/work/reports/Cordell-LOC-ML-report.pdf.

Council on Library and Information Resources (CLIR). n.d. "CLIR Postdoctoral Library Fellowship Program." https://postdoc.clir.org/.

Domingos, Pedro. 2015. *The Master Algorithm: How the Quest for the Ultimate Learning Machine Will Remake Our World.* London: Penguin Books.

Esteva, Andre, Brett Kuprel, Roberto A. Novoa, Justin Ko, Susan M. Swetter, Helen M. Blau, and Sebastian Thrun. 2017. "Dermatologist-level Classification of Skin Cancer with Deep Neural Networks." *Nature* 542:115–118. https://doi.org/10.1038/nature21056. Available at https://cs.stanford.edu/people/esteva/nature/.

Go, Goda. 2023. "This Odd ChatGPT Skill Pays $335,000/year." *YouTube,* 6.51. https://www.youtube.com/watch?v=k13v8jp8H5o.

Hervieux, Sandy and Amanda Wheatley. 2022. "The Rise of AI: Implications and Applications of Artificial Intelligence in Academic Libraries." Chicago IL: ACRL

Human Dynamics Systems Institute. 2024. "Complex Adaptive System." https://www.hsdinstitute.org/resources/complex-adaptive-system.html.

Islam, Ashfaqul, Daiyan Khan, and Rakeen Ashra Chowdhury. 2021. "An Efficient Deep Learning Approach to Detect Skin Cancer." Thesis submitted in partial fulfilment of the requirements for the Bachelor of Science in Computer Science and Engineering, 2021. BRAC University Institutional Repository. http://dspace.bracu.ac.bd/xmlui/handle/10361/15932.

Kleinveldt, Lynn. 2022. "Smarter Higher Education Learning Environments through AI: What This Means for Academic Libraries." *Trends and Issues in Library Technology: Special Artificial Intelligence Issue:* 12–15. https://repository.ifla.org/bitstream/123456789/1940/1/tilt_newsletter-June2022-RU19Final.

Kudan, Natalie. 2023. "The Difference between Labeled and Unlabeled Data." *Toloka [blog],* March 3, 2023. https://toloka.ai/blog/labelled-data-vs-unlabelled-data/.

OpenAI. [2024]. " How ChatGPT and Our Language Models Are Developed." https://help.openai.com/en/articles/7842364-how-chatgpt-and-our-language-models-are-developed.

Hart, Moritz, and Benjamin Recht. 2022. *Patterns, Predictions, and Actions: Foundations of Machine Learning*. Princeton University Press.

Nogales, Elena Sánchez, Alicia Pastrana García, and José Carlos Cerdán Medina. 2022. "Digital Transformation, Data Reuse and Heritage Collections at the National Library of Spain." *Trends and Issues in Library Technology: Special Artificial Intelligence Issue*: 16–21. https://repository.ifla. org/handle/123456789/1940.

Tschandl, Philipp. 2018. "The HAM10000 Dataset a Large Collection of Multi-source Dermatoscopic Images of Common Pigmented Skin Lesions." Harvard Dataverse, V4, UNF:6:KCZFcBLiFE5Ob-WcTc2ZBOA== [fileUNF]. https://dataverse.harvard.edu/dataset.xhtml?persistentId=doi:10.7910/ DVN/DBW86T.

Uzwyshyn, Raymond. 2016. "Online Research Data Repositories: The What, When, Why, and How." *Computers in Libraries* 36, no. 3: 18–21. http://rayuzwyshyn.net/TXU2016/OnlineDataResearchRepositoriesUzwyshyn.pdf

Uzwyshyn, Raymond. 2020. "Developing an Open-Source Digital Scholarship Ecosystem." Paper presented at the International Conference on Education and Information Technology, St. Anne's Oxford, United Kingdom. https://www.researchgate.net/publication/336923249_Developing_an_ Open_Source_Digital_Scholarship_Ecosystem.

Uzwyshyn, Raymond. 2022a. "Steps Towards Building Library AI Infrastructures: Research Data Repositories, Scholarly Research Ecosystems and AI Scaffolding." Presented at New Horizons in AI for Libraries IFLA Satellite Conference, Galway, Ireland, National University of Ireland, July 21, 2022. https://repository.ifla.org/bitstream/123456789/2062/1/s8-uzwyshyn-en-paper. pdf. PowerPoint version available at https://digital.library.txst.edu/server/api/core/ bitstreams/5f8ffd48-e76d-414d-90ba-cfeff0ca5c9c/content.

Uzwyshyn, Raymond. 2022b. "Research Data Repositories and Global Scholarly Ecosystem Possibilities." https://www.researchgate.net/publication/357286044_Research_Data_ Repositories_and_Global_Scholarly_Ecosystem_Possibilities.

Warren, Erica. 2021. "Maximize Learning: Keeping Students in the Zone of Proximal Development." *Good Sensory Learning. [blog].*March 27, 2021. https://goodsensorylearning.com/blogs/news/ scaffolding-development.

Woodie, Alex. 2023. "Prompt Engineer: The Next Hot Job in AI." *Datanami*, February 14, 2023. https:// www.datanami.com/2023/02/14/prompt-engineer-the-next-hot-job-in-ai/.

Appendix 1: Educational Resources on Artificial Intelligence

A. General Video Overviews and Introductions

The Carpentries. n.d. "We Teach Foundational Coding and Data Science Skills to Researchers Worldwide: Data Carpentry, Library Carpentry, Software Carpentry." https://carpentries.org/.

Cohere docs. n.d. "Cohere Documentation." https://docs.cohere.com/.

ColdFusion. 2018. "Why Deep Learning Now? AI Revolution Overview." *YouTube*. 13.45. https://www. youtube.com/watch?v=b3IyDNB_ciI.

DW Documentary. 2020. "Artificial Intelligence and Algorithms: Pros and Cons." *YouTube*. 42.25. https://www.youtube.com/watch?v=s0dMTAQM4cw.

DW Documentary. 2021. "Artificial Intelligence is Changing our Lives." *YouTube*. 42.25. https://www.youtube.com/watch?v=-ePZ7OdY-Dw.

Domingos, Pedro. 2016. " The Master Algorithm: Pedro Domingos: Talks at Google." *YouTube*. 1.00. https://www.youtube.com/watch?v=B8J4uefCQMc.

Domingos, Pedro. 2021. "The Ultimate Software: Machine Learning and Intelligence." The 2,444th Meeting of the Society, September 10, 2021, at 8:00 PM via Zoom Webinar *PSW Science*. 1.52. https://pswscience.org/meeting/2444/. Available at PSW Science *YouTube Channel*. 1.52. https://www.youtube.com/watch?v=7K9X2WiBvu8.

Domingos, Pedro. 2022. "Managing in the Age of AI." Transform 2022. *Vimeo*. 49.48. https://vimeo.com/694708852/9bbb077e93.

Frontline. 2021. "In the Age of AI." Full film. Tech Knowmad. *YouTube*. February 8, 2021. 1.54. https://www.youtube.com/watch?v=xFxv-nN6xWw.

Jordan, Michael I. 2020. "Machine Learning, Recommender Systems and Future of AI." Lex Fridman Podcast #74. *YouTube*.1.45. https://www.youtube.com/watch?v=EYIKy_FM9x0.

Larochelle, Hugo. 2017. "The Deep End of Deep Learning." TEDxBoston. TEDx Talks. *YouTube*. 17.59. https://www.youtube.com/watch?v=dz_jeuWx3j0.

Mitchell, Tom M. 2022. "Where on Earth is AI Headed?" Microsoft Research. MSR-IISc AI Seminar Series. *YouTube*. May 9, 2022. 1:34. https://www.youtube.com/watch?v=ij9vqTb8Rjc.

LeCun, Yann. 2018? "Heroes of Deep Learning." *DeepLearning.AI Blog*. 27.48. https://www.deeplearning.ai/hodl-yann-lecun/.

LeCun, Yann, and Lex Fridman. 2022. " Is AI Just Statistics?" *Lex Clips*. *YouTube*. 5.17. https://www.youtube.com/watch?v=iug8FAl0B1U.

Zsolnai-Fehér, Károly. n.d. "Two Minute Papers." https://users.cg.tuwien.ac.at/zsolnai/about/. Also available on *YouTube*. https://www.youtube.com/c/K%C3%A1rolyZsolnai/videos.

B. Machine Learning, Data Science and Python Online Courses

"AI & Machine Learning Lectures". 2020. This Page is a Collection of Select Recorded Lectures on AI given by Lex Fridman and Others. *Deep Learning* 2017, 2018, 2019, 2020. Self-driving cars. https://deeplearning.mit.edu/.

DeepLearning.ai. n.d. "Deep Learning Specialization." *Coursera*. Instructors Andrew Ng, Younes Bensouda Mourri, and Kian Katanforoosh. https://www.coursera.org/specializations/deep-learning.

Duke University. n.d. "Introduction to Machine Learning." Instructors: Lawrence Carin, David Carlson, Timothy Dunn, and Kevin Liang. *Coursera*. https://www.coursera.org/learn/machine-learning-duke.

Fast.Ai. 2022. "Practical Deep Learning for Coders." Practical Deep Learning: A Free Course Designed for People with Some Coding Experience…. Guide Jeremy Howard. "Practical Deep Learning for Coders part 2: Deep Learning Foundations to Stable Diffusion." https://course.fast.ai/.

FreeCodeCamp. n.d. "Legacy Python for Everybody: Python for Everybody." Course created by Charles Severance. https://www.freecodecamp.org/learn/python-for-everybody/.

Google. n.d. "Machine Learning Crash Course with TensorFlow APIs: Google's Fast-paced, Practical Introduction to Machine Learning, Featuring a Series of Lessons with Video Lectures, Real-world Case Studies, and Hands-On Practice Exercises." https://developers.google.com/machine-learning/crash-course.

Hinton, Geoffrey. 2016. "Neural Networks for Machine Learning." *Coursera. YouTube.* https://www. youtube.com/watch?v=cbeTc-Urqak&list=PLoRl3Ht4JOcdU872GhiYWf6jwrk_SNhz9.

Lateef, Zulaikha. 2024. "Artificial Intelligence with Python: A Comprehensive Guide." *Edureka. Blog.* https://www.edureka.co/blog/artificial-intelligence-with-python.

Massachusetts Institute of Technology. 2023. "MIT6.S191. Introduction to Deep Learning." http:// introtodeeplearning.com/.

Zhang, Ashton, Zachary C. Lipton, Mu Li, and Alexander J. Smola. 2023. *Dive into Deep Learning.* Interactive deep learning book with code, math, and discussions. https://d2l.ai/index.html.

Neli Tshabalala

10 Impact of Artificial Intelligence on Library Services: Reflections on a Practical Project

Abstract: The industrial revolution typology has been used to describe the impact of various technologies on all aspects of society. The fourth industrial revolution (4IR) denoting the rapid technological change which has occurred in the 21st century is seeing a transition to the fifth industrial revolution (5IR) which promulgates the integration of traditional and new technological systems along with sustainability. The technological changes and fresh perspectives have enabled a paradigm shift within libraries from the provision of traditional services to online services with implications for future library operations including the application of robotics. This chapter describes a project on the development of an autonomous robot assistant as part of new eservices and technological infrastructure integrating library systems and services to improve efficiency and effectiveness at the North-West University in South Africa. The project explored the impact of artificial intelligence (AI) within the University, examined the views and perceptions of stakeholder groups in determining and implementing innovative tools suitable for supporting teaching, learning, and research, and investigated the process and impact of implementing AI along with the legal and ethical issues and administrative concerns. The findings indicated that AI enables creative thinking that can transform library and information services to enhance user experiences. AI presents an opportunity to develop self-help tools for library users and add value to the library's online presence. Embracing automated business processes using AI within the Library improves operational efficiency. AI has the potential to transform library services and operations.

Keywords: Artificial intelligence – Library applications; Robotics – Academic libraries; Chatbots

Introduction

Schwab (2017) characterises the fourth industrial revolution (4IR) as a fusion of technologies that blurs the lines between the physical, digital, and biological spheres. Technology is everywhere and embedded in every aspect of society with global connectivity. The 4IR has had a major impact on the services provided by libraries as they seek to integrate technology to improve the student experience and match new approaches to learning. In the application of artificial intelligence (AI), academic libraries are reimagining their services and exploring new ways of providing information resources and services to meet user needs and support teaching, leaning and research activities on and off campus. Many libraries have adopted AI and robotic process applications to respond innovatively to digital transformation and to maintain competitiveness in the higher education learning landscape. Although the digital world enables the competent use of innovative technologies in various sections of the library, financial implications such as affordability, budgeting, and sustainability are of concern.

This chapter provides an overview of some of the developments in AI, describes practical applications, and examines the impact of AI on academic libraries through a project examining the use of AI in North-West University (NWU) in South Africa. The project involved the study of a humanoid robot with visual intelligence using natural language processing (NLP) algorithms to facilitate communication between library users and a knowledge-generated database. A literature review on human-like AI machines was first conducted followed by a qualitative approach to collect data on different integrative AI tools that encouraged interaction, fostered deep machine learning (ML) and addressed language diversity. The resulting data was analysed to develop an increased understanding of AI phenomena. The findings were interpreted through reflection to identify optimal applications of AI in library reference and marketing services. The aim was to implement technological solutions that would result in a measurable improvement of efficiency and effectiveness with researchers and students. The self-help tools identified included a chatbot whose components could be tightly integrated into a physical robot. The physical robot exhibited chatbot capabilities that could interact with staff and clients in a live chat environment 24/7. The chatbot could engage in small conversations. The physical robot was an autonomous assistant making use of open-source hardware and software and could freely move around the library to help patrons.

The Context

The North-West University (NWU) is a multi-campus university with eight faculties which was formed from a merger of the former University of North-West, the Potchefstroom University for Christian Higher Education, and the Sebokeng Campus of another university, Vista, in 2004 as part of the South African government's plan to transform higher education. NWU enrolled over 45,000 students in 2021 of whom 5000 were postgraduates, with just under 10% distance students. The University emphasises transformative initiatives. It has a strong values system and focus on excellence: "Where the willow trees grow and the thorn tree spreads its shade, there you will grow in knowledge". The Library and Information Service at NWU is committed to partnership in student success, open scholarship and research, and its strategic priorities for 2024 and beyond are: content discovery, innovate and integrate, inform, educate and communicate, enable and disseminate, encourage and empower, and engage and position (North-West University. Library and Information Service 2021). The Library emphasises its digital and online services and is working with the Faculty of Engineering on a prototype library robot.

Artificial Intelligence within the University and the Library

Artificial intelligent technology entails machines that perform tasks normally undertaken by human intelligence. The new technologies offer positive benefits for all. AI incorporates a range of techniques and has emerged as an agent for use in multiple environments including universities and libraries.

Artificial Intelligence within the University

Introducing AI into the university environment has resulted in innovative changes in higher education and a repositioning of the focus on learning analytics with real time dashboards that assist with decision making, optimise workflows offered through inter-connected smart devices, and support evolving curricula leading in some instances to authentic learning. There are also improved learner capabilities by use of Virtual Reality (VR) which is a computer-generated environment with scenes and objects that appear to be real, making learners feel they are immersed in their surroundings. The combination of Augmented Reality (AR) and VR, along with AI, has the potential to assist students that are struggling to understand difficult academic concepts. An enhanced version of the physical world is offered, using digital visual elements, sound, or other sensory stimuli delivered via technology. There is some evidence that the combination of the technologies improves student results. Learners embark on a learning journey and engage with experiences in ways not previously possible and obtain real-time feedback from their instructors. Appropriate use of technology can provide differentiated student experiential learning. Expert systems have been used to understand student learning needs by analysing information use patterns together with visualisation data techniques. Students can be provided with learning experiences focused on individualised learning outcomes with appropriate resources and contextual directions. Students can access digital learning resources at times and in places where they are needed.

AI has had considerable impact on research activities, primarily through improved data analysis where AI algorithms can speedily analyse vast amounts of data to identify patterns and trends. The research process can be enhanced through knowledge synthesis leading to improved research outcomes. Data mining tools can be used to transform data into knowledge. Data virtualisation techniques using dashboards can simplify data analysis as well as promote data science principles for better interpretation, use and reuse of data through the integration of various processes.

Other applications of AI are in the workforce where it has been used to automate simple lower-level tasks. Frey and Osborne (2017) stated that at least 65% of work activities could be automated with an achievement of 30% the most likely. However, it seems unrealistic that certain tasks will be completely done by machines; instead, they will be enhanced by AI and the people involved will have the opportunity to focus on the creative and social aspects of work. Seamless workflows will reduce costs and improve service delivery. AI has the potential for improving professional development through enhanced training and development opportunities, targeted personalised learning, content curation, and new learning management systems. AI can be used to identify gaps in knowledge, and to provide programmes containing content targeted to new skills and expertise required. Training can be focused and differentiated according to individual learning needs. AI can help accelerate learning and create a more productive workforce.

Artificial Intelligence within the Library

The library must respond to new directions being taken in teaching, learning and research and lead the way in encouraging innovative AI applications. Librarians are already familiar with the use of some AI applications, such as search engines that use AI, conversational agents, social networks, chatbots, and AI applications in library systems. The existing knowledge and experience of librarians provide the basis for further experimentation and implementation of AI. Incorporating innovative technologies is a unifying approach and some applications can be integrated into existing services using simultaneous discussions and online chats for enhanced eservices support. There are many AI applications of interest to the library with potential for use in process automation, collection management, online reference services with the use of chatbots and robots.

Process Automation

AI can be used with radio-frequency identification (RFID) technology to locate individual items in library collections or to track items using tags, improving the security of collections. The introduction of RFID technology has facilitated faster issuing, sorting and returning of books and the addition of robotic functionalities has added further improvements. Automated storage and retrieval systems (ASRS) are being enhanced with AI applications. Self-issue systems have become more popular as libraries adopt new technologies. Using AI tools within circulation and lending can assist in making suggestions for loans based on users' previous searches and borrowing patterns, and ensure more personalised services as well as greater accessibility to information content in both print and digital formats. Cox emphasises that "the diffusion of innovation takes time" (2021, 8). Physical access to library resources will remain significant for the foreseeable future. There are also continuing benefits to be gained from personal interactions between users and library professionals, which can be encouraged by interactive systems.

Collection Management

Use of natural language processing (NLP) which combines rule-based modelling of human language with statistical and machine learning models can facilitate automated collection management through indexing, subject classification, and assignment of subject headings as well as improving cataloguing processes. One AI application is Robotic Process Automation (RPA) which can be integrated into library processes for mundane and repetitive tasks like shelving, and book circulation. Such developments improve workflows and outcomes and contribute to the creation of a smart library that uses digital services to enable accessibility for users anywhere and everywhere. Use of intelligent techniques with services like document delivery can improve efficiency.

Online Reference Services

Expert systems were one of the early AI applications. An expert system comprises a knowledge base and an inference engine and seeks to replicate the decision making of a human expert using if-then rules. Expert systems have had many applications in libraries and have been in use since the 1980s. In some instances, they provide user interfaces for accessing existing online systems and have facilitated improved search strategies providing an intelligent front-end interface. Some expert systems provide management services, such as analytical details about users. Omame and Alex-Nmecha (2020) postulate that an expert system could manage subject index-ing and reference services that would speed up accessibility of library resources. Expert systems can also be used to provide intelligent gateways to online sources.

Machine and deep learning algorithms generate patterns to facilitate relation-ships between different data sets for ease of information retrieval. Virtual library assistance can be made available using AI and conversational agents are able to provide virtual support through tutorial platforms with the potential to transform traditional reference library services in academic libraries (Ali, Naeem, and Bhatti 2021, 14, quoting Rubin, Chen, and Thorimbert 2010, 496) "it is both timely and conceivable for ... libraries to consider adopting conversational agents to enhance – not replace – face-to-face human interaction. Potential users include library web site tour guides, automated virtual reference and readers' advisory librarians, and virtual story-tellers". Use of digital services can exploit mobile technology, social media services like Facebook, and text messaging applications and allow librarians to communicate effectively with their users.

Chatbots and Robots

Web-based tools and chatbots or virtual assistants coupled with wider availabil-ity of Wi-Fi in public spaces and wider internet access are indeed transforming the library. Robotics and chatbots are commonly used as intelligent technology to answer student queries and can promote teaching, learning, and research in support of digital scholarship. Nawaz and Saldeen (2020) posit that chatbots are cost effective as they can easily link into the library website. Libraries can expand their information services and offer virtual assistance. Chatbots appear to be con-venient for undergraduates; the anonymous interface is less threatening. They are able to provide virtual assistance, especially in relation to distance learning support and are operational outside of library opening hours. They can be linked to Ask-a-Librarian services and through automated question-answering algorithms generate responses to support users seeking guidance, support, and expertise in navigating the vast sea of information. The result is improved workflows with an automatic handover of chat responsibilities between the bot and human librarians. The chatbot can assume some, albeit not all, human librarian functions. If users obtain speedy answers to enquiries through improved customer engagement, user satisfaction levels will improve. Chatbots can have a significant effect in ensuring successful user experiences and potentially be used as a useful marketing tool with wide-ranging impact. Routine reference queries can be dealt with by the chatbot, and complex enquiries automatically escalated to library staff. Responses to users are enhanced and the content of answers provided can assist in generating a valuable knowledge base for future use.

The Project at North-West University

The NWU Library has embraced 4IR by introducing AI systems in the library. The aim was to explore technological solutions that would result in measurable improved efficiency for the benefit of the university community by providing integrated access to library resources. The 4IR cautiously makes virtual spaces infinite (Yang and Cheng 2018) and increasing customer engagement and automating mundane tasks was the main objective. The adoption of 4IR strategies propagates inclusive use and interconnected technologies and emphasises blending all activities through smart technologies rendering services accessible anytime, anywhere. Recent developments involving AI refer to the use of large amounts of data and of machines with the ability to perform repetitive tasks with limited persistent human guidance. Many useful guidelines have been provided for the implementation of AI and provided a valued approach for the NWU project.

Governance and ethical issues must be addressed. A three-phase implementation plan including discovery to ensure assessment of the most suitable AI technology for a particular purpose, an alpha phase involving training and validation, and a final beta phase for testing will ensure success. A FAST track approach involving fairness, accountability, sustainability and transparency is deemed helpful (Peets et al. 2019). The guidelines provided by Peets et al. are helpful to interested institutions such as NWU in understanding, planning, and managing AI projects and considering ethical use.

The conscious investment at NWU was in developing interactive customer platforms such as self-help services, a chatbot, and an interactive robot to provide services for the 21st century. A survey of AI activities being undertaken in libraries in 2019 found that machine learning was being commonly used in most subject fields but that libraries had been slow to introduce AI technologies. The authors encouraged libraries to get involved: "The AI revolution is not on the horizon, it is already here and libraries need to make peace with this fact and begin the process of co-existence" (Wheatley and Hervieux 2019). Wheatley and Hervieux noted that few libraries included AI in their strategic planning, let alone collaborated with other units within the university and further observed in relation to an MIT Library project that "this collaboration resulted in several online tools that are still available today, however no other partnerships have been created to work on the uses of artificial intelligence in the library". Conversations on AI have been prevalent in smaller libraries rather than larger universities where one would assume finance would be available for new technologies. In contract, NWU is a large university and has been engaged in AI conversations with other departments on campus, including the Centre for Teaching and Learning, Graphic Design within the School of Communication who designed the outside shell of the robot, and the School of Electrical, Electronic and Computer Engineering who were involved in the building of the robot, programming, and integration. Introducing digital technologies and rolling out robotics technology to other campuses at NWU is part of the five-year strategic plan. AI has created opportunities for engagement and set the pace for further work given the universities' roll-out plans and concurs with the perspective presented by Wheatley and Herview (2019).

In going forward NWU determined that a chatbot and physical robot tools and use of ML would offer integration of library services and accelerate student success, supporting individual growth and intellectual capabilities in an accessible 24/7 environment. The multiple personality context offered by the physical robot and multilingual capabilities in two other African languages, in addition to English, would provide stimulus for learning and marketing the value of library resources and services. In addition, a physical robot supports equity and inclusion since the display screen can be enlarged and is height-adjustable providing full accessibility for people in wheelchairs. It also allows for verbal and text-based interaction. People with auditory impairment can use text-based interaction through the robot screen.

The Project Details

The goal of the project was to develop an autonomous robotic assistant to answer questions from library users and to provide marketing services for the library. The key requirements were that the chatbot should be able to converse meaningfully with library users, and the physical robot must exhibit chatbot capabilities in simple conversation. The objective was to provide immediate help to library users and a knowledge database was created from the library's store of frequently asked questions (FAQ) and the responses provided to minimise initial failures which could lead to referrals.

The project was conducted by the NWU Library with the Faculty of Engineering. A homegrown artificially intelligent chatbot was chosen because it had more marketing value than a commercially available chatbot. It is easily customisable and provides for continual improvement by means of continuous learning. Since the chatbot includes machine learning elements it can learn from experience gained while it is in operation.

It was determined that the chatbot of the physical robot must be able to converse with online library users via a suitable communication channel, either WhatsApp or Telegram. Online conversations can be conducted by means of text messages. The chatbot is able to maintain more than one simultaneous discussion. The conversation with a person physically present has priority with minimal latency or response delay and more than one online conversation can be accommodated. The latency in the online chats is influenced by the number of simultaneous conversations. The latency for two simultaneous online chats should be less than 500 milliseconds, excluding communication network related delays.

Methodology

Use of open-source software reduced costs on hardware and software. The software enabled ease of maintenance and upgrades to other versions. The library robot comprised the following: mechanical structure including screen, camera fixture and battery panel, electronics, and electricals; switch panel; depth camera; sensors; software including simultaneous localisation and mapping (SLAM) code, face tracking and object recognition. Other features included a remote control panel and monitoring station. The sensor selection included various tasks, such as obstacle detection and avoidance, environmental mapping, localisation using wheel encoders, navigation, and path planning to ensure the avoidance of obstacles.

Mapping and navigating the target environment were conducted in the library environment; the design interface was finalised by building a robot shell. A controlled deployment phase was also conducted. The robot was deployed in the main campus library first to evaluate user interaction. Feedback was used for improvement in design and functionality. The last phase was to replicate the robot for other campus sites.

The Conceptual Phase

The concept generation was influenced by how 4IR ideas associated with Industry 4.0, synonymous with smart manufacturing (IBM n.d.) and Library 4.0 could be translated into the library of an African university that embraces the humanity to others philosophy of uBuntu App-centric industry 4.0. NWU nurtures the digital integration of all systems to improve efficiency in service operations. The concept of App-centric industry 4.0 contextualises inclusivity to the benefit of not only the university's internal stakeholders, but also the wider university community. It means that children in the surrounding community may participate in university community projects and have the opportunity to expand their experiences outside the classroom. In addition, the concept extends to include research and scholarship as a proactive response to the changing scholarly publishing landscape in the university. There is increased research output in the form of scholarly publishing, research and innovation endeavours through engaged collaborations.

The introduction of the two intelligent technologies, the physical robot and the chatbot, was in line with the university e-strategy to digitally transform services that would improve efficiency and customer engagement. Tight integration of services emphasised automatic handover of chat responsibilities from the bot to human librarians. The chatbot has added value to the library's online presence rather than merely being a novelty item. Cost factors were reduced by using local supply with more competitive pricing. Some mechanical components were supplied by the partner in the project, the Faculty of Engineering. Local 3D-printers were also used. The software used integrated data from the existing catalogue. The benefits were marginal maintenance and sustainability for future research development and product improvement.

The physical robot was more appealing to physical users of the library and served its marketing function, attracting more users to the library. The chatbot enhanced the discoverability of library resources with 24/7 availability across the globe and catered for distance learning students by providing virtual access. The chatbot harnessed the power of machine learning and provided continuous access to library resources.

The Development Phase

The development phase included aspects that extended robot longevity by incorporating new roles and functionality for the period 2023–2025 in line with the library strategic plan to ensure continuous improvement of the shelf life of the physical robot and updating of the content of the chatbot with 24/7 accessibility. The life of the hardware was estimated to be five to ten years. Since more commercial robots focus on English as a predominant language, product development embraced the multilingual capabilities in languages relevant to the NWU context, Afrikaans, English, Sesotho, and Setswana. All university stakeholders benefitted from the use of intelligent technologies and were able to use languages with which they felt comfortable.

As already noted, the physical robot and chatbot used open-source software. The integration process included the bot based on use of Generative NLP (Google

2022) with the same knowledge base as the library's FAQ. In addition, certain aspects of the library catalogue were incorporated to allow the chatbot to recommend references based on user requests along with library functionalities such as automated directions to specific sections of the library website. The database and software were hosted on a fast server, to prevent delays during verbal communication.

User requirements were determined through meetings held with library staff to obtain the exact specifications that would yield the desired product output. Building the physical robot involved meeting the specific requirements which have already been mentioned and included the mechanical drivetrain with electrical motors, wheels, chassis, and power supply, sensor arrays, and relevant control systems for object avoidance, human-machine interface/interaction (HMI), and mapping.

The exterior appearance of the robot was locally designed by students from the School of Electrical, Electronic and Computer Engineering within the Faculty of Engineering and graphic design students from the Faculty of Arts. Each of the three campus library robots reflected a unique feature of the campus while at the same time showcasing the university.

Multiple personality sentiment analysis was incorporated to correspond and adapt to the chatbot approach to each conversation depending on the language used. Improved customer satisfaction has been a driving principle, and the chatbot was able to escalate complex enquiries to library staff. Generation of a knowledge base for future use has allowed room for further development.

Lessons Learned

4IR has changed the way academic libraries provide services to patrons. AI is likely to replace repetitive forms of knowledge provision and service, as well as routine tasks undertaken. As a result, libraries will reengineer their operations (Marwala 2022). Implementation of AI in academic library environments could accelerate, with clear strategic positioning guided by an innovative vision and mission, where the online mode becomes the default route for providing library services in most universities in the support of teaching, learning and research. Librarians' skills and expertise must be finely tuned to respond to the level required to support both online and physical library environments. Acquiring digital skills related to the use of intelligent technologies is essential. The implementation of robotics and the chatbot simultaneously at NWU was effective both for educational purposes and access to library resources. An effective knowledge base is also an essential ingredient because data can be mapped, interpreted, and transferred to multiple environments for meaningful application. The results of the project indicated clearly that the use of intelligent technologies can improve library services given the integrative customer engagement approaches that a combination of a physical robot and a chatbot can deliver.

Opportunities for creativity abound in the digital transformation process. The questions of capacity, safe use, and security must be addressed. Luca, Narayan, and Cox (2022, 185) highlight the need to take precautions in fair use of applications and freedom of expression that will eliminate bias yet not stifle creativity. The focus must be on accelerating information access for users and professional development for staff in response to opportunities that AI and robots can offer. Understanding copyright legislation and what is legally permissible is essential. Licensing of content, and intellectual property rights are important components of the development of regulatory measures on ethical standards and policy directives concerning legal and educational compliance principles in AI. In the case of collaborative work, agreements should be in place. Reliable and secure IT infrastructure allows efficient system integration. The information architecture and knowledge organisation must be designed to enable good workflows and fast-track content discovery.

AI has the potential for positive impacts on academic libraries and can be used innovatively in reference and information services, and in the promotion of library resources. Chatbots provide numerous advantages, although they pose some limitations associated with the knowledge base and language processing. Nawaz and Saldeen (2020, 444) remark that chatbots respond to input queries previously recorded in the knowledge base which limits the conversational ability to a fixed content base and prevents responses to multiple queries simultaneously. Training for everyone involved is essential to ensure that users feel comfortable using such applications and do so effectively. The changed role of the library has made it more attractive to a new generation of users. Application of AI helps streamline library functions and results in enhanced learning, training, and skills development. Since AI reinforces learning, the quality of the knowledge base data must be updated in line with education needs and relevant library services.

AI applications must be integrated into existing library systems. The development and implementation of new applications must be collaborative working with information technology developers and information architecture and infrastructure experts along with academic support services to ensure seamless accessibility and appropriate responses to user needs. The use of AI and the transition to digitisation of library processes can improve space utilisation and enhance the user experience.

What Lies Ahead?

Varius perspectives may accelerate or slow down the broader application of AI. Developing ethical standards that incorporate intercultural understanding in institutions when adopting AI will have an impact. Design and language capabilities can enhance inclusivity and multiculturalism given the demographics of different backgrounds. Collaboration and partnerships have the capacity to strengthen engagement with AI applications, particularly in the use of robotics and conversational platforms in teaching and learning. In-house products with customisation can yield tight integration of library services and cost-effective benefits when suitably qualified professionals are involved, as in the NWU experience.

There are implications for high-end skills when planning future education strategies and changes in skills and work. AI literacy is an essential prerequisite skill for library users and librarians. Digital intelligence is also necessary for professionals to be able to evaluate the Al tools available to ensure a positive impact on library services.

The effectiveness of implementing AI in any organisation is tied to the organisation's ability to ensure that any application is fit for purpose, can be adapted for use in the environment and is capable of being applied to unfamiliar scenarios. Determining the level of response to AI within the library, and identifying the optimal interventions is challenging. The redesign and reshaping of library services have many facets. New and different types of skills are required to succeed in a fast-changing world. In some circumstances, libraries may have a role in developing new skills for displaced workers and/or improving skills so that workers can transition to new roles and responsibilities.

Conclusion

AI presents multiple options that influence the way information can be accessed, managed, and connected in exciting ways. The role of the library can be innovatively expanded through digital transformation although adversely there are issues in relation to safety and ethics including legal and administrative concerns and user authentication, AI applications have enhanced user support services. AI and big data create immersive opportunities for knowledge sharing and further opportunities for library services. Librarians will continue to play a significant role in helping clients find and use information although some aspects of the role will change. Creating an innovative, interconnected environment with secure authentication will increase the value of library services. Application of robotics and chatbots has transformed library services with integration of other technologies and inter-connected smart devices. AI multifaceted capabilities are redefining traditional library operations. AI has a pivotal role in ensuring accuracy and amplifying the efficiency of search and retrieval processes. Smart innovative AI applications tightly integrated into library services can increase customer engagement and improve teaching, learning and research in academic environments.

References

Ali, Muhammad Yousuf, Salman Bin Naeem, and Rubina Bhatti. 2021. "Artificial Intelligence (AI) in Pakistani University Library Services." *Library Hi Tech News* 38, no. 8: 12–15. https://doi.org/10.1108/LHTN-10-2021-0065.

Cox, Andrew. 2021. *The Impact of AI, Machine Learning, Automation and Robotics on the Information Professions: A Report for CILIP*. London: CILIP. https://www.cilip.org.uk/general/custom.asp?page=researchreport.

Frey, Carl Benedikt, and Michael A. Osborne. 2017. "The Future of Employment: How Susceptible are Jobs to Computerisation?" *Technological Forecasting and Social Change* 114: 254–280. https://doi.org/10.1016/j.techfore.2016.08.019.

Google. 2022. "Background: What is a Generative Model?" *Machine Learning Advanced Courses.* Last update July 18, 2022. https://developers.google.com/machine-learning/gan/generative#:~:text=A%20generative%20model%20includes%20the,to%20a%20sequence%20of%20words.

IBM. n.d. "What is Industry 4.0?" https://www.ibm.com/topics/industry-4-0#:~:text=the%20next%20step-,What%20is%20Industry%204.0%3F,improve%20and%20distribute%20their%20products.

Luca, Edward, Bhuva Narayan, and Andrew Cox. 2022. "Artificial Intelligence and Robots for the Library and Information Professions." *Journal of the Australian Library and Information Association* 71, no. 3: 185–188. https://doi.org/10.1080/24750158.2022.2104814.

Marwala, Tshilidzi. 2022. "The Fourth Industrial Revolution and Academic Library Practices." In *Academic Libraries: Reflecting on Crisis, the Fourth Industrial Revolution and the Way Forward*, edited by Anette Janse van Vuren, 1–12. Auckland Park: UJ Press. https://doi.org/10.36615/9781776402304-01.

Nawaz, Nishad, and Mohamed Azahim Saldeen. 2020. "Artificial Intelligence Chatbots for Library Reference Services." *Journal of Management Information and Decision Sciences* 23, no.S1: 442–449. Available at https://www.abacademies.org/articles/artificial-intelligence-chatbots-for-library-reference-services-9653.html.

North-West University. Library and Information Service. 2021. "Strategic Plan 2021–2025." https://library.nwu.ac.za/sites/library.nwu.ac.za/files/files/documents/lis-strategic-plan-2021-2025.pdf.

Omame, Isaiah Michael, and Juliet Chinedu Alex-Nmecha. 2020. "Artificial Intelligence in Libraries." In *Managing and Adapting Library Information Services for Future Users*, edited by Nkem Ekene Osuigwe, 120–144. Hershey, PA: Information Science Reference. https://doi.org/10.4018/978-1-7998-1116-9.ch008.

Peets, Lisa, Martin Hansen, Sam Jungyun Choi, and Chance Leviatin. 2019. "UK Government's Guide to Using AI in the Public Sector." *The Journal of Robotics, Artificial Intelligence & Law* 2: 439–443.

https://www.cov.com/-/media/files/corporate/publications/2019/11/uk_governments_guide_to_using_ai_in_the_public_sector.pdf.

Rubin, Victoria L., Yimin Chen, and Lynne Marie Thorimbert. 2010. "Artificially Intelligent Conversational Agents in Libraries." *Library Hi Tech* 28, no. 4: 496–522. DOI 10.1108/07378831011096196. Available at https://www.researchgate.net/profile/Victoria-Rubin/publication/220364240_Artificially_Intelligent_Conversational_Agents_in_Libraries/links/00b7d52fe4c722dbbd000000/Artificially-Intelligent-Conversational-Agents-in-Libraries.pdf?origin=journalDetail&_tp=eyJwYWdlIjoiam91cm5hbERldGFpbCJ9.

Schwab, Klaus. 2017. *The Fourth Industrial Revolution*. New York: Crown Business.

University of Johannesburg. Library. 2023. "Library – 4IR Technologies 4.0 @UJ." *LibGuides.* Last updated November 1, 2023. https://uj.ac.za.libguides.com/4ir/4ir#gsc.tab=0.

Wheatley, Amanda, and Sandy Hervieux. 2019. "Artificial Intelligence in Academic Libraries: An Environmental Scan." *Information Services & Use* 39, no. 4: 347–356. https://content.iospress.com/doi/10.3233/ISU-190065.

Yang, Peidong, and Yi'En Cheng. 2018. "Educational Mobility and Transnationalization." In *Higher Education in the Era of the Fourth Industrial Revolution*, edited by Nancy W. Gleason, 39–63. Singapore: Palgrave Macmillan. https://doi.org/10.1007/978-981-13-0194-0_3

Andrew Cox

11 Ethics Case Studies of Artificial Intelligence for Library and Information Professionals

Abstract: As well as offering exciting opportunities to increase access to knowledge, artificial intelligence (AI) poses many ethical issues related to bias, transparency, explainability and accountability, privacy, safety and security, and impacts on human choice and freedom. This chapter elaborates on the issues and explores how ChatGPT as an example of an AI poses many of the issues. Although high level professional codes of ethics assert relevant principles, they do not directly explain how to respond to the emerging AI concerns. Ethics scenarios can however provide short, relatable stories that pose the key dilemmas in a way which will illuminate the problems and prompt discussion. The chapter describes eight scenarios which pose the key dilemmas around AI in ways relevant to library and information professionals. The scenarios are publicly available for reuse on a CC-BY-SA licence.

Keywords: Artificial intelligence – Library applications; ChatGPT; Confidentiality; Ethics; Privacy; Scenarios

Introduction

Artificial Intelligence (AI) offers exciting possibilities for library and information professionals and the users they serve. It promises to increase access to knowledge by offering new ways to automatically describe and retrieve information from collections (Cordell 2019; Cox 2021a). It will enable adaptivity and personalisation in information provision. AI driven chatbots and voice agents can provide dialogic and supportive ways of accessing information. AI could also be applied to the analysis and prediction of user behaviour. The need to explain AI is a new dimension to information literacy.

However, AI has raised a storm of public ethical concern, especially relating to bias, intelligibility and privacy (AINow Institute 2018, 2019). Reflecting these concerns, several sites track AI ethics incidents, such as the AIAAIC Repository (AIAAIC n.d.) and the AI Incident Database (AIID n.d.). The former has reported nearly 1400 incidents from its formation in 2019 to March 2024. In response many organisations have published guidelines for ethical AI (Jobin, Ienca, and Vayena 2019). There are useful sector specific guides about how to approach the development of ethical AI in areas like education (The Institute for Ethical AI in Education 2021; JISC, 2021).

Such targeted guides are invaluable for information professionals working in particular sectors. But this chapter is written in the belief that librarians and information professionals have a unique value perspective on AI that itself needs to be fully developed. The librarian's calling to promote access to knowledge brings a unique perspective on the ethics of AI and information professionals need more resources to help think through the ethics of AI in their practice.

Professional Ethics

One of the defining characteristics of a profession is its commitment to ethical conduct. But codes of ethics published by professional bodies are increasingly aspirational (Frankel 1989): they articulate shared values at an abstract level, rather than explaining in detail how to behave in particular situations. Furthermore, they are not updated frequently enough to reflect every new ethical challenge. Advancing technologies seem to be an important locus of such new ethical dilemmas, albeit it is debatable how often they raise fundamentally new questions (Ferguson, Thornley, and Gibb 2016). Ferguson, Thornley, and Gibb's study of ethical awareness around the use of radiofrequency identification (RFID) in libraries suggests that where technologies are concerned, information professionals may be over-reliant on vendors to ensure that their use is ethical (2015). Other materials beyond broad ethics codes are needed to support professionals to think through the implications of AI in their work. Some extremely useful resources already exist. The International Federation of Library Associations and Institutions (IFLA) has published an insightful commentary on the ethical implications of AI (2020). Padilla's report for OCLC offers a guide to responsible AI development (2019). Yet there remain gaps in the tools available for the profession to explore ethical responses to new technologies.

Ethics scenarios can play an important role in posing dilemmas in relatable ways and stimulating reflection and debate about appropriate responses and actions. Scenarios tell stories and are engaging ways to open up challenging topics. They can capture everyday practical issues and are effective in promoting adult learning. There are excellent sets of ethics scenarios available for information work in general such as in Buchanan and Henderson (2009), McMenemy, Poulter, and Burton (2014) and Rösch (n.d.). However, AI is important enough to require its own set of scenarios. The purpose of this chapter is to explain the thinking behind an evolving set of scenarios of AI ethics for library and information professionals (Cox 2022). The latest edition of the scenarios is available on a CC-BY-SA licence so that they can be repurposed for the classroom or specific organisational contexts (Cox 2021b).

Ethical Aspects of Artificial Intelligence

Understanding the ethics of AI is premised on the definition of AI. However, defining AI is challenging because it is a complex and evolving idea. In essence, AI refers to computers undertaking activity akin to the thought processing and decision making normally done by humans. But achieving this ideal has been an aspiration for computer science since the 1950s. The understanding of what constitutes intelligence has evolved over time and the technologies that seem to offer some form of intelligence have also changed. Focusing only on today's technologies does not necessarily mean AI is simple to understand or define. For example, the McKinsey Global Institute's 2018 discussion paper on the skill shift required in relation to new technologies surveyed:

> ...organizations familiar with at least one automation, AI, or advanced digital technology and its application in business from the following list: big data and advanced analytics, machine learning/artificial intelligence algorithms, autonomous vehicles, image recognition, robotic process automation, virtual agents, back-office process automation, wearables, internet of things, personalized pricing and promotions, 3D printing, and blockchain and distributed ledger (Bughin et al 2018, 71)

In contrast, Lowendahl and Williams state that AI capability "consists of: robotic process automation; computer vision; machine learning; natural language text understanding; virtual agents or conversational interfaces; physical robotics; natural language speech understanding; natural language generation; and autonomous vehicles" (2018, 1). Each technology creates its own potential ethical issues. A further complexity is that because the operation of many of the technologies is premised on data, the ethics of AI encompasses many previous debates around big data ethics.

AI is much more than just a bundle of technologies, however powerful. Unlike many other technologies, AI has a strong place in the public consciousness through its popularisation in science fiction television, movies and books. AI is often presented in the media and elsewhere as a dystopian rather than as a utopian possibility. Responses to AI cannot be disconnected from responses shaped by such imaginary visions. More immediately AI is also associated with a powerful discourse that has commercial value. Society's view of AI is shaped by companies that seek to promote their products as having transformational capabilities for organisations.

Some of this may be hype for functionality that is frankly not very new. It could also be seen as linked to culturally powerful notions of technological determinism and solutionism (Mirza and Seale 2017). These ideas present technological change as inevitable and able to unproblematically solve complex social problems. They also embody sexist and racist assumptions. Rather than accepting that technology-driven change is a given, society should be thinking in ethically informed ways about choices which can be made by individuals, communities and societies. Questions should be asked about whether technology fixes the problems that need to be fixed in ways that consider human needs. Hype for AI and the power of Big Tech to drive the agenda must be challenged. In addition, there are profound social implications of datafication and dataveillance, and sustainability issues around power demands of AI. The many contentious perspectives point to the wider challenges that exist around AI.

Ethical issues around how AI is developed, governed and ultimately valued must also be acknowledged and not only its technical aspects (Greene, Hoffmann, and Stark 2019). Critics suggest that ethical implications are currently secondary in the development process, and that the Big Tech companies' statements about ethics are often no more than ethics washing. There is a sense that ethical thinking must be embedded much more deeply into the whole process of developing and using AI. Since many AI applications have widespread social impacts, there is a need for all stakeholders to participate or be represented throughout the development and implementation process. AI design must not be restricted to experts. Perhaps legal regulation is the best way for society to protect itself, rather than relying on companies to behave ethically. Ultimately, a question to ask about AI is whether an application is not just ethical, with a neutral social impact, but whether it actively promotes social justice. Such reflections point to the difficulty of easily defining AI ethics in any context.

More directly much of the debate around AI ethics has focussed on the following inter-related issues: bias, transparency, explainability and accountability, privacy, safety and security, and impacts on human choice and freedom (Fjeld et al. 2020); Jobin 2019). The media has focused on cases where AI has been shown to be biased, such as when facial recognition has failed to recognise darker skin tones. To a large extent the problems appear to arise from biases in the historic data that has been used to train an algorithm. In other cases, bias seems to arise from the composition of AI industry workforce which is predominantly made up of young white males whose narrow assumptions are reflected in the AI they produce. Another particular area of concern is around transparency, explainability and accountability. If AI tools learn to make decisions from data, rather than in ways determined by a human coder, there is an immediate problem of how to explain the process and its outcomes. The way AI functions is not necessarily clear even to the designer of the algorithm, so explaining it can be problematic. Then, if the decision making performed by AI is not transparent, there is an issue of accountability. Who is responsible when the AI makes a mistake? Indeed, how can truly informed consent be gained?

Privacy is another significant issue with AI applications related to personalisation and adaptivity which rely on bringing together personal data from many sources. Holding such personal data poses safety and security risks. AI raises fundamental issues around human agency. What is the human role when computers are making decisions? The concept of nudging where system design is geared to influencing a particular group of people is one example of the way that AI can be seen as a threat to human agency. An important dimension of automation is its impact on work, including professional work. If AI is more efficient, it may replace professionals in many roles. AI could be used to control human work and reduce rewarding work to drudgery. Equally it has the potential to expand the scope of work for professionals to focus on the more rewarding and complex aspects of their roles. The impact on jobs is an important dimension of AI ethics.

In addition to general AI ethical challenges, as already mentioned, there are issues related directly to information professional values. IFLA (2019) offers an insightful analysis of some of the main freedom of information and expression issues posed by AI. While they receive less emphasis in the wider debate about the ethics of AI, they indicate that the library and information profession is able to contribute a distinctive viewpoint on AI ethics. The personalisation and adaptivity to individual need that are often central to accounts of what AI can offer also create filter bubble effects which effectively limit free access to information. AI's use in forum moderation might limit freedom of speech, particularly when designed to over cautiously block material that might be any way controversial (Privacy International 2018). If AI's use blocks access to information in unnoticed ways, its use in creating deepfakes has far reaching potential impacts on trust in information. IFLA has pointed to AI's potential for undermining privacy and creating a fear of surveillance of what people search for and read with subsequent chilling effects. Thus, the growing use of AI can be seen as reinforcing risks of surveillance and dataveillance (Privacy International 2018).

Issues with ChatGPT

Since its launch in November 2022, Open AI's ChatGPT has greatly increased awareness of developments in AI, but also intensified concerns around AI ethics. Perhaps the reason for ChatGPT being so startling and impressive is its ability to perform a wide range of complex tasks rapidly, including writing text in different styles and also writing code. ChatGPT is a little more like a form of general AI, rather than the narrow AI we have been experiencing in previous applications. Used judiciously ChatGPT and its like offer many benefits for information work, such as the ability to produce lay summaries of complex texts and reduce the threshold to writing. But it also instantiates many of the ethical issues encountered with AI in general and discussing them offers a concrete summary of them.

The issues of bias, intelligibility and privacy, which seem to be pervasive in AI, are apparent in ChatGPT (AIAAIC 2024). Because GPT is trained partly on data from the open web, it reflects social biases that can reproduce gender stereotypes about employment, for example assuming that a doctor would be a male, and makes statements that appear to be biased against a specific religion like Hinduism (Burruss 2020). Another source of training data for ChatGPT is Reddit, which has its own biases. By using human trainers to counteract the biases in the training data, new forms of bias can be introduced (Webb 2023). Current use is further training Chat GPT, which introduces potential for further bias. ChatGPT can also be seen as unintelligible because it is far from open about what data it is based on or how it works. In terms of privacy, it was banned temporarily in Italy because it lacked privacy protection and age checks. There remain confidentiality concerns that have prompted a number of companies to warn staff from using it.

Specifically, from an information perspective, ChatGPT poses major issues. In its free version, the corpus of data on which it is based has not been refreshed since September 2021 limiting its reliability in ways that could misleading the unwary. More fundamentally, one of the features most commented upon is that ChatGPT hallucinates information, even inventing references to support statements. Chat GPT writes authoritatively and convincingly on many topics, but the information it produces is often not correct. It does not reference its sources and it is difficult to check. Repeating a search produces a different result reducing the ability to check information. The existence of a widely used tool that fails against these basic criteria of information reliability could be seen as undermining trust in information in general. With image generative AI, there is a wider risk of producing plausible falsehoods and fakes.

ChatGPT potentially violates copyright by using text and data from the Internet without permission. Arguably extracting data from publicly available sources is an act of exploitation in itself. OpenAI claims to access content under the claim of fair use, but if it reproduced something close to a previous text, it might be open to the same suits for infringement that are already in progress against other generative AI products (Dreben and Julyan 2023). There are also equity issues. As other perhaps better services behind a paywall become available, the digital divide between those who can afford such services and those who cannot will increase.

Other issues relate less to the functions of ChatGPT or how it is used, but more to how it was developed. A notable problem revealed by a *Time exposé* was that content was detoxified by Kenyan workers who were paid extremely low wages and given minimal support to deal with the disturbing content they were asked to review (Perrigo 2023). Although OpenAI was created as an idealistic not-for-profit organisation, and despite being called open, the openness of the company and its products questionable (Hao 2020). There are also issues about its environmental sustainability of GPT models (Burruss 2020; Ludvigsen 2022). Generative AI is very demanding in terms of power consumption.

At the broadest level, ChatGPT seems to have potential for wide ranging social impacts, such as threatening the livelihoods of people working in sectors such as publishing, journalism and marketing, and in software development. It is already having a significant impact on educational institutions' approach to assessment and how they teach writing, and there are many fears that it could negatively affect students' writing and critical thinking skills (Cotton, Cotton, and Shipway 2023). The effects do not appear to have been considered in releasing the service. The dramatic launch of a paradigm changing tool without concern for wider societal effects highlights the power of the Big Tech companies (Telving 2023). AINow Institute's annual landscape report focusses on the need to rein in the unregulated power of the tech giants (2023). Fears seem to be apparent within the industry, resulting in AI leaders including Elon Musk calling for a six-month AI pause in 2023 (Hern 2023). The signatories justified a pause because AI was producing impacts that "no one – not even their creators – can understand, predict, or reliably control" (Future of Life 2023).

For the information professional there are many challenges. If the implications of AI for libraries were limited to their own direct uses for information services, they could control the ethical issues. But in reality, the library has to operate in a wider information environment and use information products produced in other contexts. The library must support users in understanding how AI is impacting their lives. It is possible that regulation will control the worst excesses of AI, but it is more likely that the profession will play a role in explaining the limits of the technology and advising users to engineer higher quality responses through the best prompts.

The Scenarios

Reflecting on this discussion, it can be summarised that the following aspects need to be explored in AI ethics scenarios for the profession:

1. A sense of balance between the potential benefits of AI with its ethical challenges
2. The range of AI applications relevant to information professionals, from direct uses in information services to its use in service management and the case where information professionals might be supporting organisations to deploy AI
3. The range of different contexts of information work, for example. health, libraries, commercial and legal sectors
4. The issues relating to data reflecting AI's reliance on big data
5. Reference to the gamut of ethical dilemmas that the wider literature emphasizes, especially bias, transparency, explainability and accountability, privacy, safety and security, and impacts on human choice and freedom
6. Mention of the issues raised by the impact on jobs and professional roles.
7. Emphasis on the ethical concerns which are of particular importance to information professionals, such as those related to access to information and freedom of expression, and
8. Reference to wider issues around participation by all stakeholders in the development and use of AI and its impact on social justice and sustainability.

Scenarios are widely used to present ethics dilemmas because they encapsulate the issues in a way that promotes discussion. They are accessible stories that seek to stimulate open-ended debate about ethical choices. In designing the first iteration of the scenarios referred to in this chapter, the principles laid out by Institute of Business Ethics good practice guide (Bradshaw 2012) were followed. The principles include the recommendation to set the scenarios in relatable professional contexts yet avoid excessive detail. They should be open-ended rather than implying an obvious moral.

Having produced an initial set of scenarios, several library and information experts were consulted who suggested various further elaborations particularly to the notes supporting discussion with each scenario. The process resulted in eight scenarios (Cox 2021b). Each scenario consists of a short description of a situation and prompts for the reader to weigh up what the ethics issues are and to help them try and decide what action they would take. Accompanying notes with each scenario unpack some of the issues raised, but again without implying neat solutions. A short bibliography identifies useful references.

A short description of the scenarios follows:

1. "Supporting first responders" – set in a health context the scenario sees data managers voice objections to sharing personal data for a system to support first responders to improve interventions in an emergency situation. It raises issues around areas such as consent, privacy, security and transparency. But it also emphasises the dilemma where there are life saving benefits set against

levels of risk around issues such as privacy. There is also the question of legality: how does this interplay with ethics?

2. "Nudges" – set in a university context where the library is asked to contribute data to be processed by a tool that nudges students to change their behaviour to improve their well-being. This again raises issues of both about privacy and consent. It also poses the issue around human agency, in the context of influencing human behaviour, even if it is for proven benefit to the user. Most fundamentally there is the question of where such an app fits in the wider strategy to support student mental health and well-being.

3. "The voice assistant" – a public library offers a voice assistant service to answer questions but meets a number of objections, including the risk directly to staff jobs or changing professional roles and potential loss of human contact for users. The scenario also raises a number of issues around bias and stereotyping through the gendered naming of chatbots.

4. "A special collection" – a donation is predicated on enabling access to controversial content. This scenario prompts an exploration of issues around bias and representation in collections.

5. "Forum moderation" – imagines automation of moderation of a public forum creating issues around freedom of expression.

6. "The recommender system" – is based around responses to an imagined recommendation tool, including some relating to the chilling effects because it generates a sense of surveillance, as well as lack of transparency, privacy and bias.

7. "Stakeholders" – explores issues of representation through involvement of stakeholder communities in an AI project. Like scenario 8 this is not about a specific AI, more about governance and stakeholder involvement.

8. "Project partners" – reflects concerns about power and ethics in a joint AI project. This reflects the likelihood of library and information professionals being involved in wider organisational projects about AI and the challenges this raises.

The scenarios have been released on a CC-BY-SA licence so that library and information professionals can adapt them to local needs, such as by adjusting the sector setting and to their own organisational context.

Conclusion

In the context of growing interest in AI both applied directly in library and information professional work and in the wider organisations in which they are embedded, there is an urgent need for debate about the ethics of the technologies within the profession. This chapter has identified many of the issues and concerns. Ethics scenarios provide a way to instantiate the dilemmas encountered in relatable open-ended ways, promoting discussion and increasing understanding of AI. Seeking to encompass the range of issues identified, eight scenarios were developed. By making the scenarios available it is hoped they can be adapted for local use in organisations and by educators.

It is appropriate to end a chapter on ethics with questions rather than answers. The scenarios document closes with a set of general questions for which the reader has been prepared through analysing the eight scenarios. They reflect the depth of professional challenges posed by AI:

- How well do current codes of professional ethics help guide one through these scenarios?
- Does AI create fundamentally new challenges to the ethics and values of the profession, and if so in what ways?
- Ethics statements generally focus on the responsibilities of the individual professional, but what are the ethical challenges for the organisation?
- Do we need state regulation of AI rather than relying on organisations and individuals to follow ethics guidelines?

References

AIAAIC. n.d. "AIAAIC Repository." https://www.aiaaic.org/aiaaic-repository.
AIAAIC. 2024. "ChatGPT Chatbot." Published December 2022. Last updated February 2024. https://www.aiaaic.org/aiaaic-repository/ai-algorithmic-and-automation-incidents/chatgpt-chatbot.
AIID. n.d. "AI Incident Database." https://incidentdatabase.ai/?lang=en.
AINow Institute. 2018. "AI Now 2018 report". [by] Meredith Whittaker, Kate Crawford, Roel Dobbe, Genevieve Fried, Elizabeth Kaziunas, Varoon Mathur, Sarah Myers West, Rashida Richardson, Jason Schultz, and Oscar Schwartz. https://ainowinstitute.org/publication/ai-now-2018-report-2.
AINow Institute. 2019. "AI Now 2019 report." Authors and Contributors: Kate Crawford, Roel Dobbe, Theodora Dryer, Genevieve Fried, Ben Green, Elizabeth Kaziunas, Amba Kak, Varoon Mathur, Erin McElroy, et al. https://ainowinstitute.org/publication/ai-now-2019-report-2.
AINow Institute. 2023. "2023 Landscape; Confronting Tech Power:" [by] Amba Kak and Sarah Myers. April 11, 2023. https://ainowinstitute.org/2023-landscape.
Bradshaw, Katherine. 2012. *Developing and Using Business Ethics Scenarios*. Institute of Business Ethics Good Practice Guides. London: Institute of Business Ethics.

Buchanan, Elizabeth A., and Kathrine A. Henderson. 2009. *Case Studies in Library and Information Science Ethics*. London: McFarland.

Bughin, Jacques, Eric Hazan, Susan Lund, Peter Dahlström, Anna Wiesinger, and Amresh Subramaniam. 2018. *Skill Shift: Automation and the Future of the Workforce*. McKinsey Global Institute Discussion Paper, May 2018. New York: McKinsey & Co. https://www.mckinsey.com/featured-insights/future-of-work/skill-shift-automation-and-the-future-of-the-workforce.

Burruss, Matthew. 2020. "The (Un)ethical Story of GPT-3: OpenAI's Million Dollar Model." *Matthew Burruss Blog*, July 27, 2020. https://matthewpburruss.com/post/the-unethical-story-of-gpt-3-openais-million-dollar-model/.

Cordell, Ryan. 2020. *Machine Learning and Libraries: A Report on the State of the Field*. Washington DC: LC Labs Library of Congress. https://labs.loc.gov/static/labs/work/reports/Cordell-LOC-ML-report.pdf.

Cotton, Debby R.E., Peter A. Cotton, and J. Reuben Shipway. 2023. "Chatting and Cheating: Ensuring Academic Integrity in the Era of ChatGPT." *Innovations in Education and Teaching International*: 1–12. https://doi.org/10.1080/14703297.2023.2190148

Cox, Andrew. 2021a. *The Impact of AI, Machine Learning, Automation and Robotics on the Information Professions: A Report for CILIP*. London: CILIP. https://www.cilip.org.uk/general/custom.asp?page=researchreport.

Cox, Andrew. 2021b. *"Ethics Scenarios of Artificial Intelligence for Information and Knowledge Management and Library Professionals."* University of Sheffield. Dataset. https://doi.org/10.15131/shef.data.17081138.v1.

Cox, Andrew. 2022. "The Ethics of AI for Information Professionals: Eight Scenarios." *Journal of the Australian Library and Information Association* 71, no. 3: 201–214. https://doi.org/10.1080/24750158.2022.2084885.

Dreben, Ron, and Matthew T. Julyan. 2023. "Generative Artificial Intelligence and copyright: current issues." *Morgan Lewis Lawflash*, March 23, 2023. https://www.morganlewis.com/pubs/2023/03/generative-artificial-intelligence-and-copyright-current-issues.

Ferguson, Stuart, Clare Thornley, and Forbes Gibb. 2015. "How Do Libraries Manage the Ethical and Privacy Issues of RFID Implementation? A Qualitative Investigation into the Decision-Making Processes of Ten Libraries." *Journal of Librarianship and Information Science* 47, no. 2: 117–130. https://doi.org/10.1177/0961000613518572. Available at https://citeseerx.ist.psu.edu/document?repid=rep1&type=pdf&doi=cb59e3e082d67146eeb79760eaa5459ed1f0eb8e.

Ferguson, Stuart, Clare Thornley, and Forbes Gibb. 2016. "Beyond Codes of Ethics: How Library and Information Professionals Navigate Ethical Dilemmas in a Complex and Dynamic Information Environment." *International Journal of Information Management* 36, no. 4: 543–556. https://doi.org/10.1016/j.ijinfomgt.2016.02.012. Available at https://strathprints.strath.ac.uk/68287/1/Ferguson_Thornley_Gibb_IJIM_2016_Beyond_codes_of_ethics.pdf .

Fjeld, Jessica, Nele Achten, Hannah Hilligoss, Adam Nagy, and Madhulika Srikumar. 2020. "Principled Artificial Intelligence: Mapping Consensus in Ethical and Rights-based Approaches to Principles for AI." *Berkman Klein Center Research Publication Research Publication 2020–1*. Available at https://dash.harvard.edu/handle/1/42160420.

Frankel, Mark S. 1989. "Professional Codes: Why, How, and With What Impact?" *Journal of Business Ethics* 8: 109–115. https://doi.org/10.1007/BF00382575.

Future of Life. 2023. "Pause Giant AI Experiments: An Open Letter." March 22, 2023. https://futureoflife.org/open-letter/pause-giant-ai-experiments/.

Greene, Daniel, Anna Lauren Hoffmann, and Luke Stark. 2019. "Better, Nicer, Clearer, Fairer: A Critical Assessment of the Movement for Ethical Artificial Intelligence and Machine Learning." In

Proceedings of the 52nd Hawaii International Conference on System Sciences, 2019. Available at https://scholarspace.manoa.hawaii.edu/server/api/core/bitstreams/849782a6-06bf-4ce8-9144-a93de4455d1c/content.

Hao, Karen. 2020. "The Messy, Secretive Reality Behind OpenAI's Bid to Save the World." *MIT Technology Review,* February 17, 2020. https://www.technologyreview.com/2020/02/17/844721/ai-openai-moonshot-elon-musk-sam-altman-greg-brockman-messy-secretive-reality/.

Hern, Alex. 2023. "Elon Musk Joins Call for Pause in Creation of Giant AI 'Digital Minds'." *The Guardian,* 29th March 2023. https://www.theguardian.com/technology/2023/mar/29/elon-musk-joins-call-for-pause-in-creation-of-giant-ai-digital-minds.

Institute for Ethical AI in Education. 2021.*The Ethical Framework for AI in Education.* https://www.buckingham.ac.uk/wp-content/uploads/2021/03/The-Institute-for-Ethical-AI-in-Education-The-Ethical-Framework-for-AI-in-Education.pdf. "Annex: Developing the Ethical Framework for AI in Education." https://www.buckingham.ac.uk/wp-content/uploads/2021/03/The-Institute-for-Ethical-AI-in-Education-Annex-Developing-the-Ethical-Framework-for-AI-in-Education-IEAIED-.pdf.

International Federation of Library Associations and Institutions (IFLA). 2020 "IFLA Statement on Libraries and Artificial Intelligence." https://www.ifla.org/wp-content/uploads/2019/05/assets/faife/ifla_statement_on_libraries_and_artificial_intelligence.pdf.

Jisc. 2021. "A Pathway Towards Responsible, Ethical AI." London: Jisc [and the] British and Irish Law Education and Technology Association (BILETA). https://repository.jisc.ac.uk/8548/1/a-pathway-towards-responsible-ethical-ai.pdf.

Jobin, Anna, Marcello Ienca, and Effy Vayena. 2019. "The Global Landscape of AI Ethics Guidelines." *Nature Machine Intelligence* 1, no. 9: 389–399. https://doi.org/10.1038/s42256-019-0088-2. Available at https://arxiv.org/ftp/arxiv/papers/1906/1906.11668.pdf.

Lowendahl, Jan-Martin, and Kelly Calhoun Williams. 2018 "5 Best Practices for Artificial Intelligence in Higher Education." Gartner group. https://www.gartner.com/en/documents/3895923.

Ludvigsen, Kasper Groes Albin. 2022. "The Carbon Footprint of Chat GPT." *Medium,* December 22, 2022. Updated March 20, 2023. https://towardsdatascience.com/the-carbon-footprint-of-chatgpt-66932314627d.

McMenemy, David, Alan Poulter, and Paul Burton. 2014. *A Handbook of Ethical Practice: A Practical Guide to Dealing with Ethical Issues in Information and Library Work.* London: Chandos.

Mirza, Rafia, and Maura Seale. 2017. "Who Killed the World? White Masculinity and the Technocratic Library of the Future." In *Topographies of Whiteness: Mapping Whiteness in Library and Information Science,* edited by Gina Schlesselman-Tarango, 171–97. Sacramento, CA: Library Juice Press. Available at https://mauraseale.org/wp-content/uploads/2016/03/Mirza-Seale-Technocratic-Library.pdf.

Padilla, Thomas. 2019. *Responsible Operations: Data Science, Machine Learning, and AI in Libraries.* Dublin, H: OCLC Research. https://www.oclc.org/research/publications/2019/oclcresearch-responsible-operations-data-science-machine-learning-ai.html.

Perrigo, Billy. 2023. "Exclusive: OpenAI Used Kenyan Workers on Less Than $2 Per Hour to Make ChatGPT Less Toxic." *Time,* January 18, 2023. https://time.com/6247678/openai-chatgpt-kenya-workers/.

Privacy International. 2018. "Privacy and Freedom of Expression in the Age of Artificial Intelligence." Report by Article 19 and Privacy International. https://privacyinternational.org/report/1752/privacy-and-freedom-expression-age-artificial-intelligence.

Rösch, Hermann. n.d. "Edili: Ethical Dilemmas for Librarians and Other Information Workers: Case Studies." https://www.iws.th-koeln.de/edili/edili-start.php.

Telving, Thomas. 2023. "With ChatGPT, We All Act As Well-Behaved Children of Tech Capitalism." *DataEthics [News]*, January 23, 2023. https://dataethics.eu/with-chatgpt-we-all-act-as-well-behaved-children-of-tech-capitalism/.

Thornley, Clare, Stuart Ferguson, John Weckert, and Forbes Gibb. (2011). "Do RFIDs (radio frequency identifier devices) provide new ethical dilemmas for librarians and information professionals?" *International Journal of Information Management* 31, no. 6: 546–555. https://doi.org/10.1016/j.ijinfomgt.2011.02.006.

Webb, Michael. 2023. "Exploring the Potential for bias in Chat GPT." *Jisc. National Centre for AI*, January 26, 2023. https://nationalcentreforai.jiscinvolve.org/wp/2023/01/26/exploring-the-potential-for-bias-in-chatgpt/.

Part III: **Projects in Machine learning and Natural Language Processing**

Raymond Uzwyshyn

12 Projects in Machine Learning and Natural Language Processing in Libraries: An Introductory Overview

Introduction

Recent advancements in Natural Language Processing (NLP) and Machine Learning (ML) present amazing new avenues of discovery and innovation in the quickly transforming environment of information technology possibilities for libraries. Within an evolving framework, artificial intelligence (AI) emerges as a fundamental new driver, heralding unprecedented opportunities to foster enriched library patron experiences, novel operational efficiencies, and new possibilities for library automation. The following chapters in this section of the book review some of the developments over the past two-year period, setting the stage for the ever-evolving role of AI, large language models (LLMs) and autonomous agents for the global library sector.

In delving into these types of AI library projects, the chapters in this section explore a range of nascent and compelling library-related AI projects ranging from chatbots tailored specifically for libraries to developments offering readers a glimpse into new AI inspired recommender systems for building intelligent library patron assistants. In the realm of library systems integration, open-source solutions also promise remarkable potential in augmenting library management systems and these beginnings are highlighted. The new possibilities facilitate richer interaction with bibliographic records leveraging machine learning for more refined and focused book recommendations and these are also discussed.

Libraries are embarking on an intricate process of document analysis through ML. Some have taken on the ambitious task of automated linked data subject systems creation through AI enabled approaches to automatic indexing.Two of these types of projects are highlighted in chapters in this section: chapter 13 by Martin Malmsten and his colleagues describes work at the National Library of Sweden while chapter 14 by Anna Kasprzik presents the experiences of the *Deutsche Zentralbibliothek für Wirtschaftswissenschaften (ZBW)/German National Library for Economics*. The subject classification trajectory includes a deep dive into AI enabled topic modeling, highlighting efforts to bring more nuanced understanding for large-scale historical text-based archives with Sümeyye Akça's exploration of a project digitizing the Ottoman court registers, the Khadi registers, in chapter 15. The developments set the stage for a collaborative future where the integration of automated subject indexing promises to reshape the library search, retrieval, and research landscape. Caroline Saccucci and Abigail Potter's description of a project at the United States Library of Congress in chapter 16 and Thomas Zaragoza, Yann Nicolas and Aline Le Provost's outline of work undertaken on the union catalogue of French academic and research libraries in chapter 17 demonstrate the possibilities. In opening discussions towards these areas and the chapters to follow, it is worth briefly reflecting not only on a few tentative earlier starting points but also the blistering pace of the present and what is to come. Hopefully, these brief few pages can set wider contexts and references for present day trajectories that are recreating our world of communication, technology and information as this book goes to publication.

Historical Antecedents and Present-Day Library Possibilities

The journey towards creating virtual library assistants began with an early system, , conceived by Joseph Weizenbaum in the mid-1960s (Weizenbaum 1966). Acting as a simulated Rogerian psychotherapist, ELIZA facilitated first attempts at a sense-making, open-ended, human computer interactive questioning process. ELIZA parsed and processed simple natural language keywords through what are now regarded as primitive and basic algorithms. Remarkably, more than 50 years ago, ELIZA was able to simulate empathetic and understanding conversation. Eliza also utilized reflective thinking using a psychodynamic reference model, synthesizing algorithmic possibility with technological infrastructures. This monumental stride marked the first early incursions into an AI domain. Machines could potentially mirror or, at least, mimic human-like interactions offering a glimpse of future possibilities. Chat + computer processing could offer assistance and guidance.

The early work on ELIZA provided a historical legacy that still finds resonance in today's library AI reference infrastructure beginnings. It is important to remember that virtual reference and question and answer through computers began with humanistic psychodynamic principles of self-reflection to focus user/patient/patron questions. Virtual reference leaned heavily on the foundational human-centered, principle of focusing attention on keywords. This principle instituted by ELIZA and later Boolean keyword searching was carried forward by AI large language models in a paper on transformer models (Vaswani et al. 2023). The abstract idea of reflection was originally famously formulated by René Descartes in the expression "*Cogito ergo sum*/I think therefore I am" contained in his *Discours de la méthode/*

Discourse on the Method in 1637 with the mind reflecting on itself. The abstract idea of reflection was expressed in early AI thinking with feedback loops. Servers watched and reflected on each other to improve, adjust, and correct performance. The approach continues with current thinking involving the next level of large language model AI development and autonomous agents (Wang et al. 2023).

Large Language Models

As libraries and others have navigated the new millennium, they have found the AI tipping point. Transformative changes mark the moment underscored by the advent of large language models nurtured through deep learning and neural network technologies. A critical inflection point was vividly epitomized in OpenAI's public announcement of GPT-3.5 in November 2022 and GPT-4 in early 2023 (OpenAI 2024). This monumental sea change in the AI and technology landscape of today's global village denoted not just a staircase evolutionary step but a phase change or, as Kuhn would call it, a paradigm shift. The turnaround occurred through the combined synthesis and expansive power of neural network possibility, logarithmically increasing processing power and the unexpected revelations and emergent properties of what very large, connected data sets with associated repositories and training can accomplish.

Autonomous Agents

The various but intricately connected burgeoning developments introduce a new generation of virtual assistants, products, and infrastructures. They will together fundamentally reshape our global landscape. Library and information science and all libraries are inevitably included in the huge sea change occurring. Virtual assistants and AI inspired developments have changed all aspects of information creation, discovery, access, and use. All research, learning, and reference systems are evolving into sophisticated multi-level forms with AIs and autonomous agents (Wang et al. 2023). The new approaches are proficient in guiding users and provide unprecedented access to knowledge and information. Precision and personalization of knowledge and information are available on a multiplicity of levels and can be used to conduct increasingly complicated tasks. The developments are leading to what some are calling AGI or Artificial General Intelligence (Bubeck 2023). The empowerment and augmentation of human intelligence is courtesy of deep learning neural net mechanisms. These neural net layer outputs leverage vast trillion parameter data content archives to connect nodes. Connections open ever more nuanced responses to complex questions. The neural net multi-trillion parameter distillations are able to provide insight into arcane problems and challenges. Just a few years ago, these levels of discovery and insight were thought impossible for technology to fathom.

This new 21st century birth comes from stochastic and statistically based probabilistic paradigmatic AI technology models. The models represent the evolution of linguistic-based human cognitive capabilities. They evoke whispers of the hopes and anxieties of AGI. The emerging large language models become incredibly powerful as a group working together, reflecting evolving, learning, adapting, and improving at an iterative pace impossible for humans to fathom in their layers of complex connection. New philosophical, pragmatic 21st century toys of AI's large language models have offered the world a deceptively simple search box user conversational interface that is also quickly shifting to smart phone voice recognition. This type of AI human/language model question/answer model will now respond instantly from a phone on any topic possible. This new interface and question/answer conversation represents a paradigm shift. The previous 25-year dominance of the keyword search and retrieval screen is now displaced to sidelines. The new interface is deceptively intuitive and simple but also richly layered. It is also incredibly powerful, facilitating in-depth possibilities and new insights and discoveries. Questions now arising are: How soon will AI developments give rise to radically different future library models? How soon will present online vendor database infrastructures and applications all change? Information retrieval has shifted from a keyword task to a conversation and an interactive conversation and experience with an artificial intelligence.

Prompt Engineering and Multimodal Artificial Intelligence

The search and retrieval process requires what is termed prompt engineering. The prompting quickly becomes an immersive experience requiring a new set of specialized skills. AI is rapidly synthesizing the intricate web of human text-based knowledge contained in ever larger datasets with the language models processing power through AI's deep learning brain-like neural nets. Language models are quickly evolving to more human-like polyphonic cognitive modalities. They are moving to incorporate and process all other media including images, video, and data along with other lesser thought about modalities of human communication and interaction with the world using tactile, phatic, and robotic means to ingest, process, analyze and create responses. These novel approaches utilize human-associated semiotic linguistic structures in various modalities for their systems of organization and response. Global activity and dynamic responses are quickly deepened, enriched, detailed, and personalized for what is now termed the AI orchestration of multi-modal human perspectives. New lines of research and systems promise a future trajectory where libraries and indeed the globe transform into vibrant imaginative learning hubs. The new knowledge and information systems will nurture and kindle human curiosity in areas yet unexplored. They will foster a deeper, richer understanding of the world and the people within it through new AI-powered lenses. The exciting new possibilities whisper through the early reflective aspirations kindled by human computer interaction trailblazers, like Weizenbaum's humanly self-reflective ELIZA algorithm.

Libraries and the New Artificial Intelligence Paradigms

In navigating the intricate topography of the present shifts, there are fascinating synergies developing among new open-source AI toolkits and library automation systems. The open-source relationship is deeply steeped in historical technological cooperation and global library communal software development. The open-source software community has long been a stalwart ally to libraries, offering vital tools and systems. DSpace, Koha, Harvard's Dataverse and other open-source library related systems have fortified libraries' operational efficiencies and capabilities over the years. Today, the collaborative spirit is flourishing anew with the integration of AI and AI toolkits. Hugging Face (2023), Gemini, LangChain, Voyager, Llama2 and other new products or services emerge daily and are crystallized through new browser plugins, open APIs and an ever-evolving digital ecosystem infrastructure. The kaleidoscope of new possibilities and developments like Gutenberg3 open fertile ground for new library exploration with interdisciplinary possibilities for using bibliographic records and content, paving the way for AI enhanced query and retrieval functionalities where deep, rich contextual insights are readily accessible.

The expansive embrace of AI technologies is not just transformative but necessary for the competitive survival of today's dominant library vendors. Library IT vendors across the spectrum are scrambling to rapidly come up to speed with AI enhanced product roadmaps. If they wade into new AI waters, they can hopefully make a speedy transition with new strategies to encapsulate the boundless opportunities presented by large language models and other AI utilities. The shifts to new ways of working and providing service herald a new era for libraries, especially those already embracing robust digital resource directions. Libraries and their information stores will be more dynamically connected not just as passive repositories but as interactive conversing entities. They will evolve to maximize the use of new technological AI possibilities and adapt to the changing informational and AI technological landscape. The new landscape promises a spectrum of enriched library and archival experiences along with research and learning possibilities. New AI services will be tailored to multimedia and multimodal needs of postmodern or fourth industrial revolution patron expectations.

Library Recommender Systems

Going forward, the emphasis in new developments is gravitating towards breaking deeper ground for new possibilities for AI recommender systems and patron query research responses in libraries. Sophisticated AI setups, fostered by large language model deep learning algorithms, are steering away from the conventional pathways of previous 20th century subject access compartmentalization of disciplinary areas. New offerings will usher in more fluid domains and subject constellations replete with a richer and more connected interdisciplinary tapestry of information categories customized for users and user needs. New AI systems bear the potential to revolutionize patron research and browsing experiences. They will provide platforms where focused user interests are not just met but are enriched, expanded, and rethought on the fly through a web of interrelated interdisciplinary content and focused contextual suggestions. The new possibilities wield the capacity to turn a curious mind towards unexpected yet aligned avenues of exploration, entertainment, and research, fostering a nurturing more personalized environment for learning, research, insight, and discovery.

Artificial Intelligence Topic Modeling and New Metadata Possibilities

This section focuses on and explores the less trodden realm of topic modeling and subject clustering. Topic modeling utilizes applied mathematical modeling methodology to unlock unprecedented depths in content analysis. The methods facilitate the unearthing of unrealized connections, ushering in fresh perspectives through the identification and clustering of keywords into discernible subjects. Topic modeling provides a more nuanced and dynamic lens through which to view and engage with content. The approach unveils a network of subject connections, offering users a pathway to delve deeper and find strong subject associations that would remain obscured in a traditional cataloging environment. The area stands as a promising frontier in the ongoing pursuit of accessing and synthesizing knowledge and providing insights into large archives previously more difficult to access.

Present possibilities of topic modeling allow better access and division into intuitive, fluid, and interconnected frameworks. They nurture a space where learning is not linear but richly layered and a multidimensional subject access journey. It is through these innovative techniques that libraries can begin to participate in the continually evolving AI landscape. It is also a landscape which adapts to the diverse needs of its patrons and offers not just resources but also vibrant new ecosystem possibilities for exploration and discovery.

Audiovisual Media, Libraries and Artificial Intelligence

Chapters in this text herald the next burgeoning frontier for AI in media, unfolding within libraries a vibrant locus for not only image and video analysis but also for delving into potentialities engendered by generative AI technologies such as Adobe Firefly, Midjourney, DALL-E and Stable Diffusion. The sophisticated new tools available stand as testimony to the advanced cognitive abilities of current AI systems. They are equipped to both classify and generate visual and multimedia content with an unprecedented depth and nuance. They also open questions about which new methodologies should be selected for appropriate archiving, creating, and retrieving multimedia resources in libraries, and how they might best be used.

The advances in AI are poised to catalyze a seismic shift in the way business is done in library special collections and archives, especially multimedia collections. The advancements promise a renaissance where historical video footage, photographs, and complex art works can be analyzed, annotated, and remixed. Libraries are nurturing grounds for digital literacy and knowledge dissemination. They play auspicious roles in fostering new competencies in new digital literacies, equipping patrons with the skills and tools to not only navigate but actively engage, create, and recreate within a dynamically evolving media and multimodal landscape of resources available.

Conclusion

As libraries and librarians begin to find a path through an era of groundbreaking change and augmentation for the library sphere, this section heralds glimpses of a future brimming with potential but also raises questions about the present and the past. The chapters paint a portrait of an emerging epoch where library possibilities are overflowing traditional bounds and metamorphizing beyond prescribed definitions to enable creative production in innovative digital and algorithmic ways. Libraries, their knowledge stores, access gateways and warehouses are evolving into intelligent ecosystems pulsating with life, capable of fostering environments where user information and knowledge seeking experiences are dynamically personalized and tailored, intuitive, and richly responsive and immersive to the unique individual posing the questions. Through the advanced lens of AI, libraries are becoming crucibles and incubators for new genres of artifacts. These developments all speak to the necessity of digital and algorithmic literacy for librarians and patrons. There are new domains where patrons will need to be empowered to engage with content in a more immersive, interactive, and creative way than they do currently. Hopefully, the developments will nurture larger global learning and professional communities to harness the transformative power of AI in understanding and generating new media and learning narratives for knowledge on both local and global levels. The current era marks the dawn of a new AI horizon. Libraries stand in their historical role but are also now positioned towards the necessities of innovative engagement, offering new enriched, personalized journeys through a digital landscape. It is up to all to use the new tools wisely, adopt a fresh philosophic stance, and optimize AI's potential to create, research and understand the world and the people within it.

References

Bubeck, Sébastien, Varun Chandrasekaran, Ronen Eldan, Johannes Gehrke, Eric Horvitz, Ece Kamar, Peter Lee, Yin Tat Lee, et al. 2023. "Sparks of Artificial General Intelligence: Early Experiments with GPT-4." *ArXiv*: 2303.12712 [cs.CL]. https://arxiv.org/abs/2303.12712. https://doi.org/10.48550/arXiv.2303.12712

Hugging Face. n.d. "The AI Community Building the Future." https://huggingface.co.

Michelson, Annette. 1984. "On the Eve of the Future: The Reasonable Facsimile and the Philosophical Toy." *October* 29, Summer: 3–20. https://www.jstor.org/stable/778304?origin=crossref. https://doi.org/10.2307/778304.

Open AI. 2024. "GPT-4 is OpenAI's Most Advanced System, Producing Safer and more Useful Responses." https://openai.com/gpt-4.

Vaswani, Ashish, Noam Shazeer, Niki Parmar, Jakob Uszkoreit, Llion Jones, Aidan N. Gomez, Lukasz Kaiser, and Illia Polosukhin 2023. "Attention Is All You Need: The LLM Transformer Model." *Arxiv*. Cornell University. Submitted 12 Jun 2017, last revised 2 Aug 2023. https://arxiv.org/abs/1706.03762. https://doi.org/10.48550/arXiv.1706.03762.

Wang, Lei, Chen Ma, Xueyang Feng, Zeyu Zhang, Hao Yang, Jingsen Zhang, Zhiyuan Chen, Jiakai Tang, Xu Chen, Yankai Lin, Wayne Xin Zhao, Zhewei Wei, and Ji-Rong Wen. 2023. "A Survey on Large Language Model Based Autonomous Agents." *ArXiv*: 2308.11432. Submitted on 22 Aug 2023 (v1), last revised 7 Sep 2023. https://arxiv.org/abs/2308.11432.

Weizenbaum, Joseph. 1966. "ELIZA – A Computer Program for the Study of Natural Language Communication between Man and Machine." *Communications of the ACM* 9, no. 1: 37–45. https://dl.acm.org/doi/10.1145/365153.365168. Available at https://web.stanford.edu/class/cs124/p36-weizenabaum.pdf.

Martin Malmsten, Viktoria Lundborg, Elena Fano, Chris Haffenden,
Fredrik Klingwall, Robin Kurtz, Niklas Lindström, Faton Rekathati
and Love Börjeson

13 Without Heading? Automatic Creation of a Linked Subject System

Abstract: Can problems with library subject headings systems designed and operated by humans be mitigated by machine learning? This chapter discusses work undertaken at *Kungliga biblioteket*/National Library of Sweden (KB) to explore the use of an automated system for identifying subjects that would sidestep the need for fixed headings from a controlled vocabulary. The new approach taken combined the natural language processing (NLP) capacities of large language models (LLM) with topic modelling, to cluster and order texts according to topics derived from the material, rather than any pre-defined terms reflecting existing biases. The chapter explains how BERTopic was tested on a text corpus compiled from KB's digital collections and presents and analyses the results. The value of such critical exploration is to illuminate the shortcomings of existing systems that might otherwise remain unnoticed.

Keywords: Subject headings; Knowledge organization in subject areas; Machine learning; Linked data

Introduction

How can libraries create order and provide effective access to information in an era of Big Data? While traditional means of knowledge organisation and document arrangement used by libraries such as subject headings and classification systems are useful, they demand considerable resources to maintain and are prone to bias given their rigid nature in an ever-changing context. A more dynamic option stems from recent developments within machine learning (ML), where the emergence of transformer models has enabled a subject system that is content-based, can be created and re-created at a moment's notice, and allows its biases to be measured. Can such an automated approach complement, enhance, or even replace existing systems?

This chapter describes a project exploring the possibility of fully automating the creation of a subject heading system, albeit without the actual headings. To achieve the desired outcome, novel methods from natural language processing (NLP) were combined with topic modelling techniques to create vector-based clusters derived from the content of the collections under consideration. Subjects could thereby be defined without the constraint of using words or phrases to denote a pre-existing and inherently biased concept. While opening up new forms of granular and empirically-driven indexing, the new approach retains the functional requirements of a traditional subject headings system, including the ability to expose the system as linked data and to provide a useful search tool for users. Allowing ML methods to create particular topics based on the specifics of the material under consideration suggests one way in which the arbitrary role of human bias in existing systems of subject indexing might be countered.

This chapter provides a vision of how an automated linked subject system without predetermined headings might work. The first part offers a brief contextualising discussion of subject analysis and topic modelling, pointing to various ways in which the problems of the former could be mitigated by the advantages of the latter. The consideration of both manual and automated approaches stems from the multidisciplinary character of the project group, which combined expertise in manual indexing systems on the one hand with innovative perspectives of AI and data science on the other. The second part of the chapter explains how a sentence BERT language model trained at KBLab, the digital research infrastructure at *Kungliga biblioteket*/National Library of Sweden (KB) (Börjeson et al. 2023) as the basis for a new transformer-based approach to topic modelling called BERTopic (Grootendorst 2022). A description of how the approach was tested on a text corpus compiled from the library's digital collections is provided before a discussion and evaluation of the results. The chapter concludes with broader reflections on the value of such experimentation in illuminating the shortcomings of existing systems that otherwise tend to be normalised to the point that problems are no longer noticed.

Subject Analysis of Library Collections

The history of libraries readily demonstrates the suggestion that "to classify is human" (Bowker and Star 1999, 1). Since at least as far back as the ancient Babylonian library of Ashurbanipal (Finkel 2009) some form of subject analysis has been used in libraries. The concept of aboutness has received considerable attention in the literature (Beghtol 1986; Hutchins 1978; Yablo 2014). In this chapter, the terms *subject, theme, aspect, topic* and *cluster* are all used in relation to aboutness. *Topic* and *cluster* are used to denote topics extracted using topic modelling techniques, whereas *subject* is used to refer to existing subjects in a subject heading system. The terms are not entirely equivalent, but in this context and in actual usage they are similar enough. Any attempt to distinguish them further could lead to an ontological rabbit hole from which it would be difficult to escape. Similarly, *theme* or *aspect* is used to designate the actual subject matter of a particular topic or subject.

Catalogues and subject systems have been utilized by both library professionals and users to organise, navigate and search large collections. Such tools greatly reduce the time needed to query a collection for resources in a given category, and together with classification schema have played a crucial role in creating order. The principal value of using words and controlled vocabularies to embody a subject is to convey its boundaries to a user or, with the addition of a scope note, a librarian, based on the assumption that the receiver of the information will use language and general knowledge to quickly grasp the intended scope and meaning of the subject. It depends, in short, on a common understanding of the world to communicate, receive and understand information in a highly compressed form.

A subject heading system is useful when exposing library data as linked data, making it machine readable (Malmsten 2009). Knowledge organisation systems for subjects are easily modelled and can map relationships and connections to other subjects, indicating if a subject is broader, narrower, or somehow related. Many subject headings systems with controlled vocabularies have been developed throughout the world, the most well-known being the Library of Congress Subject Headings (LCSH). Specialist subject headings lists or thesauri exist in specific subject areas, for example Medical Subject Headings (MESH). The various systems can be linked. For example, the *Svenska ämnesord*/Swedish subject headings (SAO) terms can be connected with LCSH.

Yet subject heading systems are not without their problems. The most obvious is the lack of shared understanding. As soon as more than one person is involved in classifying a subject area or searching for information, it becomes apparent that people have slightly, or wildly, differing ideas about the nature of a subject, both when choosing a heading within the system to apply to an item, or when using it to search. "Indexers do not agree with each other nor themselves" (de Keyser 2012, 47). One could say the same for people in general. And the problem is only exacerbated when linking subject heading systems from differing origins. Moreover, there is the ever-looming question of bias. People building subject systems are biased; people applying subject terms are biased; and the people using the systems are biased (Knowlton 2005; Olson 1998). One might argue that knowledge organisation formalises bias, based on the mistaken assumption that everyone shares the same biases. Martin notes that bias can have significant consequences: "Naming controls what can and cannot be easily talked about, grappled with, and faced" (Martin 2021, 282).

Beyond Machine Indexing

In Bloomfield's cutting terms, "Machine indexing is noted as 'rotten' and human indexing as 'capricious'" (2002). Even if human indexing is unreliable, can machine indexing or automated subject indexing still be dismissed? The answer is not necessarily. While techniques for automatic clustering and indexing of text have existed for some time, recent developments in ML offer potentially transformative new possibilities. Topic modelling is an example. It refers to a technique where topics are extracted automatically from a corpus of text fragments (Blei 2012). Each text fragment is then assigned to one or more of the topics. Topics deemed close to one another can be clustered to create broader topics.

> Topic modeling algorithms are statistical methods that analyze the words of the original texts to discover the themes that run through them, how those themes are connected to each other, and how they change over time... [T]he topics emerge from the analysis of the original texts. Topic modeling enables us to organize and summarize electronic archives at a scale that would be impossible by human annotation (Blei 2012, 77–8).

Topic modelling produces a structure similar to that of a subject headings system that can be exposed in a machine-readable way. It previously required a large amount of pre-processing and tended to be regarded as a qualitatively inflected method demanding substantial prior knowledge of the corpus to apply it correctly. However, the emergence of large, transformer-based language models like BERT has changed the situation dramatically (Devlin et al. 2019). Using the new models significantly reduces the need for pre-processing and specific corpus knowledge. In short, topic modelling has been made far easier since the incorporation of BERT (Fano and Haffenden 2022).

The project hypothesised that new AI techniques could be leveraged to achieve benefits similar to those of existing subject headings systems but without some of the drawbacks. The lack of commensurability that besets systems created and applied by humans could be mitigated by a fully automated approach in which a single neural network provides a type of cohesive universal understanding. By exploring such an alternative, the value of hand-crafted subject heading systems when used by end users would also be questioned. Experience has shown that users deploy the headings unknowingly when searching and do not browse the subjects *per se* (Antell and Huang 2008). Users rarely understand the systems they are using which suggests that if the second order effects of a subject heading system can be replicated, the system itself does not need to be legible to a user.

In using BERTopic, the approach differed from other efforts to automate subject indexing within predetermined frameworks (Golub 2021). Systems like Annif in Finland (Suominen 2019) and more recently Kratt in Estonia (Asula et

al. 2021) produce a form of semi-automated subject indexing that assigns documents to given subject headings or controlled vocabularies. In essence, they replace
manual indexing with automation but reproduce existing practices and forms
from established knowledge organisation systems. By contrast, it is precisely these
practices themselves that could be flawed, and rather than emulating them they
should be replaced by an alternative, ML-based system that can be applied in an
unsupervised manner. The Swedish project critically probed the suggestion that
"algorithms are really not able to entirely replace the intellectual work of subject
indexing professionals" (Golub 2021, 703). The framework used by professionals
may be part of the problem and any solution must be found outside the box.

Subject Analysis in Sweden

KB maintains the primary subject heading system used in Sweden: *Svenska ämnesord*/Swedish subject headings (SAO). SAO is used in the Swedish union catalogue
Libris by all types of libraries including academic, public and special libraries and
other cultural institutions like museums and broadcasting companies for analysing
materials ranging from books to videogames. SAO is a subject heading system that
is based on international principles (Chan 1990), including:
- Current usage; the preferred terms should mirror what a subject is usually
  called
- Literary warrant; there is at least one resource in Libris for each heading
- Uniform heading; one heading per subject
- Unique heading; one subject per heading
- Specific and direct entry; the most precise term naming the subject
- Stability; a heading is changed only when authoritative sources consistently
  use a new term
- Consistency; regarding form and structure for similar heading, and
- References and relationships; synonyms are recorded as variants and the
  subject headings are placed in hierarchies with relationships to related terms.

The indexing guidelines follow international principles such as depth, covering the
main points, and assigning headings only for topics that comprise at least 20% of
the work, and specificity, assigning headings that precisely represent the subject
content.

The purpose of using controlled subject headings is to provide standard subject
access to resources in a given collection. By using a controlled vocabulary based on
the principles outlined, there is a predictability regarding the indexing that should

enable the user to find everything about a given subject. Indexing in Libris using the SAO system is undertaken by human cataloguers. Some are librarians who work with cataloguing on a full-time basis; some work part-time for only a few hours a week; and others conduct indexing as part of their jobs.

In practice, indexers use subject heading systems in slightly different ways, which tends to lead to inconsistency. Not all resources about the same topic are analysed in the same way. There are many reasons for the different approaches:

- Not all indexers have studied the subject heading manual or read the individual scope notes connected to specific subject headings
- The subject heading system allows for subjects and related subjects to be described in more than one way. For example, a resource about gender inequality in the job market may be indexed with some or all of these headings: Women—Employment; Sex discrimination; Equality; Women; Men; Men and women; Labour market; Labour market—Gender aspects
- The tools that cataloguers use to find appropriate subject headings are not optimised. There are challenges in indicating specific narrower terms and understanding scope notes when choosing headings
- The search options for finding related bibliographic records on the same subject might be limited which is also an issue for users, and
- Indexers are human individuals with diverse life and education experiences.

In commenting previously on inconsistency in human indexing, the wording "tends to" was used. There is no specific research regarding the quality of the manual subject indexing in Libris, but more general studies on indexing such as de Keyser's have noted the issues (de Keyser 2012, 40–47).

The SAO system was not constructed from scratch using the above-mentioned principles. Rather, it was launched as a subject heading list in 2000 based on a Swedish classification system's subject index and has since grown into a more thesaurus-like form. Hierarchies and LCSH-mapping have been added in piecemeal fashion over the years, and there are still some parts of the system that consist of single terms with no relationship to other terms. The isolated terms are at higher risk of not being found and used by cataloguers. Another challenge is that maintaining a manual subject heading system is a costly enterprise. SAO is maintained by one full-time member of staff, but even so keeping the 36,000 subject headings and 2000 genre/form terms up-to-date can prove a challenge.

Topic Modelling with BERTopic

Topic modelling has already been introduced in this chapter. It is a text mining technique used to determine which topics are represented in a collection of documents without manually reading them. The most popular algorithm used has been Latent Dirichlet Allocation (LDA) where topics are represented as a set of words with different probabilities, and documents are understood as being generated by a distribution of different topics (Blei 2012). When a topic model is fitted to a collection of texts, it denotes the words relevant for a given topic and indicates the documents in the collection most representative of that topic.

BERTopic is a modelling technique based on clustering document embeddings generated by a transformer model. "BERTopic generates document embedding with pre-trained transformer-based language models, clusters these embeddings, and finally, generates topic representations with the class-based TF-IDF procedure" (Grootendorst 2022). It therefore leverages the language understanding of the language model to find similar documents and build topics.

The first step when building a model with BERTopic is to run a SentenceBERT model on the corpus to obtain embeddings for each document. The BERTopic library allows different kinds of backend models to generate representations for clustering, but SentenceBERT is the recommended method since it is a transformer model that can embed entire documents at once. The project used a Swedish Sentence-BERT trained in-house at KBLab and available through Huggingface (Rekathati 2023).

Once the document embeddings are ready, their dimensionality must be reduced for the clustering algorithm to work properly. BERTopic uses a dimensionality-reducing algorithm called UMAP that preserves both global and local information to an adequate degree. The representations of the documents are then clustered using an algorithm called hierarchical density-based spatial clustering of applications with noise (HDBSCAN) which is a density-based clustering method that is good at detecting outliers and is particularly suited to noisy data like natural language text.

The result of the clustering algorithm is a number of clusters that correspond to topics, but they are still virtually uninterpretable at this stage. The next step is to use an adapted version of term frequency, inverse document frequency (TF-IDF), to extract relevant words from each cluster and label the topics. For the purpose of class-based TF-IDF, all documents in the cluster are treated as a single document, and then TF-IDF is applied to the whole text to find words that are important for that cluster. A ranking algorithm called maximal marginal relevance (MMR) can then be applied to diversify the words that represent each topic and make sure that they form a coherent but non-overlapping representation.

Topic modelling is regarded as a tool to gain general insights about a corpus to be followed by a deeper dive as required. It previously involved many modelling choices which can have a significant impact on the end results. Documents must be pre-processed to maximise the information content of the words to be modelled with a range of parameters in place to control the modelling behaviour. BERTopic greatly simplifies both aspects of the process. Since document representations are generated through a pre-trained language model, the need for pre-processing is greatly reduced. Transformer models leverage transfer learning to output high-quality representations of text data, in this case accepting whole paragraphs as input. They take into account both semantics and syntax while generating representations, whereas regular topic models usually operate on a bag-of-words basis. The traditional components of an NLP pipeline like tokenising, part-of-speech tagging and lemmatising (Tech Gumptions 2023) are not required, as single words are not used as features in this kind of modelling.

In terms of parameter settings, BERTopic comes with a number of default parameters that are automatically optimised and yield consistent modelling outcomes. For instance, one of the main challenges in traditional topic models is determining the number of topics. This has to be done manually and is usually based on some coherence measures and/or knowledge of the subject matter. BERTopic provides an automatic setting to let HDBSCAN determine the number of topics based on optimal distance between the clusters. The alpha and beta parameters to control topic word density and document topic density are absent in BERTopic, as the clustering is handled by HDBSCAN instead of latent Dirichlet allocation.

In summary, BERTopic offers a higher degree of automation compared to traditional topic modelling, while also allowing for some flexibility by letting the user override the default settings.

Embeddings

To understand the mechanics of the project approach, the role of a BERT model in enabling the automated clustering that underpins it requires further explanation. A class of models called sentence transformers, s-BERT, is used to convert text sequences into exact numerical vector representations which are referred to as embeddings. The term sentence is used loosely to refer to a sequence of text of arbitrary length, rather than its traditional linguistic meaning.

Using neural networks to compute continuous numerical vector representations of words was introduced in word2vec (Mikolov et al. 2013). Depending on configuration, the networks were challenged to predict either the current word given its surrounding context, or the surrounding context of words given the current word. The idea and the expectation were that words frequently co-occur-ring within some context length N would also be semantically related to each other, which would manifest itself in the form of vector representations of similar words moving more closely together during training. The concept of word embeddings would later be extended to documents in another NLP tool doc2vec (Le and Mikolov 2014; Shperber 2017).

While being effective, word2vec produced only a static word embedding for each word. Static embeddings could not account for words having several different definitions nor for changes in their meaning based on surrounding context, such as the presence or absence of negations and other modifiers. Transformer models addressed the shortcomings of static embeddings through the use of another set of network layers with the purpose of contextualising the embeddings (Vaswani et al. 2017). In these models, word embeddings representing the same word start out the same in the input stage, but end up with different numeric representations depend-ing on the influence of the surrounding context.

As already noted, BERT (Devlin et al. 2019) is a transformer architecture that incorporates both previous and future context in a sequence in computing output embeddings. Prior architectures focused either on machine translation or language modelling tasks (Radford et al. 2018), gaining a general language understanding through challenging the models to predict the next word in a sequence while only considering the context of previous words in the sequence. BERT modified the pre-training objective to a masked language modelling (MLM) task (Briggs 2021). As opposed to predicting the next word, its approach relied on trying to fill in and predict a proportion of words in the sequence that had been masked out while being able to consider the full context of the sequence. Considering the full context of a sentence, paragraph, or sequence when making a prediction proved an advan-tage on many downstream tasks such as extractive question answering and sen-tence similarity.

The manner in which BERT initially was fine-tuned and adapted for sentence similarity tasks meant a sequence pair would be passed to it as input and it would then be tasked with producing a similarity score for the pair. In the training setup, the two sequences would be passed to the network together, and contextual infor-mation from both sequences would be used in producing the output embeddings needed to determine the similarity score. While incorporating information from both sequences yielded strong results, it unfortunately suffered from an impracti-cal inference procedure. Involving the neural network in the computation of every single similarity score between a sentence pair was computationally expensive.

Ideally, performing inference on a set of documents would use a model that outputs a meaningful document embedding which can be later used for similar-ity computations or clustering algorithms. Unfortunately, the original BERT training setup did not produce a representative sentence embedding, since during its training it always cross-encoded information from two sequences. Sentence-BERT (Reimers and Gurevych 2019) modified the training setup to pass sequences independently and separately to the network. By isolating the two inputs in a bi-encoder setup, the BERT model could learn to output meaningful sentence embeddings.

Practical Details of the Project

The techniques outlined above were used to create topics from the corpus. Most of the heavy lifting was carried out by the sentence-BERT language model in producing embeddings. Once the embeddings were produced, the standard algorithms already mentioned, UMAP and HDBSCAN, could be applied to the embeddings. The tools are further packaged in BERTopic making the process easy to experiment with through testing different parameters. The parameters included the minimum distance between topics to determine whether closely related topics should be merged or not. Since the aim was the exposure of the created topic system as linked data between topics rather than a balanced list of terms, having many similar topics was not a problem.

Sentence-BERT was used to make the model for the embeddings and BERTopic was used to fit the model to the data to find clusters of paragraphs. The resulting clusters became the topics. The language model does not operate on a word level, but uses embeddings which means that the model can handle synonyms, and even though a particular word might be chosen to represent the cluster it does not have to be present in the paragraphs. It is likewise important to note that each paragraph is not only clustered into a single topic, but also is distributed over all topics with an attached score. Paragraphs that deal with many themes receive a high score for multiple topics.

The Corpus

To create and evaluate topics, a corpus was extracted from 954 titles from the Swedish publishing foundation Natur och Kultur. Fiction and biographies were filtered out. The remaining titles comprised a corpus of roughly 65,000 paragraphs. Metadata from the Swedish union catalogue, Libris, was used for filtering and to find the attached subject headings from the existing system.

A SPARQL-query (Prud'hommeaux and Seaborne 2008) was used to obtain a list of title, ISBN, topics and genre/form for all monographic texts matching the criteria. An overwhelming percentage had been catalogued with any of the three description levels: Full Level, Abbreviated Level, and Minimal Level, where Abbreviated Level does not require subjects or genre/form. Only controlled terms were used for the project and non-internationalised resource identifier (IRI) types were filtered out, which also excluded post-coordinated complex subjects. Corpus details are contained in Table 13.1.

Table 13.1: Corpus disposition

Titles	954
Paragraphs	65165
Subject headings from SAO	522

Project Results and Findings

The result with most parameters set to the defaults was a system with 1211 topics covering 50% of the paragraphs. The seemingly high number of unclassified paragraphs is in line with previous experiments. Given a particular text, the model provided output values or topic loadings that represent the distribution topics for that text. Since there is no gold standard for comparison, it is not feasible to evaluate the automatically created subject system using quantitative metrics such as precision and recall and the F1 score, the harmonic mean of the precision and recall. Instead, qualitative evaluation and proxy measurements were used. Topics were assigned per paragraph while subjects were assigned per work, which made the task of comparison more complicated.

Optimally, both systems would be evaluated against real-world use-cases with actual users. The effects of the systems could thereby be measured rather than examining similarities. However, this is unfortunately beyond the scope of this chapter. To create a sample for evaluation, topics were first chosen at random, and paragraphs then sampled from the topics. A small number of works was chosen. The resulting sample contained twenty-five topics, 125 paragraphs and ten works.

Representing Topics as Strings

It is difficult for human beings to recognise what a generated topic represents. It would be possible to read all of the paragraphs in a topic and then come up with a term, that is, a subject heading. But since the project's aim was sidestepping human involvement to counter the problem of divergent judgement in existing systems, this strategy was not deployed. Another approach to the problem is to find words in each topic that are disproportionately common compared to the rest of the corpus. Traditionally this has been done using TF-IDF where the frequency of a term in relation to a topic is divided by the frequency of the term globally. Taking the top ten words for each topic and concatenating them creates a string that gives some idea of what the topic is about. It is important to note that the string is not a subject heading in that it does not necessarily represent the topic. The string provides a sense of what the topic encompasses, as shown in Table 13.2.

Table 13.2: Words selected using TF-IDF for sample clusters

Topic	#0	#34	#112	#710
Words	religious, god, religion, humanity, spiritual, christian, gods, faith	stage, tour, driver, armstrong, anquetil, kilometer, france, desgrange	lens, light, eye, mirror, figure, reflection, ray, rays	russian, rolf, women, men, woman, petersburg, russia, kalle, sune, romantic

As an initial, fail fast attempt to evaluate the results, the words chosen are examined for apparent affinity. At first sight, the results are inconclusive. While topics often have words that are clearly related, some are a mix of seemingly random words as shown in Table 13.2. However, on further inspection it becomes apparent that the seeming randomness is an effect of the method. In retrospect, the class of words should have been considered, since names, for example, are often disproportionately common in a text while not being connected to the actual topic.

Topic Cohesion

The degree to which a topic collects paragraphs that are similar indicates the extent of clarity of topic definition. If the paragraphs seem to have no connection to each other, the cohesion is low, whereas if the paragraphs have a clear common denominator, then the topic cohesion is high. From sampling and evaluating paragraphs, three distinct categories of topics were identified:

1. Topics that mapped well to existing subject headings such as religion or alcoholism (Table 13.3).
2. Topics that mapped to observable themes or aspects in the text, but where the work spanned multiple seemingly disparate subjects, for example client, parents, and time. These topics can show up in any work that has such a theme.

3.   Topics for paragraphs that have a particular form and content such as intro-
     ductory texts, instructions and acknowledgements. These paragraphs do not
     relate to the subject matter and can therefore show up in a work regardless of
     the subject (Table 13.4, especially topic #27).

An option for differentiating the three categories is to examine how closely they
map to subjects using entropy (Stevens et al. 2012). Entropy is low when a topic
maps cleanly to a single or a few subjects and high if it maps equally to many or all
topics. If the goal is to find topics that map to subjects, then using an entropy threshold is effective. It was not appropriate for the project because it was not concerned
with reifying existing subject terms.

After manual evaluation of the sample, topic cohesion in all three categories
was deemed to be high. Even though topics might not cleanly map to subjects, there
was often something observable that indicated why paragraphs had been clustered
together.

Table 13.3: Topics with an apparent subject

#	Words	Comment
104	Drugs, metabolize, effect, side effect, liver, concentration, dosage, uses, oral, anesthesia	Paragraphs all deal with the effect of drugs
400	Algorithm, dataism, data, human, google, decision, data processing	Computer science
302	God, my, mine, me, father, gods, mercy, felt	Paragraphs in this topic contain multiple themes, but they all also deal with religion

Table 13. 4: Examples of topics that do not align with traditional subject headings or themes

#	Words	Comment
27	Thank, thank you, book, my, helped, editor, me, contribute	This cluster very precisely contains acknowledgements where the author thanks family members, and the editor
94	Psychologist, psychotherapist, university, psychology, clinical, dr, karolinska, professor, institute	Introductory texts and description of authors. For example, "Adam Smith is therapist at the Center for Mental Health, he has [...]" is a good example of when the selected words do not give a good indication of the topic. The cluster shows high topic cohesion
165	Copy, cid, questions, students, read, whiteboard	Paragraphs contain task instructions for students

Mapping Topics to Subjects

The existence of the first category of topics, those with low entropy mapping to subjects, indicates that the method operates similarly to human creation of a system manually. If there had been no correlation the appropriateness of the method might be in question. Such correlation could be used to map generated topics for new works to existing subjects, in a similar vein to existing automated or semi-automated approaches to subject headings. While this aspect was neither within the scope nor the intention of the work with BERTopic, it can still be useful as an aid to cataloguers.

Aggregating Topics for Whole Works

Given the entire set of paragraphs for a single work, all topics can be aggregated to obtain a work-level topic distribution. The distribution is more stable than that from a single paragraph since any noise from paragraphs that do not deal with the topic(s) are fewer by comparison, assuming that one or more distinguishable topics exist in the work.

Mapping from topics to subject can be used to determine the aggregated subject heading. The approach is more effective than using a paragraphs distribution, because it deals with the topic of one paragraph only. For example, a book with the subject heading "chemistry" might contain a paragraph about physics which will result in a topic connected to physics even though the broader subject of the work is chemistry. However, when aggregating the topic distribution of all paragraphs, one single paragraph will not influence the total in any meaningful way (Figure 13.1). There is evidence that topics at the aggregate level can be used to propose, or automatically add, subject headings if required.

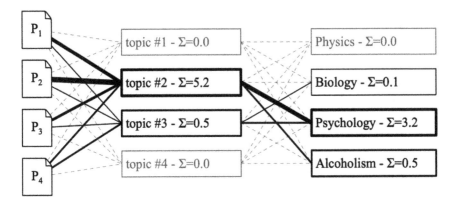

Figure 13.1: Example of aggregated topic distribution for multiple paragraphs and optional mapping back to subjects

Linked Data

Following the development of topics and mapping through paragraphs to works, both the topic system and its relationships can be easily exposed as linked data (Bizer et al. 2008). Because HDBSCAN is a hierarchical clustering algorithm, topics are grouped into increasingly broader topics until there is only one overarching topic. The process creates a tree of topics that can be exposed as linked data. Dublin core (DC) was used for links between topics and works and Simple Knowledge Organization System (SKOS) was also applied using sKOS:Concept for topics and skos:broader for links (Figure 13.2).

The resulting Resource Description Framework (RDF) data can be imported into Libris and examined further by users and cataloguers. This is possible since the infrastructure underpinning the Swedish union catalogue, Libris XL, is based on linked data (Wennerlund and Berggren 2017) facilitating data sharing among libraries and interfaces using Libris.

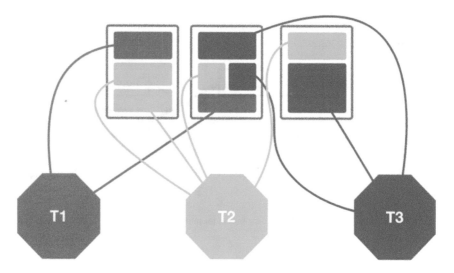

Figure 13.2: A visual representation of paragraphs and their connected topics, with the different colours showing the paragraphs where the respective topics can be found in the works

Other Findings

A surprising side-effect of evaluating the BERTopic approach was the insights into the workings and application of the existing subject headings system that it provided. Comparing topics to subjects in paragraphs led to questions about why a particular subject had been used. The answer could be custom and habit, or that the subject heading system had been co-opted for another purpose, making it a general-purpose solution for tagging content. An example is the use of the subject "Swedish as a second language" to tag resources that are suitable for readers with Swedish as a second language, rather than being about Swedish as a second language as might be expected. On the other hand, BERTopic would probably not have found the particular aspect or generated a topic for it. In this particular instance, it would be advantageous to target the specific intended use and analyse the text to determine its suitability for people with limited language understanding, rather than focus on the topic/subject system.

Conclusion

The project undertaken at KB and described in this chapter examined whether problems with library subject headings systems designed and operated by humans might be overcome by the use of machine learning. The work undertaken showed that the fully automated creation of a linked subject system using BERTopic is possible. It also suggested that such a topic modelling approach to indexing need not reproduce the headings of prevailing systems for knowledge organisation, with their inherent layers of bias. It is possible to develop a machine-learning based approach that enables users to search and navigate according to their interests without relying on fixed headings from a controlled vocabulary. Whether such a system is used to replace, extend or support existing practices will ultimately depend on the usage of the current subject heading system at any given institution.

During the evaluation of the topic modelling approach, multiple problems with existing approaches were discovered. Working through the data provided insights into the manual subject heading system. There was evidence that subject headings are sometimes seen as a golden hammer, an available tool used for purposes for which it was not designed. If all one has are subject headings, everything will look like a subject. The problem was highlighted with the example of the "Swedish as a second language" heading which had been liberally applied to refer to the style of content rather than its subject matter.

Another broad outcome of the project was the reinforcement of the importance of digitisation in libraries, not only as a means of preserving and representing physical objects and improving access. Digitising books facilitates the creation of metadata and subject analytical data created using the text itself. The findings in relation to the advantages of digital data point to a "digitise first and ask questions later" approach. Since the new system does not rely or expand on the current one, the experiment carried out in Sweden with BERTopic means that a valuable additional tool has been gained to examine both the current system and its application. Critical exploration using new methods and techniques helps to illuminate shortcomings of existing systems that might otherwise remain hidden.

Next Steps

The pilot project undertaken at KB investigated the practical and technical feasibility of creating an automated subject system without fixed headings using BERTopic. To build on the work and capitalise on the experience gained, there are three directions in which future efforts could usefully be directed:

- Incorporate a user experience (UX) perspective and determine how the system might work from a user perspective
- Test at scale by examining how the topic modelling approach might function with a larger corpus than considered in the pilot, and
- Conduct qualitative interpretation and assessment.

While the lack of benchmarks makes assessment of performance a challenging issue, further attention must be directed towards comparing the effectiveness and efficiency of manual and automated systems used to analyse the content of library collections.

Acknowledgements

The authors would like to thank the National Library of Sweden (KB) for providing metadata, the KBLab for providing resources, *Natur & Kultur* for providing the full texts for the corpus and Maarten Grootendorst for creating BERTopic. Part of the development work for this project was carried out within Huminfra, the Swedish national infrastructure for digital and experimental work in the humanities.

References

Antell, Karen, and Jie Huang. 2008. "Subject Searching Success: Transaction Logs, Patron Perceptions, and Implications for Library Instruction." *Reference & User Services Quarterly* 48, no. 1: 68–76. https://www.jstor.org/stable/20864994.

Asula, Marit, Jane Makke, Linda Freienthal, Hele-Andra Kuulmets, and Raul Sirel. 2021. "Kratt: Developing an Automatic Subject Indexing Tool for the National Library of Estonia." *Cataloging & Classification Quarterly* 59, no. 8: 775–93. https://doi.org/10.1080/01639374.2021.1998283.

Beghtol, Clare. 1986. "Bibliographic Classification Theory and Text Linguistics: Aboutness Analysis, Intertextuality and the Cognitive Act of Classifying Documents." *Journal of Documentation* 42, no. 2: 84–113. https://doi.org/10.1108/eb026788. Available at https://edisciplinas.usp.br/pluginfile. php/7880387/mod_resource/content/0/BEGHTOL_1986_Bibliographic%20classification%20 theory%20and%20text%20linguistics....pdf.

Bizer, Christian, Tom Heath, and Tim Berners-Lee. 2011. "Linked Data: The Story so Far." In *Semantic Services, Interoperability and Web Applications: Emerging Concepts*, edited by Amit Sheth, 205–27. Hershey, PA: IGI Global. Reprinted in *Linking the World's Information: Essays on Tim Berners-Lee's Invention of the World Wide Web*, edited by Oshani Seneviratne and James Hendler, 115–143. New York, NY: Association for Computing Machinery, 2023. https://doi.org/10.1145/3591366.3591378.

Blei, David M. 2012. "Probabilistic Topic Models." *Communications of the ACM* 55, no. 4: 77–84. https:// doi.org/10.1145/2133806.2133826.

Bloomfield, Masse. 2002. "Indexing – Neglected and Poorly Understood." *Cataloging & Classification Quarterly* 33, no. 1: 63–75. https://doi.org/10.1300/J104v33n01_07.

Bowker, Geoffrey C., and Susan Leigh Star. 1999. *Sorting Things Out : Classification and Its Consequences.* Cambridge, Mass.: MIT Press.

Börjeson, Love, Chris Haffenden, Martin Malmsten, Fredrik Klingwall, Emma Rende, Robin Kurtz, Faton Rekathati, Hillevi Hägglöf, and Justyna Sikora. 2023. "Transfiguring the Library as Digital Research Infrastructure: Making KBLab at the National Library of Sweden." *SocArXiv Papers.* Accepted for publication in *College & Research Libraries.* December 8, 2023. Anticipated publication date 2025. https://osf.io/preprints/socarxiv/w48rf.

Briggs, James. 2021. "Masked-Language Modeling With BERT." *Medium*, May 20, 2021. https://towards-datascience.com/masked-language-modelling-with-bert-7d49793e5d2c.

Chan, Lois Mai. 1990. *Library of Congress Subject Headings : Principles of Structure and Policies for Application.* Annotated version. Washington, D.C.: Cataloging Distribution Service, Library of Congress. Available at https://babel.hathitrust.org/cgi/pt?id=mdp.39015057586136&seq=9.

de Keyser, Pierre. 2012. *Indexing : From Thesauri to the Semantic Web.* Oxford: Chandos Publishing. Available at https://www.comecso.com/wp-content/uploads/2019/05/Indexing-from-thesauri-to-the-Semantic-Web.pdf.

Devlin, Jacob, Ming-Wei Chang, Kenton Lee, and Kristina Toutanova. 2019. "BERT: Pre-Training of Deep Bidirectional Transformers for Language Understanding." In *Proceedings of the 2019 Conference of the North American Chapter of the Association for Computational Linguistics: Human Language Technologies,* Volume 1 (Long and Short Papers), 4171–86. Association for Computational Linguistics. https://doi.org/10.18653/v1/N19-1423.

Fano, Elena, and Chris Haffenden. 2022. 'The KBLab Blog: BERTopic for Swedish: Topic Modeling Made Easier via KB-BERT'. https://kb-labb.github.io/posts/2022-06-14-bertopic/.

Finkel, Irving. 2019. "Assurbanipal's Library: An Overview." In *Libraries Before Alexandria: Ancient Near Eastern Traditions* edited by Kim Ryholt and Gojko Barjamovic, 367–89. Oxford: Oxford University Press.

Golub, Koraljka. 2021. "Automated Subject Indexing: An Overview." *Cataloging & Classification Quarterly* 59, no. 8: 702–19. https://doi.org/10.1080/01639374.2021.2012311.

Grootendorst, Maarten. 2022. "BERTopic: Neural Topic Modeling with a Class-Based TF-IDF Procedure." *arXiv*:2203. 05794. https://doi.org/10.48550/arXiv.2203.05794.

Hutchins, William J. 1978. "The Concept of 'Aboutness' in Subject Indexing." *Aslib Proceedings* 30, no. 5: 172–181. https://doi.org/10.1108/eb050629. Available at https://citeseerx.ist.psu.edu/document?repid=rep1&type=pdf&doi=ddaeb42ad5889edf6e3eba808133ee0066c4fea2

Knowlton, Steven A. 2005. "Three Decades Since Prejudices and Antipathies: A Study of Changes in the Library of Congress Subject Headings." *Cataloging & Classification Quarterly* 40, no. 2 123–145. Available at https://steven-knowlton.scholar.princeton.edu/sites/g/files/toruqf3746/files/steven.a.knowlton/files/knowlton_three_decades.pdf.

Le, Quoc, and Tomas Mikolov. 2014. "Distributed Representations of Sentences and Documents." *PMLR*: *Proceedings of Machine Learning Research* 32:1188–96. Proceedings of the 31st Machine Learning Research, Beijing, China, 22–24 Jun 2014. https://proceedings.mlr.press/v32/le14.html.

Malmsten, Martin. 2009. "Exposing Library Data as Linked Data." Paper presented at the IFLA Satellite Preconference sponsored by the Information Technology Section. https://citeseerx.ist.psu.edu/document?repid=rep1&type=pdf&doi=2e0791d88a65cb2517e284c2bfca02b7c6660f30.

Martin, Jennifer M. 2021. "Records, Responsibility, and Power: An Overview of Cataloguing Ethics." *Cataloging & Classification Quarterly* 59, no. 2–3: 281–304. https://doi.org/10.1080/016393

74.2020.1871458. **Available at** https://api.mdsoar.org/server/api/core/bitstreams/c204d913-b186-46b6-8ecd-409ef215adc4/content.

Mikolov, Tomas, Kai Chen, Greg Corrado, and Jeffrey Dean. 2013. "Efficient Estimation of Word Representations in Vector Space." *arXiv*:1301.3781 (cs.).Submitted January 16, 2013 (this version), latest version 7 Sep 2013 (v3)]. https://arxiv.org/abs/1301.3781.

Olson, Hope A. 1998. "Mapping Beyond Dewey's Boundaries: Constructing Classificatory Space for Marginalized Knowledge Domains." *Library Trends* 47, no. 2: 233–254. https://www.proquest.com/docview/220452238?sourcetype=Scholarly%20Journals. **Available at** https://core.ac.uk/download/pdf/4817546.pdf.

Prud'hommeaux, Eric, and Andy Seaborne. 2008. "SPARQL Query Language for RDF." *W3C Recommendation*, January 15, 2008. https://www.w3.org/TR/rdf-sparql-query/. **New Version Available:** SPARQL 1.1 (Document Status Update, 26 March 2013) https://www.w3.org/TR/sparql11-overview/.

Radford, Alec, Karthik Narasimhan, Tim Salimans, and Ilya Sutskever. 2018. 'Improving Language Understanding by Generative Pre-Training'. https://cdn.openai.com/research-covers/language-unsupervised/language_understanding_paper.pdf.

Reimers, Nils, and Iryna Gurevych. 2019. "Sentence-BERT: Sentence Embeddings Using Siamese BERT-Networks." https://arxiv.org/abs/1908.10084.

Rekathati, Faton. 2023. "Swedish Sentence Transformer 2.0." *The KBLab Blog*, January 16, 2023. https://kb-labb.github.io/posts/2023-01-16-sentence-transformer-20 /.

Shperber, Gidi. 2017. "A Gentle Introduction to Doc2Vec." *Medium*, July 26, 2017. https://medium.com/wisio/a-gentle-introduction-to-doc2vec-db3e8c0cce5e.

Stevens, Keith, Philip Kegelmeyer, David Andrzejewski, and David Buttler. 2012. "Exploring Topic Coherence over Many Models and Many Topics." In *Proceedings of the 2012 Joint Conference on Empirical Methods in Natural Language Processing and Computational Natural Language Learning*, Jeju Island, Korea. 952–61. Association for Computational Linguistics, https://aclanthology.org/D12-1087/.

Suominen, Osma. 2019. "Annif: DIY Automated Subject Indexing Using Multiple Algorithms." *Cataloging & Classification Quarterly* 29, no. 1: 1–25. https://doi.org/10.18352/lq.10285.

Tech Gumptions. 2023. "Natural Language Processing (NLP) Pipeline." *Medium*, October 15, 2023. https://medium.com/@tech-gumptions/natural-language-processing-nlp-pipeline-e766d832a1e5.

Vaswani, Ashish, Noam Shazeer, Niki Parmar, Jakob Uszkoreit, Llion Jones, Aidan N. Gomez, Lukasz Kaiser, and Illia Polosukhin. 2017. "Attention Is All You Need." In *Advances in Neural Information Processing Systems*, edited by I. Guyon, U. Von Luxburg, S. Bengio, H. Wallach, R. Fergus, S. Vishwanathan, and R. Garnett, 30. [Presented at] 31st Conference on Neural Information Processing Systems (NIPS 2017), Long Beach, CA. https://proceedings.neurips.cc/paper/2017/file/3f5ee243547dee91fbd053c1c4a845aa-Paper.pdf.

Wennerlund, Bodil, and Anna Berggren. 2019. "Leaving Comfort Behind: A National Union Catalogue Transition to Linked Data." Paper presented at IFLA WLIC 2019, Athens, Greece. Libraries: dialogue for change in Session S15 - Big Data. In: Session S15 Data Intelligence in Libraries: The Actual and Artificial Perspectives, 22-23 August 2019, Frankfurt, Germany. https://library.ifla.org/id/eprint/2745/.

Yablo, Stephen. 2014. *Aboutness*. Princeton, NJ: Princeton University Press.

Anna Kasprzik

14 Transferring Applied Machine Learning Research into Subject Indexing Practice

Abstract: Subject indexing is one of the core activities of libraries. It is no longer possible to intellectually analyse and annotate with human effort every single document of the millions produced, which is why the potential of automated processes must be explored. At ZBW – Leibniz Information Centre for Economics / *ZBW – Leibniz-Informationszentrum Wirtschaft*, the efforts to automate the subject indexing process began as early as 2000 with experiments involving external partners and commercial software. The conclusion from the first experimental period was that supposedly shelf-ready solutions would not meet the requirements of the library. In 2014 the decision was taken to establish a doctoral candidate position and to do the necessary applied research in-house. However, the prototype machine learning solutions developed were not yet integrated into library operations. Subsequently in 2020 an additional position for a software engineer was established and a pilot phase initiated with the goal of building a software architecture that would allow for real-time subject indexing with trained models integrated into the workflows at ZBW. This chapter addresses the question of how to transfer results from applied research effectively into an operational service. The provisional conclusion is that there are still no shelf-ready open source systems for automated subject indexing. Existing software must be adapted and updated continuously which requires various forms of expertise. However, the problem is here to stay, and librarians are witnessing the dawn of an era where subject indexing will be done at least in part by machines, and the respective roles of machines and human experts will shift considerably. The collaborative work with subject librarians is described as well as its expected trajectory into the future.

Keywords: Subject headings; Indexing; Metadata; Libraries – Automation; Machine learning; Artificial intelligence; Organisational change – Management

The Context

Subject indexing is:

the act of describing or classifying a document by index terms, keywords, or other symbols in order to indicate what different documents are about, to summarize their contents or to increase findability. In other words, it is about identifying and describing the subject of documents (Wikipedia 2024a).

The term metadata is used to refer to the descriptive and analytical information in records created or used by libraries to identify and access content in documents. The semantic enrichment of metadata records with descriptors is one of the core activities of libraries. It is not possible to manually index or annotate every single one of the plethora of documents available in multiple formats anymore which leads to the necessity of exploring the potential use of automated means on every level. A wide range of automated approaches can be and is already being used ranging from simple measures using basic scripts and straightforward routines for metadata manipulation to the use of complex techniques from artificial intelligence (AI), notably from the domain of machine learning (ML).

The ZBW – Leibniz-Informationszentrum Wirtschaft/ZBW – Leibniz Information Centre for Economics is a member of the Leibniz Association in Germany and functions as the German National Library for Economics and the world's largest research infrastructure for economic literature, online as well as offline. ZBW is heavily engaged in the support of open access, providing users with millions of documents and research results in economics, partnering with many international research institutions to create an open portal to economic information, EconBiz. ZBW has a strong research emphasis in its activities, including the development of innovative approaches to librarianship.

At ZBW the efforts to automate the subject indexing process started as early as 2000. Two projects with external partners and/or commercial software yielded some insights into the state of the art at the time but mostly showed that the evaluated solutions would not suffice to cover the requirements of the library and that there were still many hurdles to overcome both with respect to the quality of the output and to the technical implementation (Gross and Faden 2010). However, abandoning the endeavour was not an option since the need for automation became ever more obvious and pressing over time. A reorientation phase around 2014 led to the decision that the necessary applied research should be done in-house and only open source software should be used and created. To this purpose, a full-time position for a researcher with appropriate qualifications and the option of obtaining a doctoral qualification in computer science was established within the library. The first phase of the new approach, Project AutoIndex, was launched. Following a personnel change in 2018, the role of coordinating the automation of subject indexing was upgraded to a permanent full-time position and a computer scientist with additional library training, the author of this chapter, was recruited.

However, the prototype ML solutions developed in project AutoIndex were not ready for integration into productive operations at the library. To take the project to the next stage and to respond effectively to the challenges, several adjustments were made at the strategic level. Most importantly, the automation of subject indexing at ZBW was declared no longer a project but a permanent task dubbed

AutoSE. A pilot phase was scheduled from 2020 until 2024 with the goal of transferring results from applied research into a productive service by building a suitable software architecture that allowed for real-time subject indexing with the trained models and integration thereof into the other metadata workflows at ZBW. To meet the requirements, AutoSE was allocated an additional position so that the resulting team comprised three people encompassing the roles of leadership and coordination, applied research, and development of the software architecture and its components.

Developing the Models

From the ML perspective, subject indexing of documents is a multi-label classification task assigning several labels or subject headings to each publication. Developments in AI have ebbed and flowed resulting in so-called AI winters. The current AI summer has seen the emergence of many usable ML models with many of them available as open source software. In the precursor project of AutoSE, AutoIndex, the prototype fusion approach developed towards automated subject indexing combined several methods and filtered the resulting output using additional rules (Toepfer and Seifert 2018a). At the same time, a team at the *Kansalliskirjasto/National-biblioteket*/National Library of Finland (NLF) commenced work on the creation of the open source toolkit Annif (NLF 2024) which offers various ML models for automated subject indexing and also allows the integration of one's own models. ZBW and NLF regularly exchanged information about their respective developments.

At the beginning of the pilot phase the AutoSE team adopted Annif as a framework for combining several state-of-the-art models. The following four are currently used: two variants of Omikuji, Parabel and Bonsai, which are tree-based machine learning algorithms (Dong n.d.), fastText (Facebook Inc. 2020), which uses word embeddings, and Stwfsapy, a lexical algorithm based on finite-state automata, which was developed at ZBW (n.d.a). Stwfsapy is optimised for use with the *Standard-Thesaurus Wirtschaft*/STW Thesaurus for Economics (ZBW 2023a), the thesaurus for economics hosted and used for subject indexing at ZBW, but can be used with other vocabularies as well. The output from the models is aggregated using another model called nn-ensemble (NLF 2023) to balance the results, yielding a final set of subject headings that have all passed a given confidence threshold. For AutoSE the models are trained with short texts from the metadata records underlying the ZBW research portal *EconBiz*, specifically titles and author keywords if available of publications in English. Experiments in the AutoSE context have shown that the use of author keywords in addition to titles improves the results considerably. Applied research continues in parallel to explore other ML methods beyond the classical ones, including approaches from deep learning (DL), notably the fine-tuning of pretrained large language models (LLM) (Wikipedia 2024b) which are particularly promising for multi-lingual subject indexing.

The AutoSE team has been actively involved in the continuous advancement of Annif, checking with NLF at regular intervals to examine whether results from the AutoSE context can be integrated as new functionalities in Annif, assisting NLF with giving tutorials, and providing other institutions with advice on how to deploy Annif in practice, including the *Deutsche Nationalbibliothek*/German National Library. The AutoSE team has complemented the ZBW instance of Annif with its own components for setting up experiments, hyperparameter optimisation, various quality control mechanisms and APIs to communicate with internal and external metadata workflows.

Productive Operations

The first version of the AutoSE service went into operation in 2021. The software runs on a Kubernetes cluster of five virtual machines employing technologies including Helm, GitLab, Prometheus and Grafana for software deployment, continuous integration, and monitoring. The research continues with the team integrating additional requirements into the system and supplementing it with enhancements. The architecture is constantly evolving and its modular design retains flexibility for future developments beyond the pilot phase.

The output of the service is used for two purposes at present. The first is fully automated subject indexing for publications in English that would otherwise not be annotated with any subject headings from the STW thesaurus. The *EconBiz* database is checked every hour for new eligible metadata records which are then enriched by AutoSE with STW subject headings and written back into the database immediately. If a publication belongs to the core set of literature earmarked for annotation by human specialists at ZBW, the AutoSE subject headings are subsequently suppressed both in the search index and in the single display page for the publication once the intellectual subject indexing has taken place. The connection between AutoSE and the *EconBiz* database was activated in July 2021, and in the first six months of operations, over 100,000 machine-annotated metadata records were entered into the database via direct write access. In contrast, approximately 20,000 records receive subject indexing by humans every year. The total number of records enriched by AutoSE methods in the database is higher than the numbers presented because the team processes large numbers of records retrospectively which are written back into the database via a batch process. As of September 2024, the *EconBiz* database contained over 1.7 million records with AutoSE subject indexing, which corresponds to about a quarter of ZBW holdings.

The second purpose of the output of the service is machine-assisted subject indexing: the subject headings generated by AutoSE are made available as suggestions to *Digitaler assistent* (DA-3) (Eurospider 2023), the platform used for intellectual subject indexing at ZBW via an API for the first time in 2020. Within DA-3, AutoSE suggestions are marked as machine-generated for reasons of transparency and can be adopted by a single click of an add button during the annotation of a publication. Freshly annotated records are stored in the union catalogue and mirrored back into the *EconBiz* database where the AutoSE team collects them and computes the F1-score (Wikipedia 2024c) from the difference between those annotations and the AutoSE suggestions to monitor performance. The F1-score is the harmonic mean of precision and recall and the highest possible value is 1.0. It represents one option for measuring the overall quality of machine-generated subject indexing.

Figure 14.1 shows the data flows between the service and other metadata systems.

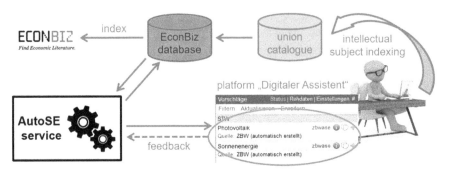

Figure 14.1: Data flows of machine-generated subject indexing using the AutoSE service

Milestones yet to be completed within the pilot phase include:

– Preparing for the use of abstracts and potentially also tables of content in addition to titles and author keywords. Besides gathering the necessary amount of training data for experiments to develop models that are optimised for these kinds of text materials, clarification of rights issues related to text and data mining in abstracts since most licences do not mention the use of abstracts for non-commercial productive purposes such as the AutoSE service, even if the use for research purposes is explicitly allowed

-   Preparing the integration of solutions for languages other than English with potential approaches including an upstream machine translation before subject indexing and, as one of the most promising options, the use of previously mentioned large language models
-   Finalising and publishing a web user interface which provides an interactive demonstration of the backend, statistics concerning current and past performance of the AutoSE service and additional information about the methods used.
-   Automating various machine learning processes such as hyperparameter optimisation and training to be able to retrain the models more easily when sufficient new metadata records have accumulated or a new version of the STW thesaurus is available, and
-   Documenting the requirements of future operations in terms of personnel, software, and computing power to enable long-term availability and development.

Plans beyond the pilot phase include extending the architecture to integrate automated metadata extraction workflows to generate additional input for AutoSE, and combining machine learning with symbolic approaches to incorporate semantic information from STW and from external sources to check the plausibility of the output of the trained models. Once the subject indexing process is at least partly automated, it may pave the way for moving towards cataloguing and subject indexing practices based on entities and formalised relationships between them as defined by the Resource Description Framework (RDF), and not on string-based entries in a database.

Quality Assurance and Quality Management

The Technical Aspects

The automation of subject indexing is a change prompted by new technological possibilities but it also affects subject indexing practices on a cultural level. In an automation endeavour such as this, quality control is key both because of the positive or negative effects of metadata quality on retrieval and because stakeholder approval of service output, in particular by subject indexing experts, is vital to long-term acceptance, development, and use.

The AutoSE team has been working on a comprehensive quality assurance plan using different approaches to guarantee an overall subject indexing quality that is as high as possible. On the technical side the approach includes working with metrics commonly used in ML with the aim of maximising the F1-score but with future evaluation potentially using differently weighted combinations of precision and recall or other metrics such as normalised discounted cumulative gain or metrics that take the hierarchy of the thesaurus into account as well and identify reasonable thresholds, for example the minimum level of confidence required. Following the automated subject indexing process, the thresholds are applied to the output along with other filters such as blacklists and mappings. Since 2022, quality control for AutoSE has featured the application of an ML-based approach for the prediction of overall subject indexing quality for a given metadata record. The Qualle method predicts the recall for a record by drawing on confidence scores for individual subject headings and additional heuristics such as text length, special characters, and a comparison of the expected number of labels with the actual number of labels that were suggested. The code was based on a prototype described in Toepfer and Seifert (2018b) but re-implemented for practical use from scratch (ZBW 2023b). Before launching Qualle, the AutoSE team asked ZBW subject indexing experts for an assessment of the output in order to ensure that the new method would outperform the previous method. A much coarser semantic filter had been previously applied for quality control on the metadata record level: The output was required to contain at least two subject headings from one of the two economic core domains modelled as two sub-thesauri in STW. In contrast, Qualle learns from the training data what appropriate subject indexing should look like without discriminating between sub-thesauri. This shows that, if trained on suitable data, a machine-learning-based method can be more flexible than an intellectually postulated rule.

The Human Aspects

One of the most essential components of quality assurance is and will remain the human element. The ML domain has coined the phrase human-in-the-loop to examine "the right ways for humans and machine learning algorithms to interact to solve problems" (Monarch 2021). Human beings are involved at various levels in ML. Training data is typically annotated by humans as it is in AutoSE. Knowledge organisation systems and mappings between them are usually created and maintained by humans, which applies to STW as well. There is machine-assisted subject indexing using machine-generated suggestions, and there are various ways of making use of intellectual feedback such as online machine learning where a machine directly retrains itself in response to additional available data and active machine learning where a machine interactively requests annotations or assessments from a human at certain points.

In the AutoSE context, several strategies have been used to gather human analytical feedback. One strategy has been to conduct an annual review with a group of ZBW subject indexing experts to assess the quality of machine-generated subject headings. The group typically consists of seven or eight people who assess approximately 1000 publications using an interface called Releasetool (ZBW n.d.b) that was originally developed in the earlier ZBW project AutoIndex. It allows experts to view the relevant metadata, access the full text via a link, navigate the list of records (Figure 14.2), and assign one of four quality levels both to each individual subject heading: "how well does this subject heading describe an aspect of the content of this publication?" and to the sum of subject headings for a document: "how well does the sum of subject headings suggested cover the content of this publication?". Note that there can be individual subject headings that describe one aspect of a publication very well but that the sum of subject headings may omit aspects or lack specificity and the overall assessment for a publication can be poor.

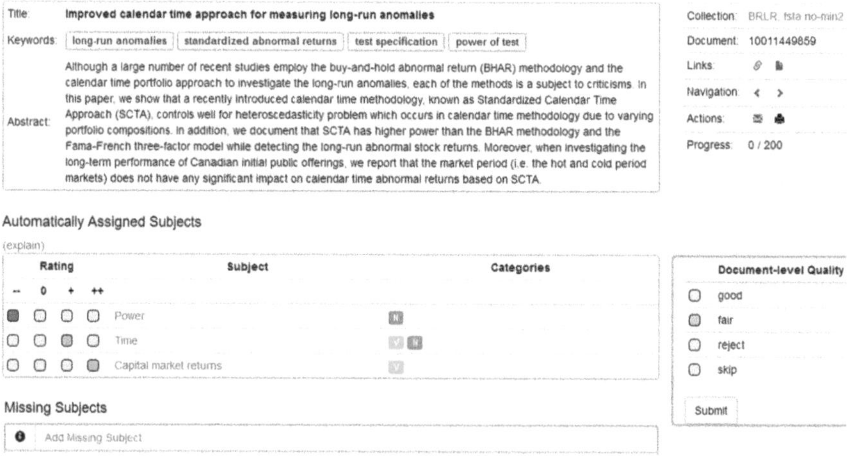

Figure 14.2: Releasetool interface

After every review the AutoSE team conducted an extensive debriefing where the experts reported individual observations and perceived biases in the output of AutoSE and over several reviews, systematic divergences from the desired outcome were identified and remedied. For example, several reviewers pointed out that the subject headings for "theory" and "USA" wrongly appeared in the output more frequently than other subject headings, due to overrepresentation in the training data. As a temporary fix, the team implemented a filter such that the subject "USA" was subsequently blocked if it was not explicitly contained in the title or the author keywords. For the "theory" issue, the AutoSE team asked the subject experts to compile a list of more specific subject headings pertaining to economic theories. A filter was constructed to block "theory" from the output if another subject heading from the compiled list was also present. However, maintaining hand-crafted filters is tedious and error-prone and ideally should serve only as short- to medium-term solutions to be superseded by improvements in ML methods in the long term.

The reviews kept the subject indexers informed about the automation activities that were effected or planned, provided transparency in the methods employed by the AutoSE team, and made clear that the subject experts' accumulated expertise in knowledge organisation and semantic annotation would still be needed at essential points in the system, albeit in a modified, unfamiliar form. Such an approach may prove an important psychological factor in the change management processes that will continually be necessary at any institution to secure the support of the in-house subject experts for changes and disruptions in their accustomed workflows due to progressing automation.

Continuous Reviews and Other Evaluation Strategies

Another way of gathering feedback is to compare AutoSE output with human indexing of the same publication where possible. The team developed a means for achieving this outcome: The addition of STW subject headings by a subject indexer to a metadata record in the *EconBiz* database that had already been enriched with machine-generated subject headings automatically triggers a notification in the AutoSE system, the two sets of subject headings are compared, and an F1-score is computed from the difference. The human subject indexing is taken as the desired output against which the machine-generated output is tested. The process enabled the team for example to gather evidence that a new backend performed better than the previous one before launching it into productive operations by comparing F1-scores on parallel operation of the two backends over a certain period of time (Figure 14.3).

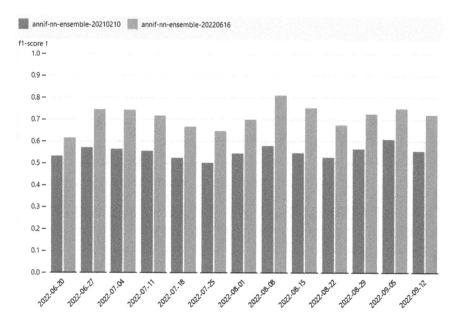

Figure 14.3: Comparison of F1 scores computed from subsequent human subject indexing for two backends over time

While the F1-score is an accepted performance indicator in classification tasks, it is of limited value given that it is determined by verifying whether a machine-generated subject heading is present in the human-generated set and whether a human-generated subject heading is missing from the machine-generated set, but it does not indicate whether a machine-generated subject heading not chosen by the human indexer is too general or completely incorrect, for example. Given the challenges of the review process, the AutoSE team collaborated in early 2022 with the provider of the DA-3 platform to integrate a solution into DA-3 so that subject librarians could give graded feedback. As a consequence, subject indexing experts are now able and strongly encouraged to submit quality assessments via DA-3 continuously during their everyday work. As in the annual reviews, the experts can rate subject headings individually and their sum for a given publication (Figure 14.4).

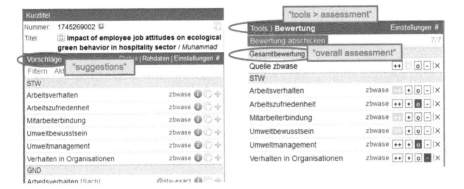

Figure 14.4: Partial screenshot of DA-3 where users can see and assess machine-generated suggestions during their subject indexing work

Missing subject headings are computed from differences between AutoSE suggestions and the human subject indexing entered into a record. The larger amount of assessment data collected by this means affords the team a more effective evaluation of AutoSE performance and facilitates targeted improvements. Dynamically generated visualisations of the data can be displayed via a web user interface to increase transparency for all parties involved.

Next Steps

Future plans with respect to the implementation of a more advanced human-in-the-loop relationship include exploring how the feedback data might be used for incremental online learning with the machine retraining itself on receiving the feedback. Another interesting concept to pursue is active learning with a machine interactively requesting annotations or assessments of individual data from a human at certain points. So far, automated and human subject indexing represent quasi-separate lanes with machine-generated subjects discarded as soon as human-generated ones are available even if the latter is inspired by the former. Exploring the possibilities of more interactive modes for machines and humans to solve the task of subject indexing together, exploiting their respective strengths, is an approach with a lot of potential. Automated solutions are still designed to emulate intellectual ones as closely as possible although machines may be able to identify subtle patterns and differences where traditional rules for intellectual subject indexing are too coarse. According to the current roadmap for the future, the AutoSE team plans to explore various large language models for subject indexing at ZBW and to identify aspects in which the models struggle with specific local challenges for example when dealing with training data sets that are small and/or messy. The team also plans to examine approaches to overcome those challenges where the machine autonomously requests annotations for data sets from human experts. The feasibility and usefulness of each potential strategy must be investigated through carefully designed studies to ensure that any suggested changes in practices and workflows are sustainable and tailored to the needs of users and various stakeholders.

Conclusion

Experience from the pilot phase of AutoSE has demonstrated that challenges in automated subject indexing remain. There are no shelf-ready open source automated systems available. Existing software must be adapted and maintained continuously. Various forms of expertise are required and although LLMs have been hailed by some as the game changers awaited by all, LLM-based applications must be prevented from providing fictitious or irrelevant data by integrating information from established knowledge bases. Also, the models must be finetuned to the respective datasets and use cases in libraries. On the strategic level, leaving the project format behind in favour of the commitment of a permanent task has proven to be worth the effort. The search for automation solutions for subject indexing and other related processes is a permanent task that will stay with libraries for many years to come. Implementation of new approaches and innovative operations must be based on thoroughly established long-term concepts and accompanied by adequate financial and staffing resources, along with the necessary software, computing power and infrastructure.

At ZBW, applied research and software development for AutoSE are conducted within the library as part of ZBW's core business and not in a separate research or IT development department. This approach has been greatly beneficial because it allows close collaboration and communication between researchers, developers, and subject librarians. It is essential to include subject indexing experts as stakeholders in the process, both for their expertise in the areas of information and knowledge organisation and to increase acceptance of new research-based solutions within the workplace. Transparency helps dissipate reservations and concerns and a collaborative approach establishes a basic trust in the technology and especially in the way it will be used. In summary, the implementation of methods from AI can assist libraries in their continued mission to prepare and provide information resources while remodelling their data processing practices in a novel way. The concept of the human-in-the-loop offers a possible approach for retaining human subject indexing expertise while combining it with ML-based methods and transferring state-of the-art technology into current library practice.

References

Dong, Tom. n.d. "Omikuji." Version 0.5.1. October 30, 2023. https://github.com/tomtung/omikuji; https://www.wheelodex.org/projects/omikuji/.

Eurospider. 2023. "Subject Indexing Using the DA." https://www.eurospider.com/en/relevancy-product/digital-assistant-da-3.

Facebook. 2020. "fastText." Version 0.9.2. April 28, 2020. https://github.com/facebookresearch/fastText/.

Gross, Thomas, and Manfred Faden. 2010. "Automatische Indexierung elektronischer Dokumente an der Deutschen Zentralbibliothek für Wirtschaftswissenschaften." *Bibliotheksdienst* 44, no. 12: 1120–1135. Available at https://pub.zbw.eu/dspace/bitstream/11108/9/1/2010_Gross_Indexierung.pdf.

Kansalliskirjasto/Nationalbiblioteket/National Library of Finland (NLF). 2023. "Backend: nn_ensemble." *Annif.* https://github.com/NatLibFi/Annif/wiki/Backend%3A-nn_ensemble.

Kansalliskirjasto/Nationalbiblioteket/National Library of Finland (NLF). 2024. "Annif." Version 1.0.2. February 2, 2024. https://github.com/NatLibFi/Annif.

Monarch, Robert (Munro). 2021. *Human-in-the-loop Machine Learning: Active Learning and Annotation for Human-centered AI*. New York: Manning. https://www.manning.com/books/human-in-the-loop-machine-learning.

Toepfer, Martin, and Christin Seifert. 2018a. "Fusion Architectures for Automatic Subject Indexing under Concept Drift: Analysis and Empirical Results on Short Texts." *International Journal on Digital Libraries* 21: 169–189. https://doi.org/10.1007/s00799-018-0240-3. Available at https://ris.utwente.nl/ws/portalfiles/portal/248044709/Toepfer2018fusion.pdf.

Toepfer, Martin, and Christin Seifert. 2018b. "Content-Based Quality Estimation for Automatic Subject Indexing of Short Texts Under Precision and Recall Constraints." *Digital Libraries for Open Knowledge,* edited by Eva Méndez, Fabio Crestani, Cristina Ribeiro, Gabriel David, and João Correia Lopes, 3-15. TPDL 2018. Lecture Notes in Computer Science LNISA, volume 11057. Berlin: Springer. https://doi.org/10.1007/978-3-030-00066-0_1.

W3C. 2014. "Resource Description Framework (RDF)." *Semantic Web Standards.* https://www.w3.org/RDF/.

Wikipedia. 2024a. "Subject Indexing." Wikimedia Foundation. Last modified February 3, 2024. https://en.wikipedia.org/wiki/Subject_indexing.

Wikipedia. 2024b. "Large Language Model." Wikimedia Foundation. Last modified March 5, 2024. https://en.wikipedia.org/wiki/Large_language_model.

Wikipedia. 2024c. "F-score." Wikimedia Foundation. Last modified February 25, 2024. https://en.wikipedia.org/wiki/F-score.

ZBW – Leibniz-Informationszentrum Wirtschaft/ZBW – Leibniz Information Centre for Economics. n.d.a. "Stwfsapy." https://github.com/zbw/stwfsapy.

ZBW – Leibniz-Informationszentrum Wirtschaft/ZBW – Leibniz Information Centre for Economics. n.d.b. "Releasetool." https://github.com/zbw/releasetool.

ZBW – *Leibniz-Informationszentrum Wirtschaft/*ZBW – Leibniz Information Centre for Economics. 2023a. "*Standard-Thesaurus Wirtschaft/*STW Thesaurus for Economics." Version 9.16. November 20, 2023. https://zbw.eu/stw/version/latest/about.en.html.

ZBW – *Leibniz-Informationszentrum Wirtschaft/*ZBW – Leibniz Information Centre for Economics. 2023b. "Qualle." Version 0.2.0. May 4, 2023. https://github.com/zbw/qualle.

Sümeyye Akça

15 Topic Modelling in the Ottoman Kadi Registers

Abstract: The Qāḍī/Qadi/Kadi is the judge who renders decisions in Islamic Shariah law. The registers documenting the court decisions by the Kadis also describe daily events in the life of the Ottoman Empire and are of great importance for Ottoman research. The data recorded in the registers highlighted the problems of social life of the period and provide modern-day researchers and interested people the opportunity to penetrate the details of the cultural life of the Ottoman state. Using computational methods enables a close reading of the records by historians and other social researchers which significantly enhances the value of the registers and leads to improved research outcomes. Natural Language Processing (NLP) methods like topic modelling and clustering have been used to identify topics in large document collections and the relationships between them. This chapter outlines the work undertaken in a project which used topic modelling to analyse the Kadi registers. The resulting modelling identified connections between the descriptive words used to record the subject matter in each record within the register and the connections were used to form a subject clustering list. Topics identified were compared with previously determined subjects and the semantic links between registers revealed. The project goal was to enable an effective approach for ensuring effective searching and information retrieval in the Kadi registers database.

Keywords: Qadi registers; Kadi registers; Natural language processing; Ottoman empire – Social life and customs; Topic modelling

The *Qāḍī*/Qadi/Kadi Registers

The *Qāḍī*/Qadi/Kadi is the magistrate or judge of an Islamic *sharīʿa* court, who also exercises extrajudicial functions. The Kadis recorded their decisions in registers or notebooks which constitute the court records and can be defined as "a book which has the records of any document created as a result of the legal cases heard by *kqadis* (Islamic judge) as well as administrative and legal activities of qadis" (Aydin and Tak 2019). Kadi Registers contain a wide range of information on the life and times in which court decisions were recorded and shed light on social life in the Ottoman Empire. They are one of the most important sources for today's historians (Akça 2005). They were written in Turkish, Arabic, and Persian and maintained in book format. The books, which were maintained and updated from the second half of the 15th century through to the first quarter of the 20th century, are one of the key sources of information on Turkish culture and history, and are also closely linked to Turkish economic and political life. Over the last 50 years many researchers in Turkey have been transcribing the content of the Kadis to the Latin (Roman) alphabet to facilitate studying the wealth of content contained in the registers.

A significant project, the Istanbul Kadi Registers Project, was undertaken by the *İslam Araştırmaları Merkezi/* Centre for Islamic Studies (İSAM) working with other organisations and resulted in the transcription of a large corpus of 60 note-books from 1557–1911, with a large body of the content available in an online database, the *İstanbul Kadı Sicilleri/*Istanbul Kadi Registries." In addition to being historical data, Kadı Registers are an extremely important and reliable source for many scientific fields such as law, economics, geography, sociology and psychology" (Istanbul Kadi Registries n.d.). Each book contains records for every unique event, giving clues to the legacy structure of the Empire. Although to date there has been significant effort to transcribe the notebooks, some still await transcription into the Latin alphabet.

Following transcription into the Latin alphabet, a subject descriptor has been assigned by the transcriber to each record in the register. Researchers can search the indexed registers by subject and retrieve relevant content. However, one record may refer to more than one subject area, and in some cases, a particular event may be covered by more than one record. Assigning appropriate subject headings to the content of each entry in the registers through the use of a thesaurus of terms opens up the content to researchers. Creating subject authority files is considered valuable in terms of providing the basis for indexing the content of the notebooks thereby rendering the content discoverable, accessible and available to wider audiences. It is important to define and analyse the content of information resources according to subject authority files to provide more effective results in information retrieval. Subject authority files are important sources in the field of information science. They provide standard terms from a controlled vocabulary and can be used by indexers and users alike to understand how content can be described or sought (Gültekin 2020, 47).

The aim of the project described in this chapter was to automatically assign a topic to each record in the Kadi registers using the topic modelling method and to reveal the distinctive dominant word groups of the topics by examining the common word groups used for each topic. The multiple records pertaining to a specific subject area can provide valuable insights into the structure and content of the Kadi registers. Analysing the descriptive terms associated with each record and examining word frequency allows for the identification of interconnected subject clusters. When users search using specific terms, a structured hierarchy provides researchers with access to a broader range of topics, including records related to those terms. It is crucial to ensure that the Kadi registers, which hold significant historical value, are effectively used by a diverse audience of users. A comparison was made with topics tagged during manual transcription. The project involved the creation of an authority file that could be used when describing the content of the records contained. The ultimate goal of the project is to facilitate discovery and access of the information contained in the Kadi registers.

Machine Indexing and Analysis of Historical Documents

Projects in which computer or computational methods have been used on historical data and documents have been carried out with the intention of making the data and information contained in the documents easier to understand and interpret. Grant et al. (2021) used topic modelling to undertake an historical analysis of global policies on refugees within approximately 55,000 pages from the 1970s of typewritten and digitally born documents stored in archives from the UK and US governments and the United Nations High Commissioner for Refugees (UNHCR). Standard optical character recognition (OCR) was used to scan the documents and natural language processing (NLP) topic modelling was adopted as the means of identifying topics within the documents and their relationships. Topic modelling is a text-mining tool used to identify semantic structures in a given body of text by statistically examining the occurrence of particular words. A document typically refers to several topics in unequal proportions. Clusters of similar words are captured using topic modelling. Topic modelling can help organise the plethora of written material produced today which cannot be analysed by human means and contribute to understanding large collections of unstructured text. The study analysing the documents on refugees identified the main topics in each document and investigated the transmission of the topics between organisations and over time to suggest areas for further study. Major themes and varying organisational approaches were identified. Researchers were then able to analyse the roles of the various people and organisations involved and their discourse, as well as the results of resettlement programmes.

In another study, Yang, Torget, and Mihalcea (2011) applied topic modelling to the content of newspapers published in Texas US between 1829 and 2008. The study examined the difficulty historians experience when working with the huge quantity of digital data available for analysis which has been generated from the projects transferring newspaper content to the digital environment. Topic modelling was used to cluster topics within the digital texts to identify the most important and potentially interesting topics, and/or to discover unexpected topics through unusual patterns over a given period of time. Researchers can use the clusters to focus on the topics most closely identified with their research. Schöch (2017), used topic modelling to examine French drama texts between the years 1610-1810, examined whether different dramatic genres had distinctive dominant themes and whether sub-genres have their own specific plot patterns. Schöch's study looked at the extent to which clustering and classification methods based on subject scores produced results consistent with traditional genre distinctions. The various studies undertaken have demonstrated that topic modelling is an effective means of analysing historical documents for further research examination.

Digitisation of Ottoman Manuscripts

Making Ottoman manuscript documents and books readable and accessible by computer is a process that requires serious effort. There is no system that works with a high accuracy rate among existing studies. For various reasons, Ottoman manuscripts seem particularly difficult to read by machine. There are issues with the handwriting and language used and with the condition of the manuscripts themselves. The language of *Osmanlı Türkçesi*/Ottoman Turkish has particular issues being based on Arabic. One of the most significant difficulties is that Ottoman manuscripts were not written on paper with a satisfactory flat surface or plane, which makes scanning of the content challenging.

In the literature, there are studies using different methods to render irregularly written manuscript historical documents machine-readable and accessible. With advanced information technology, it is possible to extract data from documents by using machine learning (ML) algorithms. Existing common techniques based on handwritten text recognition (HTR), combined with deep learning (DL) recurrent neural networks (RNN) have greatly contributed to the ability of machines to scan, recognise, analyse and store the content of complex manuscripts. DL architectures are used to detect line and page structures of documents, and various projects have applied techniques to extract line and page structures with methods such as masking used with convolutional neural networks (CNN), RNNs and graph neural networks (GNN). CNNs and RNNs have different architectures with one feeding data forward and the other back and are commonly used to solve problems involving spatial data, such as images. RNNs are better suited to analysing temporal and sequential data, such as text or videos (Craig and Petersson 2023). Masking refers to skipping missing data during machine processes (Zhu and Chollet 2023).

Deep neural networks and artificial intelligence have significantly accelerated the automatic transcription of historical manuscripts. Various studies have adopted the techniques mentioned to analyse handwritten texts (Andrés et al. 2022; Ares Oliveira 2018; Gao et al. 2019; Gilani et al. 2017; Prasad et al. 2019; Qasim, Mahood, and Shafait 2019; Siddiqui et al. 2019). These studies have demonstrated effective use of artificial intelligence techniques to the analysis of text but clearly also demonstrate the need to use structured automated methods that take the context into account to reduce both layout analysis errors and text recognition errors (Prieto et al. 2023). Existing HTR implementations are not error-free (Andrés et al. 2022).

Software and platforms using HTR and DL technology like Transkribus have been developed and used for various projects. "Transkribus is an AI-powered platform for text recognition, transcription and searching of historical documents – from any place, any time, and in any language" (Read Co-op 2023). However, varying document layouts, types of handwriting or fonts used, and differences due to the person writing the article make the task of effective transcription and analysis challenging even with the use of appropriate software (Lang et al. 2018). In particular, document image understanding is a difficult pattern recognition problem extracting and distinguishing relevant data that requires complex models based on ML. The problem is even more demanding for document images with complex layouts, such as tables. The reading order is often inherently ambiguous and, as a result, the context is often unclear (Prieto et al. 2023). Document layout analysis focuses on identifying and categorizing the regions of interest in the scanned image of a text document and recent developments have potential for improvements in image analysis with geometric and logical layout analysis, and top-down approaches which divide a document into columns and blocks based on white space and geometric information in addition to bottom-up approaches which examine the raw pixel data. Accuracy rates in pattern recognition above average have been found in trials using the hidden Markov model (Motawa, Amin, and Sabourin1997; Onat, Yildiz, and Gündüz 2008). The improvements give impetus to undertaking further studies on the viability of automated means of analysing Ottoman manuscript documents.

Since printed works have a page layout, it seems easier to digitise them through machine-readable means by scanning and use of AI techniques, and make the content more widely accessible. A successful Turkish project has been:

> Wikilala, nicknamed as Google of Ottoman Turkish, is a Turkish digital library of Ottoman Turkish textual materials. Wikilala, which is currently in its beta version, consists of more than 109,000 printed Ottoman Turkish textual materials, including over 45,000 newspapers, 32,000 journals, 4,000 books and 26,000 articles. Wikilala, provides its users with full-text search through its database using Ottoman Turkish alphabet or Turkish alphabet (Wikipedia 2024).

The issues with digitising and transcribing Ottoman Turkish based on Arabic have been mentioned. A *Luggat Osmanlica Türkçe Sözlük*/Luggat Ottoman Turkish Dictionary with Arabic and Persian spelling and Ottoman pronunciations and detailed explanations has been developed and provides support (*Luggat Osmanlica Türkçe Sözlük* n.d.). Another project impacting on the Kadi register project has been the development of an Ottoman transcription tool.

> Akis is carried out in cooperation with DH Lab and VERİM (Data Analytics Research and Application Center). Our aim is to develop recognition technologies that can transcribe Ottoman Turkish handwritten and printed works written in Arabic and Persian script into Latin script. Thus we want to make texts in Ottoman archives and libraries written in Ottoman Turkish more accessible to researchers and general users from different disciplines (*Sabancı Üniversitesi* n.d.).

Various issues encountered in working with digitisation in relation to Ottoman manuscripts were highlighted in the study undertaken by Kirmizialtin and Wrisley (2022). Their study of a digital newspaper collection printed in Arabic-script Ottoman Turkish in the late 19th and early 20th centuries emphasised the difficulties of automated transcription of non-Latin script languages along with difficulties in training HTR models, particularly with writing systems which have experienced change over time. Synthetic data and other data have been used in studies to augment data available for input to ML models. A test of data augmentation on printed works in Ottoman Turkish found that the system could be improved if there was a larger database (Bilgin Tasdemir 2023).

In projects carried out all over the world, documents and records that cannot be read by machine due to line and page formats and other issues continue to be transcribed and made accessible by volunteers. Crowdsourcing is currently the most likely method for extending the digitisation and analysis of manuscripts. Zooniverse hosts projects for people-powered research where volunteers work with researchers to build datasets for analysis. FromThePage is a crowdsourcing platform for archives and libraries where volunteers transcribe, index, and describe historic documents.

Data Set and Research Methods Used

This section outlines the details of the project involving the Kadi registers which focused on one of the registers, the book of Üsküdar, a district within Istanbul. It covers the years 1561-1563, and had previously been transcribed by the author. The register contains important information about the social life of Üsküdar, with 648 *hüccets*/court records such as purchase and sale transactions, cases about fugitive slaves, and murders (Akça 2015, 9). In the transcribed version of the book, a manual classification had been given for the topic of each court record, with an index consisting of subject, person, event and place information. A topic modelling algorithm was run on the text to machine-classify the topics of the court records in the text and to compare them with previously assigned topic headings.

As previously outlined in this chapter, topic modelling is an unsupervised approach to finding groups of words in a text document. The topics are made up of words that often occur together and share a common theme. Topics with a pre-defined set of words can be used as phrases to describe the entire document. To improve the identification of the subject of each record, Latent Dirichlet allocation (LDA) was run on the text using Python software. LDA is a type of topic modelling algorithm where each document is considered a collection of topics with each word in the document corresponding to one of the topics.

The study commenced by importing the data and running pre-processing tools on the text. The initial clean function was used to remove the punctuation marks on the text and change uppercase letters to lowercase. In addition, word tokenization was used to demarcate words and symbols with spaces. The stop word removal function was used to remove the most commonly used words in a language. The open-source Gensim library was used to create the corpus and a dictionary. Gensim is an open-source library for unsupervised topic modelling and NLP using modern statistical ML.

To apply topic modelling, the number of topics must be determined. There are many approaches currently available for this task. The approaches generally look at the distributions of LDA such as subject-terms, document-subjects, and calculate the distances between pairs of topics and determine the most appropriate number of topics (Akbulut 2022, 29). Four metrics were used to determine the most appropriate number of topics for the LDA algorithm to be applied on the Kadi register. The metrics included statistical calculations based on topic and document calculations on the text, and each metric was run in R-project over a single code. As a result, the most suitable number of topics for the model to work on the data set was determined to be thirty (Figure 15.1).

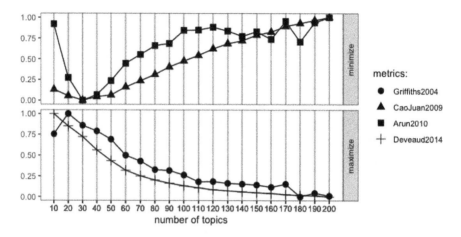

Figure 15.1: Four metrics used to determine the optimal number of topics for the LDA model

The topic models were then created and the results analysed. PyLDAvis was used to visualise the results. PyLDAvis is designed to help users interpret topics in a topic model as appropriate to a collection of text data. It provides an interactive web-based visualisation with information from the LDA topic model. Finally, an evaluation was made by determining which topic was dominant for each record. To validate the results, the output gives the most appropriate topic for each text data. The topic ratios with their keywords can easily be seen. Through the model, a range of topics or recurring themes and the extent to which each document addresses the issues has been explored on the Kadi Registers.

Findings and Discussion

The phrases used in the Kadi registers and the most frequently used words can be easily viewed in the graphic created by the LDA model. Indicators of time and place names and the name of the office where the court was held are among the most used words in the data set (Figure 15.2).

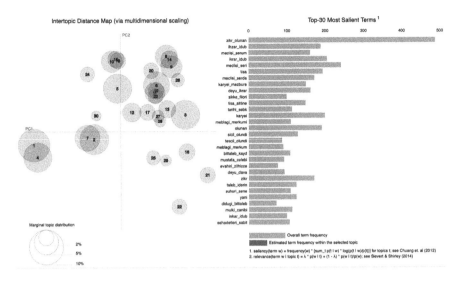

Figure 15.2: LDA algorithm on the Kadi Registers representing all clusters

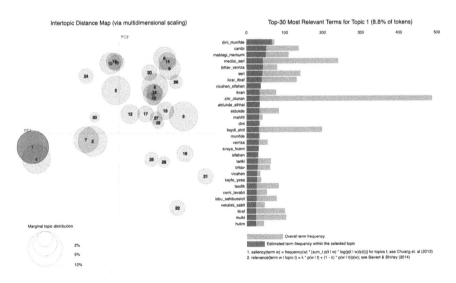

Figure 15.3: The first clusters of the LDA Model on the Kadi Registers

The first set of the LDA model shows that the most common records in the data set are *alım-satım (bey')*/commercial transaction cases which are represented by(the widest circle. The frequency of the words used in the first cluster in the whole document, red and blue, can be easily observed in Figure 15.3. Looking at the previous topic tagging, buying-selling cases constitute approximately 16% (101) of the total individual cases.

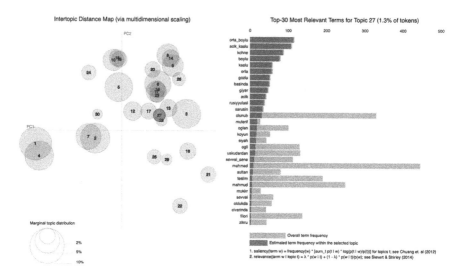

Figure 15.4: The 27th cluster of the LDA model on the Kadi Registers

In Figure 15.4, words used in the topic cluster, which are rarely mentioned in the whole data set, are seen. In a detailed reading, the topics of *iltizam*/tax farming, *kaçak köle*/fugitive slaves and *niza (kavga)*/ hostility) in the records of the Kadi registers were gathered in a cluster and indicate that the words used in the topics are related or that these topics can be included together under one record. In the LDA model figure, the cluster circles are smaller and the frequency of use of the words within this cluster in the entire data set has a distinctive character (Figure 15.4). The manual topic labelling made by the author on the Kadi register also confirms the outcomes. Accordingly, *iltizam*/tax farming is mentioned twenty-one times and the issue of *kaçak köle*/fugitive slaves forty times in the book (Akça 2005).

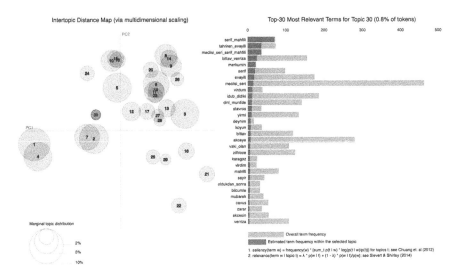

Figure 15.5: The 30th cluster of the LDA model on the Kadi Registers

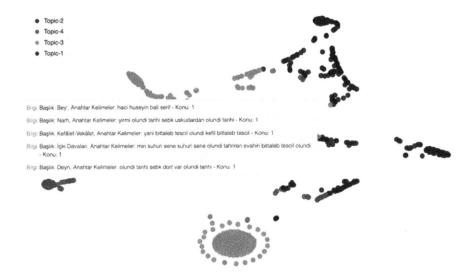

Figure 15.6: t-SNE algorithm on the dataset

The most distinctive issue in the data set is seen as the *kefil*/guarantor cases. Since the words used in *kefil*/guarantor or surety cases are generally names including foreign names and non- Muslim names, they have formed a separate cluster of words that are rarely used in the entire document universe (Figure 15.5). For a closer look at the LDA model and to examine each case, the t-distributed Stochastic

Neighbour Embedding (t-SNE) algorithm was applied to the data set. In Figure 15.6, the status of each case is visualised in two dimensions according to its topic. One of the important points is that the approach differentiates subjects which are unalike and unique in the data set and which subjects are similar to each other. Figure 15.6 identifies subjects which converge with each other and relate on the basis of easily used words. The words used in *alım-satım (bey')*/commercial transaction, *borç (deyn)*/debt, *narh*/pricing, *kefil*/surety deputation and *alkol*/alcohol cases are seen as related words.

Conclusion

The LDA topic modelling process used for analysing historical texts has emerged as an effective method that enables readers and researchers to comprehend content and identify subject matter for further examination. The results are presented in an efficient and contextualised way. AI and other means of automated analysis enhance the context and improve access to historical records. Computer methods provide significant improvements not only to the work of historians and social science researchers but also enhance social and cultural life and understandings. The results of this study can be used to guide future similar projects and also to enhance searching and information retrieval from the Kadi registers database and similar Ottoman document stores.

Acknowledgement

I would like to thank Dr Müge Akbulut for her support in the study.

References

Akbulut, Muge. 2022. *"Bilgi Erişimde İlgi Sıralamalarının Artırımlı Olarak Geliştirilmesi/* [Incremental Refinement of Relevance Rankings in Information Retrieval]." Unpublished doctoral dissertation, *Hacettepe Üniversitesi*, Ankara. https://bby.hacettepe.edu.tr/yayinlar/Muge_Akbulut_PhD_Tez.pdf

Akça, Sümeyye. 2005. *"Üsküdar Kadılığı 23 Nolu ve H. 968-970 Tarihli Sicilin Diplomatik Yönden İncelenmesi: Metin ve İnceleme."* Unpublished Master's thesis, *Marmara Üniversitesi*/Marmara University, İstanbul, Turkey. http://hdl.handle.net/11424/212437.

Andrés, José, José Ramón Prieto, Emilio Granell, Verónica Romero, Joan Andreu Sánchez, and Enrique Vidal. 2022, "Information Extraction from Handwritten Tables in Historical Documents." In

Document Analysis Systems: Proceedings of the 15th IAPR International Workshop, DAS 2022, La Rochelle, France, May 22–25, 2022, edited by Seiichi Uchida, Elisa Barney, and Véronique Eglin, 184–198. Berlin: Springer Verlag. https://doi.org/10.1007/978-3-031-06555-2_13.

Ares Oliveira, Sofia, Benoit Seguin, and Frederic Kaplan. 2018. "DhSegment: A Generic Deep-learning Approach for Document Segmentation." In *Proceedings of the 16ᵗʰ International Conference on Frontiers in Handwriting Recognition (ICFHR) Niagara Falls, NY, USA, 2018*, 7–12. doi: 10.1109/ICFHR-2018.2018.00011. Available at https://doi.org/10.1109/ICFHR-2018.2018.00011.

Arun, Rajkumar, et al. 2010. "On finding the natural number of topics with latent dirichlet allocation: Some observations." In *Advances in Knowledge Discovery and Data Mining: 14th Pacific-Asia Conference, PAKDD 2010, Hyderabad, India, June 21-24, 2010. Proceedings. Part I 14*. Springer Berlin Heidelberg.

Aydin, Bilgin, and Ekrem Tak. 2019. "Istanbul Sharia Court Registers." In *History of Istanbul* by the Türkiye Diyanet Foundation İslam Araştırmaları Merkezi/ Center for Islamic Studies (İSAM). Translated from the Turkish. Vol.2. https://istanbultarihi.ist/434-istanbul-sharia-court-registers?q=istanbul%20registers.

Bilgin Tasdemir, Esma F. 2023. "Printed Ottoman Text Recognition Using Synthetic Data and Data Augmentation." *International Journal on Document Analysis and Recognition* (IJDAR) 26: 273-287. https://doi.org/10.1007/s10032-023-00436-9. Available at https://assets.researchsquare.com/files/rs-2275909/v1_covered_f6102db4-105b-44e6-ad96-0713492be767.pdf?c=1697491252.

Cao, Juan, et al. 2009 "A density-based method for adaptive LDA model selection." *Neurocomputing* 72, no. 7–9: 1775–1781.

Craig, Lev, and David Petersson. 2023. "CNN vs. RNN: How Are They Different?" *TechTarget*, August 8, 2023. https://www.techtarget.com/searchenterpriseai/feature/CNN-vs-RNN-How-they-differ-and-where-they-overlap#:~:text=CNNs%20are%20commonly%20used%20to,such%20as%20text%20or%20videos.

Deveaud, Romain, Eric SanJuan, and Patrice Bellot. 2014. "Accurate and effective latent concept modeling for ad hoc information retrieval." *Document numérique* 17.1: 61-84.

Gao, Liangcai, Yilun Huang, Hervé Déjean, Jean-Luc Meunier, Qinqin Yan, Yu Fang, Florian Kleber, and Eva Lang. 2019. "ICDAR 2019 Competition on Table Detection and Recognition (cTDaR)." In *Proceedings of the International Conference on Document Analysis and Recognition (ICDAR), Sydney, NSW, Australia, 2019*, 1510–1515. doi: 10.1109/ICDAR.2019.00243.

Gilani, Azka, Shah Rukh Qasim, Imran Malik, and Faisal Shafait, 2017. "Table Detection Using Deep Learning" In *Proceedings of the 14ᵗʰ IAPR International Conference on Document Analysis and Recognition, 2017*, 771–776. https://tukl.seecs.nust.edu.pk/members/projects/conference/Table-Detection-Using-Deep-Learning.pdf.

Grant, Philip, Ratan Sebastian, Marc Allassonnière-Tang, and Sara Cosemans. 2021. "Topic Modelling on Archive Documents from the 1970s: Global Policies on Refugees." *Digital Scholarship in the Humanities* 36, no. 4: 886–904. https://doi.org/10.1093/llc/fqab018. Available at https://philip-grantlinguistics.net/docs/am_topic-modelling-dsh-2021.pdf.

Griffiths, Thomas L., and Mark Steyvers. 2004. "Finding scientific topics." *Proceedings of the National Academy of Sciences* 101, no. 1: 5228–5235. https://doi.org/10.1073/pnas.0307752101

Gültekin, Vedat. 2020. "Konu Otorite Dizini Nedir? Nasıl Oluşturulur?" *Türk Kütüphaneciliği/[Turkish Librarianship]* 34, no. 1: 46–64. https://dergipark.org.tr/tr/pub/tk/issue/53283/687062.

İstanbul Kadı Sicilleri. n.d. https://kadisicilleri.istanbul/.

Kirmizialtin, Suphan, and David Joseph Wrisley. 2022. "Automated Transcription of Non-Latin Script Periodicals: A Case Study in the Ottoman Turkish Print Archive." *Digital Humanities Quarterly* 16, no. 2. https://www.digitalhumanities.org/dhq/vol/16/2/000577/000577.html.

Lang, Eva, Joan Puigcerver, Alejandro Héctor Toselli, and Enrique Vidal. 2018. "Probabilistic Indexing and Search for Information Extraction on Handwritten German Parish Records." In *Proceedings of the 16th International Conference on Frontiers in Handwriting Recognition (ICFHR), Niagara Falls, NY, USA, 2018*, 44–49. https://doi.org/10.1109/ICFHR-2018.2018.00017. Available at https://jpuigcerver. net/pubs/lang_icfhr2018.pdf.

*Luggat Osmanlica Türkçe Sözlük/*Luggat Ottoman Turkish Dictionary. 2024. Istanbul: EURODMC Dijital Marka Çözümleri Tic. Ltd. Şti. https://www.luggat.com/.

Motawa, Deya, Adnan Amin, and Robert Sabourin. 1997. "Segmentation of Arabic Cursive Script." In *ICDAR '97: Proceedings of the 4th International Conference on Document Analysis and Recognition, Ulm, Germany, August 1997*, 625–628. doi: 10.1109/ICDAR.1997.620580. Available at https:// en.etsmtl.ca/ETS/media/ImagesETS/Labo/LIVIA/Publications/1997/sabourin97arabic.pdf.

Onat, Ayşe, Ferruh Yildiz, and Mesut Gündüz. 2008. "Ottoman Script Recognition Using Hidden Markov Model." *International Journal of Computer and Information Engineering* 2, no. 2: 462–4. Available at https://citeseerx.ist.psu.edu/document?repid=rep1&type=pdf&doi=f1d05b6257a661a 788529f85579d39552f59391e.

Prasad, Animesh, Hervé Dejean, and Jean-Luc Meunier. 2019. "Versatile Layout Understanding Via Conjugate Graph." In *Proceedings of the International Conference on Document Analysis and Recognition, ICDAR, Sydney, Australia, 20-25 September, 2019*, 287–294) doi: 10.1109/ ICDAR.2019.00054. Available at https://animeshprasad.github.io/resources/c4.pdf.

Prieto, Jose Ramón, José Andrés, Emilio Granell, Joan Andreu Sánchez, and Enrique Vidal. 2023. "Information Extraction in Handwritten Historical Logbooks." *Pattern Recognition Letters* 172: 128-136. https://doi.org/10.1016/j.patrec.2023.06.008.

Qasim, Shah Rukh, Hassan Mahmood, and Faisal Shafait. 2019. " Rethinking Table Recognition Using Graph Neural Networks." In *Proceedings of the International Conference on Document Analysis and Recognition, ICDAR, Sydney, Australia 2019*, 142–147. https://doi.ieeecomputersociety.org/10.1109/ ICDAR.2019.00031. Available at https://doi.org/10.48550/arXiv.1905.13391.

Read Co-op. 2023. "Transkribus: Unlock Historical Documents with AI." https://readcoop.eu/ transkribus/.

Sabancı Üniversitesi Dijital Beşeri Bilimler Laboratuvarı/ Sabanci University Digital Humanities Laboratory. n.d. "Akis: Ottoman Transcription Tool." https://dhlab.sabanciuniv.edu/en/akis-os-manlica-transkripsiyon-araci.

Schöch, Christof. 2017. "Topic Modeling Genre: An Exploration of French Classical and Enlightenment Drama." *Digital Humanities Quarterly* 11, no. 2. https://www.digitalhumanities.org/dhq/ vol/11/2/000291/000291.html. Also available at https://doi.org/10.48550/arXiv.2103.13019.

Siddiqui, Shoaib Ahmed, Imran Ali Fateh, Syed Tahseen Raza Rizvi, Andreas Dengel, Sheraz Ahmed. "DeepTabStR: Deep Learning Based Table Structure Recognition." In *Proceedings of the International Conference on Document Analysis and Recognition, ICDAR, Sydney, Australia, 2019*, 1403–1409. doi: 10.1109/ICDAR.2019.00226. Available at https://www.dfki.de/fileadmin/user_ upload/import/10649_DeepTabStR.pdf.

Wikipedia. 2024. "Wikilala." Last updated February 24, 2024. https://en.wikipedia.org/wiki/Wikilala.

Yang, Tze-I, Andrew J. Torget, and Rada Mihalcea. 2011. "Topic Modeling on Historical Newspapers." In *Proceedings of the 5th ACL-HLT Workshop on Language Technology for Cultural Heritage, Social Sciences, and Humanities, Portland, OR. June 2011*, 96-104. Association for Computational Linguistics. https://aclanthology.org/W11-1513.pdf

Zhu, Scott, and Francois Chollet. 2023. "Understanding Masking & Padding." *TensorFlow Core Guide*, July 24, 2023. https://www.tensorflow.org/guide/keras/understanding_masking_and_padding.

Caroline Saccucci and Abigail Potter

16 Assessing Machine Learning for Cataloging at the Library of Congress

Abstract: Born-digital content is being produced by all and collected by libraries at an increasing rate. Workflows for cataloging this material continue to evolve and have the potential to be augmented by automated technologies. To explore the potential of machine-generated cataloging methods, the Library of Congress is undertaking phased research and experimentation through a specific project: *Exploring Computational Description.* First, using thousands of cataloged ebooks, five different machine learning models are being trained, tested, and documented. The most promising approaches will be applied to uncatalogued ebooks and evaluated. Building on the first phases of experimentation, additional potential automated workflow improvements will be tested. The process of evaluation will result in foundational quality benchmarks for automated methods along with detailed benefits, risks, and costs. Outcomes of the experiment will be used to inform the future development of born-digital cataloging workflows at the Library of Congress and potentially elsewhere. The experiment utilizes a set of tools developed by the LC Labs team to plan, document, analyze, prioritize, and assess AI technologies. The chapter includes a review of the AI planning tools being used and reports on the experiment in progress.

Keywords: Machine learning models; Data processing documentation; Cataloguing workflows

Introduction

In August 2022, the Library of Congress (LoC) of the United States initiated an experimental project, *Exploring Computational Description*, with the help of a third-party vendor, Digirati, to investigate machine learning (ML) processes to create or enhance bibliographic records for born-digital content. The experiment, jointly coordinated by staff in the Library's Office of the Chief Information Officer and the Acquisitions and Bibliographic Access Directorate, provides a mechanism for evaluating five potential models for using ML methods in metadata description and two cataloging workflows to assist catalogers in describing digital content. This chapter describes the background and early details of the experiment.

Artificial Intelligence and Machine Learning: The Next Wave of Technological Change

Machine learning (ML), a subfield of artificial intelligence (AI), was defined in the 1950s as "the field of study that gives computers the ability to learn without explicitly being programmed." ML processes are trained to recognize patterns, predict patterns, and make suggestions about what actions to take (Brown 2021). Machine learning is dependent on algorithms or models that are trained on data. Very simply, training data are tagged or marked up according to the desired pattern. The models are trained, tested, tweaked, and retrained on training and test data, then applied to larger volumes of untagged target data, and asked to recognize similar patterns.

ML technologies have been in use in libraries, archives, and museums (LAMs), primarily in the form of Optical Character Recognition (OCR), for decades. Providing machine-readable historic texts using OCR techniques to capture the content of books and manuscripts has enabled the digital humanities to grow into a recognized world-wide field of study. Applying data science techniques to large corpuses of digital text has spurred new kinds of analysis and research. OCR has also enabled powerful search and discovery tools to connect digital collections to a wide variety of users. Advances in the capabilities and availability of ML tools that could be applied to a larger scope of LAM content beyond text, such as images, audio-visual, born-digital manuscript collections, web archives, and recorded sound, could have similar broad impacts.

Specific Challenges for Libraries, Archives and Museums

The LAM community and LC Labs, a digital strategy team within the Library's Office of the Chief Information Officer, have been intentionally collaborating, experimenting, and sharing results of small-scale AI projects since 2019 (LoC LC Labs n.d.). There is a universal challenge in moving any of the small-scale experiments to operationalized technologies. Most institutions do not currently have the technical expertise or literacies to develop and test custom AI tools, and they must rely on vendor-provided or commercial solutions. Typically, commercial, or free-use options are not open source, and specifics around the nature of the models and training data that are utilized are not shared. Commercial tools and data may also only be available when used on a commercial cloud platform.

In tests by the LAM community, many of the widely available commercial tools do not perform well with historic, digitized, or formatted materials. As noted in a report on the LC Labs experiment using the Amazon transcribe tool and a Speech to Text viewer, the transcripts based on "regional and older styles of speech" were inaccurate because the particular style of speech was likely not present in the training sets (Adams and Kim 2020).

> These issues are inherent to some collections; even listening and understanding what is being said can be very difficult. Additionally, many items had gone through previous necessary physical carrier migrations before being digitizing, resulting in . . . poor "signal-to-noise" ratios, with artifacts like crackling. The accuracy of contemporaneous born-digital audio, in contrast, was high (Adams and Kiim 2020).

The report David Smith and Ryan Cordell released in 2018: *A Research Agenda for Historical Multilingual Optical Character Recognition*, called out this same problem with text-based OCR stating "While large-scale scanning projects have generally used off-the-shelf OCR products, several researchers on a smaller scale have found that domain-specific training and modeling provide significant gains in accuracy" (Smith and Cordell 2018, 11).

LAMs are sources for authoritative and trusted information and they act for the public benefit. The collections they steward are complex and contain a wide variety of physical and analog formats with restricted, private, or sensitive content. Highly trained staff with deep knowledge and expertise have always been, and will continue to be, the bridge between collections, services, and the public. Automated technologies could disrupt the operational principles of LAMs. For example, errors in description about sensitive content that show up on a Library of Congress MARC record could have greater repercussions for users, staff, and the organization than that same error showing up on a search result page of a commercial search engine. The machine-readable cataloging record format (MARC) has driven automated cataloguing developments since the 1960s and continues to do so (Library of Congress 2023). However, a justified desire to implement AI responsibly coupled with a lack of direct experience or practical guidance on implementing AI in LAMs might slow down adoption.

To move beyond small-scale experimentation in AI and take an active role in how this influential technology will shape the field, LAMs must develop shared quality standards, governance structures, and clear requirements for how AI tools need to perform to support the content and principles that are inherent to LAMs. The values and aspirations which shaped the adoption of digitization and digital preservation technologies must be reflected in AI implementation within LAMS. The new environment requires the development of targeted tools to understand the specific risks, benefits, and mitigation approaches for implementing AI at a human-scale and perhaps at a slower pace.

Developing Human-centered and Domain-specific Applications of Artificial Intelligence Responsibly

The LOC is not alone in considering ways to implement AI technologies responsibly. The community of technical and subject matter experts brought together by the Artificial Intelligence for Libraries, Archives and Museums (AI4LAMs) group is a network of peers from similar organizations who are sharing the lessons learned as they experiment with AI (AI4LAM n.d.). AI4LAM sponsors events, comprises working groups and chapters, and produces an Awesome List of AI Resources. The Office of the White House in the United States Government has made a call for articulating the concerns and rights of humans in AI systems (White House 2022). Its blueprint for an AI Bill of Rights embraces five principles: safe and effective systems; algorithmic discrimination protections; data privacy; notice and explanation; and human alternatives, consideration, and fallback.

Various actions by organizations add credibility to the emerging best practices around creating documentation for AI data. The Data Nutrition Project "seeks to create tools and practices that encourage responsible AI development, partners across disciplines to drive broader change and builds inclusion and equity into our work" (n.d.). It has produced a dataset nutrition label to ensure transparency, seeking to replicate the nutrition labels on food. A group within the ML community has proposed the use of a datasheet for each dataset, mirroring the datasheets in the electronics industry. The dataset datasheet would include composition, collection process, and recommended uses (Gebru et al 2021). Further work on ensuring responsible use of AI has been undertaken at OCLC. A research agenda proposes seven areas for investigation including commitment to responsible operations, sharing of methods and data, machine-actionable collections, workforce development, and interprofessional and interdisciplinary cooperation (Padilla 2019). The activities of the various groups directly influence and inspire the development of the LC Labs AI planning and assessment tools.

Artificial Intelligence Planning and Assessment Tools

LC Labs has prepared planning and assessment tools to be used on their various projects. The goals of the tools are to gain specificity, establish baseline performance metrics, and build in pauses to assess project alignment with stated LAM principles and goals. Another important aspect of the tools is the act of gathering a diverse set of stakeholders with internal and external perspectives, including those groups who have the potential to be impacted by an AI system, to collaborate in the planning process. The tools are being used for the first time with the *Exploring Computational Description* experiment, and they will continue to be refined. Two of the tools are described in detail below. The two tools are the Organizational Profile and the Data Processing Plan.

Organizational Profile

The National Institute for Standards and Technology (NIST) AI Risk Management Framework (NIST 2023) includes an examination of the risks of AI implementations. These include reliability, validity, security, resilience, accountability, and transparency, explainability, interpretability, and fairness. The framework proposes core functions: govern, map, measure and manage, and use-case profiles. Building an organizational profile or functional profile to map and define potential uses of AI in an organization is a recommendation in the NIST framework. This step helps to define the specific AI tasks and methods in the context of an organization or its users.

For example, in an initial organizational profile for LC Labs, four functional areas emerged:

– Enabling discovery at scale
– Enabling research use
– Enhancing collections processing and data management for internal workflows and business cases, and
– Augmenting user services

The first, *Enabling Discovery at Scale,* relates to generating metadata for items, papers, articles, paragraphs, or objects to enhance search and discovery with example tasks of processing digitized collections with OCR, speech to text transcription, and named entity linking. The next *Enabling Research Use* emphasizes making data and guides available for researchers and other users to analyze and includes processes to create and process datasets or research corpora for use by external users. Users may request the creation of datasets, so they can run AI or ML techniques like natural language processing (NLP), text mining, or sentiment analysis. A library may also run the processes to answer specific researcher requests. The next area in the initial profile *Enhancing collections processing and data management for internal workflows and business cases* concerns the support of local content management, reporting, and analysis. A subcategory might be the management, processing, and preservation of born-digital collections, such as web archives, email archives, and other born-digital manuscript materials and include automatic classification, segmenting documents, creating automated workflows, and humans-in-the-loop (HITL) processing which involves combining human review with machine learning in a workflow. The final functional area in the initial mapping is *Augmenting User Services,* which includes tools for public-facing services like recommending systems, chatbots, and voice searching.

By mapping out and organizing specific tasks, it is possible to gain insight into the risks and benefits of a functional area that may be similar to or distinct from others. For example, in the area of collections processing and data management, the users of the system are internal staff, and feedback and input from staff are essential in designing systems. Additionally, high visibility tasks in collection processing areas are designed for different levels of staff oversight and HITL workflows. Mapping an organizational profile helps in prioritizing where to focus effort. Hypothetically, LC Labs has undertaken foundational experimentation in one of the functional areas, *Augmenting User Services.* If a broad base of experimentation were the goal, testing out technologies and gathering baseline information about voice search or chatbots could be a next step. The *Exploring Computational Description* experiment fits into the management and processing of born-digital collections sub-category. The users are catalogers and digital collection managers who constitute the people who will review deliverables from the project and integrate any findings into future planning.

Data Processing Plan

The Data Processing Plan (DPP) is a template that vendors, partners, or staff can complete to document data transformations, specifically transformations using AI or ML technologies. It brings together emerging AI documentation standards like Google's model cards (GoogleCloud n.d.) and data coversheets (Gebru et al. 2021) and includes LAM-specific sections for documenting data provenance, potential gaps in data, and potential risks to people, communities, and organizations. Risk management is a required deliverable for experimental data processing in Library of Congress contracts. An initial plan is required before LoC data are processed to outline the intent of the processing, the preparatory and processing steps, the descriptions of the data used in the experiment, and the models with expected performance information. At the end of an experiment, a final DPP is required to document the actual performance and delivered data.

At the time of writing, the initial DPPs have been delivered for the *Exploring Computational Description* experiment. They provide an incredible amount of detail and specificity about the ML models and data that are being tested. When the series of experiments is completed, the final DPPs will provide foundational information about performance requirements and expectations for specific models and how each performs. Compiled over time on a variety of models and LAM data formats, DPPs and other similar documentation can contribute to the development of shared quality standards for AI/ML processing.

Table 16.1 shows an excerpt of the DPP for the Annif model, one of the five models being tested and one of the initial DPPs submitted for the *Exploring Computational Description* experiment. Annif is a tool for automated subject indexing developed at the National Library of Finland.

Table 16.1: Data processing plan for Annif

---

1) Please describe the purpose of this dataset with relation to the ML/AI workflow. Explicitly address if it is being used as training, validation, or test data.

Where possible, we will use cross-evaluation when training models on LoC data in order to avoid introducing selection bias or overfitting the model to the training set. If this is not possible, the dataset will be explicitly split into training, validation, and test data without cross-evaluation. The split will be random, and follow a standard 80/10/10 split. We would expect the training, validation, and test data to comprise examples from all four of the sub-divisions (CIP, OA, E Deposit, Legal Reports) within the dataset. However, we would expect that for the majority of the experiment the dataset will be split randomly and any specific ebook (and associated MarcXML) could be used for training, validation, or test.

b) For training data:
1.   if the model is pre-trained, describe the data on which it was trained
2.   if the model will be fine-tuned, outline the data involved in this process
3.   if the model is being trained from scratch, outline the plan for creating training data.

We would expect to:
1.   *Train the model(s) based on the training subset of the LoC ebook dataset*
2.   *Testing the LoC-trained models on a test subset of the LoC ebook dataset.*
3.   *Produce scores/metrics for each record, and for the collection in aggregate for each testing cycle.*
Each of the training and fine-tuning steps will use the text from the books and the MarcXML records.

c) If creating training data or validating training data using volunteers or paid participants (e.g. via crowdsourcing), please describe the workflow and incentive structure.
This experiment does not include data generated or collected from volunteers or paid participants.

d) Document any known gaps in the dataset, such as missing instances or forms of representation. Address possible sources of vias in the dataset resulting from these discrepancies.

1. Describe any steps taken to remediate or address gaps or bias in a dataset used in the ML/AI processing or in the experiment overall.

For this experiment, the goal is to test, in a time-limited period, the success of these models in matching existing human catalogers at generating bibliographic metadata from ebooks. The type of task being carried out in this experiment is less likely to surface bias, as we are primarily looking for existing text in an existing record, and will be fine-tuning models based on existing catalog records.

To the extent that any biases show up in the data outputs, these will be reflected in lower scores (where the bias leads to misclassification).

Details of the *Exploring Computational Description* Experiment

Exploring Computational Description is a year-long experiment to test multiple ML models in their ability to generate MARC record catalog metadata from the contents of digital materials, specifically ebooks. The technical work is being done by the firm Digirati. It is the first in a series of ML experiments that are gathering baseline performance and quality data for generating priority catalog metadata. The research questions for the initial experiment are:

- What are examples, benefits, risks, costs, and quality benchmarks of automated methods for creating workflows to generate cataloging metadata for large sets of Library of Congress digital materials?
- What technologies and workflow models are most promising to support metadata creation and assist with cataloging workflows? and
- What similar activities are being employed by other organizations?

Table 16.2 provides an overview of the experiment's scope of research, targets for quality review and key deliverables.

Table 16.2: *Exploring Computational Description* Experiment

Scope of research	Targets for LoC quality review	Key deliverables

Test five ML models or methods to detect or generate full level bibliographic records.
 	
All models are open source
	Expected generated fields:
	  – titles
	  – author names
	  – unique identifier
	  – date of issuance
	  – date of creation
	  – genre/form, and
	  – subject terms
		– Data Processing Plans
		– Performance reports + data
		– All data utilized or generated in the experiment

Test two additional ML techniques to augment cataloging workflows Test most promising models on uncatalogued ebooks	– Subject classification workflow – Proper name disambiguation workflow – Review for potential use in LOC systems – Use for further tests	– Data Processing Plans – Rough prototype – All data utilized or generated in the experiment – Delivery of MARC21 and BIBFRAME metadata
What ML or other automated processes are similar organizations using?		– Findings and recommendations report

Data Involved in the Experiment

LoC has delivered data to the contractor to train and test the models. The training data consisted of a total of 23,130 items and their existing catalog records and included 13,802 Cataloging in Publication (CIP) titles, 5,835 open access ebooks, 403 edeposit ebooks, and 3,750 legal reports containing a mix of digitized and born-digital content. The five different models being tested are being trained on these data. The models yielding the most results will be used to generate MARC records for approximately 50,000 uncatalogued ebooks. The LoC will review and test the automatically generated records for potential use in its systems; however, it is more likely that the data will primarily be used for further experimentation.

Machine Learning Processes to Be Tested

Five ML models are being trained and tested in their ability to create high-quality MARC records. The description of the model capability is provided by the vendor in the initial DPPs. A mix of text extraction and visual analysis approaches will be tested. Each model, with some in combination, will be tested in how well each can generate the key MARC record fields. The five models are:

1. GROBID (GeneRation Of Bibliographic Data) is a machine learning library for extracting, parsing, and re-structuring raw documents such as PDF into structured extensible markup language (XML)/text encoding initiative (TEI) encoded documents with a particular focus on technical and scientific publications. The extraction includes bibliographical information, for example title, abstract, authors, affiliations, and keywords, along with the text and document structure. GROBID will be used to provide initial benchmarking with an off-the-shelf tool, and the model then trained to be more tailored to LoC data. GROBID is also useful for generating XML files which can be used for text input for subsequent experiments.

2. Annif: automated subject indexing toolkit, a tool from the National Library of Finland which is designed for automated subject cataloging. Annif provides access to multiple ML backends facilitating trials of different ML models and approaches, including term frequency - inverse document frequency (TF-IDF) and multi-modal language model (MLLM), and benchmarking a wide range of approaches to subject and genre cataloging.

3. Spacy. Spacy is an industry standard NLP library in Python, with extensive abilities to be trained and customized with additional pipeline steps for LoC catalog metadata, and can be used for the full range of metadata for the experiment, including subjects, genres, and bibliographic metadata.

4. Bidirectional Encoder Representations from Transformers (BERT) testing and training a wide range of BERT-derived LLMs including BERT, RoBERTa, and distilBERT, and transformer-based approaches for token classification, identifying words or phrases in text like titles, authors, and dates, and for text classification which classifies a body of text like assigning subjects and genres.

5. NLP with Layout features. The use of this approach would supplement either the fourth or the fifth model, depending on the outputs of the earlier experiments, with layout data such as page position, text size, text location, page number, and recto/verso, to identify whether visual information can add additional weighting to the NLP models and to further refine data extraction for titles, authors, and other fields that have distinct positions, or formatting within the document.

DPPs accompany each model to be tested and the results will provide baseline information on which models perform well with LoC data and which models do not. LoC catalogers and digital collection managers will review the data and use the insights for further experimentation and to inform technical and performance requirements for potential future systems.

Assisting Cataloging Workflows

Based on the performance of the models, the LoC has asked the vendor to select and test an additional two ML methods to assist catalogers in workflows for digital content. After a series of stakeholder and user workshops, the following ML workflows were selected:

- Text Classification which would generate subject and genre data labels from the text and supplement the outcome with text summaries and taxonomies for subject classification, and
- Token Classification which would identify specific entities within the text and generate data and keywords, including coinciding entities, and use data from the Program for Cooperative Cataloging (PCC)
- Name Authority File and elsewhere to disambiguate named authorities.

The tests will result in a basic prototype which catalogers will use to select ML-generated terms. LoC catalogers and digital collection managers will review the output and provide feedback on the information provided in the prototype. Insights will inform future experiments and planning efforts for future development of born-digital cataloging workflows.

Next Steps

The next steps in the experiment are to review the performance reports and data from the tests, define quality review criteria and plans, pause for assessment and alignment, plan for future task orders, and share outputs from the experiment widely.

Conclusion

Experimenting with machine learning models for bibliographic description enables the Library of Congress to make strategic resource decisions for cataloging large quantities of digital content. Contracting with an external vendor for experimental work provides the LoC with experts in machine learning to test out various possibilities without taking staff resources away from production cataloging. As the current experiment progresses and with follow-on experiments waiting to be implemented, the Library of Congress will continue to explore computational description while assessing machine learning to provide discovery and access to even more of the Library's rich digital resources.

References

Adams, Chris, and Julia Kim. 2020. "Experimenting with Speech to Text and Collections at the Library." *Library of Congress Blogs. The Signal Blog: Digital Happenings at the Library of Congress.* Posted by Leah Weinryb-Grohsgal. June 18, 2020. https://blogs.loc.gov/thesignal/2020/06/experimenting-with-speech-to-text-and-collections-at-the-library/.

Artificial Intelligence for Libraries, Archives and Museums (AI4LAM). n.d. http://ai4lam.org/.

Brown, Sara. 2021. "Machine Learning, Explained." MIT Sloan School of Management. April 21, 2021. https://mitsloan.mit.edu/ideas-made-to-matter/machine-learning-explained#:~:text=

The Data Nutrition Project. n.d. https://datanutrition.org/.

Gebru, Timnit, Jamie Morgenstern, Briana Vecchione, Jennifer Wortman Vaughn, Hanna Wallach, Hal Daumé III, and Kate Crawford. 2021. "Datasheets for Datasets." V8. arXiv:1803.09010. Top of Form https://arxiv.org/abs/1803.09010.

GoogleCloud. n.d. "Model Cards: The Value of a Shared Understanding of AI Models." https://modelcards.withgoogle.com/about.

Library of Congress (LoC) LC Labs. n.d. "AI at LC." https://labs.loc.gov/work/experiments/machine-learning/.

Library of Congress (LoC) Network Development and MARC Standards Office. 2023. "MARC Format for Bibliographic Data." 1999 Edition Update No. 1 (October 2000) through Update No. 37 (December 2023). https://www.loc.gov/marc/bibliographic .

National Institute of Standards and Technology (U.S.). 2023. "Artificial Intelligence Risk Management Framework (AI RMF 1.0)". Washington, DC: US Department of Commerce NIST. January 31, 2023. https://nvlpubs.nist.gov/nistpubs/ai/NIST.AI.100-1.pdf.

Padilla, Thomas. 2019. *Responsible Operations: Data Science, Machine Learning, and AI in Libraries.* Dublin, OH: OCLC Research. https://doi.org/10.25333/xk7z-9g97.

Smith, David A., and Ryan Cordell. 2018. *A Research Agenda for Historical and Multilingual Optical Character Recognition.* Boston MA: Northeastern University NULab for Texts, Maps & Networks. With the support of the Andrew W. Mellon Foundation. https://repository.library.northeastern.edu/downloads/neu:m043p093w?datastream_id=content.

The White House Office of Science and Technology Policy (OSTP). 2022. "Blueprint for an AI Bill of Rights: Making Automated Systems Work for the American People." October 2022. https://www.whitehouse.gov/wp-content/uploads/2022/10/Blueprint-for-an-AI-Bill-of-Rights.pdf.

Thomas Zaragoza, Yann Nicolas and Aline Le Provost

17 From Text to Data Inside Bibliographic Records: Entity Recognition and Linking

Abstract: The *Système Universitario de Documentation* (Sudoc)/University Documentation System catalogue is the French higher education union catalogue. It is run by *Agence bibliographique de l'enseignement supérieur*/Bibliographic Agency for Higher Educations (Abes). Like any large database, Sudoc with 15 million records has quality issues that can negatively impact the user experience or database maintenance efforts, for example the process towards an IFLA Library Reference Model (LRM) compliant catalogue. Quality issues are diverse: data might be inaccurate, ambiguous, miscategorised, redundant, inconsistent or missing. Details might not really be missing but hidden or lost in text inside the bibliographic record itself. This chapter describes efforts to extract structured information about contributors and their roles from statements of responsibility to generate automatically data in access points: last name, first name, relator code and optionally identifier, to link to the French higher education authority files. The first step in the process was a named entity recognition task implemented through a machine learning (ML) approach. The second step was an entity linking task. The pipeline is for Abes a first experience in adopting machine learning and building a generic approach to AI uses in cataloguing.

Keywords: Cataloguing; Entity-relationship modelling; Machine learning; Text analysis (Data mining)

Introduction

The *Système Universitaire de Documentation* (Sudoc) catalogue is the union catalogue of French academic and research libraries and it is managed and maintained by *Agence bibliographique de l'enseignement supérieur* (Abes)/Bibliographic Agency for Higher Education. Library catalogues are old, large and highly structured databases, created and maintained by professionals with a strong quality ethos. The development of new information technology paradigms has stressed the importance of data quality. On a web of linked data, the pollution of good data by less good data is a permanent risk and predictive models and decision making algorithms require the best possible training data to optimise results and minimise the generation of additional erroneous data.

As in any large database, quality issues in Sudoc's 15 million bibliographic records are diverse: data may be inaccurate, ambiguous, miscategorised, redundant, inconsistent or missing. Data are not necessarily missing; they might be implicit, hidden or lost in text inside the bibliographic record itself. Inaccurate or incomplete data impinge on the usefulness of the catalogue to its users and also inhibit future maintenance and moves to new approaches and conceptual models like the IFLA Library Reference Model (LRM) (Riva, Le Boeuf, and Žumer 2018).

This chapter focuses on one important and interesting aspect of so-called missing data. Contributor names and roles are transcribed from a document to the appropriate MARC descriptive field statement of responsibility, referred to throughout this chapter as the SoR. Most names and roles have corresponding access points that contain the normalised name and a function relator code to express the role, optionally the identifier of an authority record. But in Sudoc, many records have contributor mentions in descriptive fields that are not identified in access points. There are 300,000 existing person access points which lack a relator code.

This chapter describes the current effort being undertaken to extract structured information or data about contributors and their roles from text in the SoRs. The objective is to generate automatically, or correct, access points containing the last name, first name, function relator code, and optionally identifier, to link to the authority files maintained by Abes and used by the French higher education catalogue Sudoc. The authority files known as *Identifiants et Référentiels pour l'Enseignement supérieur et la Recherche* (IdRef)/Identifiers and Repositories for Higher Education and Research (Abes n.d. a) provide a variety of records within its database:

An open and reusable database, IdRef provides more than 6 million authority records of different types:
- Nearly 4 million individuals
- More than 400,000 local authorities (legal entities) and congresses
- More than 120,000 geographic locations
- ...

In the documentation ecosystem, authority records are used to control certain information that is common to several bibliographic records. They are used to identify, describe, aggregate, bounce back and disambiguate the resource being described.

The richness of authority records is also expressed in the quality and completeness of the links that unite them to bibliographic records, which makes it easy to establish an author's bibliography (Abes n.d.b).

The work being undertaken has two parts. The first is the creation and evaluation of a named entity recognition (NER) model to extract person and role entities from the SoRs. The second is linking the extracted role to the UNIMARC controlled vocabulary of roles via text classification. A pre-existing generic model has been employed for the recognition of names and retrained with ad hoc data marked up by librarians through a dedicated annotation tool. For the extraction of roles, a model was generated from scratch. The linking of contributor names has been achieved using a logical rule based artificial intelligence (AI) framework which is currently still being debated with a preference for either an entity linking model or a classification model over a rule-based approach. This project is a work in progress and the last section of the chapter provides an overview of further work to be done.

Incomplete Bibliographic Records

For various reasons, many bibliographic records contain incorrect and/or incomplete data. Some examples are provided of such records. The following UNIMARC bibliographic record has as its statement of responsibility (SoR):

> 200 1 $aHawking$fStephen Finnigan, réalisation$gStephen Hawking,
> Stephen Finnigan, Ben Bowie, scénario$gJoe Lovell ; Tina Lovell ;
> Arthur Pelling [et al.] acteurs

B200$f and B200$g UNIMARC fields encode the SoR as found on the document with the title frame as a source for a motion picture or the title page for a book. The SoR transcribes and records the original text found on the document, with minimal structuring and a separate SoR per role or function. A unique SoR can mention more than one person, for example:

> $gStephen Hawking, Stephen Finnigan, Ben Bowie, scénario

The following UNIMARC fields deal with access, not description. This highly structured data comes from the intellectual analysis of the document by the cataloguer, not the transcription of the title page:

> 700 1 **$3**241177782 **$a**Finnigan **$b**Stephen **$4**300
> 701 1 **$3**028590295 **$a**Hawking **$b**Stephen **$4**690
> 701 1 **$3**241177286 **$a**Lovell **$b**Joe **$4**005
> 701 1 **$3**241177421 **$a**Lovell **$b**Tina **$4**005
> 701 1 **$3**241177588 **$a**Pelling **$b**Arthur **$4**005

Each line is called an access point and refers to a unique person. In 701 1 $3241177421 $aLovell $bTina $4005, the subfields respectively refer to the linked authority record (Abes n.d.b) the last name, the first name and the UNIMARC role code (IFLA 2021) of the person related to this document. It is easy to peruse the previous SoRs and count the number of different persons mentioned, that is six, and then compare this number with the number of access points, that is five and come to the conclusion that the record lacks access points. But this conclusion is not trivial to reach automatically. In the process of encoding the five access points, the cataloguer extracted person names from the three SoR fields, but seems to have dismissed or forgotten one person, Ben Bowie. The project intention is to rely on machines to extract the named person missing, and to predict the precise role or function Ben Bowie plays in the work.

There are 300,000 author access points which lack a relator code and constitute lacunae that the ML project will try to fill. Missing access points in the Sudoc database are more difficult to find and require knowing how many different names are mentioned in the SoR. That is precisely one of the objectives of the project and can be accomplished using a named entity recognition model.

Named Entity Recognition and Extraction

Named Entity Recognition (NER) is an application of Natural Language Processing (NLP) on large amounts of unstructured text to extract entities. The application chosen for the purpose was an open-source model offered by spaCy. The model used was fr_core_news_lg, that had been trained on 7200 high quality, hand annotated French articles from Wikipedia, WikiNER (Nothman et al. 2013), and over 3000 French sentences from UD French Sequoia v2.8 (Candito et al. 2014). It can be used to extract persons, organisations and locations but not roles. For the latter, a new model was created and trained from scratch.

When applying the initial model on the statement of responsibility:

Stephen Finnigan, réalisateur, the result is:

Stephen Finnigan PER , réalisateur

And whilst offering promising outcomes in a broad context, the result does not translate well into a bibliographic context. Statements of responsibility are not written as naturally as the articles and sentences on which the model was trained. The model also ignores the role entity. Retraining of the model in a bibliographical context would be required using a large quantity of annotated bibliographic records. To accomplish this task, the annotation tool Prodigy was used which facilitated speedy and easy annotation of a large amount of data with spaCy's models built-in for training and retraining. SpaCy's capacity for recognising people can be retained, but it has no capacity to recognise roles. After annotating 10,000 bibliographical records using Prodigy, spaCy's model was retrained to extract person entities and to begin extracting role entities.

Evaluation

A new model can be evaluated using three metrics: precision, recall and accuracy. The metrics can be visualised using a confusion matrix (Figure 17.1).

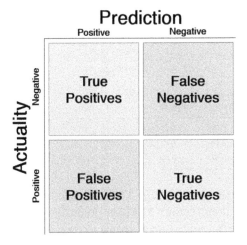

Figure 17.1: Confusion matrix example

Precision is the chance for a prediction to be true and is calculated by dividing the number of true positives by the sum of true positives and false positives. Recall is the chance for an entity of a certain class to be predicted as such. It is calculated by dividing the number of true positives by the sum of true positives and false negatives. Finally, the overall accuracy of a model is the sum of true positives and true negatives divided by the sum of all four.

To return to the previous problem, after retraining the model, the results shown in Figure 17.2 were obtained:

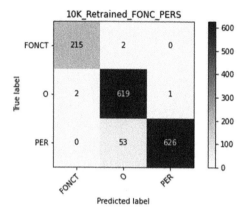

Figure 17.2. Confusion matrix of retrained spaCy model

Table 17.1: Results with retrained spaCy model

	Precision	Recall	F1-Score	Support
Fonct (Role)	0,99	0,99	0,99	217
O (Outside)	0,92	0,99	0,96	622
Per (Person)	0,99	0,92	0,96	679

The retrained model provides good performance (Table 17.1) and was able to detect 99% of person and role or fonct entities of which 99% of its predictions were correct. In the table, O indicates outside of an entity, and it is a token or a word that is neither role nor person. The model proved sufficiently efficient for tackling the next objective while still being able to further retrain the model, given additional annotated data. To reiterate, a suitable NER model was available to analyse statements of responsibility to detect the people mentioned and the keywords representing their roles in the creation of the catalogued document.

Linking Role Keywords

The next step in the process was to link role keywords to their controlled role codes. The example previously used illustrates the issue:

Stephen Finnigan, réalisateur

There are approximately 155 different relator codes. For a human, it is quite easy to link *réalisateur*/director in the context of a movie to the function relator code

300 - Movie director. But there can be difficulties clearing ambiguity without sufficient context. A director could also be 632 - Artistic director or 727 - Thesis Director.
To automatically remove the ambiguity, the first approach was an entity-linking
model, which links entities of a text to a controlled ontology. The problem encountered with this approach was that it relied on a rules-based system, which could
produce excellent results, but also required a larger quantity of effort which lacked
viability within the project context. Instead, a text classification approach was
chosen.

Text classification is a machine learning technique that assigns a set of pre-
defined categories to open-ended text through variables like word count frequencies and other predefined features and requires no set of rules. The human work is
limited to choosing features, extracting data, creating training sets, and choosing an
algorithm that provides the best result for our problem. It was decided to provide
the following features initially: role keywords with the entities extracted by the
NER model including directed, written or illustrated; the document content type
from a list including text, still image, animated image, and video; the position of the
mention of responsibility relative to other SoRs in the same record; and the document type in relation to its being a thesis or academic paper, or not.

Creation of the Training Dataset

To obtain the features outlined and create a training set, the entries for the
UNIMARC fields 200$ (SoR), 70X$ (access points), 181$c (content type), 608$3 (ID of
the authority record of the form/genre of the document), 105$a (textual resources
types) and 503$a (form title) were extracted from the Sudoc database. With the
NER model, the role keywords and the person names were extracted from the SoR
and subsequently paired with the persons in the access points to provide a relator
code answer for the training of the model. Following extraction of the raw data, the
position of each SoR was noted, including whether the document was a thesis or
not. Table 17.2 outlines the entries obtained. The content type, tdi, refers to biodi-
mensional animated image.

Table 17.2: Extraction of data

Bibliographic Record ID	SoR	Position	Access Points	Content type	Thesis
236018256	Stephen Finnigan, director	0	Finnigan Stephen 300 Hawking Stephen 690 Lovell Tina 005 Lovell Joe 005 Pelling Arthur 005	tdi	False
236018 256	Stephen Hawking, Stephen Finnigan, Ben Bowie, scénario;	1	Finnigan Stephen 300 Hawking Stephen 690 Lovell Tina 005 Lovell Joe 005 Pelling Arthur 005	tdi	False
236018256	Joe Lovell, Tina Lovell, Arthur Pelling [and al.] auteurs	2	Finnigan Stephen 300 Hawking Stephen 690 Lovell Tina 005 Lovell Joe 005 Pelling Arthur 005	tdi	False

The most complex step is executing the NER model on the SoRs to extract persons and roles keywords. The keywords are linked to the appropriate persons using a simple Person* + Role* / Role* + Person* pattern (Figure 17.3):

Figure 17.3: Statement of responsibility example pattern link

A string comparison of the person entity was made with the persons in the access points taking in consideration abbreviations, composite names and typos using the Levenstein distances between the two names. Given that the NER model has correctly extracted the entities, and that the extracted name and access point name have been paired, a training set can be created (Table 17.3).

Table 17.3: Training set example

Keywords	Position	Content type	Thesis	Label
réalisateur	0	tdi	False	300
scénario	1	tdi	False	690
acteurs	2	tdi	False	5

The approach has its limits. Since it is vital that the training set is as accurate as possible any ambiguity encountered that could not be removed was ignored. For example, the correctly completed bibliographic record, Stephen Finnigan, would have the following roles: 300 and 690. And in such case, it would be impossible to distinguish between the associated keywords and function relator codes in the entry (Table 17.4).

Table 17.4: Ambiguous bibliographic record example

Bibliographic Record ID	Keywords	Position	Content type	Thesis	Label
236018256	Directeur, scénario	0,1	tdi	False	300,69

Directeur could be associated with the role code 300 or 690, and it requires a choice between the two which is the objective of the model. It poses a conundrum as the model's predictions cannot be used to create its own training set. At least not yet.

The inability to differentiate between multiple role codes is limiting and potentially discriminatory in the training of the model as some roles have a greater chance of appearing in conjunction with others than alone and tend to have fewer training entries. Nonetheless a training set was constructed with 1000 entries per function for thirteen of the most common functions: 005 – Actor , 065 – Auctioneer, 070 – Author, 100 – Original Author, 230 – Composer, 300 – Movie director, 340 – Scientific publisher, 365 – Expert, 440 – Illustrator, 651 – Publication director, 727 – Thesis director, and 730 – Translator. A limit of 1000 entries was set. Whilst there are hundreds of thousands of annotated training entries of certain classes like the role code 070 – Author, there are only thousands of entries of minority classes like the role code 300 – Composer. A balanced training set must be created to avoid bias in a predictive model. The easiest and safest method to do so was to downscale, which entailed creating a training set with an equal number of entries per role code. The number chosen must be the highest possible while remaining lower than the number of training entries from the lowest count class. Once the training set was created, it was then used to train a k-nearest neighbours algorithm model.

K-Nearest Neighbours Algorithm (KNN)

"If it looks like a duck, if it sounds like a duck, then it probably is a duck."

The k-nearest neighbours algorithm (KNN) was implemented initially to evaluate the feasibility of the approach before branching out and experimenting with various different algorithms to choose the most appropriate, because the KNN algorithm is simple to comprehend and constitutes a simple introduction to the world of machine learning and decision-making algorithms.

The entries in the training set are encoded into numerical values that can be computed by the model. Each training entry constitutes a point in a universe. For example, if a KNN model is trained with k=3 and two classes, author in red and illustrator in blue, any attempt to predict the classification of a new point, in this case grey, will look for the three nearest neighbours and predict the majority, in this case, the role of illustrator in blue (Figure 17.4).

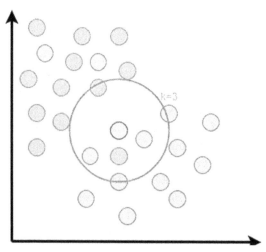

Figure 17.4: Prediction by KNN model with k=3

Evaluation

After training the model, the results can be visualised in Table 17.5, and in the confusion matrix (Figure 17. 5).

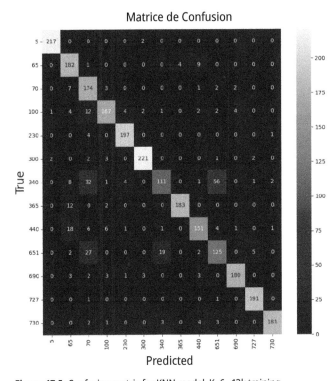

Figure 17.5: Confusion matrix for KNN model, K=6 , 13k training

Table 17.5: Evaluation table

Label	Precision	Recall	F1-Score	Support
005	0,99	0,97	0,98	224
065	0,93	0,78	0,85	211
070	0,44	0,91	0,6	196
100	0,96	0,81	0,88	217
230	0,99	0,98	0,98	179
300	0,92	0,98	0,95	191
340	0,95	0,61	0,74	201
365	0,97	0,9	0,93	181
440	0,96	0,78	0,86	197
651	0,81	0,6	0,69	58

Label	Precision	Recall	F1-Score	Support
690	0,94	0,96	0,95	206
727	0,95	0,99	0,97	207
730	0,99	0,89	0,94	205

The greatest discrepancy is in the 070 - Author column of predictions. This class has a poor precision measurement of 0.444 which is due to the nature of the class. Being the most common and principal role in the Sudoc, often in first position. and not introduced by a role keyword, the conclusion is implicitly reached that the said person is the author. The lack of role keywords makes the author class a collective bin for other entries that lack role keywords due to either a mistake by the NER model or initial cataloguing, or differences in the average entry of its class. In practice since the class 070 – Author is a majority role (Figure 17.6), the fact that it is the de facto prediction for sparse entries is the least damaging to overall efficiency. The satisfactory recall and precision scores for other classes lend assurance to accurate prediction for more specific and least common classes. Overall, the model appeared to be satisfactory, particularly given the limited amount of data used to train and test it.

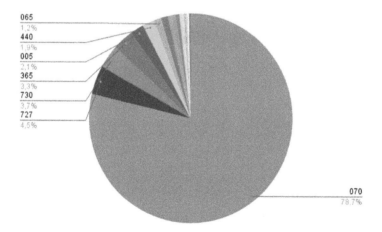

Figure 17.6: Pie chart of the distribution of function relator codes

As previously mentioned, there are over 100 roles that the model must differentiate which is considerably more than the thirteen roles in the training set. The current approach may well be flawed. Another model was trained, this time differentiating between thirty-five classes, and different results emerged (Table 17.6).

Table 17.6: Evaluation table with 35 classes

Label	Precision	Recall	F1-Score	Support
003	0.67	0.01	0,03	114
005	0.9	0.99	0,94	192
010	0.84	0.69	0,76	146
040	0.15	0.24	0,18	169
065	0,81	0,78	0,79	185
070	0.37	0,9	0,53	194
080	0,84	0,81	0,83	199
100	0,74	0,74	0,74	196
180	0,96	0,93	0,95	222
205	0.5	0.78	0,61	218
212	0.82	0.8	0,81	175
220	0.76	0.59	0,66	136
230	0.91	0.94	0,93	203
273	0.47	0.44	0,45	213
300	0.92	0.95	0,94	198
340	0.67	0.35	0,46	204
350	0.62	0.86	0,72	196
365	0.96	0.88	0,92	199
410	0.93	0.87	0,9	190
440	0.83	0.62	0,71	213
460	0.76	0.64	0,69	181
470	0.71	0.37	0,49	147
550	0.92	0.88	0,9	132
555	0.38	0.08	0,14	173
595	0.53	0.25	0,34	201
600	0.97	0.72	0,83	199
651	0.61	0.47	0,53	185
673	0.21	0.86	0,34	217
690	0.97	0.86	0,91	222
710	0.88	0.59	0,7	192
727	0.85	0.08	0,16	198
730	0.99	0.88	0,93	210
956	0.88	0.51	0,65	192
958	0.82	0.48	0,61	205

The cells with a score lower than 0.7 have been highlighted and it can be inferred that there are many more collective bins, due in part to the similarities between roles that did not exist in the previous model. Figure 17.7 charts and simplifies the mispredictions.

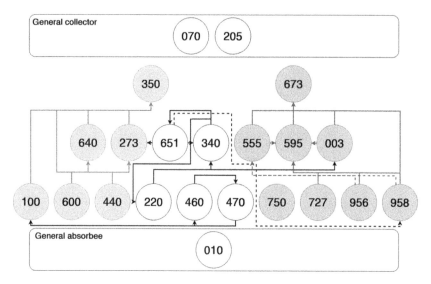

Figure 17.7: Prediction graph of function relator codes

Two specialised collective bins for classes 350 – Engraver, and 673 – Director of the research team, emerged representing respectively the artistic and academic classes. The existence of the collective bins indicates insufficient features to distinguish satisfactorily between similar roles. Further diagnostic work is required to determine if and how the results can be improved.

Further Work

The next stage of the work is to optimise and improve on the results achieved and work accomplished. There are over one hundred function relator codes. The text classification model implemented was able to predict only thirty-three function relator codes. And the results obtained justified an eventual implementation of the models on a grand scale for only thirteen function relator codes among the thirty-three function relator codes. To improve results, it is planned to vastly increase the amount of data allocated to the text classification model's training. To overcome the current constraint of keeping the classes balanced, the number of bibliographical records extracted and used to automatically create training entries will be significantly increased and/or records will be manually extracted including the lacking function relator codes to create specific training entries.

It is also planned to increase the number of features on which a model may rely when making its decisions to enhance the quality of the prediction and to differentiate more accurately between similar function relator codes. The technical team is working closely with a team of cataloguing experts to analyse the false predictions and explore potential new features. Another possible solution is the creation of different models for different needs. Multiple specialised models targeting specific categories of documents could be created and trained rather than using a large all-encompassing model. Class constraints in creating balanced training sets would be reduced and differentiated models would be able to discriminate between similar role codes through focusing on finer details and differences. Another possibility is the exploration and implementation of different classification algorithms apart from KNN to find one better suited to the requirements.

The implementation of an additional decision-making algorithm above the current prediction model would increase the accuracy. The aim would be to analyse the score given by the initial prediction model and act upon it only at a certain threshold. To present this idea in simpler terms, the prediction would be taken into consideration only if it were sure enough and ignored if deemed unsure. Precision would be enhanced at the cost of recall, which would be a sacrifice worth making given the nature of the project. There would also be the option of accepting multiple predictions instead of one. The hierarchy between roles should also be taken into consideration. For example, 350-engraver is a more specific type of author 070. Finally, the generation of missing access points must be implemented. Differentiation between first and last names to link the person names to their idRef identifier could be undertaken using the logical rules-based system tool Qualinka (Le Provost 2020). If the linking is not possible, first and last names will still need to be differentiated when creating UNIMARC zones and subzones for access points.

Conclusion

The objective of the project was to teach models to analyse the text of statement of responsibility to automatically generate missing access points for contributors or add the function relator code when missing in an existing access point. It first required the extraction of two types of entities: persons and roles. The standard Spacy model used for the task gave excellent results with a precision > 0.99 and recall > 0.92 after being re-trained on 10,000 manually annotated records. The annotation task, critical but often time-consuming, was efficiently achieved with the help of a dedicated annotation web tool. Librarians can use AI to produce more reliable training data which will feedback into further improvement of the AI.

When the persons and roles are extracted and paired, the next arduous task is to find the right function relator code among UNIMARC relators. Our first results with KNN as classification algorithm will be completed and hopefully enhanced in various ways: more data, more features, more specialised models, more algorithms; and more librarians to analyse the predictions and work with the data scientist.

This project is still a work in progress. If the end result is satisfactory, it could be used in production to create new access points for bibliographic records or check if the existing ones are correct. But no matter what the final conclusion of the project might be, it will have taught Abes a great deal both as a bibliographic agency and as a data steward of massive quantities of data. Abes has a duty to understand and adopt machine learning approaches as quickly as possible to fulfil its traditional missions. Abes with the help of efficient tools to annotate and prepare the data, and with librarians in the loop (Lieber, Van Camp, and Lowagie 2022), can achieve real progress both in terms of data quality and human resource development, two main issues for libraries.

Acknowledgments

The authors are grateful to Pascal Poncelet, University Montpellier, Abes colleagues who helped us to extract and analyse data, and Stephen Finnigan.

References

Agence bibliographique de l'enseignement supérieur (Abes). n.d.a. "IdRef: Identifiants et Référentiels pour l'Enseignement supérieur et la Recherche/Identifiers and Repositories for Higher Education and Research." https://www.idref.fr/autorites.jsp.

Agence bibliographique de l'enseignement supérieur (Abes). n.d.b, "Données d'autorité et référentiels." https://abes.fr/reseaux-idref-orcid/le-reseau/.

Candito, Marie, Guy Perrier, Bruno Guillaume, Corentin Ribeyre, Karën Fort, Djamé Seddah and Éric de la Clergerie. 2014. "Deep Syntax Annotation of the Sequoia French Treebank." In Proceedings of Language Resources and Evaluation Conference 2014, Reykjavík, Iceland. https://inria.hal.science/file/index/docid/971574/filename/deep_sequoia.final_with_keywords.pdf. Updated dataset used posted 2023 https://github.com/UniversalDependencies/UD_French-Sequoia?tab=readme-ov-file

International Federation of Library Associations and Institutions (IFLA). 2021. "Appendix B: Relator Codes." In *UNIMARC Bibliographic Format Manual (online ed., 1.0, 2021).* https://www.ifla.org/wp-content/uploads/2019/05/assets/uca/unimarc_updates/BIBLIOGRAPHIC/u_b_appb_update2020_online_final.pdf.

Le Provost, Aline, and Yann Nicolas. 2020. "IdRef, Paprika and Qualinka. A Toolbox for Authority Data Quality and Interoperability" *ABI Technik* 40, no. 2 : 158–168. https://doi.org/10.1515/

abitech-2020-2006. Available at https://abes.fr/en/publications/articles-et-contributions/idref-paprika-and-qualinka/.

Lieber, Sven, Ann Van Camp, and Hannes Lowagie. 2022. "A LITL More Quality: Improving Library Catalogs with a Librarian-in-the-loop Linked Data Workflow." Semantic Web in Libraries (SWIB) Conference, November 28, 2022. Presentation by KBR, Royal Library of Belgium. *YouTube.* Video. 27.31. https://www.youtube.com/watch?v=r29W73vle2I

Nothman, Joel, Nicky Ringland, Will Radford, Tara Murphy and James R. Curran. 2013. "Learning Multilingual Named Entity Recognition from Wikipedia." *Artificial Intelligence* 194: 151-175. https://doi.org/10.1016/j.artint.2012.03.006. Dataset used posted October 3, 2017 at https://figshare.com/articles/dataset/Learning_multilingual_named_entity_recognition_from_Wikipedia/5462500.

Riva, Pat, Patrick Le Boeuf, and Majal Žumer. 2018. "IFLA Library Reference Model: A Conceptual Model for Bibliographic Information." The Hague: International Federation of Library Associations and Institutions (IFLA) Functional Requirements for Bibliographic Records (FRBR) Review Group. https://repository.ifla.org/handle/123456789/40.

Part IV: **Artificial Intelligence in Library Services**

Edmund Balnaves

18 Artificial Intelligence in Library Services: An Introductory Overview

In the 1990s, the library management system (LMS) reigned supreme as the expression of information technology in the library. It was the culmination of many years of evolution in automation of library service delivery. The internet and the evolution of online search and discovery, exemplified by Google, represented the first in many transformations that have seen information usage migrate wholesale to electronic and online delivery. The technological landscape for libraries has seen rapid transformation rapidly since the turn of the century.

New categories of library services have emerged to support the role played by libraries in a radically online era. The evolving services include discovery systems grounded in massive electronic journal resources, research management systems, digital library systems, and digital repositories. The integration of library systems with other services such as the learning management system has become integral to library service delivery.

The emergence of open source as a rival to traditional commercial software delivery has impacted many library services. The open-source LMS, Koha, originated in New Zealand in 2000, the same year which saw the emergence of the open-source DSpace digital library system and several other key software services used by libraries. Koha, like other open-source software, has a large, diverse, international community of contributors, service providers and libraries adopting the system.

Artificial intelligence (AI) has represented another change in the library information technology landscape and has seen like other software developments within libraries the use of open source. Open source has been central to innovation within AI. Most of the earliest toolkits for AI were developed in open source, most notably in the Python programming language.

Client behaviour has dramatically changed in recent years, and the era of AI has raised a new set of expectations about the capabilities of libraries to deliver information resources that make best use of technology available. User experience (UX) techniques focusing on the interaction between the user and a service provider has shaped new services being provided.

Finally, the emergence of cloud computing has provided a platform for rich technological resources as a playground for innovation and service delivery. The availability of highly proficient cloud services has opened up opportunities for library service delivery.

Libraries are engaging with the various new technologies by use of cloud service delivery and integration using application programming interfaces (APIs). The API has become central in cross integration of the many services the library now manages. The long history of strong standards in the library community has fostered the rapid evolution of integrated services.

This section explores the ways in which libraries can engage with the emerging services using AI in libraries. Patrich Cher from the National Library Board Singapore explores the integration of ChatGPT using APIs and its own custom knowledge base. Imam Khamis explores the elements of building AI in libraries. Helen Cheung, Alex Chan and Kenny Kwan from the HKSKH Minghua Theological College explore the ways in which AI games can be deployed in learning AI literacy. Itai Veltzman and Rael Elstein discuss the integration of AI into the Ex Libris platform. Finally, Edmund Balnaves provides an illustrated journey in the playground of AI facial recognition tools in the context of library services.

This section provides a taste of the ways in which AI is already used in library services and an insight into the ways in which the AI toolset can be applied and explored in the delivery of library services. AI will increasingly be present across many of the software platforms that the library deploys, whether the libraries have introduced it themselves or applied software received via commercial or open-source systems implementation. Whichever way AI reaches the library, this book provides a solid introduction to librarians seeking to prepare the library to engage with a new era of software.

Patrick Cher

19 Empowering Library Services: Building a ChatGPT Chatbot

Abstract: In an era characterised by rapid technological advancements, libraries have evolved to meet the everchanging demands of their patrons. Artificial Intelligence (AI) has emerged as a transformative tool. This chapter delves into the multifaceted realm of AI's applications in library and reference services, with a particular focus on ChatGPT-based chatbots enhanced by custom knowledge bases. The chapter contains an introduction to AI technology and its implications in contemporary library services and encapsulates the profound impact of AI on resource accessibility, data accuracy, efficient management, cultural heritage preservation, innovative user engagement, and the crucial ethical considerations that underpin responsible AI deployment. ChatGPT's capabilities are explored with the aim of equipping library professionals with the knowledge and resources required to harness AI through tailored chatbot solutions and outlines the basic competencies necessary for constructing customised chatbots that cater to the unique demands of libraries and their users. A demonstration chatbot was prepared for presentation at the International Federation of Library Associations and Institutions (IFLA) 88th World Library and Information Congress (WLIC) in Rotterdam, The Netherlands, in August 2023. The step-by-step instructions and guidance for building this chatbot are provided. In summary, this chapter embarks on an exploration of AI's transformative potential within libraries, outlining the knowledge and tools required to navigate the evolving landscape of AI-driven library services while adhering to ethical principles, and provides practical guidance to building a chatbot.

Keywords: Artificial intelligence; ChatGPT; Chatbots; Library reference services; Libraries – Information technologies

Introduction

In the ever-evolving landscape of libraries, where information is not just sought but expected at the speed of thought, the integration of Artificial Intelligence (AI) has emerged as a transformative force. Among the diverse AI technologies, generative AI, with its ability to create human-like text and engage in natural language conversations, stands at the forefront of innovation. At the heart of the AI revolution lies ChatGPT, a remarkable example of generative AI, poised to reshape library and reference services in ways previously unimagined.

Artificial Intelligence, Machine Learning, Deep Learning and Generative AI

Artificial Intelligence pertains to the theory and advancement of computer systems with the capability to execute tasks typically demanding human-like intelligence (Stripling 2023). AI has transcended the boundaries of science fiction to become an integral facet of contemporary life. It has permeated diverse sectors, optimising processes, providing data-driven insights, and even demonstrating creative capacities.

Within the expansive realm of AI, machine learning (ML) has emerged as a pivotal subfield. Machine learning enables computers to learn from data, recognise patterns, and make intelligent decisions without explicit programming (Stripling 2023). Deep learning is a subset of ML that uses neural networks with many layers, deep neural networks, to model and solve complex problems. Deep learning has gained significant attention and success in recent years due to its ability to automatically learn hierarchical representations from data, making it particularly well-suited for tasks like image and speech recognition. AI, ML and deep learning are integrated (Figure 19.1).

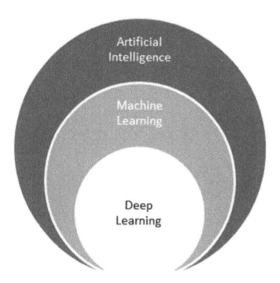

Figure 19.1: Relationship between AI, ML and deep learning

Generative AI is a technique associated with deep learning. Generative AI uses deep neural networks to create new data, such as text, images, music or other forms of content, based on patterns and structures learned from existing data. ChatGPT falls into this category, with its ability to understand and create content through human-like conversations.

Relevance of Artificial Intelligence in Today's Libraries

AI is playing a significant role in libraries today, exemplified by initiatives presented at the International Federation of Library Associations and Institutions (IFLA) World Library and Information Congress (WLIC) in 2023:

- SeTA@OP: Developed by the Publications Office of the European Union (EU), SeTA@OP employs ML and knowledge graphs to semi-automatically index EU publications. It improves information accessibility, accuracy, and ethical management, benefiting users by facilitating faster and more reliable resource discovery (Küster 2023).
- Visboeck CuratorBot: A conversational agent (Gukuma 2023) created by Delft University of Technology (TU Delft) Future Libraries Lab employs OpenAI's ChatGPT application programming interface (API) to engage users with cultural heritage objects, such as digitised drawings from *Het Visboeck*/[Book of Fish], a 16th century publication by Adriaen Coenen (Figure 19.2) It explores the application of natural language technology within cultural heritage, enhancing user education and interaction (Love, Gu, and Vandommele 2023)
- Poem Booth by Vouw: An AI Poetry machine that transforms portrait photos into personalised poems (Figure 19.3), fostering user engagement with literature and encouraging local writers to participate in library activities (Little Robots 2023; Vouw 2023).

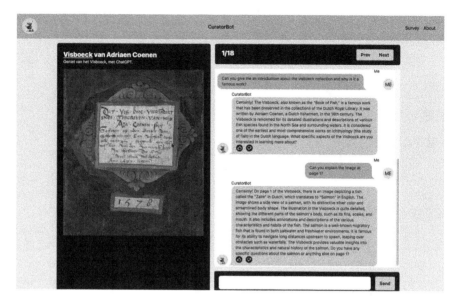

Figure 19.2: Visboeck CuratorBot (CuratorBot 2023)

Figure 19.3: Poem Booth (Vouw n.d.)

The advantages of use of the technology include enhanced accessibility, accuracy, efficiency, preservation and innovative engagement.

– Accessibility: AI-powered tools like SeTA@OP significantly enhance the accessibility of information within libraries. They automate the process of indexing and categorising publications, making it easier for library users to search, discover, and access relevant materials quickly. The result is a profound impact on the overall user experience, ensuring that library resources are effectively utilised.

– Accuracy: AI can play a crucial role in maintaining the accuracy and quality of information within library collections. Through the automation of tasks such as indexing, metadata generation, and content validation, AI can minimise susceptibility to human error. By using reliable and high-quality training data, AI can impart information to library users that is not merely accessible but also dependable and of superior quality, thereby enhancing the library's standing as a reliable font of knowledge.

– Efficient management: AI has the capacity to assist libraries in efficiently managing their digital collections. ML algorithms can identify duplicate materials, streamline cataloguing processes, and ensure that digital resources are organised effectively. Valuable time and resources are conserved freeing library personnel for other activities and digital assets deployment is optimised.

– Cultural heritage preservation: Initiatives like the *Visboeck* CuratorBot highlight how AI can contribute to the preservation and exploration of cultural heritage. AI-driven conversational agents engage users in meaningful and educational conversations about historical artefacts and documents, not only bringing cultural heritage to life but also fostering a deeper appreciation and understanding of the past, aligning with the mission of libraries to educate and inform.

– Innovative engagement: AI-powered projects like the Poem Booth add a novel dimension to library services. By using AI to turn portrait photos into personalised poems, libraries can engage users in creative and interactive ways and encourage a deeper connection with literature. Libraries can use such services to promote the participation of local writers in library activities, fostering a sense of community and creativity within the library environment.

AI applications enrich library services by ensuring effective resource utilisation, increasing user satisfaction, and promoting access to digital cultural heritage.

What is ChatGPT

ChatGPT, an AI-driven chatbot created by OpenAI, operates on the advanced foundation of the generative pre-trained transformer (GPT) machine learning architecture. ChatGPT belongs to the class of large language models (LLMs) in the realm of ML for natural language processing (NLP). LLMs process vast volumes of text data, extracting intricate word relationships from the text. The performance of LLMs is related to the scale of their input datasets and parameter space. It is crucial to recognise that ChatGPT, despite its significant promise, is not impervious to substantial limitations. Concerns have arisen regarding instances where it generates responses that deviate from factual accuracy and may inadvertently perpetuate societal biases. The various concerns have prompted rigorous examination and widespread discussions within the international community.

Training Data

The model used for ChatGPT underwent training utilising extensive textual datasets sourced from the internet. The training encompassed an extensive corpus of data amounting to 570 gigabytes derived from various sources such as ebooks, web texts, Wikipedia, online articles, and assorted written materials accessible on the internet (Hughes 2023). To provide precise granularity, the training data comprised a staggering volume of 300 billion words that were input into the system for learning and model development (Hughes 2023).

How Does ChatGPT Work?

At its core, ChatGPT is like a virtual librarian capable of understanding and responding to natural language queries. At first glance, the technological premise of ChatGPT appears straightforward. It receives user requests, questions, or prompts and promptly delivers corresponding answers. However, it is imperative to underscore that the underlying technology facilitating the interactions is considerably more intricate than initial impressions may suggest. Figure 19.4 provides a high-level overview of the processes.

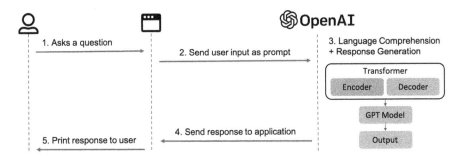

Figure 19.4: High level flow of ChatGPT

As an LLM, ChatGPT operates probabilistically, predicting the subsequent word in a sentence. To attain proficiency, the model underwent a phase of supervised testing as shown in Figure 19.5.

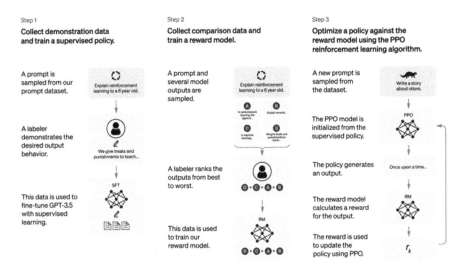

Figure 19.5: An Overview of ChatGPT's Learning Process (OpenAI 2022)

Step 0 – Initial Pre-Training

ChatGPT's training commences with the foundational step of pre-training. During this phase, a substantial neural network architecture, denominated as the GPT, is subjected to training on an extensive corpus of publicly accessible textual content derived from the internet. The pre-training serves as the bedrock upon which the model acquires fundamental linguistic attributes, encompassing grammatical constructs, language structure, factual knowledge, and rudimentary reasoning capabilities. This phase does not impart task-specific knowledge to the model.

Step 1 – Supervised Fine-Tuning

Subsequently, ChatGPT progresses to supervised fine-tuning. This phase entails the generation of a dataset where human AI trainers engage in simulated conversations, assuming dual roles as both user and AI assistant. Additionally, the trainers are furnished with model-written suggestions to aid in composing responses. The objective is to imbue ChatGPT with conversational prowess and responsiveness. The model learns from human-generated conversations and is fine-tuned to generate contextually appropriate responses based on the conversations it has seen in the training data.

Step 2 – Reinforcement Learning from Human Feedback

After supervised fine-tuning, ChatGPT proceeds to the reinforcement learning from human feedback (RLHF) phase. AI human trainers evaluate responses generated from diverse models and rank them based on perceived quality. The evaluative feedback serves as the foundation for the creation of reward models that quantitatively gauge the superiority of various model responses. The reward models crystallise the notion of what constitutes a better or more contextually relevant response.

Step 3 – Fine-Tuning with Proximal Policy Optimisation

The next step is proximal policy optimisation PPO) which is employed to fine-tune ChatGPT's response generation policy. The reward models informed by human evaluator feedback guide the model's behaviour. Specifically, PPO orchestrates refinements in the model's response generation strategy, fostering the production of responses that closely align with those receiving higher rankings from human evaluators. The RLHF phase, complemented by PPO fine-tuning, is often an iterative journey. Multiple rounds of fine-tuning occur to continually improve the model's performance. The ultimate goal is to enable ChatGPT to generate responses characterised not only by grammatical accuracy but also by contextual relevance, thereby conforming to the criteria of high quality set forth by human standards.

The Custom Knowledge Base

This section explains LLMs and the concept of a custom knowledge base through an illustrative analogy. Imagine a scenario where the objective is to impart specific skills to a canine for the purpose of executing diverse tasks. In this metaphorical framework, the dog serves as a representative metaphor for an AI model, and the competencies it acquires correspond to the proficiencies inherent in the AI model.

LLMs (Large Language Models)

Using the dog analogy, an LLM may be conceptualised as akin to the innate attributes and abilities of a dog. The training of a dog relates to basic skill: sit, come, down and stay (Figure 19.6). Certain dog breeds are renowned for distinct traits, such as agility or intelligence. Similarly, LLMs, exemplified by models like GPT-3, exhibit inherent linguistic capabilities. Through exhaustive training procedures, the LLMs attain an expansive comprehension of language, akin to how specific dog breeds naturally incline toward particular aptitudes.

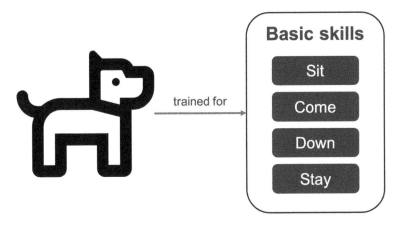

Figure 19.6: Dog's innate abilities

Custom Knowledge Base

Extending the dog analogy, the custom knowledge base can be compared with the supplementary training and information administered to the canine. In practice, dogs can be meticulously trained to execute particular tasks with special services skills as a police, guide or hunting dog, and provide specialised assistance to individuals, for example, people with disabilities (Figure 19.7). In a parallel vein, the custom knowledge base embodies the specialised tutelage imparted to an LLM, thereby enabling it to demonstrate proficiency within a designated domain. The reservoir of knowledge comprises curated datasets, factual information, and contexts specific to a chosen field, mirroring the tailored training received by a dog to excel in precise roles and functions.

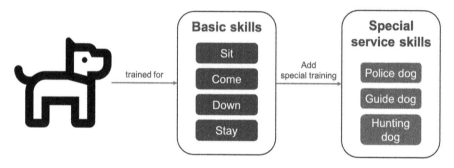

Figure 19.7: Special service skills training for dogs

In ways similar to how canine performance is augmented through rigorous training, an LLM's competencies undergo refinement through the process of fine-tuning with a custom knowledge base. The iterative procedure empowers the LLM to furnish responses that are not only more precise but also contextually pertinent within a specific domain, analogous to the manner in which a well-trained dog excels in its designated tasks. Through the allegorical lens of canine training, the interplay between LLMs and custom knowledge bases becomes more readily comprehensible to readers seeking a nuanced understanding of this sophisticated AI technology.

Setting Up the Environment

A demonstration chatbot was prepared for presentation at the International Federation of Library Associations and Institutions (IFLA) 88th World Library and Information Congress (WLIC) in Rotterdam, the Netherlands, in August 2023. An overview of the work undertaken and guidelines on how to construct such a chatbot are provided in this chapter. Included are details on setting up the environment and building the chatbot.

Setting up the environment addresses the technology stack, a combination of software tools and technologies, used for the demonstration chatbot project as well as the specifics and explanations of their development. The technology stack used for this demonstration comprised a meticulously selected ensemble of tools and libraries, each playing a distinctive role in facilitating the development and deployment of a sophisticated ML model. The technology inclusions are delineated in Figure 19.8 and comprise Python as the programming language, gpt-3.5-turbo as the GPT model, Gradio as the ML model and Google Drive for the storage.

Python	gpt-3.5-turbo	Gradio	Google Drive
Programming language that has one of the most comprehensive GPT and LLM libraries	GPT model optimized for chat interfaces	Build web interface to demo machine learning model that can be used by anyone	File storage for project resources

Figure 19.8: The technology stack

Prior to delving into the intricacies of configuring and executing Python source code for a ChatGPT chatbot, it is essential to recognise the two environments available: web-based notebook platform and the integrated development environment (IDEs) (Nehme 2023). Executing Python code within a web-based notebook platform like Google Colaboratory (Colab) through a web browser affords users several advantages. It encompasses convenience and universal accessibility across devices, streamlined access to pre-installed libraries for efficient code development, and the availability of powerful graphics processing units (GPUs) and tensor processing units (TPUs) that can substantially augment computational performance (Nehme 2023). Conversely, an IDE like Microsoft Visual Studio provides greater privacy and security, as data and code reside locally, mitigating exposure to potential online vulnerabilities. A local development setup empowers users to harness the full potential of their hardware resources without constraints. It is pertinent to mention that setting up and configuring an IDE adds an additional layer of complexity (Nehme 2023).

The choice between the two environments depends on factors like convenience, resource requirements, collaboration needs, and data security considerations, with each approach having its own strengths and trade-offs. To facilitate the exploration of building ChatGPT chatbots within the context of this chapter, the web-based notebook approach has been adopted.

The Google Colab Environment

Google Colab is a cloud-based platform tailored to facilitate the creation and execution of Python code with minimal setup (Google n.d.). Access to the platform is straightforward, requiring a Google account, and it offers the flexibility to create new Python notebooks or access existing ones (Google n.d.b). Figure 19.9 shows the user interface.

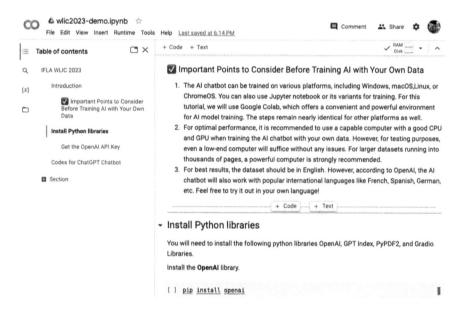

Figure 19.9: Screenshot of Google Colab's interface

Google Colab distinguishes itself by providing pre-configured computational environments and complimentary access to GPUs and TPUs which is particularly advantageous for computationally intensive tasks like training MLMs. It seamlessly integrates with Google Drive for data storage and collaborative sharing, executing code at the cell level while automatically preserving all work within Google Drive which makes Google Colab an appealing choice for individuals seeking a Python development environment without the need for local installations, while also benefiting from the capabilities of robust cloud-based computing resources.

Setting Up Google Colab Notebook

Creating a Google Colab notebook is a straightforward process which is described in the following five steps:

6. Access Google Colab. Firstly, open a web browser and navigate to the <u>Google Colab website</u>

7. Sign in to your Google Account if not already signed in and proceed to a Google account so that notebooks can be accessed and saved on Google Drive

8. Create a notebook. On the Google Colab homepage, click on the New Notebook button under File. This action will initiate the creation of a new Colab notebook.

9. Name the Notebook (Optional). Naming the notebook can be helpful for organisation. Click on "Untitled" at the top left of the notebook interface and provide a meaningful name.

10. Setup the file storage and structure. Click on Mount Drive, the third button underneath the Files title which will seek permission to store and retrieve files in Google Drive.

Once permission has been granted, navigate to drive >MyDrive > Colab Notebooks, and create a folder to store all files required for the chatbot project. Ensure that the newly created notebook is stored in the folder (Figure 19.10). In the same folder, create a docs folder and upload the documents for the custom knowledge base as indicated in Figure 19.10. Take note of the file path for the construct_index function which will be covered in this chapter.

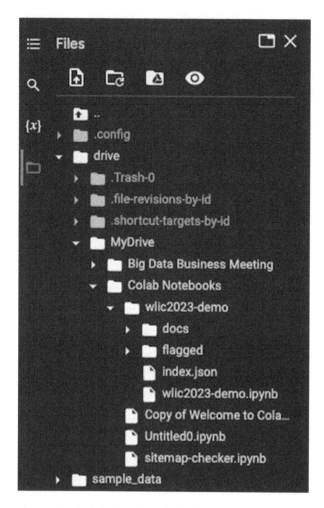

Figure 19.10: File interface at Google Colab

Obtaining an OpenAI API

OpenAI's API enables users to integrate ChatGPT-style AI capabilities into their own applications and tools. OpenAI offers users a seamless process for obtaining an API key, complete with a US$5 free credit upon registration (OpenAI 2023). To initiate the integration of the OpenAI capabilities, an API key can be obtained from OpenAI by following the steps outlined:

1. Create account and sign-in. To embark on the journey of obtaining an OpenAI API key, access the official OpenAI developer platform website (OpenAI n.d.). In the absence of an existing account, prospective users are required to initiate the account creation process by adhering to the straightforward registration protocol detailed on the website. For pre-existing users, a conventional sign-in mechanism is available through registered email credentials and associated passwords. Alternatively, users may opt to employ Google or Microsoft accounts for authentication (Figure 19.11).
2. Access the user account. Upon successful authentication, the user's name and profile icon will be visible at the top-right corner of OpenAI's platform homepage. Click on the user's name, and a dropdown menu containing various options is revealed (Figure 19.12).

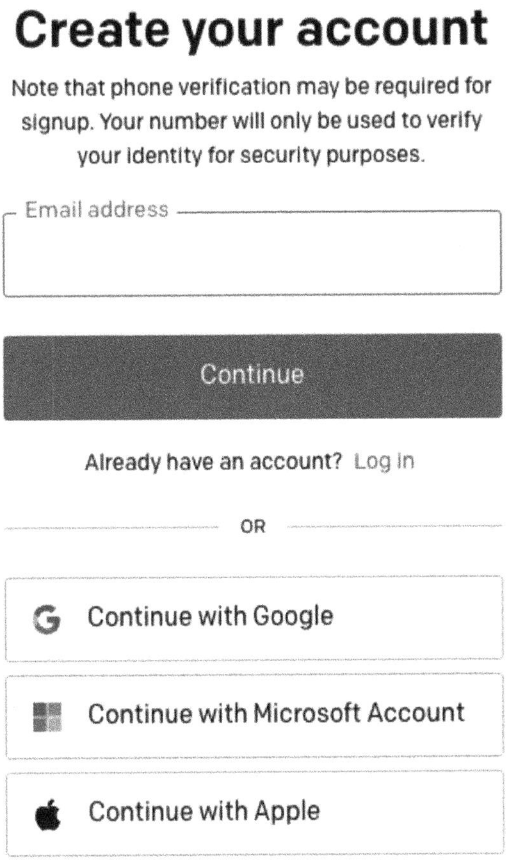

Create your account

Note that phone verification may be required for signup. Your number will only be used to verify your identity for security purposes.

Email address

Continue

Already have an account? Log in

———————— OR ————————

G Continue with Google

▦ Continue with Microsoft Account

🍎 Continue with Apple

Figure 19.11: Account creation page on OpenAI website

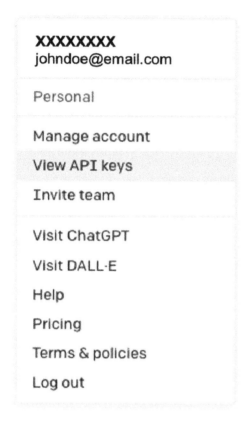

Figure 19.12: Account dropdown menu

3. Within the dropdown menu, select the View API keys option (Figure 19.12). API keys listing in OpenAI platform which will redirect to a page for the management of API keys. Should a new API key need to be generated, a conspicuous button named "Create new secret key" situated centrally on the page will initiate the procedure for the generation of an API key. It is imperative to promptly save the API key once it is generated and essential to acknowledge that closing the window displaying the API key will irreversibly lead to an inability to retrieve the key thereafter. Consequently, it is of utmost importance that the API key is securely stored (Figure 19.13) to ensure uninterrupted and continuous access to OpenAI's comprehensive suite of services.

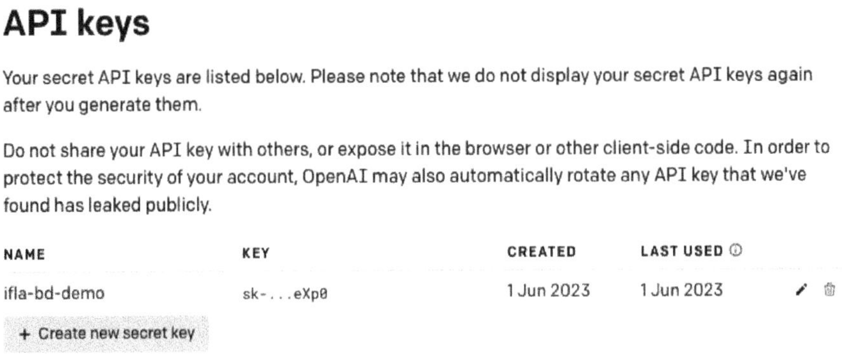

API keys

Your secret API keys are listed below. Please note that we do not display your secret API keys again after you generate them.

Do not share your API key with others, or expose it in the browser or other client-side code. In order to protect the security of your account, OpenAI may also automatically rotate any API key that we've found has leaked publicly.

NAME	KEY	CREATED	LAST USED ⓘ	
ifla-bd-demo	sk-...eXp0	1 Jun 2023	1 Jun 2023	✏ 🗑

+ Create new secret key

Figure 19.13: API keys listing in OpenAI platform

Installation of Python Libraries

In the code cell of the Google Colab Notebook, run the code snippet:

```
1 !pip install openai
2 !pip install gpt_index==0.4.24
3 !pip install langchain==0.0.148
4 !pip install PyPDF2
5 !pip install gradio
```

Figure 19.14: Install the Python libraries required for the demonstration chatbot

Pip is the package installer for Python (Figure 19.14). You can use pip to install packages from the Python package index and other indexes. The code snippet can be likened to assembling the necessary ingredients and equipment in a kitchen before cooking a meal. The code snippet guides the computer to obtain essential software tools like Openai, Gpt_index, LangChain, PyPDF2, and Gradio from the Internet and ensures that the computer has all the required tools readily available for use when executing the subsequent code snippets, much the same as having all the ingredients and utensils at hand before starting the cooking process.

Prerequisite Python Libraries

- *Openai* is a software package that facilitates interaction with OpenAI's services and APIs. It empowers developers to integrate OpenAI's AI capabilities, including NLP and text generation, into their applications.

- *Gpt_index* is a framework designed to facilitate the development of LLM applications. It offers essential tools, including data connectors for ingesting data sources, data structuring capabilities, and an advanced retrieval and query interface.
- *LangChain* is a framework designed for building applications that harness language models. It offers customisable components, facilitating the creation of structured chains for specific tasks and includes interfaces for various modules.
- *PyPDF2* is a software package that provides developers with tools for working with Portable Document Format (PDF) files programmatically. It offers functionalities for reading, manipulating, and extracting data from PDF documents.
- *Gradio* is a software package that provides developers with tools and functionalities to quickly build and deploy interactive web applications that display ML models.

Building the Chatbot

Once the environment has been set up, the groundwork for building the chatbot is laid. In the following step, the newly installed libraries would be imported into the Google Colab Notebook, OpenAI API key is integrated to unlock ChatGPT capabilities, Google Drive is linked to store the generated index for knowledge retrieval, and a user interface is built to enable interaction with the demonstration chatbot.

Importing Prerequisite Library Packages

In the code cell of the Google Colab Notebook, run the code snippet:

```
 1 # import libraries dependencies
 2 from gpt_index import (SimpleDirectoryReader, GPTListIndex,
 3                         GPTVectorStoreIndex, LLMPredictor, PromptHelper)
 4 from langchain.chat_models import ChatOpenAI
 5 from google.colab import drive
 6 from tenacity import (retry, stop_after_attempt, wait_random_exponential)
 7 import gradio as gr
 8 import sys
 9 import os
10
```

Figure 19.15: Import the dependent libraries in Google Colab Notebook

The code snippet (Figure 19.15) ensures that everything essential for the functioning of the chatbot application is readily available. The tools are used for file reading, working with specialised models, and interfacing with Google Drive. Additionally, the code includes a tool for error handling, and another tool for creating a web-based interface for the demonstration chatbot to function.

Specifying OpenAI API Key

```
11 # API key
12 os.environ["OPENAI_API_KEY"] = 'REPLACE WITH YOUR OPEN AI API KEY HERE'
13
```

Figure 19.16: Specify OpenAI API key in Google Colab Notebook

The line of code configures the storage of the OpenAI API key (Figure 19.16) in the computer's memory, reserving a designated location where the computer securely retains a confidential code, known as the API key. The key is essential for executing tasks requiring access to OpenAI's AI capabilities, including responding to prompts and training a customised knowledge base. Substitute the text PLACEHOLDER FOR API KEY with the previously acquired API key enclosed within the single quotation marks.

Connecting Google Drive

```
14 # Mount Google Drive
15 drive.mount('/content/drive/', force_remount=True)
16
```

Figure 19.17: Connect Google API for accessing and storing files in Google Colab Notebook

The line of code directs the computer to use a file path to connect with a place called /content/drive/ within Google Drive (Figure 19.17), and makes sure the connection is established even if previously disconnected so that the computer can access files and data stored.

Ingesting Documents and Creating an Index for Knowledge Retrieval

```
17 # Function to construct index
18 # Retrying with exponential backoff avoids rate limit by performing a short
19 # sleep when a rate limit error is hit, then retrying the unsuccessful request
20 @retry(wait=wait_random_exponential(min=1, max=60), stop=stop_after_attempt(6))
21 def construct_index(directory_path):
22     max_input_size = 4096
23     num_outputs = 512
24     max_chunk_overlap = 20
25     chunk_size_limit = 600
26
27     prompt_helper = PromptHelper(max_input_size, num_outputs, max_chunk_overlap,
28                                  chunk_size_limit=chunk_size_limit)
29
30     # 1. Temperature 0-0.4 (focused, conservative),
31     #                 0.5-0,7 (balanced),
32     #                 0.8-1 (more creative, unexpected)
33     # 2. gpt-3.5-turbo model was optimised for dialogue
34     # 3. max_tokens determine the length of the response provided
35     # by the bot (0.75 words per token)
36     llm_predictor = LLMPredictor(llm=ChatOpenAI(temperature=0,
37                                                 model_name="gpt-3.5-turbo",
38                                                 max_tokens=num_outputs))
39
40     # Load the docs for training the model
41     documents = SimpleDirectoryReader(directory_path).load_data()
42
43     # Generate and save the index
44     index = GPTVectorStoreIndex(documents, llm_predictor=llm_predictor,
45                                 prompt_helper=prompt_helper)
46     index.save_to_disk(
47         '/content/drive/MyDrive/Colab Notebooks/wlic2023-shared/index.json')
48
49     return index
50
```

Figure 19.18: Create the function to ingest documents and create index in Google Colab Notebook

The code defines a function named construct_index. The function is designed to create an index, which is like a digital library catalogue, by processing the collection of documents located in the specified folder on Google Drive. The created index helps the chatbot quickly find and retrieve information from the documents when needed. It is similar to how a library keeps track of its books so that users can easily find the one to read. The code is preparing the index to answer questions based on the contents of specified documents.

The process to generate an index involves several tasks:
- Setting parameters like input size, the number of desired outputs, and other factors that influence the indexing process
- Preparing a helper tool called Prompt Helper to assist with generating prompts for the language model

- Configuring a language model known as gpt-3.5-turbo to be used for generating responses with the predefined temperature and response length within the index. Temperature is a parameter that controls the creativity or randomness of the text. A higher temperature results in a diverse output, while a lower temperature makes the output more focused
- Loading the documents from the specified directory for training the model, and
- Creating and saving the index, which helps in organising and retrieving information from the documents.

The construct_index function (Figure 19.18) is designed to handle errors effectively, as indicated by the @retry decorator. When the function encounters a problem during the indexing process, it does not give up right away but instead, tries repeatedly, up to six times, with a random pause of one to 60 seconds between each try, to ensure that the process eventually succeeds, even if there are temporary issues.

Execute the following code snippet to invoke the construct_index function:

```
65 # Call the construct index function.
66 # This can be skipped if there is an existing index that can be used
67 index = construct_index(
68      "/content/drive/MyDrive/Colab Notebooks/wlic2023-shared/docs")
69
```

Figure 19.19: Invoke the construct_index function in Google Colab Notebook

The code should be executed whenever there is a need to update the model with changes to the custom knowledge base, such as adding, removing, or updating documents, or performing the initial model training. It is essential to run this code snippet (Figure 19.19) to ensure that any modifications made to the knowledge base are properly integrated into the model's index. The execution of the construct_index function may require some time to complete. When dealing with a relatively small custom knowledge base consisting of approximately 2,000 textual PDF articles, ranging from 1,000 to 2,000 words in length, the process may take around 45 minutes. Users should be prepared for a potentially lengthy execution time, especially when working with larger or more extensive knowledge bases.

Providing Responses to Users' Prompts

```
51 # Function to load the generated index to generate responses from
52 def chatbot(input_text):
53     index = GPTVectorStoreIndex.load_from_disk(
54         '/content/drive/MyDrive/Colab Notebooks/wlic2023-shared/index.json')
55     response = index.query(input_text, response_mode="compact")
56     return response.response
57
```

Figure 19.20: Create the chatbot function in Google Colab Notebook to load the generated index file to generate responses to users' questions submitted in the demonstration chatbot

The code defines a function called chatbot that takes an input text as an argument. Inside the function, a pre-existing index consisting of a structured collection of data from a specific location on Google Drive is loaded and used to process the input text, generate a response. and return the response (Figure 19.20). The code creates a chatbot that can understand and respond to user input based on the data stored in the index.

Creating the User Interface with Gradio

```
58 # Create the Gradio local interface
59 iface = gr.Interface(fn=chatbot,
60                     inputs=gr.components.Textbox(lines=7,
61                                             label="Enter your text"),
62                 outputs="text",
63                 title="WLIC 2023 Demo AI Chatbot")
64
```

Figure 19.21: Create the User Interface with Gradio in Google Colab Notebook

The code sets up the visual and interactive components for engaging with the AI chatbot in a formal and user-friendly manner. Users can input up to seven lines of text in the text box, and the chatbot responds with text. Access to the user interface is limited to the web-based notebook. After successfully executing the provided code (Figure 19.21), users will have access to a web-based user interface. Figure 19.22 provides a screenshot illustrating an interaction between a user and the chatbot, showcasing the seamless engagement facilitated by the interface.

WLIC 2023 Demo AI Chatbot

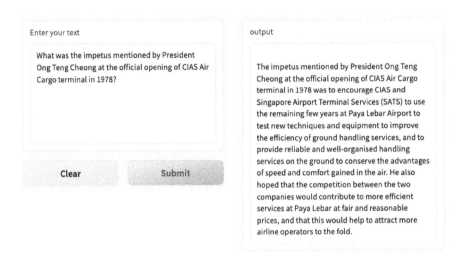

Figure 19.22: User interface of the chatbot

Run this code snippet to create a public link:

```
70 # Launch the Gradio site with share option set to True
71 # The share option allows you to determine whether a public link is created
72 iface.launch(share=True)
```

Figure 19.23: Optional step to create a public link for the chatbot user interface in Google Colab Notebook

The code snippet (Figure 19.23) is optional and can be invoked when needed. The share=True part means that the chatbot user interface can be shared via a public Uniform Resource Locator (URL) accessible by multiple users over the Internet.

Ethical Considerations

In the development and deployment of AI technologies such as ChatGPT chatbots, adherence to ethical principles is of utmost importance in library services. Libraries must prioritise ethical guidelines to establish trust and uphold responsible AI practices throughout the system design and development phases. Google's 2018 guidelines for AI development underscore societal benefit, fairness, safety, accountability, privacy, scientific excellence, and responsible use and are in their <u>fifth revised edition</u> (Google 2023). The commitment to avoiding harmful and unethical uses of AI demonstrates a responsible approach. It also reflects an awareness of the potential risks and consequences associated with AI technologies.

The <u>IFLA Statement on Libraries and Artificial Intelligence</u> recognised the potential for libraries to encourage the use of responsible AI by others in 2020, as well as adopting principles for use within libraries and emphasised two key ethical considerations: privacy and bias (IFLA 2020). Privacy concerns arise from the extensive use of data for AI training and decision-making, encompassing both non-personal and personally identifiable information. AI-driven analysis outputs may also expose sensitive data, raising questions about individual privacy and data protection rights (Cox, Pinfield, and Rutter 2019). Libraries employing AI solutions, such as ChatGPT, must prioritise data privacy, obtain informed consent for personal data processing, enhance transparency, and implement flexible consent mechanisms.

An example of a consent mechanism can be found in <u>Singpass</u>, the Singapore government's digital identity service, which facilitates the secure sharing of government-verified personal data with government agencies and businesses for transactions (Singpass 2023a). It exemplifies a robust approach to respecting individuals' data privacy rights while ensuring the responsible use of AI-driven services (Figure 19.24).

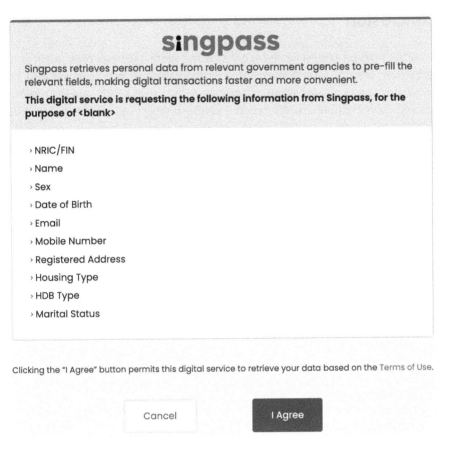

Figure 19.24: Consent request in Singpass (Singpass 2023b)

Bias is another significant ethical concern. Unfair outcomes must be avoided (Latonero 2018). Unintentional biases may infiltrate AI development during problem framing, data labelling, or attribute selection, often perpetuating societal inequalities (Borgesius 2018). Addressing biases involves proactive measures such as conducting practice exchanges, organising bias management symposia, and establishing committees to guide responsible AI engagement (Padilla 2019). It is imperative to scrutinise the AI model training processes of external vendors and raise concerns related to ethics, privacy, or bias. The effectiveness of ethical principles and measures hinges on their diligent implementation and enforcement. Ensuring transparency and accountability in adhering to standards and measures is crucial for their practical application.

Conclusion

Artificial intelligence developments are growing apace. Libraries must adapt and adopt new ways of service provision. Library staff must gain competencies in developing and applying various approaches to the use of AI. The use of chatbots has particular usefulness in libraries and simple strategies can maximise their use. Libraries also have a particular responsibility to ensure that continuous observance of ethical principles are in place with regard to evolving AI technologies to ensure their sustainability, relevance and effectiveness over the long term. Libraries deploying AI-driven service must prioritise ethical principles, uphold trustworthiness, and promote transparency, aligning their AI initiatives with societal objectives and fostering public welfare and innovation in library services.

References

Borgesius, Frederick Zuiderveen. 2018. "Discrimination, Artificial Intelligence, and Algorithmic Decision-making." Strasbourg: Council of Europe. https://rm.coe.int/discrimination-artificial-intelligence-and-algorithmic-decision-making/1680925d73.

Cox, Andrew M., Stephen Pinfield, and Sophie Rutter. 2019. "The Intelligent Library: Thought Leaders' Views on the Likely Impact of Artificial Intelligence on Academic Libraries." *Library Hi Tech* 37, no. 3: 418–435. https://doi.org/10.1108/LHT-08-2018-0105. Available at https://eprints.whiterose.ac.uk/136552/1/file.PDF/1000.

CuratorBot. 2024. "Visboeck van Adriaen Coenen: Geniet van het Visboeck, met ChatGPT." https://visboeck.vercel.app/.

Google. n.d.a. "Google Colab - Frequently Asked Questions." https://research.google.com/colaboratory/faq.html.

Google. n.d.b. "Google Colaboratory." https://colab.google/.

Google. 2023. "AI Principles Progress Update 2023." https://ai.google/static/documents/ai-principles-2023-progress-update.pdf.

Gukuma, Eric. 2023. "Visboeck: CuratorBot (CB): Specifications and Details." [Developed by H. Gu and J.S. Love at TU Delft]. https://github.com/gukuma/VisboeckGPT.

Hughes, Alex. 2023. "ChatGPT: Everything You Need to Know About OpenAI's GPT-4 Tool." *BBC Science Focus*, September 26, 2023. https://www.sciencefocus.com/future-technology/gpt-3.

International Federation of Library Associations and Institutions (IFLA). 2020. "IFLA Statement on Libraries and Artificial Intelligence." https://repository.ifla.org/bitstream/123456789/1646/1/ifla_statement_on_libraries_and_artificial_intelligence-full-text.pdf.

Küster, Marc W. 2023. "SeTA@OP - Semi-automatic Indexing of EU publications; Combining the Power of Machine Learning, Knowledge Graphs, and Human Intelligence." Presentation at the 88th IFLA World Library and Information Congress, 21-25 August 2023, Rotterdam, The Netherlands. https://iflawlic2023.abstractserver.com/program/#/details/presentations/404.

Latonero, Mark. 2018. "Governing Artificial Intelligence: Upholding Human Rights & Dignity." Data & Society report. https://datasociety.net/wp-content/uploads/2018/10/DataSociety_Governing_Artificial_Intelligence_Upholding_Human_Rights.pdf.

Little Robots. 2023. "The Tech Behind the Poem Booth." [Blog]. Posted by Hugo September 7, 2023. https://www.littlerobots.nl/blog/the-tech-behind-the-poembooth/.

Love, Jeff, Heng Gu, and Jeroen Vandommele. 2023. "The Visboeck Curatorbot: Discussing Heritage Collections with Machines." Poster presented at 88th IFLA World Library and Information Congress (WLIC), 2023 Rotterdam. https://repository.ifla.org/handle/123456789/3058.

Nehme, Adel. 2023. "6 Best Python IDEs for Data Science in 2023." *Datacamp. Tutorials.* Updated February 2023. https://www.datacamp.com/tutorial/data-science-python-ide.

OpenAI. n.d. "Welcome to the OpenAI Developer Platform." https://platform.openai.com/.

OpenAI. 2022. "Aligning Language Models to Follow Instructions." https://openai.com/research/instruction-following.

OpenAI. 2023. "Usage Openai API, 5 Dollar Free Gift." *OpenAI. Documentation. API Reference.* OpenAI Developer Forum. November 2023. https://community.openai.com/t/usage-openai-api-5-dollar-free-gift/512163.

Padilla, Thomas. 2019. "Responsible Operations: Data Science, Machine Learning, and AI in Libraries." Dublin, OH: OCLC. https://www.oclc.org/content/dam/research/publications/2019/oclcresearch-responsible-operations-data-science-machine-learning-ai.pdf.

Singpass. 2023a. "Discover What You Can Do With Singpass." https://www.singpass.gov.sg/main/individuals/.

Singpass. 2023b. "User Journey Template for Integrating with MyInfo." https://public.cloud.myinfo.gov.sg/dpp/frontend/assets/api-lib/myinfo/downloads/user-journey-template.pptx.

Stripling, Gwendolyn. 2023. "Introduction to Generative AI." *Google Cloud Tech*. AI and Machine Learning with Google Cloud. Video. 22.07. https://www.youtube.com/watch?v=G2fqAlgmoPo.

Vuow. n.d. "Poem Booth: An AI Poetry Machine That Turns Portraits into Poems." https://www.vuow.com/poem-booth.

Iman Khamis

20 Fundamentals of Artificial Intelligence for Libraries

Abstract: Artificial intelligence (AI) developments are impacting on business and libraries in their operations and service delivery. There are many facets of AI including machine learning (ML), recommender systems, natural language processing (NLP), speech recognition and text analytics. Speech recognition technology is relevant to many businesses and to libraries. It provides customer service benefits and enriches the customer experience. The chapter explores ML, recommender systems, and NLP. Chatbots have emerged from NLP developments and allow uninterrupted interactions between organisations and their clients and ideally enhance the overall user experience. Chatbots offer libraries the opportunity to improve user engagement and operational efficiency, and potentially to reduce costs. This chapter discusses the fundamentals of AI technologies using the development of a chatbot as the context.

Keywords: Chatbots; Artificial intelligence - Library applications; Machine learning

Introduction

Machine learning (ML) refers to the development of algorithms that enable machines to mimic human intelligence and has led to the development of many artificial intelligence (AI) applications. Natural language processing (NLP) helps humans to communicate with computers that can read, hear and understand. Chatbots are software applications or web interfaces which simulate human conversation and facilitate communication between a person and a machine through text or voice interactions. Chatbots are growing in importance as tools in business and in libraries because of their capacity to offer effective and individualised support to customers. Chatbots are likely to become a popular method for addressing the demands of library users as a result of the development of digital technologies and the rising demand for remote services. Chatbots can assist with a variety of requests and tasks by leveraging AI and NLP applications. Chatbots can help in many areas ranging from responding to straightforward questions about library hours and services to helping with more complicated research requests for detailed information on specific topics. Additionally, chatbots can run continuously, allowing libraries to offer users round-the-clock support. In general, chatbots have proven to be a priceless tool for libraries looking to improve user experience and their digital products and offerings.

Building a chatbot can seem to be a difficult task. However, with the right tools and appropriate knowledge, the construction can be simplified. Chatbots have the capacity to improve users' experiences and have emerged as a popular solution for organisations looking for seamless customer service. Libraries are no exception to the trend. In this chapter, the steps needed for building a chatbot for a library are outlined, from understanding ML to selecting the appropriate tools and programming languages. Overall, this chapter provides insight into the fundamental knowledge and resources needed to create a successful chatbot for a library.

Basic background information on the concepts involved in understanding ML and NLP is provided. Guidance is then given on how to construct a chatbot using an intent JavaScript Object Notation (JSON) file. Intent is a messaging object for requesting an action from another app component and facilitates communication. JSON is an open standard file and data interchange format. The intent file will document and answer the questions users have in mind. It ensures that the chatbot will work properly and that the chatbot has the ability to analyse intent and provide a successful interaction.

Machine Learning

Machine learning (ML) refers to the development of algorithms that enable machines to mimic human intelligence. Machine learning technology has recently been used in many fields such as image recognition, biomedical applications, natural language processing, and prediction. In 1958, Rosenblatt developed the first neural network that mimicked neural cells in the human brain (Rosenblatt 1958). In 1975 another breakthrough was made by Werbos when he came up with back-propagation making neural networks and ML more efficient (IBM Developer 2023). He developed the multilayer perceptron (MLP). MLP is a neural network that consists of fully connected layers that can produce a set of outputs from inputs (Werbos 1994). In 1986, Quinlan developed another ML technology known as decision trees (Quinlan 1986), followed by Cortes and Vapnik's invention of support vector machines (SVMs) (Cortes and Vapnik 1995). ML technology has grown exponentially through the development of many accompanying algorithms, inventions, and models such as Adaboost, random forests, and multilayer perceptron.

Arthur Samuel was the first to refer to machine learning in 1959 as a computer's capacity to be programmed and learn on its own:

> The studies reported here have been concerned with the programming of a digital computer to behave in a way which. if done by human beings or animals, would be described as involving the process of learning. While this is not the place to dwell on the importance of machine-learning procedures. or to discourse on the philosophical aspects, there is obviously a very large amount of work. now done by people. which is quite trivial in its demands on the intellect but does, nevertheless, involve some learning. We have at our command computers with adequate data-handling ability and with sufficient, computational spend to make use of machine-learning techniques. hut our knowledge of the basic principles of these techniques is still rudimentary. Lacking such knowledge, it is necessary to specify methods of problem solution in minutes and exact detail a time-consuming and costly procedure. Programming computers to learn from experience should eventually eliminate the need for much of this detailed programming effort. (Samuel 1959, 535).

Bernard in writing for the World Economic Forum on ML referred to the work of Samuel: "In 1959, MIT engineer Arthur Samuel described machine learning as a "Field of study that gives computers the ability to learn without being explicitly programmed", and added "Machine learning is all about sorting through those troves of collected information to discern patterns and predict new ones" (Bernard 2017). ML can also be explained as:

> **Definition**: A computer program is said to learn from experience E with respect to some class of tasks T and performance measure P, if its performance at tasks in T, as measured by P, improves with experience E. (Mitchell 1997, 2)

Another definition is "Programming computers to optimize a performance criterion using example data or experience" (Eick 2024). All the various definitions have a commonality; machine learning is about how computers are taught to perform advanced tasks by inputting sufficient data for effective learning.

Recommender Systems

Machine learning techniques are classified into supervised and machine unsupervised learning techniques. Supervised ML refers to ML algorithms that perform accurate predictions based on input-out pairs. Recommender systems work on the same concept. The most important feature of supervised learning methods is that they are adaptable to various regression tasks. Regression analysis is the most used technique in recommender systems because it aims to organise the content and order it according to a ranking system. In recent years, the need for recommender systems has increased. With vast amounts of information available on the internet, selection of appropriate and accurate information has become more difficult. Making the right choice from the plethora available has led to confusion and an inability to decide on what is best. There is an increasing need for tools that can effectively prioritise the available options according to specific criteria that will match user needs. Recommender systems were born to solve the problem by searching the vast majority of options available for users, filtering the content, and dynamically generating personalised options for each individual (Isinkaye, Folajimi, and Ojokoh 2015). Recommender systems have been around for a long time, and it is no exaggeration to suggest that the ideas about targeted responses to inquiries emerged initially with the invention of the computer and even perhaps with Alan Turing's question in 1950 which has become known as the Turing Test: "Can machines think?"

In 1979, Elaine Rich addressed the problems related to computers treating their users in a personalised way and described a system called Grundy which simulated the behaviour of a successful librarian and dealt with enquiries from stereotyped models of users constructed on the basis of a small amount of knowledge about them. An analysis of Grundy's performance recommending novels to users demonstrated the effectiveness of the user models in guiding its performance (Rich 1979). Grundy might well be a first in the field of recommender systems (Rich 1979). In the 1990s, GroupLens Research, a human-computer interaction laboratory at the University of Minnesota created the GroupLens recommender, which set up an automatic collaborative filtering system collating user ratings of articles from *Usenet News* (Konstan et al. 1998). A recommender system, MovieLens was set up to collate ratings from users on movies and to provide recommendations to users of the system based on user profiles (Konstan et al. 998).

Perhaps the best-known recommender system is the one used by Amazon who created its famous collaborative filtering method initially for book selection. The filter system created by Amazon engineers was a user-based collaborative system that analysed users based on their purchase history and browsing behaviour, established groups, and developed a recommender system which suggested purchases based on the search histories of the users themselves and other similar users (Ekstrand, Riedl, and Konstan 2011). Collaborative filtering has gained prominence since the success of Amazon's approach changing customer behaviour with personalised experiences particularly in the e-commerce field. User-based collaborative filtering to identify users with similar tastes and preferences based on their historical behaviour has become a standard approach and interest in recommender systems has increased driven by the demands of e-commerce and online shopping.

Schafer, Konstan, and Riedl (1999) highlighted the importance of recommender systems in e-commerce as they made the user experience easier, increased sales of products across the store, and enhanced customer loyalty. Browsers became buyers and purchased additional products. In e-commerce, the essential role of a recommender system is to automatically generate the right suggestions for the right users based on users' interests and search history to make the experience of shopping more pleasant. However, recommender systems require a large amount of data and learning time to train the models to understand user interests. Recommender systems are considered very powerful tools as they navigate millions of items to select only the item/s which match individual needs to suggest for each user. However, each system is evaluated based on the user's interaction with the suggested recommendation and feedback is provided to the system to retrain the model for more accurate suggestions in the future where matching has been unsatisfactory (Singh 2022).

Research papers have been published on the advantages and difficulties of recommender systems. Some of the issues mentioned that need to be addressed are:

- With the rapid increase in the amount of data produced by users on the Internet, scalability has become a problem and systems that can process large-scale datasets with high accuracy and steady performance need to be built (Ricci, Rokach, and Shapira 2011)
- Computers sometimes find it difficult to comprehend Internet users. A user might choose an item that is out of her/his interest. Many users are not willing to fill out questionnaires. These factors make it difficult for computers to classify user choices correctly. The models must learn to understand the implicit and explicit preferences of users to be able to recommend items that might be of interest
- Privacy is an extremely sensitive matter when gathering user data, and maintaining confidentiality and security of data has become a problematic yet essential feature of recommender systems, and
- Systems might fail to make suggestions and limit or restrict users' choices, preventing them from exploring the variety of items available. Diversity of offerings must be part of the system to ensure the recommender system remains a help rather than a hindrance (Qomariyah 2018).

Natural Language Processing

Natural language processing is one of the core pillars of the AI and data science field.

> Natural language processing, or NLP, combines computational linguistics—rule-based modeling of human language—with statistical and machine learning models to enable computers and digital devices to recognize, understand and generate text and speech (IBM n.d.a)

NLP uses different methods and algorithms to enable successful communication between computers and humans. NLP is where computer science, linguistics, and mathematics come together to convert the natural language of humans to commands that can be understood, executed and regenerated by a machine.

NLP comprises two primary research areas natural language understanding (NLU) and natural language generation (NLG). NLU emphasises making human natural language comprehensible and understandable to a computer by extracting valuable information from text that is said or written. NLG is the opposite where the computer generates a natural language that is understandable by humans from some underlying representation of information or unstructured data (Kang et al. 2020; McDonald 2010; Schank1972). NLP focuses primarily on classification problems rather than regression and uses classification algorithms, such as random forest classification or support vector machines (SVMs). The first step in this process is to represent the data numerically through techniques such as vectorisation (Science Direct 2024), embedding (Barnard 2023), bagging, (IBM n.d.b), or the bag-of-words model. Some of these approaches are explored further in the next section of this chapter.

The purpose of language models is to understand natural language and to predict the probability of the occurrence of a sentence or the next word. Language models can also be used for text generation, which is particularly useful in translation applications. Various techniques, such as counting the frequency of words, and recurrent neural networks (RNN) including long short-term memory (LSTM), can be employed for this purpose. To understand natural language, knowledge graphs are extracted, and inductive and deductive reasoning applied. Deductive reasoning helps the model understand grammar and language rules. It is crucial to comprehend the differences between taxonomy, ontology, and graphs. Understanding the differences between the three will help in data organisation, and information retrieval. Taxonomy provides a hierarchical classification system, while ontology adds meanings and relationships between concepts; finally graphs represent complex relationships between entities. This knowledge is essential for structured data management, accurate data analysis, and facilitating interoperability.

Taxonomy involves naming concepts or entities and organising them based on shared characteristics and can take various structural forms, including hierarchies, and is primarily focused on classification. Ontology involves defining the properties, relationships, and classes used to describe concepts or entities in a specific domain and captures the underlying structure, semantics, and complex relationships within the domain. Graphs are a data structure used to represent relationships between entities or concepts. While they can be used to represent hierarchical structures, they are versatile and can depict various types of connections and structures beyond hierarchies.

Before constructing knowledge graphs, the information must first be extracted from unstructured data. This involves three steps: named entity recognition (NER), named entity linking (NEL), and relation extraction. NER involves labelling words into predefined categories, such as places or objects. NEL links entities to real-world identities, while relation extraction involves extracting knowledge from unstructured data. A knowledge graph is a knowledge base or set of sentences that uses a structured model to store descriptions of entities and their relationships or underlying semantics. A triple is a sequence of three entities, subject, predicate, and object, that codifies a statement. The triples can be stored in a relation description format (RDF), extensible markup language (XML), or graph format. More detail is now provided on some of the topics mentioned in relation to NLP: vectorisation, clustering and support vector machines.

Vectorisation

Vectorisation is the process of converting an algorithm from operating on a single value at a time to operating on a set of values at one time. Term Frequency-Inverse Document Frequency (TF-IDF) assigns a value to each term in a document based on its frequency and inverse document frequency, indicating the importance of the term in the document and its relationship to the collection of documents, bearing in mind that some words appear more frequently in general. The TF-IDF matrix is a numerical measure that indicates the significance of a word in each corpus. Compared to simply counting the frequency of a word, TF-IDF focuses on how often a term is mentioned in the document.

To conduct a more comprehensive analysis and reduce the input dimensions, less significant words can be eliminated in future steps by plotting the components of the TF-IDF matrix and k-means clusters on a two-dimensional plane. Doc2vec is used to create a model that converts groups of words into a single unit for vectorisation. Numeric representations are necessary for machine analysis and TF-IDF or Doc2vec matrices can be used to represent any text document numerically. To avoid issues with word similarity based on frequency, latent semantic analysis (LSA) can be used to analyse the corpus of the document and simulate the meaning of words and passages based on topic similarity rather than frequency. Additionally, latent Dirichlet allocation (LDA) can be used to extract topics from the documents and map them to their respective documents as a probabilistic distribution.

As already mentioned, K-means clustering can be used to reduce the input dimensions. K-means clustering can also be used to discover patterns within the data, to group data points together and to identify underlying structures in the dataset. K-means establishes the centroids for each cluster and assigns the data points to the nearest cluster. By iterating and recalculating the centroids, the algorithm accurately clusters the points in a specific group. K-means clustering is capable of accurately clustering 250 documents in a thousand-dimensional space within minutes.

Support Vector Machines (SVM)

The support vector machines (SVM) classification technique is highly robust due to its use of the kernel method to map data from lower to higher dimensions, enabling the identification of a decision boundary. The approach maximises the width of the decision boundary, ensuring effective discrimination between positive and negative instances. SVM is not only a linear classification model but can also be used for regression problems. To separate data into classes, SVM creates a hyperplane, and the SVC (Support Vector Classifier) function, which is the classification variant of the SVM algorithm, is utilised to fit the data in the TF-IDF matrix and train the corpus of data with TF-IDF-weighted word frequencies. The function returns the best-fit hyperplane that divides or organises the data.

Building a Chatbot

To build a chatbot, there needs to be a bank of answers which can be provided to the questions expected. The chatbot will classify and map questions into a group of appropriate responses. The intent JSON file contains a variety of questions that library users might ask in a typical customer service situation and will contribute to developing appropriate answers to the questions users have in mind. The questions can be mapped against a group of appropriate responses. The tag on each dictionary in the file indicates the group to which a customer's message would belong. The neural network will be trained to analyse the words in a sentence and classify it to one of the tags in the JSON file. The chatbot will be able to take a response from the groups and display the correct answer to the customer.

    The greater the number of tags, responses, and patterns that can be provided to the neural network, the better the chatbot answers will be. Neural networks can be edited, layers added, hyperparameters changed and the network edited to achieve better performance. Convolutional neural networks (CNN) (IBM n.d.c) or recurrent neural networks (RNN) (IBM n.d.d) are recommended for building chatbots locally. And there needs to be lots of data. Larger quantities of data will improve the learning and the outputs. There are various frameworks that can be used: Keras,

PyTorch, TensorFlow, and Apache Spark. Particular frameworks will suit particular situations.

Conclusion

No doubt there will be improvements in NLP approaches, frameworks and techniques that can be applied to the development of chatbot services. Developments in areas like named entity recognition will add more features to the capacity of chatbots. Sentiment analysis could be used to determine whether data is positive, negative or neutral which would help in understanding client needs and could also be used to encourage emotional engagement with a chatbot (Amazon Web Services n.d.). Much more data must be added to the neural networks underpinning the chatbots. Advances in ML, recommender systems, NLP, and associated AI applications have led to significant growth in the use of chatbots in libraries which are capable of providing personalised services to users in multiple languages. "Chatbots are increasingly replacing some of the traditional library services provided by humans, and their role in libraries is expanding rapidly with the evolution of artificial intelligence" (Aboelmaged et al. 2024). Libraries must be openly innovative to capitalise on the opportunities available and ensure that staff are led from an awareness of the technologies to adoption of them and the development of personalised online services for the benefit of library users.

References

Aboelmaged, Mohamed, Shaker Bani-Melhem, Mohd Ahmad Al-Hawari, and Ifzal Ahmad. 2024. "Conversational AI Chatbots in Library Research: An Integrative Review and Future Research Agenda." *Journal of Librarianship and Information Science*. First published online February 6, 2024. https://doi.org/10.1177/09610006231224440

Amazon Web Services. n.d. "What is Sentiment Analysis?" https://aws.amazon.com/what-is/sentiment-analysis/#:~:text=Sentiment%20analysis%20is%20the%20process,social%20media%20comments%2C%20and%20reviews.

Barnard, Joel. 2023. "What is Embedding?" *IBM [Blog]* December 22, 2023. https://www.ibm.com/topics/embedding.

Bernard, Zoë. 2017." Here's What Machine Learning Actually Is." *World Economic Forum*. *Artificial Intelligence*, November 28, 2017. https://www.weforum.org/agenda/2017/11/heres-what-machine-learning-actually-is/.

Cortes, Corinna, and Vladimir Vapnik. 1995. "Support-vector Networks." *Machine Learning* 20: 273-297. http://dx.doi.org/10.1007/BF00994018.

Eick, Christoph F. 2024. "A Gentle Introduction to Machine Learning." [PowerPoint Presentation]. University of Houston. https://www2.cs.uh.edu/~ceick/ai/4368-ML-Intro.pptx.

Ekstrand, Michael D., John T. Riedl, and Joseph A. Konstan. 2011. "Collaborative Filtering Recommender Systems." *Foundations and Trends® in Human–Computer Interaction* 4: 81-173. http://dx.doi.org/10.1561/1100000009.

IBM. n.d.a. "What Is NLP?" https://www.ibm.com/topics/natural-language-processing.

IBM. n.d.b. "What is Bagging?" https://www.ibm.com/topics/bagging.

IBM. n.d.c. "What Are Convolutional Neural Networks?" https://www.ibm.com/topics/convolutional-neural-networks.

IBM. n.d.d. "What are Recurrent Neural Networks?" https://www.ibm.com/topics/recurrent-neural-networks.

Isinkaye, Folasade Olubusola, Yetunde Oluwatoyin Folajimi, and Bolanle Adefowoke Ojokoh. 2015." Recommendation Systems: Principles, Methods, and Evaluation." *Egyptian Informatics Journal* 16: 261-273. https://doi.org/10.1016/j.eij.2015.06.005.

Jones, M. Tim. 2017. "Cognitive Neural Networks: A Deep Dive." *IBM Developer*. July 24, 2017. https://developer.ibm.com/articles/cc-cognitive-neural-networks-deep-dive/.

Kang, Yue, Zhao Cai, Chee-Wee Tan, Qian Huang, and Hefu Liu. 2020. "Natural Language Processing (NLP) in Management Research: A Literature Review." *Journal of Management Analytics* 7, no. 2: 139–172. https://doi.org/10.1080/23270012.2020.1756939.

Konstan, Joseph A., John Riedl, AI Borchers, and Jonathan L. Herlocker. 1998. "Recommender Systems: A GroupLens Perspective." In *AAAI Conference and Symposium Proceedings. Workshop Papers 1998*, 60-64. Association for the Advancement of Artificial Intelligence. https://aaai.org/papers/060-ws98-08-016/.

McDonald, David D. 2010. "Natural Language Generation." In *Handbook of Natural Language Processing* edited by Ninit Indurkhya and Fred J. Damerau. 2nd ed., 121–144. New York: Chapman and Hall.

Mitchell, Tom M. 1997. *Machine Learning*. New York: McGraw-Hill. Available at http://www.cs.cmu.edu/~tom/files/MachineLearningTomMitchell.pdf .

Qomariyah, Nunung Nurul. 2018. "Pairwise Preferences Learning for Recommender Systems." PhD diss., University of York, England. https://etheses.whiterose.ac.uk/20365/1/Main.pdf

Quinlan, John Ross. 1986. "Induction of Decision Trees." *Machine Learning* 1: 81-106. https://doi.org/10.1007/BF00116251. Available at https://hunch.net/~coms-4771/quinlan.pdf.

Ricci, Francesco, Lior Rokach, and Bracha Shapira. 2011. "Introduction to Recommender Systems Handbook." In *Recommender Systems Handbook*, edited by Francesco Ricci, Lior Rokach, Bracha Shapira, and Paul B. Kantor. 1-35. New York: Springer. https://doi.org/10.1007/978-0-387-85820-3_1.

Rich, Elaine. 1979. "User Modeling Via Stereotypes." *Cognitive Science* 3: 329-354. https://onlinelibrary.wiley.com/doi/epdf/10.1207/s15516709cog0304_3.

Rosenblatt, Frank. 1958. "The Perceptron: A Probabilistic Model for Information Storage and Organization in the Brain." *Psychological Review* 65, no. 6: 386–408. https://doi.org/10.1037/h0042519. Available at https://sci-hub.se/10.1037/h0042519.

Samuel, Arthur L. 1959. "Some Studies in Machine Learning Using the Game of Checkers." *IBM Journal of Research and Development* 3, no. 3: 210–229. doi: 10.1147/rd.33.0210. Available at https://ieeexplore.ieee.org/stamp/stamp.jsp?tp=&arnumber=5392560.

Samuel, Arthur L. 1988. "Some Studies in Machine Learning Using the Game of Checkers. II - Recent Progress." In *Computer Games I*, edited by David Neil Laurence Levy, 366-400. New York: Springer. https://doi.org/10.1007/978-1-4613-8716-9_15. Also published in *IBM Journal of Research and*

Development 11, no. 6: 601–617 (1967). https://doi.org/10.1147/rd.116.0601. Available at https://www.cs.virginia.edu/~evans/cs6501-s13/samuel.pdf.

Schafer, J. Ben, Joseph Konstan, and John Riedl. 1999. "Recommender Systems in E-Commerce." In *EC '99: Proceedings of the 1st ACM Conference on Electronic Commerce*, edited by Stuart I. Feldman and Michael P. Wellman, 158-166. Denver: Association for Computing Machinery. https://doi.org/10.1145/336992.337035.

Schank, Roger C. 1972. "Conceptual Dependency: A Theory of Natural Language Understanding." *Cognitive Psychology* 3: 552–631. https://doi.org/10.1016/0010-0285(72)90022-9.

Science Direct. 2024. "Vectorization." https://www.sciencedirect.com/topics/computer-science/vectorization.

Singh, Pramod. 2022. "Recommender Systems." In *Machine Learning with PySpark: With Natural Language Processing and Recommender Systems*, edited by Praod Singh, 157-187. Berkeley: Apress. https://doi.org/10.1007/978-1-4842-7777-5_8.

Werbos, Paul John. 1994. *The Roots of Backpropagation: From Ordered Derivatives to Neural Networks and Political Forecasting.* New York: John Wiley & Sons.

Helen Sau Ching Cheung, Alex Hok Lam Chan, Kenny Ka Lam Kwan
and Yoko Hirose

21 Developing Digital Literacy Using Mini-AI Games

Abstract: The use of digital technologies has transformed learning, teaching, and research Topics like digital humanities have emerged. Artificial intelligence (AI) after initial slow development is becoming embedded in all aspects of life, including education. Students and teachers at all levels are learning coding to use new information and communication technologies (ICT) effectively. Digital literacy has become an important consideration in ensuring that students and faculty have the knowledge and skills required to adopt new approaches and use the various technologies available effectively. Many novice library users lack experience and confidence in their abilities to use ICT effectively in their studies, and find it difficult to learn new techniques. This chapter discusses the need for digital literacy and describes work undertaken as part of an international initiative at the Hong Kong Sheng Kung Hui (HKSKH) Ming Hua Theological College Library (MH Library). Three mini-AI games containing fun elements and embedded library resources were developed as learning materials and used in an innovative library user education programme. The results of the programme have been positive. Participating students and library staff gained additional skills and knowledge in AI and other areas and showed interest in digital literacy.

Keywords: Digital literacy; Artificial intelligence; Programming languages (Computers); Digital humanities; COVID-19 (Disease)

Introduction

The Hong Kong Sheng Kung Hui (HKSKH) Ming Hua Theological College (MH College), serves the Anglican Church in the Province of Hong Kong and Macau following Hong Kong. The Anglican Communion in Hong Kong is known as Hong Kong Sheng Kung Hui (SKH), and also as the Hong Kong Anglican Church (Episcopal). It encompasses over one hundred schools including kindergarten, primary, and secondary schools, tertiary colleges, and churches in Hong Kong. MH College is a tertiary educational institution that provides degrees and diploma programmes, including two separate joint degree programmes with Charles Sturt University (CSU) in Australia and Virginia Theological Seminary (VTS) in the US. The MH College Library houses electronic resources and printed materials on the topics of

Christianity, theology, philosophy, church history and humanities. MH Library has participated in collaborative projects with others in their community and with Japanese parties since 2016.

The COVID-19 pandemic has changed lives, studies, and work models. In developing responses to rapidly developing new situations, MH Library has partnered with local and international parties on a project to work collaboratively to develop training programmes for library users to improve their information use skills in a digital world. The user education project was titled *Connect the World via Libraries* and emphasised online activities and digital experiences. The partners included the Library Fair Management Committee in Japan, RapidsWide in Japan, and the Libraries Research Group (LRG) at Charles Sturt University (CSU) in Australia. The Library Fair Management Committee in Japan is held annually and the exhibition is the largest trade show, information exchange, and exchange place in the library world. RapidsWide is a company providing consulting services for libraries and professional librarians in Japan and overseas. The LRG at CSU focuses on key issues affecting libraries and examines ways in which library and information services can be improved, and library collections enhanced, as well the role of libraries and librarianship in contemporary society.

The Project and its Aims

Librarians in universities, schools, and special libraries, students, faculty, and professionals in Hong Kong, Japan, and Australia are working together through international partnerships to develop a series of library programmes and activities emphasising online and digital experiences to improve the information skills and knowledge of library users. The experiences include tours and talks and the uses of ICT tools and are designed for worldwide online audiences. The project known as *Connect the World via Libraries* aims to:

- Develop new models for educating library users based on fun
- Develop students' digital literacy skills, including ICT skills and subject knowledge, and
- Enhance the visibility and role of librarians and libraries, focusing on the changing roles of librarians in the digital age.

This chapter is a description of a case study of one of MH Library's activities, the development of a mini-AI games programme for user education. Two presentations were made on the project with one at a forum at the Library Fair in 2022 and the second at an AI seminar IFLA mid-term meeting in Singapore in 2023.

Digital Literacy

With an ever-increasing digital environment, many people use technology widely in their daily lives, for study, work, and in their professions. There has been huge growth in online education and the pandemic saw an expansion of delivery of educational and training programmes online throughout the world. Libraries have seen significant growth in e-resources and in online information services. To use technology effectively, people must gain relevant skills. A high level of digital literacy has become essential for people to lead successful lives. Digitally literate people have more economic, educational, professional and social opportunities available to them. Kelly, McGrath and Hubbard in an excellent review of digital skills and coding pointed out "The skill and knowledge to use digital tools is essential both for individuals specifically and for communities generally to take advantage of the opportunities of these technologies" (2023, 488) and highlighted the work and suggestions of other writers (Hadziristic 2017; Roberts, Farrington, and Skerratt 2015; Townsend et al. 2013). "The more digital literacy people have and the higher their skill in using these technologies, the more digital opportunities they pursue" (Kelly, McGrath, and Hubbard 2023, 488). The much-reported digital divide of unequal access to digital technology has been studied in relation to children and young people. Demographic, use and expertise variables are significant factors and contribute to inclusion and exclusion (Livingstone and Helsper 2007). "For children and young people, it seems, the more literacy, the more opportunities are taken up" (Livingstone and Helsper 2007, 647).

Digital literacy has no single definition. In the mini-AI games programme under study, digital literacy is defined as the ability to search, locate, evaluate, and use information, and the use of technology applications effectively, ethically, and with creativity. The approach draws on ideas developed within the United States and Hong Kong (ALA 2021; Hong Kong 2024).

Artificial Intelligence, Digital Humanities and Library User Education

Artificial Intelligence

In general, AI is defined as: "It is the science and engineering of making intelligent machines, especially intelligent computer programs. It is related to the similar task of using computers to understand human intelligence, but AI does not have to confine itself to methods that are biologically observable" (McCarthy 2007, 2).

Digital Humanities

Digital humanities was examined by Kirschenbaum who accepted that the definition provided by Wikipedia was a reasonable one:

> a field of study, research, teaching, and invention concerned with the intersection of computing and the disciplines of the humanities...[involving]investigation, analysis, synthesis, and the presentation of information in electronic form ... (Kirschenbaum 2010, 1-2).

Wikipedia's current definition of digital humanities is slightly different:

> Digital humanities (DH) is an area of scholarly activity at the intersection of computing or digital technologies and the disciplines of the humanities. It includes the systematic use of digital resources in the humanities, as well as the analysis of their application. DH can be defined as new ways of doing scholarship that involve collaborative, transdisciplinary, and computationally engaged research, teaching, and publishing. It brings digital tools and methods to the study of the humanities with the recognition that the printed word is no longer the main medium for knowledge production and distribution (Wikipedia 2024).

AI is impacting on all areas of knowledge and has great potential in exploring teaching, learning, and research. There are many AI developments in digital humanities, such as the use of AI in archaeology and cultural heritage.

> The beginning of the 21st century marks an era of ubiquitous digital technology, big data, and artificial intelligence (AI). Even traditionally technology-hostile domains are now strongly assisted by innovations of advanced digital technology. Archaeology and cultural heritage belong to a particular domain that, although once technology-phobic, has rapidly become digital and advanced technology assisted (Pavlidis 2022, 26).

Library User Education

The aim of library user education is to help users gain skills in effectively using library resources and services (Harisanty, Diba, and Layyinah 2020; Onah et al. 2021). "Library User Education (LUE) is expected to have various positive effects on students' learning outcomes, research practices, and self-motivation for independent learning" (Liu et al. 2019, 9). Libraries of all types provide wide-ranging educational programmes for their users ranging from online library guides in specific subject areas or on targeted topics online videos based on topical areas. The new learning environment based on information technology sets new challenges for teachers, student and librarians. Vast amounts of data collected by educational institutions about and for their students provide the basis for new approaches to learning, teaching and research in education. Library user education is intertwined with digital literacy to ensure that library users gain the skills and knowledge required to find and use information effectively in a digital age. Data mining, machine learning, and other techniques related to AI are being used for academic analysis and prediction (Gómez-Pulido et al. 2023). Libraries are responding to the changes in the educational environment and to new methods of teaching, learning and research and providing user education related to improved skills in the use of digital tools in all subject areas, including digital humanities, and in many techniques which can be used, including coding (Martin 2017; Prato 2017). In response to new ways of knowing, learning, and researching, the mini-AI games project of the MH Library aimed at developing an effective learning model for library user education and digital literacy which would build users' knowledge and skills in discovering, accessing, and using information effectively. The mini-AI games project of the MH library added digital humanities, coding, and AI approaches to information literacy training.

The Changing Roles of Librarians

Society and libraries are undergoing digital transformation. New needs are emerging. The roles and required skills of librarians are changing as they face the new challenges. The changed requirements are reflected in the titles of positions in libraries and in job duty statements with new types of librarians emerging, such as digital humanities librarians, digital scholarship librarians, and librarians in specific subject areas like science, technology, engineering and mathematics (STEM), and enhanced and redeveloped liaison librarian functions. The pedagogical role of librarians has come to the fore as they ensure that teachers and researchers acquire new digital skills which will prepare them for effective performance in new information contexts (Sanches 2019). Crucial digital literacy competencies for librarians include searching for and retrieving information across all information environments, using a wide variety of digital tools including AI, critical thinking, organising ideas, building knowledge collaboratively, and marketing. Professional development for librarians must address all these areas (Novo, Bastos, and Vasconcelos 2017). Since the introduction of computers into libraries, some librarians have developed a knowledge of computer programming, or coding as it is frequently known. Programming languages used to be complex but with the development of simpler techniques, coding skills have become easier for librarians to acquire, and with digital developments and AI techniques, such skills have become more essential as part of the knowledge and skills base and many librarians are acquiring expertise in coding (de la Cruz and Hogan 2016).

Coding

By learning to code, learners not only acquire knowledge in the programming language itself, but also in building digital confidence, and enhanced creativity, critical thinking and problem-solving (Kelly, McGrath, and Hubbard 2022) with Woodward and Fayed suggesting that it should be at the centre of the curriculum (2016). Many novices experience difficulties with learning text-based programming languages, perhaps because of the learning environment or experience used (Mladenović, Boljat, and Žanko 2018). As a result, it has been suggested that block-based programming languages (BBPL) be used to develop students' coding skills with various articles reporting on the use of different languages. Scratch is one language (Resnick et al. 2009); MIT App Inventor is another (da Cruz Alves, Gresse von Wangenheim, and Rossa Hauck 2020); and mBlock is a third (Peng, Bai, and Siswanto 2020). Studies have shown the positive results of using BBPL for students, including the use of friendly interfaces, attractive graphics, and animation functions (Xinogalos, Satratzemi, and Malliarakis 2017). BBPL are effective as introductory programming languages. They have many advantages in improving learning because they avoid syntax errors and allow students to develop creative and logical thinking via block design and games and facilitate students' progression to text-based programming languages (Cárdenas-Cobo et al. 2021; Lin and Weintrop 2021; Simpkins 2014).

The Mini-AI Games Project Details

The broad aims of the project have already been stated. MH Library's involvement related to the development of a fun mini-AI games programme for user education which would develop digital literacy skills and knowledge and enhance the role of the library and its librarians. A demonstration and explanation of the coding elements used in the three mini-AI games can be found in the Appendix to this chapter. The three mini-AI games (Figure 21.1) were:

- Book suggestions by facial expressions, built using mBlock
- Learning Japanese with a shooting game, built using Scratch, and
- SealFinder app for seal script characters, built using the MIT App Inventor (Figure 21.1).

The book suggestions game included recommendations of library books based on users' emotions, happy, bored, or surprised. The second game related to learning the Japanese language and the third game focused on understanding seal script characters, a formerly used style of writing Chinese languages.

Aims

The aims of the mini-AI games by MH Library were:
- Develop a learning model incorporating gamification to enable students to develop digital literacy, basic coding skills, and subject knowledge
- Promote library collections and library user education programmes, and
- Use the mini-AI games as teaching materials for librarians and library staff to use as templates to edit and further develop their own apps and teaching materials.

Participants

The programme divided users into two groups: university students and high school students. The period from August 2022 to July 2023, the MH Library term, was held for programme delivery to the university students, while the period from the summer of 2023 focused on secondary school students. This chapter explores the learning outcomes of the university students who took part in the three mini-AI games, which the MH Library team designed and developed. The MH Library team consisted of a librarian, an IT officer, and student interns, who were university students from engineering, library and information sciences, and humanities subjects from four universities/colleges in Hong Kong.

Design

The mini-AI games embed library user education in digital literacy, coding, and digital humanities to achieve learning goals. When students develop the mini-AI games, they learn and apply the following skills:

–   Digital literacy: identify, search for, evaluate, and use information to develop the games
–   Block-based programming languages: Scratch, mBlock, and App Inventor
–   Basic programming concepts: variables, conditionals, loops and algorithms
–   Subject knowledge: humanities and languages.
–   MH library collections: students need to select library books for the book recommendation AI game. and
–   Other skills: problem-solving, presentation, creativity, and collaboration.

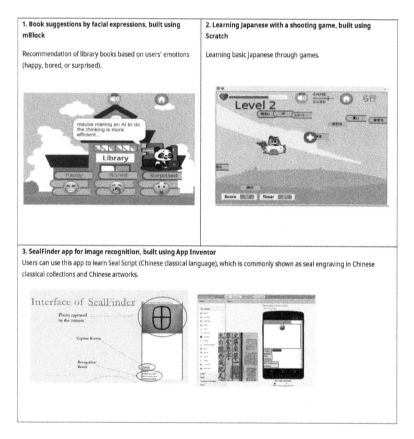

Figure 21.1: The three mini-AI games

The Learning Process

The first phase took place in August 2022. The MH Librarian provided on-the-job training to participating student interns, including digital literacy, such as searching for and evaluating information effectively, demonstrations of Scratch, mBlock, and App Inventor; and an introduction to digital humanities and library collections, including special collections in Chinese classical collections and Japanese books, to give students some ideas for the topics of the mini-AI games.

The second phase was held from September to November 2022. Student interns worked together to design and develop the mini-AI games. Two engineering students used App Inventor, Scratch, and mBlock to develop the games. Another five students from the humanities, the library, and information science provided assistance in preparing materials, such as booklists, and carried out usability tests. When the students had completed the prototypes of the mini-AI games, several librarians from universities and schools in Hong Kong and Japan provided feedback. Following the feedback, the MH Library team adjusted the mini-AI games.

The third phase commenced in November 2022. The mini-AI games programme is part of the international project *Connect the World via Libraries* and was presented online at the Japan Fair in November 2022. The MH Library team including the librarian and the student interns gave an online presentation to demonstrate the three mini-AI demo games to worldwide audiences. The presentation was in English, with Japanese subtitles added for Japanese speakers. Most of the online audiences were librarians, students, and faculty members in Asia, with some audience members from Australia, Europe, and North America. The presentation at the Japan Fair resulted in positive outcomes and feedback; for example, after the online event, a secondary school in Hong Kong used the mini-AI games as templates, adapting them for use on their library's open day.

The fourth phase was held from December 2022 to July 2023. The MH Library team enhanced and developed the final versions of the three mini-AI games and prepared how-to-use videos as teaching materials in English, Chinese, and Japanese, in cooperation with libraries in Hong Kong and Japan. A presentation was also made at an IFLA seminar on AI in Singapore in March 2023.

Outcomes and Lessons Learned

The mini-AI games programme works effectively as a creative learning framework for collaboratively building knowledge by combining elements of digital literacy including coding, with subject knowledge, and library collections. Intuitive blocks of Scratch, mBlock, and App Inventor and add-on functions, such as the AI block in mBlock and image classifier in App Inventor, are helpful in building the skills and confidence learners need to take the first steps in coding. Overall, the programme benefitted students, librarians, and international partnerships.

Student Benefits

When developing the SealFinder app, students have to search for and access accurate seal script images as training data. In the beginning, students sourced incorrect script images from an unreliable website. With the guidance of the librarians, the students became aware of the importance of using reliable e-resources and how to evaluate information. The students also enhanced their knowledge of citation styles, referencing, and plagiarism.

The humanities students and library and information science students involved in this project, who were novices in programming and coding, learned concepts such as variables, loops, and algorithms. To overcome the limitations of BBPL, such as the accuracy and functions of mini-AI games, text-based programming languages, such as Python, were required. This motivated the engineering students involved in the project to progress, learn more source code, and create advanced functions, such as deep learning. They also enhanced their problem-solving skills, such as debugging.

Students expanded their knowledge in humanities subjects via the mini-AI games and learned about Chinese classical language through the seal script characters and also learned Japanese. The students acquired knowledge about the library collections by, for example, selecting the library collections as source material for the book suggestion AI game.

Other student skills were enhanced. They gained skills in graphics and creativity, which are necessary to create the interface, storyline, and dialogue of the games. They also learned to work independently and as members of a team. Their writing skills improved along with public speaking, through making presentations to online audiences.

The Changing Role of the Librarian

The mini-AI games programme under study makes evident the multiple roles of librarians as instructors in digital literacy, academic writing, citation styles, and referencing skills for students, as researchers, designing and evaluating the programme, an as teammates when developing the games with students. To adapt to new technology, librarians must shape multiple skills in various areas, such as coding and research, actively market library services, design innovative user education programmes, and adopt the role of lifelong learners.

International Partnerships

Through international partnerships, librarians can provide learning materials for the programme in three languages: English, Chinese, and Japanese. This could benefit and attract people from around the world to join the programme. Librarians, faculty, professionals, and students from various countries and locations can share knowledge, expand learning experiences and research areas, and develop a global framework for developing essential skills, such as digital literacy and coding skills.

Conclusion

Ensuring digital literacy for all in today's high tech big data environment is essential. Digital humanities is an important component of today's academic environment and students and librarians alike require sophisticated ICT skills to participate actively in teaching, learning, and research activities. Educational programmes for library users and professional development activities for librarians can provide opportunities for gaining the knowledge and skills required. The study of coding is one way of gaining skills in digital literacy to be applied in various environments, and studying the skills has many other benefits related to personal and professional development. The mini-AI games under study have enabled the development of a model combining digital literacy, coding, digital humanities, and library collections for user education with positive outcomes. This study has shown that BBPL are useful as an introduction to coding, to the AI world, and to creating apps. BBPL are also useful in the digital transition that facilitates learners' progression to advanced coding languages. Libraries of all types can provide BBPL workshops to a wide range of library users, not only for children and young people, but also for adults. Library schools and professional associations providing training should consider adding BBPL courses to library and information science programmes for librarians.

Acknowledgments

Thank you to all facilitators, audiences, and participating institutions involved in this study. We would also like to thank Professor Fumiko Kohama and Ms Asami Tanaka, The Rare Book Library, Rissho University; Ms Sachiko Kamakura; Ms Hikaru Nakano at the Senri International School of Kwansei Gakuin; Mr Kenji Yagi; Ms Inger Kwok at the Diocesan Girls' School; Principal Pang Yiu Kwan and Ms Kwok Wing Yan at Caritas Chong Yuet Ming Secondary School; Ms Ma Wai Ling at SKH Tsang Shiu Tim Secondary School; Dr Sam Chu at the University of Hong Kong; Associate Professor Mary Carroll, Dr Jane Garner, Dr Mary Anne Kennan, the Libraries Research Group at Charles Sturt University; and Professor Yuriko Nakamura at Rikkyo University.

References

American Library Association (ALA). 2011. "Digital Literacy." Office of Information Technology Policy (OITP). Digital Literacy Task Force. https://alair.ala.org/handle/11213/16260.

Cárdenas-Cobo, Jesennia, Amilkar Puris, Pavel Novoa-Hernández, Águeda Parra-Jiménez, Jesús Moreno-León, and David Benavides. 2021. "Using Scratch to Improve Learning Programming in College Students: A Positive Experience from a Non-WEIRD Country." *Electronics* 10, no. 10: 1180. https://doi.org/10.3390/electronics10101180.

da Cruz Alves, Nathalia, Christiane Gresse von Wangenheim, and Jean Carlo Rossa Hauck. 2020. "Teaching Programming to Novices: A Large-Scale Analysis of App Inventor Projects." In *2020 XV Conferencia Latinoamericana de Tecnologias de Aprendizaje (LACLO)*, 1–10. Ithaca: IEEE. https://doi.org/10.1109/LACLO50806.2020.9381172.

de la Cruz, Justin, and Joshua Hogan. 2016. " 'Hello, World!': Starting a Coding Group for Librarians." *Public Services Quarterly* 12, no. 3: 249–256. https://doi.org/10.1080/15228959.2016.1197082. Available at http://hdl.handle.net/20.500.12322/auc.rwwlpub:0009.

Gómez-Pulido, Juan A., Young Park, Ricardo Soto, and José M. Lanza-Gutiérrez. 2023. "Data Analytics and Machine Learning in Education." *Applied Sciences* 13, no. 3: 1418. https://doi.org/10.3390/app13031418.

Hadziristic, Tea. 2017. *The State of Digital Literacy in Canada: A Literature Review.* Toronto: Brookfield Institute for Innovation + Entrepreneurship. Working paper. https://brookfieldinstitute.ca/wp-content/uploads/BrookfieldInstitute_State-of-Digital-Literacy-in-Canada_Literature_WorkingPaper.pdf.

Harisanty, Dessy, Aulia Farah Diba, and Khoirotun Layyinah. 2020. "The Effectiveness Program of User Education at University of Malaya's Library." *Library Philosophy and Practice (e-journal)*: 4227. https://digitalcommons.unl.edu/libphilprac/4227.

Hong Kong. Education Bureau. 2024. "Information Literacy for Hong Kong Students: Learning Framework." https://www.edb.gov.hk/attachment/en/edu-system/primary-secondary/applicable-to-primary-secondary/it-in-edu/information-literacy/il_learningframework/informationliteracyforhongkongstudentslearningframework(2024)_eng.pdf.

Kelly, Wayne, Brian McGrath, and Danielle Hubbard. 2023. "Starting From 'Scratch': Building Young People's Digital Skills Through a Coding Club Collaboration With Rural Public Libraries." *Journal of Librarianship and Information Science* 55, no. 2: 487–499. First published online May 3, 2022. https://doi.org/10.1177/09610006221090953.

Kirschenbaum, Matthew. 2010. "What is Digital Humanities and What's it Doing in English Departments?" *ADE Bulletin* 150: 1–7. https://www.uvic.ca/humanities/english/assets/docs/kirschenbaum.pdf.

Lin, Yuhan, and David Weintrop. 2021. "The Landscape of Block-Based Programming: Characteristics of Block-Based Environments and How They Support the Transition to Text-Based Programming." *Journal of Computer Languages* 67: 101075. https://doi.org/10.1016/j.cola.2021.101075.

Liu, Qianxiu, Bradley Allard, Patrick Lo, Qingshan Zhou, Tianji Jiang, and Hiroshi Itsumura. 2019. "Library User Education as a Window to Understand Inquiry-Based Learning in the Context of Higher Education in Asia: A Comparative Study Between Peking University and the University of Tsukuba." *College & Research Libraries* 80, no. 1: 8–31. https://doi.org/10.5860/crl.80.1.8.

Livingstone, Sonia, and Ellen Helsper. 2007. "Gradations in Digital Inclusion: Children, Young People and the Digital Divide." *New Media & Society* 9, no. 4: 671–696. https://doi.org/10.1177/1461444807080335. Available at https://eprints.lse.ac.uk/2768/1/Gradations_in_digital_inclusion_%28LSERO%29.pdf.

Martin, Crystle. 2017. "Libraries as Facilitators of Coding for all." *Knowledge Quest* 45, no. 3: 46–53. Available at https://eric.ed.gov/?id=EJ1125376.

McCarthy, John. 2007. "What is Artificial Intelligence?" http://www-formal.stanford.edu/jmc/whatisai.pdf.

Mladenović, Monika, Ivica Boljat, and Žana Žanko. 2018. "Comparing Loops Misconceptions in Block-Based and Text-Based Programming Languages at the K-12 Level." *Education and Information Technologies* 23, no. 4: 1483–1500. https://doi.org/10.1007/s10639-017-9673-3. Available at https://www.researchgate.net/publication/321332296_Comparing_loops_misconceptions_in_block-based_and_text-based_programming_languages_at_the_K-12_level.

Novo, Ana, Glória Bastos, and Ana Isabel Vasconcelos. 2017. "Effects of a Virtual Learning Environment on Librarians' Information Literacy and Digital Literacy Competences." In *Information Literacy in Everyday Life, 6th European Conference, ECIL 2018, Oulu, Finland, September 24–27, 2018, Revised Selected Papers*, edited by Serap Kurbanoğlu, Sonja Špiranec, Yurdagül Ünal, Joumana Boustany, Maija Leena Huotari, Esther Grassian, Diane Mizrachi, and Loriene Roy, 655–664. Springer International Publishing. https://doi.org/10.1007/978-3-319-52162-6_64. Available at https://www.scribd.com/document/353050896/10-1007-2F978-3-319-52162-6-64.

Onah, Jude Chidike, Ebubechukwu Arinze Okonkwo, Nwando Ogochukwu Eseni, and Fatima O. Momohjimoh. 2021. "Adopting Flipped Classroom Model for Effective Library User Education in Nigerian Universities: Challenges and Strategies." *Library Philosophy and Practice (e-journal)*: 5028. https://digitalcommons.unl.edu/libphilprac/5028.

Pavlidis, George. 2022. "AI Trends in Digital Humanities Research." *Trends in Computer Science and Information Technology* 7, no. 2: 26–34. https://doi.org/10.17352/tcsit.000048.

Peng, Li Hsun, M. H. Bai, and I. Siswanto. 2020. "A Study of Learning Motivation of Senior High Schools by Applying Unity and mBlock on Programming Languages Courses." *Journal of Physics. Conference Series* 1456, no. 1: 012037. https://doi.org/10.1088/1742-6596/1456/1/012037.

Prato, Stephanie C. 2017. "Beyond the Computer Age: A Best Practices Intro for Implementing Library Coding Programs." *Children & Libraries* 15, no. 1: 19–21. https://doi.org/10.5860/cal.15n1.19.

Resnick, Mitchel, John Maloney, Andrés Monroy-Hernández, Natalie Rusk, Evelyn Eastmond, Karen Brennan, Amon Millner, et al. 2009. "Scratch: Programming for All." *Communications of the ACM* 52, no. 11: 60–67. https://doi.org/10.1145/1592761.1592779.

Roberts, Elisabeth, John Farrington, and Sarah Skerratt. 2015. "Evaluating New Digital Technologies through a Framework of Resilience." *Scottish Geographical Journal* 131, no. 3–4: 253–264. https://doi.org/10.1080/14702541.2015.1068947.

Sanches, Tatiana. 2019. "Changing Roles for Research and Information Skills Development: Librarians as Teachers, Researchers as Learners." In *Information Literacy in Everyday Life, 6th European Conference, ECIL 2018, Oulu, Finland, September 24–27, 2018, Revised Selected Papers*, edited by Serap Kurbanoğlu, Sonja Špiranec, Yurdagül Ünal, Joumana Boustany, Maija Leena Huotari, Esther Grassian, Diane Mizrachi, and Loriene Roy, 462–471. https://doi.org/10.1007/978-3-030-13472-3_44.

Simpkins, N. K. 2014. "I Scratch and Sense But Can I Program?: An Investigation of Learning with a Block Based Programming Language." *International Journal of Information and Communication Technology Education* 10, no. 3: 87–116. https://doi.org/10.4018/ijicte.2014070107. Available at https://oro.open.ac.uk/39215/1/21_VisualProgrammingInvestigationInlineImagesRevised.pdf .

Townsend, Leanne, Arjuna Sathiaseelan, Gorry Fairhurst, and Claire Wallace. 2013. "Enhanced Broadband Access as a Solution to the Social and Economic Problems of the Rural Digital Divide." *Local Economy* 28, no. 6: 580–595. https://doi.org/10.1177/0269094213496974.

Wikipedia. 2024. "Digital Humanities." Last edited March 18. 2024. https://en.wikipedia.org/wiki/Digital_humanities.

Woodward, John R., and Marwan Fayed. 2016. "Why Everyone Should Have to Learn Computer Programming." *The Conversation*, July 13, 2016. https://theconversation.com/why-everyone-should-have-to-learn-computer-programming-62328.

Xinogalos, Stelios, Maya Satratzemi, and Christos Malliarakis. 2017. "Microworlds, Games, Animations, Mobile Apps, Puzzle Editors and More: What is Important for an Introductory Programming Environment?" *Education and Information Technologies* 22, no. 1: 145–176. https://doi.org/10.1007/s10639-015-9433-1.

Appendix: Demonstration and explanation of coding elements in three mini-AI games

How the authors of the mini-AI games define the basic programming concepts in their works:

Variables, conditionals, loops, and algorithms

Variables

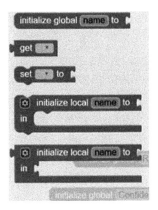

Variables are abundant in all kinds of programmes. A name is first assigned to the variable, and then the variable is used to store values that will be referenced and manipulated in the programme. Variables can also be used to label data in order to enhance the readability of the code. Declared variables can be used throughout the computer programme.

Conditionals

Conditionals are one of the control methods in a programme. Conditionals are used to instruct the computer programme to execute a command if some given conditions are fulfilled. The most common and entry-level conditional statements are if–conditionals and if–else–conditionals. If the condition is fulfilled, the result 'True' is returned and the command will be executed. Otherwise, the result 'False' is returned and the command will not be executed. To increase the number and complexity of the judging conditions, the conditional statements can be nested, that is, enclosed inside other conditional statements to include more layers of judging conditions.

Loops

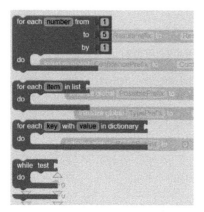

A loop is another control method in a programme. The operation of a loop is a continuous cycle of certain procedures. Common loops include for–loop and while–loop: for–loop is a loop with a counter that will operate a number of times based on its parameters; and while–loop is a loop with conditions that will operate continuously as long as the conditions are fulfilled.

Algorithm

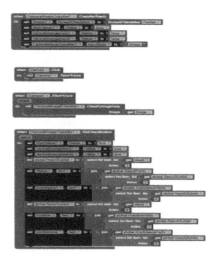

An algorithm is the structure and problem-solving approach of one procedure or even the whole programme. Depending on the complexity of the algorithm, it can be a combination of variables, conditions, and loops. Any set of steps of logical statements, such as codes, that aims to solve a certain problem or achieve a certain goal can be referred to as an algorithm.

Integrative feature

Applications are created for users. The user interface is important for users to be able to utilize the functions. The user interface is an integration with graphic design and programming functions where the code is written to control the components of the app.

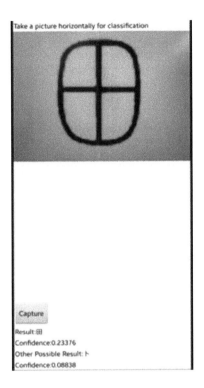

i) Book suggestions by facial expressions, built mBlock

Interface

Block coding

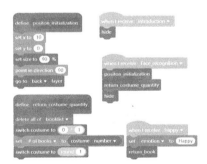

Variables

The facial expression of the user is used as an input variable for book recommendations.
AI is used to determine the facial expression of a library user. The pre-trained weight of typical facial expressions is deployed to determine the user's facial expression, which in turn is used to recommend books in the corresponding category.

Conditional if–statements

The main structure of the book recommendation is composed of if–statements, which control the output for each facial expression.

Loops

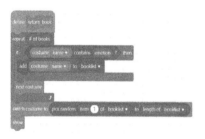

A loop is used to construct the sorting algorithm, as explained below. The purpose of a loop is to execute a certain range of a code or a function multiple times with specified criteria fulfilled. Here, since the sorting algorithm must be chekked among all the books in the booklist, the loop is used to repeat the process until the checking of the entire booklist is complete.

Sorting algorithm

A sorting algorithm is applied to categorise the books into their corresponding facial expressions.

The programme uses a name-matching sorting technique to categorise every book in the booklist. For example, if books in the "happy" category are required, the sorting algorithm will be executed to sort all the "happy" books in the booklist. To enlist a book into a specific category, its name must be renamed with a specified format: (emotion) + (index).

Integrative

In the integration of several elements into a single unified platform, the book recommendation feature is part of the whole project. Individual features are integrated into a single platform to mimic the offering of library services via a library platform, such as the library website.

It is necessary to apply programming concepts with flexibility and consistency.

ii) A shooting game for learning Japanese, built using Scratch

Interface

Block coding

Variables

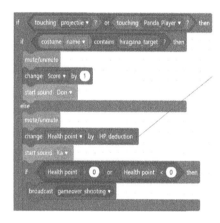

Variables are abundant in any kind of programme. The picture here shows one of several uses of variables in the shooting game.

Variables here include the score, health points, and health points (HP) deductions, which are important parameters in the game. The meaning of individual variables is as their name suggests. Throughout the gameplay, the value of the abovementioned variables will change and affect the gameplay experience.

Conditionals

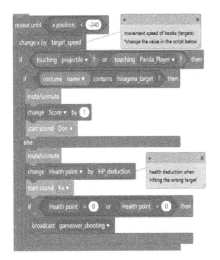

The use of nested if–statements is involved on multiple occasions in the shooting game, for example in the hit detection and timer. Nested statements, in which the output is judged by more than one condition, are common.

Algorithm

A sorting algorithm is used to control specific types of books in the book list. In the shooting game, the spawn probability of target books is enhanced around 2.5 to 3 times that of non-target books, so players can become more attached and kept busy in their gameplay. The particular type of each book is sorted in every unique game to increase the respective spawn probability.

Integrative

The integration of computer knowledge, art, and creativity in game development are interdisciplinary skills that are crucial to making any product appealing to users.

iii) Seal Finder, built using App Inventor

1. Interface Design

2. Block coding

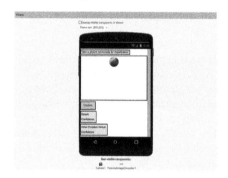

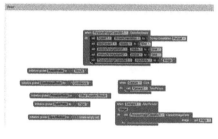

Coding elements demonstrated in the Seal Finder App

Variables – photo input and data output

Variables – photo input and data output

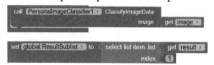

The photo captured using a phone camera is an independent variable and acts as an input to the app so that the programme can read the photo and generate the recognition result.

The recognition result is a dependent variable that is a list of results, including the confidence of different possible instances of recognition.

Conditionals – workflow control

The workflow of the app is controlled by the when function in App Inventor and is similar to if–conditionals. The if–conditionals are used to decide which action the app should perform next.

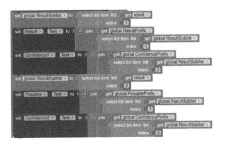

Algorithm – Greedy algorithm

The algorithm of the app uses a Greedy algorithm to give the best result in each layer of the decision-making condition. Each instance of text recognition goes through a chain of decision-making processes and eventually returns the result with the highest level of confidence. After the classification process, only two results with the highest level of confidence will be shown.

The algorithm can run efficiently, as the decision-making process is simple, and so this algorithm is common. However, the algorithm may not produce the optimal solution because it makes decisions before validating all solutions and may miss better possible solutions.

Integrative functions – User Interface (UI)

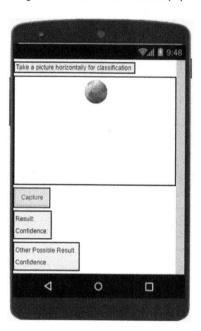

The elements in the user interface are integrated with programming blocks, where the blocks determine the behaviour of different parts on the screen, such as buttons and text.

Itai Veltzman and Rael Elstein

22 How Ex Libris Uses Artificial Intelligence and Smart Services to Transform Libraries

Abstract: Ex Libris is a member of the Clarivate group and with three decades of involvement in the business of academic institutions, libraries and technology companies, works closely with its stakeholder community, user groups and partners to provide services which manage access to and delivery of scholarly content and enhance goal achievement of the organisations and individuals concerned. Ex Libris is working to embrace generative AI and new technologies in the implementation of value-added products which ensure the effective, accurate and responsible implementation of new services by its client groups. This chapter explores some of the initiatives being examined and offered by Ex Libris.

Keywords: Library management systems; Artificial intelligence in libraries; Transformation; Information retrieval systems

Introduction

Ex Libris™, a part of Clarivate™, is a leading global provider of intelligent and forward thinking library solutions, empowering libraries, academic institutions and research organisations. With a rich history and an extensive portfolio, Ex Libris is at the forefront of technological advancements, including artificial intelligence (AI) serving a diverse customer base worldwide, comprising academic libraries, national libraries, library consortia, research institutions and museums. Ex Libris solutions are trusted by thousands of institutions in over 90 countries, enabling optimisation of operations, improvement of user experiences and smart, data-driven decisions by utilising best-fit modern technologies, such as AI.

> With three decades of continuous innovation and together with our global community of industry leaders from academic institutions, libraries, and technology powerhouses, we are embracing generative AI, linked open data and conversational discovery. Leveraging the latest innovation to optimize library management, research, teaching and learning across the entire higher education ecosystem (Ex Libris n.d.a).

With a strong commitment to innovation, Ex Libris' primary focus is ensuring that modern technologies such as AI are used to solve real challenges, resulting in exciting new developments in recent months. For example, over the past year students have increasingly incorporated the use of generative AI in their research and homework, often with unreliable results. In response, Ex Libris has developed the Primo Research Assistant which provides immediate answers to natural language queries and offers visibility into dependable resources and references, emphasising transparency, proper accreditation, and intellectual property rights. Ex Libris is also prioritising the automation of simple but time-consuming tasks for library staff with products such as Specto that harnesses AI technology to enhance metadata records for resources like digital collections, to expedite cataloguing and discovery of valuable insights and information.

By empowering libraries with cutting-edge technologies, Ex Libris plays a pivotal role in facilitating the discovery, access and preservation of knowledge in today's digital age. As part of its growth strategy, Ex Libris is continuously looking to develop exciting new opportunities and directions for libraries, made possible through the responsible implementation of new information technologies such as AI and machine learning (ML).

Clarivate is home to Ex Libris, Innovative™ and ProQuest™, as well as industry-leading solutions such as the Web of Science™, engaging students, research and faculty in all learning environments. A Clarivate data science team has been created to support Clarivate's mission to advance the success of people and organisations through transformative intelligence and trusted partnerships.

> Clarivate is a global leader in trusted and transformative intelligence. We bring together enriched data, insights, analytics and workflow solutions, grounded in deep domain expertise across the spectrum of knowledge, research and innovation. Whether it's providing insights to transform the water industry or accelerating the delivery of a critical vaccine, our aim is to fuel the world's greatest breakthroughs by harnessing the power of human ingenuity (Clarivate 2024a).

The organisation uses AI and other technologies to facilitate customer insights, enhance user experience and boost efficiency.

As part of the Clarivate family, Ex Libris benefits from the synergy with other best-in-class solutions, services and trusted content offered by Clarivate, a global leader in connecting people and organisations to intelligence. Clarivate curates trusted, diversified content and services; is committed to data privacy; supports unified and personalised discovery; and connects library technology, powered by AI and linked data.

AI has the potential to revolutionise the world, but its effectiveness relies heavily on the quality of the data manipulated and massaged. With billions of trusted and curated articles, books, documents and propriety best-in-class data points, the Clarivate family is well-placed to lead the market in making the most of the opportunities presented. The AI landscape is changing rapidly. Clarivate and Ex

Libris keep all developments under close observation to think innovatively and to plan ahead no matter what new technologies might emerge, with clients and customers confident in their reliance on the organisations for partnerships which will take libraries forward in meeting emerging needs.

Library Services

Ex Libris library services span nearly all areas that academic and non-academic libraries require in order to provide innovative tools and deliver better experiences to librarians, researchers and users. The following lists the Ex Libris services and relevant terminology to be used subsequently in this chapter. The services outlined include, but are not limited to discovery and delivery, metadata management, support of teaching and learning, and support of research:

–   Discovery and delivery
    –   Discovery refers to all patron-facing or end-user interfaces providing search and discovery services within the library catalogue to access physical, digital, and electronic resources and information content, both locally held and/or globally managed, and
    –   Delivery refers to all librarian-facing or internal library interfaces providing services to manage the library's collection of physical, digital, and electronic resources, both locally held and globally accessed, from acquisition to fulfilment, including all supporting services within libraries and between libraries as part of consortium agreements or other collaborations which might exist.
–   Metadata management
    Ex Libris products and services support the management of content solely on the metadata level, while the content itself may be stored or hosted on various other platforms, such as catalogues or databases provided by the library or external content providers. The services of Ex Libris support large-scale metadata management within its KnowledgeBase which contains multiple databases from many providers, and stores article, book, and journal-level metadata for collection management, access permissions and fulfilment purposes, amongst others
–   Support of teaching and learning
    Teachers and learners within academic institutions require professional support and rely on library resources and services to conduct and participate in lessons and courses. For example, educators and librarians create reading lists for courses taught within educational institutions to make information content and learning materials easily discoverable, accessible and available

to students and learners from within the library and information resources held or accessed remotely at no personal charge to users because access to or ownership of the information resources has already been purchased by the library, and
– Support of research
  Research is the backbone of many academic institutions. Researchers require support not only for searching, discovering, and accessing relevant content but also in the preparation of research outputs, communication, and collaborative activity with other researchers both within their own institutions and externally, and funding for research projects. Various services can assist in these activities both for librarians and the researchers themselves.

Technological Developments

With AI technological and conceptual advancements over recent years, Ex Libris, like other library software solutions providers, has been continuously developing tools and features powered by AI to provide better support for the customer community and to address new challenges and needs.

AI tools are just one of the ways in which Ex Libris can augment its products, tools and services. AI has great potential to change the entire world. Whether its impact is for better or worse depends on legislative frameworks, organisational strategies and how service providers and users engage with and deploy new tools and technologies. Everyone wants to ensure that the use of AI technology solves real problems and community needs and Ex Libris wishes to ensure that its customers are confident in purchasing new products and optimising functionality of existing services so that any critical decisions made will result in successful outcomes mitigating any risks involved. Importantly, most AI tools are only as good as the data input to them. For many years Ex Libris has been actively researching and implementing AI across its portfolio to enhance its services and solutions. Ex Libris is mindful of the massive potential of such applications, while being fiercely protective of data from all sources to ensure the privacy and security of customers and partners, as well as users of services.

The following sections outline several examples of AI technologies which have been implemented in various Ex Libris products, ranging from rules-based responses to ML advancements, and research into deep learning technologies. Four products are examined: Data Analysis Recommendations Assistant (DARA); Esploro; Use of Knowledge Graph in the Ex Libris Central Discovery Index (CDI); and Rialto Selection Plans.

Data Analysis Recommendation Assistant (DARA)

Data Analysis Recommendation Assistant (DARA) is used in Alma. Alma is one of the few unified library services platforms in the world which manages print, electronic, and digital materials through a single interface. It is a library management system (LMS) or integrated library system (ILS) that provides secure, scalable end-to-end library software for managing the acquisition, sharing, cataloguing, discovery, access and use of all kinds of information resources.

Released back in 2019, DARA is an early example of a rules-based AI engine hot that provides users of Alma with smart recommendations to improve workflows and optimise usage of Alma. DARA also explains how and why a specific recommendation is generated, and provides a service to implement the recommended action, all in one. If action is required by the user, DARA will guide the user through the process to ensure it is completed successfully. The success and usefulness of DARA within the Alma product is due to its recommendations being powered by a large data input of community best practices and optimal workflows.

Ex Libris is looking to develop DARA further and to upgrade its engine from a rules-based approach to incorporate ML technology. This advancement will enable the system to offer a greater variety of smart recommendations from workflow optimisation to collection management insights based on anonymised data collected within Alma (Ex Libris n.d.b).

Esploro

Esploro is a research information management solution which drives research impact and improves efficiency and effectiveness. "Esploro Research Portal and Profiles automatically captures publications and datasets, connecting all information into one portrait of your institution" (Clarivate 2024b). It breaks down data silos, linking comprehensive scholarly information across all academic disciplines. Institutional or research repositories assemble, organise and disseminate the research outputs of organisations to publicise their research. Esploro facilitates the automatic capture of research output and data, improving an institution's ability to showcase its research, enrich its reporting, and relieve the administrative burden. Smart harvesting AI is at the heart of how Esploro facilitates keeping research repositories and researcher profiles comprehensive, accurate and always up to date. It uses AI to manage accurate and complete research information.

The strength of Esploro lies in the connections it facilitates between authors, researchers, and the associated content of their publications and communications. Those connections are driven by smart harvesting from the Central Discovery Index

(CDI) for author identification and matching based on multiple data points, such as name and ORCID ID to import an author's list of known publications from the CDI:

> The Ex Libris Central Discovery Index (CDI) is a central, unified index, for scholarly and academic material worldwide. It contains over 5 billion records and many different resource types from thousands of publishers, aggregators, and repositories. CDI is content neutral and indexes any type of subscribed, purchased or open access content that is of use for research, teaching, and learning. While CDI primarily focusses on metadata, it also indexes full text for part of the content. In addition to what is indexed, CDI encompasses a suite of services available via an API and our discovery systems, Primo and Summon (Ex Libris n.d.c).

When there are missing data or no ORCID ID, Esploro will continue cross-referencing and searching to find the correct author, based on name, subject area and research affiliation, and will then indicate the probability of the match when associating publications to the researcher's profile (Ex Libris n.d.d, 2022).

Use of Knowledge Graph in the Ex Libris Central Discovery Index (CDI)

As already mentioned, the Central Discovery Index (CDI) is a central, unified index for scholarly and academic materials produced worldwide which is created and maintained by Ex Libris. With over 5.26 billion records, the CDI manages a vast variety of resource types from thousands of publishers, aggregators and repositories. Its goal is to provide smart services for excellent information discovery, access and use experiences. CDI powers the Ex Libris Primo and Summon discovery search engines, as well as other products that rely on this extensive database. The CDI has been developed and designed with the foresight for it to support contextual relations based on a knowledge graph or semantic network approach (IBM n.d.) for effective search and discovery, both intentional and serendipitous. Based on contextual connections, whether derived from formal or informal relations, CDI and the search engines it powers can generate smart services, relevant search recommendations, glanceable associations on the screen and insightful discovery paths.

It must be noted that any and all data-generated insights rely solely on the existing metadata and content available within the CDI itself. The CDI content scope is maintained and carefully curated by Ex Libris in collaboration with the customer community to ensure that any ingested content serves organisational and client joint goals of making relevant, appropriate, and high-quality content available to library patrons.

CDI and the knowledge graph enable discovery beyond searching by using contextual relations. Contextual relationships can be expressed in a variety of ways, including formal, informal and curated. Formal connections are the most familiar classic connections, such as a book and the chapters within it. Informal connections are more tangential, like co-usage within the bX article recommender, which "captures anonymous usage information from millions of scholars around the world, then leverages this data to enrich and expand the user discovery experience with relevant recommendations for articles and ebooks" (Ex Libris n.d.e). Exploratory content that other users have looked at is recommended. Curated relationships are empirical connections such as the citation trail which draws on articles citing each other, or reading lists and collections created by the library or others, thereby fashioning associations between content.

Rialto Selection Plans

ProQuest's product Rialto™ is a one-stop vendor-neutral marketplace for academic content from a variety of publishers, aggregators and platforms. "Built on the Ex Libris Higher-Ed cloud platform, Rialto creates a seamless, unified and end-to-end library workflow from requests and searches to selection, acquisition, and discovery" (Ex Libris n.d.f). Applying next generation technology and innovative thinking to address the challenges of legacy approval collection management and selection plans in managing profiles, the Rialto selection plans have been created, predicting spending and coordinating disparate profiles. The Selection Plans are library-configured queries, and contain rules and spending caps that allow libraries to prioritise the purchase of the highest-value titles available at any time. At each purchase interval, Rialto identifies relevant content, sorts and ranks results on outcomes as determined by the library, chooses actions to take on those titles and presents details for review by librarians before final action is taken. Further information is available about the Selection Plans in a white paper on Rialto (ProQuest n.d.).

What Next?

In looking to the future and the immense possibilities surrounding the use of AI and other new technological advances, the basic tenet remains that AI tools are just one of the many ways used by Ex Libris to augment its products, tools and services. There are many real-world challenges that can benefit from AI-powered solutions. Ex Libris is excited to be at the forefront, investigating the enormous potential for AI and examining how AI can benefit the user community.

The following is an illustrative list of initiatives that are being actively pursued based on current expectations of future developments and on information currently available. But the area is rapidly evolving and final results may differ materially from current expectations. Three areas are addressed: Discovery, Collection Development, and Metadata Management.

Discovery

Within discovery, developments are expected to cover conversational search and discovery, additional resource recommendations, recommendations for related articles and citation extraction from syllabi files.

Conversational Search and Discovery

The need for and knowledge of Boolean queries and exact searches is occurring less frequently and becoming less commonplace. A simplified approach to search and discovery such as that provided by Google's search engine is recognised to be highly intuitive and one of the most common ways users interact with everyday search enquiries. Conversational searches, such as questions and prompts, are easier for users to generate and Ex Libris is looking at generative AI technologies and partnerships to match users' approaches and enable them to search intuitively and easily.

How search results are displayed is also evolving. Based on trends in the consumer industry, users expect bundled responses with informative summaries that are both useful and efficiently obtained. AI technologies can be used to generate quick, extensive, and accurate summaries based on vast amounts of data. Yet not all data are equal; AI outputs can only be as good as the input data. It is important that trusted, reliable scholarly content, including references and citations, is the foundation for generating AI-powered results. Ex Libris is seeking to enable intuitive academic conversational search and discovery which is specifically designed to foster excellence and drive success for students and researchers, while adhering to core academic principles and values, working both independently as a company and through strong partnerships with industry leaders in the field of AI.

Additional Resource Recommendations

Once a search is performed and results are returned, Ex Libris is hoping to expand the user experience by supplying recommendations for additional relevant content and resources, based both on the original search query and the needs of individual users. Serendipitous navigation and movement within a database can yield deeper and more relevant results and findings. Anonymised big data and smart analysis of similar and identical past searches from users across the Ex Libris products, can generate tailored recommendations for additional content the user may find beneficial. Expanding on the existing bX article recommendation service with advanced AI technology will power future recommendations and smart analysis based not only on the search query itself but also specific needs of individual users and their areas of interests while remaining mindful of data privacy and anonymisation to protect users' interest.

Recommendations for Related Articles

For researchers and academics who would like to pursue specific areas of interest further and expand their knowledge and information resource base, establishing an Esploro portal that will generate content recommendations based on researchers' areas of expertise, interest and investment is being explored. Many academic libraries are known for championing certain research areas and an enhanced portal has the potential to support the enrichment of researchers' work and analyses.

Citation Extraction from Syllabi Files

Many instructors and teachers create course reading lists based on course syllabi which they have carefully constructed and curated. Leganto is the Ex Libris course resource list solution, and it is developing an AI-based tool that will extract citations from an uploaded syllabus file and generate course reading list suggestions based on the course's content. Instructors will be able to review the resulting suggestions as well as adjust for variables such as learning objectives, diversity, equity and inclusion considerations, scholarly vs popular publications, and more.

Collection Development

Collection development is a major component in library activity. Ensuring an appropriate lifecycle for collection content is vital and determines the current and future availability of and access to content for patrons. Libraries must be able to assess the appropriateness and effectiveness of existing content and collections spanning all formats including physical and digital content held locally or accessed remotely, in addition to the platforms available for accessing content and various service offerings, such as centrally-managed content and/or various content sharing agreements.

AI technology can assist libraries in reviewing the effectiveness of collection development by clustering existing collections into categories and comparing them across the collective collection and other benchmarks determined by the library, to offer insights and recommendations. DARA has already been referred to in this chapter. It provides an existing rules-based recommendation assistant in the Ex Libris Alma product, supplying primarily workflow efficiency recommendations. Upgrading the DARA engine to run on ML technology would enable it to offer a greater variety of smart recommendations, including collection management insights based on anonymised data collected within Alma. DARA exists on an infrastructure level within several Ex Libris products, and the potential for determining how recommendations already available might be extended to benefit users of other products in the Ex Libris portfolio is being investigated with a view to driving efficiency in additional areas for user communities.

Automated decision making in relation to processes undertaken in library collection acquisition and development is also under investigation to improve efficiency for library operations. New ways to collaborate with textbook publishers and regional copyright agencies to automate and expedite manual processes using robotic process automation (RPA) are being investigated. Such collaboration could introduce a new automated command-driven efficiency tool that would be able to execute basic repetitive time-consuming activities like copy-and-paste and moving files, improving operational efficiency and effectiveness for libraries and librarians so that they can deliver quality experiences to patrons, students and faculty.

Metadata Management

Future developments in relation to improvements based on AI in metadata management relate to title matching, subject enrichment, and automated data record creation.

Title Matching

Titles are not always unique and a single item's title may be described and catalogued differently by various publishers, aggregators, individual libraries, or the authors themselves, as well as differently across resource formats either physical or digital. There are many solutions and workarounds that address the challenge, primarily through unique identifiers such as ISSNs and ISBNs. Yet the use of these identifiers cannot always resolve the full end-to-end issue of connecting a single resource across multiple platforms, products, and companies, considering the variety in content levels, such as a journal vs a journal article. AI tools can enable smart analysis of titles and intelligent connections and provide the means for advanced cross-product and cross-platform resource sharing, shared cataloguing, collective collection analysis, and more.

Subject Enrichment

Subject headings are the mainstay of library approaches to bibliographic description and cataloguing involving MARC standards and BIBFRAME, creating the basis for major and minor connections and correlations between pieces of content, based on shared understandings of content classification. Currently, most subject headings are created and added manually by skilled cataloguers working with the Library of Congress and other national bibliographic authorities individually, albeit on a collective basis, to grow the interconnecting subject relationships. Yet it is a complex, time-consuming and highly skilled task, and cataloguers face large volumes of new incoming content requiring analysis and processing, occasionally involving delays or perhaps incomplete or inaccurate results. An AI-based ML tool using the available data within the full-text record to determine relevant subject headings would free up the time of cataloguers and allow them to focus on areas requiring their specific expertise and the provision of value-added services based on unique experience. Ex Libris is working on the development of such tools and there is already research in the industry supporting the processing and cataloguing of legal deposit material, which might be expanded to academic content as well.

Automated Metadata Record Creation

Title matching and subject heading enrichment are examples of how AI technology can generate high quality metadata for specific fields. There are prospects for expanding this approach to the AI-driven automated creation of a basic metadata record. When AI technology can generate a basic metadata record based on its fulltext, the role of the cataloguers will no longer involve focusing on the creation of basic metadata, but rather on record enhancement to improve the quality of analysis and the provision of additional value based on expert treatment of complex materials. Basic metadata records generated by AI would be built to support linked data structures, thereby ensuring that flexibility of data generation and input and preparation for incorporation in a knowledge graph database. AI-generated records would be able to take the structures into account at the point of creation, creating semantic records that are supported by the next generation of database management systems, as well as remaining compatible with the existing tools and databases used by libraries.

Conclusion

Ex Libris, a part of Clarivate, is committed to working closely with its community, user groups, and partners, to ensure the effective, accurate and responsible development and implementation of all technologies, including the exciting opportunities around AI. Ex Libris aims to empower users with the tools they need to gain insights from the ever-growing volume of scholarly content, while upholding academic integrity and observing ethical standards. By responsibly utilising new AI-powered services being offered, progressive institutions will be at the forefront of improved teaching and learning experiences and enhanced research activity.

Ex Libris has implemented AI across its product portfolio to enhance the tools and solutions which have been provided for decades and is adopting forward-thinking and progressive approaches to ensure the use of emerging new technologies, both independently and through strong partnerships with leading AI innovators. By bringing clarity to the complex, Ex Libris can give library customers the confidence to make critical decisions sensibly and smartly, to navigate roadblocks encountered with the best tools and to achieve their goals.

Details have been provided of some existing Ex Libris products, tools and features available across the extensive Clarivate portfolio that are currently driven by AI technology. They range from librarian workflow efficiency tools to patron discovery recommendations. The products and tools described already exist, and it is only the beginning. Building towards the future involves the continuation of investment in new AI technologies and partnerships to deliver better and more enriched experiences to librarians and patrons across their daily interactions with the library. Due to the rapidly changing nature of the AI landscape, continuous review is the operational focus along with evolving internal processes and guidelines to ensure a full awareness of the potential benefits and possible risks when researching and implementing new technologies. To advance, progress,and best serve the librarian community, Ex Libris continues to evaluate and research how AI technologies can best transform the world. AI can be used to transform librarians and library systems from data management to knowledge management and beyond.

References

Clarivate. 2024a. "Connecting You to Intelligence with the Power to Transform Our World." https://clarivate.com/about-us/.

Clarivate. 2024b. "Research Funding and Analytics: Esploro." https://clarivate.com/products/scientific-and-academic-research/research-funding-and-analytics/esploro/.

Ex Libris. n.d.a. "Transforming the Future of Library Solutions, Today." https://exlibrisgroup.com/.

Ex Libris. n.d.b. " DARA – Data Analysis Recommendation Assistant." https://knowledge.exlibrisgroup.com/Alma/Product_Documentation/010Alma_Online_Help_(English)/050Administration/090DARA_%E2%80%93_Data_Analysis_Recommendation_Assistant.

Ex Libris. n.d.c. "An Overview of CDI." https://knowledge.exlibrisgroup.com/Primo/Content_Corner/Central_Discovery_Index/Documentation_and_Training/Documentation_and_Training_(English)/CDI_-_The_Central_Discovery_Index/010An_Overview_of_the_Ex_Libris_Central_Discovery_Index_(CDI).

Ex Libris. n.d.d. "Smart Harvesting AI: Growing Your Research Information Hub." https://discover.clarivate.com/ExLibris_esploro-smart-harvesting-ai.

Ex Libris. n.d.e. " bX Article Recommender." https://exlibrisgroup.com/products/bx-recommender/.

Ex Libris. n.d.f. " Introduction to Rialto Marketplace: Overview." https://knowledge.exlibrisgroup.com/Rialto/Product_Documentation/010Introduction_to_Marketplace/010About_Rialto_Marketplace.

Ex Libris. 2022. "Smart Harvesting AI: A Hands-free Approach to Growing Your Research Information Hub." https://discover.clarivate.com/ExLibris_esploro-smart-harvesting-ai.

IBM. n.d. "What is a Knowledge Graph?" https://www.ibm.com/topics/knowledge-graph.

ProQuest. n.d. "Rialto: The Future is Selection Plans: Rialto's Innovative Solution to Legacy Approvals." https://about.proquest.com/globalassets/proquest/files/pdf-files/whitepaper-rialto-selectionplans.pdf.

Edmund Balnaves
23 Artificial Intelligence in Libraries on $5 per Day: Image Matching with Koha

Abstract: This chapter takes the reader on a journey through artificial intelligence (AI) integration with a well known open-source library management system, Koha. A case study explores the integration of an open-source AI toolkit with an open-source library management system. By leveraging open source and cloud services, the integration of an image recognition AI toolkit is demonstrated on a budget of under $5 per day. This chapter explores the strengths and opportunities in open-source AI projects and provides an example of integrating library and information services using a widely implemented open-source library management system.

Keywords: Open source software; Images; Library management systems (Computer systems); Koha

Introduction

The union of image capture from cameras with image recognition software has opened up new opportunities for many client-facing applications. When applied to libraries, the use of image recognition techniques to achieve image matching offers potential both in the semantic recognition of image and video assets held by the library, and in the enhancement of client-facing library applications.

This chapter explores the implementation of a facial recognition system using open-source toolkits when integrated with an open source library management solution. Open source refers specifically to projects – that have source code provided and allow royalty-free redistribution and modification of the code within the bounds of normal open-source licences (Balnaves 2012).

Many AI toolkits have their origins in open source, written either in Python or C++ programming languages. The use of open source allows inspection of the techniques used, and the nature of the community of developers allows an agile approach to development and testing of the fit of the tools developed to the tasks for which they are being employed. Most toolkits for AI have wrappers that allow them to be embedded using popular programming languages, including Python, Java and C++. Examples of AI open-source software include:
- OpenCV, a popular computer vision library that includes tools for face detection and recognition (OpenCV 2024)

- <u>DLib C++</u> Library, a C++ library that includes Python bindings for facial land-mark detection, face detection, and face recognition (DLibC++ Library 2022)
- <u>Tensorflow</u>, a machine learning framework that includes tools for face recognition (Tensorflow n.d.)
- <u>Face_recognition</u>, a simple Python face recognition library that wraps around <u>dlib</u> (Geitgey 2021)
- <u>PyTorch</u>, another Python machine learning framework that includes tools for face recognition (PyTorch 2024)
- <u>Keras</u>, a high-level deep learning application programming interface (API) that includes tools for face recognition (Keras n.d.)
- <u>Apache MXNet</u>, a deep learning framework that includes tools for face recognition. It is now retired and available in the attic (Mxnet 2022)
- <u>Scikit-learn</u>, a machine learning library that includes tools for facial recognition using <u>support vector machine</u> (SVM) and other algorithms (Scikit-learn 2024)
- <u>Caffe</u>, a deep learning framework that includes tools for face recognition (Caffe n.d.), and
- <u>CodeProject AI</u>, locally installed and self-hosted for any platform and any language. Runs as a Windows service or as a <u>docker container</u> (CodeProject AI 2024b).

Some of the software tools listed are used as building blocks for other software applications and make use of features from other applications.

An open-source implementation of AI tools has a range of privacy benefits to the library. Images and digital content are not sent to external services where the national hosting and privacy of content may be uncertain. One of the ethical considerations in the adoption of AI is the degree to which the algorithmic elements of the solution used can be scrutinised, tested and understood. In the case of open source, the library has agency over the algorithmic design of the AI implementation.

This chapter outlines a case study exploring the process of integrating an open-source AI toolkit with an open-source library management system. The process adopted explored the use of cloud services for storage to provide the proof-of-concept platform for the whole solution at low cost.

Choosing the Platform and Toolkit

Cloud platforms provide an environment that allow for low-cost proof of concept design of systems without having to invest in infrastructure in the first instance.

This case study chose the cloud infrastructure in Amazon Web services to demonstrate the use of its facilities and to illustrate the implementation of the proof-of-concept integration with the installation of a Koha library management system and the AI toolkit, using Koha plugins to bring the two solutions together. Such an approach allows free testing of solutions and services from an infrastructure perspective.

The implementation of the final solution can be done within the normal infrastructure of the institution. There are several advantages to implementing the initial trial solution within a cloud infrastructure. It allows the formulation and trialling of the final technical architecture required without having to commit to the architecture during the design stages. The solution sets can therefore be created and taken down quite easily while the project is in evolution. The cloud infrastructure allows experimentation with solution options without large upfront investment. The security architecture around the solution can be safely tested outside the target implementation environment.

The use of cloud platforms for initial proof of concept testing has many benefits. During the initial exploratory stage with software experimentation, the final target hardware environment may be unknown as different packages are tested for their suitability. In this case several open-source image recognition packages were explored before arriving at using the CodeProject AI toolkit. The CodeProject AI software was chosen because it:
- Installed easily
- Passed initial image testing well, and
- Provided a representational state transfer (REST) API for integration with other applications, which was the key requirement for the cross-platform integration in this case study.

Image Recognition Toolkit

Docker is a platform that allows lightweight installation of software based on containers that are pre-baked or prepared with the solution being installed. The beauty of docker is that it is platform-agnostic. Linux docker images can be installed on Windows systems for example, or Windows docker images can be installed on Linux systems, even though one is in open source, and one is proprietary to Microsoft. In the library and information science business, and in testing environments, docker images can be used to rapidly run in and test solutions. Docker images can also be used for some production solutions when thoroughly tested.

Docker lives on top of the host platform on which it is being run, and contains within its own system only the data which is sufficient for the operating system environment that is being used by the application in order to run the application. It is lightweight and because of this characteristic, it is easy to deploy. Docker provides an excellent method for undertaking software throw-away trials to test the suitability of software, and also for production deployment of software in scalable solutions.

For the purpose of the proof of concept in this case study, the image recognition toolkit sought required a good API and a web interface for testing purposes, and facial recognition features. Fortunately, in the AI space, there are many open-source solutions in both machine learning and image recognition some of which are listed earlier in this chapter.

The case study undertook its exploration of integration using a kit recently released by CodeProject. "CodeProject is a community of Software Developers joined together with certain common goals: to learn, to teach and to have fun. Members from all over the world come together to share code, tutorials and knowledge for free to help their fellow Software Developers" (CodeProject 2024a). CodeProject makes available a range of solution kits for developers to experiment with new technologies. One of the recent solution toolkits is CodeProject AI, an implementation of Python open-source image recognition technologies within a Windows or Linux environment (CodeProject 2024b). The CodeProject AI solution has a docker install. There are many others, for example, FaceNet-Object-Detection-Net (Pandeyer 2024) and projects like Real Python (Stratis 2023).

The deployment of the CodeProject AI server was accomplished with a single command:

```
docker run -p 32168:32168 --name CodeProject.AI-Server -d -v /usr/share/
CodeProject/AI:/usr/share/CodeProject/AI codeproject/ai-server:1.6.8.0
```

Use of one command:
- Downloads the docker project
- Unpacks the docker images, and
- Launches the docker processes.

CodeProject AI makes its toolkit by default available via a web server and provides set up advice: "CodeProject.AI Server provides the glue, the infrastructure and the front-end to bundle together whatever AI project you wish to expose to your applications (Maunder 2024). They also kindly provide a web testing interface at a locally running API server with an internal address of http://localhost:32168/vision.html (Figure 23.1).

Figure 23.1: Web interface for CodeProject

The web interface (Figure 23.1) provided was used to trial some initial face recognition. The function allows upload of an image and testing recognition of image variants. The web interface has corresponding APIs which are the methods for integrating with other systems, in this case Koha.

Cloud Server Setup

Cloud servers are available from many vendors and are increasingly positioned globally across most continents and larger industrial centres. A cloud server provides a platform which can be used to create and run computing resources on a fractional basis with micro-billing tied to the amount of resources used. For this reason, they provide a good environment for concept testing software architectures. A proof of concept of a new software solution can be tested in a an inexpensive throw-away environment without large upfront hardware expenditure. The final deployment may or may not be in a cloud platform.

This chapter focuses on the concept used to demonstrate the implementation of Koha version 21.11 on an AWS Ubuntu 20.04 server with integration to AI capabilities of CodeProject's AI docker images. It is easy to create an AWS server for throw-away testing. Creating the AWS instance requires that one:

- Registers an AWS account, free, but linked to a credit card, and
- Creates a server, EC2 in AWS terminology, and in this instance using the standard AWS Ubuntu 20.04 server open-source base. However, there are many flavours of computer operating systems that can be deployed at differing costs.

Koha and CodeProject were installed initially on a free tier eligible server following the standard installation guidelines for Koha on Debian (Koha 2024) using the Ubuntu 21.11 pathway (Figure 23.2).

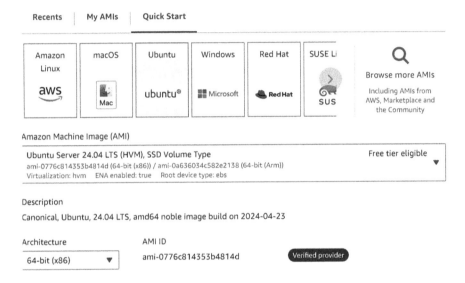

Figure 23.2: AWS Ubuntu server

In this project a small instance was created in the free tier layer. However, in the testing it was soon found that the image recognition software could not be installed in the smallest instance. The target installation required at least 4GB of memory. The problem was discovered when the server hung while launching the CodeProject docker image at the same time as the Koha server. The throw-away server just created was discarded and started again with a larger image. Final deployment took place on an 8GB (EC2 type "T3 large") server after creating and throwing away several server instances. The final cloud server had 2 x CPU and 8GB x memory. The path taken led successfully to a minimum architecture for the deployment environment, and to a minimal operational cost of $5 per day for the entire application operation including Koha.

Implementation of Koha

Koha is one of the most widely implemented library management systems in the world. It is an open-source library management solution supported by a rich community of developers, service providers and librarians around the globe. It runs on Debian, Ubuntu or other flavours of Linux and has a well-documented installation process (Koha 2024). Koha was installed on the EC2 instance alongside the docker CodeProject instance. It took twenty minutes to install and deploy Koha on the server with the advantage of familiarity.

Integrating with Koha

Koha provides a plugin system that allows integration of features within the application. The plugin system means that the developer does not have to touch the code base of the application. The plugin system itself has API hooks and hooks to place code within the application. In the case of this project, a plugin was developed based on existing community published plugins. The concept of plugins is common across many applications and allows extension of an application with local customisations without having to modify the underlying application. The development of this plugin was realised using readily available code examples for Javascript webcam integration, Koha plugin development and the CodeProject AI example integrations.

The plugin created achieved two minimal functions for the project integration task:
- An integration hook between the OPAC login page and the AI server to
  - Scan an image
  - Send the image to CodeProject AI, and
  - Authenticate the use on Koha based on a successful match, and
- An integration hook on the patron page to allow transfer of an uploaded patron image to CodeProject AI

Both development tasks essentially involved injecting JavaScript into the login page and librarian's patron editing page to upload images using the Koha Plugin API integration as follows (Figure 23.3):

- The OPAC login page shows JavaScript to capture an image using the webcam
- The JavaScript code sends the webcam image mage to the Koha server using the custom Koha Plugin integration with the Koha API, and

– The Koha plugin sends the image to the Code Project AI server for validation or registration.

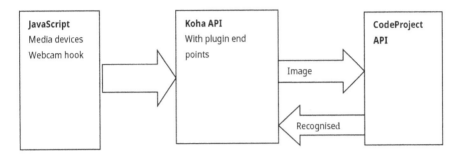

Figure 23.3: Koha integration

By relying heavily on existing plugin examples, and using the APIs in JavaScript, Koha and CodeProject, the proof of concept development took two days to complete and was the most complex programmatic task in the proof of concept. It involved software development focussed primarily on interacting with the Koha plugin functions and the CodeForLibAI functions.

Login with photo

Powered by Koha
Hosted by Prosentient

Figure 23.4: Online Public Access Catalogue (OPAC) login page

The online public access catalogue (OPAC) login page offers the user a choice in logging in and offers the use of the camera and image creation for sign in (Figure 23.4).

Testing the Toolkit

Artificial Intelligence systems rely on models of the real world of one sort or another. Image recognition for example can use many occurrences of sample images to train a model for subsequent recognition of similar occurrences. The larger the sample sizes available and the greater the amount of data included, the better the matching will be. When applying a real-world occasion against a model, the matching process is always an approximation: the image match is looking for equivalence or similarity in characteristics between the query image and the model and the resulting match is evaluated for performance. The match equals *this much* which is the level of confidence. The confidence level measures probability of accurate detection.

The matching confidence levels are crucial in the context of authenticating facial image recognition. If there is too low a confidence level accepted from the matching algorithm, any face is happily accepted in the authentication process. If an exceptionally high confidence level is reuired, it may be functionally impossible to log in. Initial explorations indicated a confidence level of > 0.75 as a minimum confidence.

An important aspect in using AI of any kind is the algorithm used and the methodology for use, and whether levels of confidence are provided at any of the modelling or processing layers. The benefit of using open source is that the whole process is open to scrutiny. The CodeProject AI yields a confidence level on its image and facial matching which can be used to good effect in the overall testing.

CodeProject AI does not store the original image once it has captured and processed the image. It simply stores a vector representing the face captured. Exploring the source reveals an SQLITE database. CodeProject itself is an application wrapper. It makes use of other open source projects to provide a simple interface to access a range of AI functions – which greatly simplifies the integration process with existing applications. CodeProject AI uses ObjectDetectionYolo (You Only Look Once) which itself uses OpenCV (Kundu 2023) and illustrates the ways in which open source allows progressively more complex solutions of tool kits from a wide collection base.

How does the toolkit store the facial image? No image is saved by the toolkit. Instead, it stores a vector defining the unique points defining the face, using the underlying image recognition software. It stores the vector in a database table, which can be explored (Figure 23.5). Note that this vector contains personally sensitive data as it provides defining facial recognition.

```
apt install SQLite
sqlite3 ./faceembedding.db
.tables
List the table
Select * from TB_EMBEDDINGS
```

Figure 23.5: Vector in database table

There is a set or a vector array that describes the unique points for a face (Figure 23.6).

```
0.026341065674227185, 0.03604118525981903, 0.05735778045518771,
-0.04988788140183555, -0.001674302271567285, 0.028918949887155787,
-0.006237712223018781, 0.008357822452184116, 0.08690883219222096,
0.03714309023022652, 0.03508520871400833, 0.016281576706784135,
```

```
……
```

```
0.057015251785516739, 0.008849352598190308, 0.06125432997941971,
-0.00867899414151907, 0.042281255453185, -0.010691865347325802,
-0.02570171467959881, -0.01565711200237274, -0.03459269553222928,
-0.011747458018362522, -0.03084883838891983, -0.05788338112831116,
-0.09049146135759354, -0.020388029515743256, -0.061122243144919586,
0.026703915790077972, 0.0673513263463974, 0.04039162260029793,
0.018179498612880707]
```

Figure 23.6: Example of a vector array for a face N.B. It does not represent a real face

The API call returns matched the facial identifications and produced the confidence level for the match. The application using the toolkit is left to make a decision on what to do based on the confidence levels of the match.

Webcam Integration, Secure Server and Image Scanning

To be useful within the Koha application, it is necessary to allow Koha to take an image snapshot to send to the server. Accessing the webcam from the browser to scan facial images might have been the trickiest part of the project:. Fortunately, the problem was solved several years ago with the browser introduction of Hypertext Mark Up Language 5 (HTML5) and media functions for the browser which allow JavaScript functions to access and manipulate images from the webcam.

One of the first integration issues with the web interface for Koha concerned accessing the webcam. For good security reasons, one cannot access the webcam from a non-SSL website. The reason for this is sound: anyone on the local network could watch or listen to a video or audio stream if the stream were not sent through a secure connection. Firefox and Chrome disable access to webcam functions if the web page itself is not secure.

Secure socket layer (SSL) is the technology used to create a secure information interchange between the browser being used whether it be Chrome, Firefox or some other, and the server to which one is connecting. Websites use public certificates shared with the browser during a search to create a secure connection.

Creating an SSL (https) protected website is an additional step required for proof of concept for the project being undertaken. While there are options for what are called self-signed certificates, they do not always overcome the obstacle of using secured components of the browser. To create an SSL-protected website there are two components:

–   Creating a domain name, which will be the public web domain of the website on which Koha will be hosted. The domain name chosen was aidemo.intersearch. com.au. Creating a domain name requires the use of a domain registration company like GODADDY or one's own organisation if it has the capability, and
–   Installing a secure certificate for the domain. An SSL certificate needs to be installed on the server being used. The certificate is time limited and is currently one year and must be created through a well-known registration system that is widely recognised on client computers and devices. There may be a fee associated with the certificate creation, but some sites provide the certificate for free as part of the hosting.

The project described in this case study had control of an existing domain, intersearch.com.au, and two sub-domains for Koha were registered: aidemo.intersearch.com.au and aidemoadmin.intersearch.com.au. The two domains translated to the cloud web server and the following domains were created, and certificates registered for them: https://aidemo.intersearch.com.au, and https://aidemoadmin.intersearch.com.au.

Fortunately, there is a free certificate service called Let's Encrypt (https://letsencrypt.org/) which provides an open-access method for registering certificates at no charge. The excellent service provides a solid and robust means for encryption of a website and its existence and activities have been responsible for a much greater level of systematic website encryption. Let's Encrypt is a non-profit authority which accepts sponsorships and donations. Support for this wonderful service is greatly to be encouraged. Let's Encrypt's products can be integrated with the servers very easily with a tool certbot (Inmotion Hosting Support Center 2023). It takes three steps in Linux:

–   *Install snapd:*
    –   sudo apt install snapd
    –   sudo snap install core; sudo snap refresh core

- *Install Certbot with snapd:*
  - sudo snap install --classic certbot
- *Create a symlink to ensure Certbot runs:*
  - sudo ln -s /snap/bin/certbot /usr/bin/certbot

Once installed, the certbot tool can be used to create certificates that are automatically renewed on the server. With encryption enabled on the web server, the integration with the computer webcam followed naturally.

Ethical Review

Any project that captures biometric data, or data that might be interpreted as biometric, raises ethical considerations in relation to retention, access, appropriate use and consent:

Retention: For how long is the image data to be retained? Will the image data be removed after its relevant usage or when the client is no longer a library subscriber? While the AI image processor does not retain the original image, the vector definition of the face in itself constitutes sensitive personal data and should not be retained once the client is no longer a member of the library. The client must be able to remove all representations of personal biometric data. Koha provides this capability.

Access: Who can access the library subscriber data, especially where it contains biometric information such as the patron image? Are there security controls to access, or example two factor authentication).

Use: Is the captured image data used appropriately and only for designated permitted purposes? In this case its purpose was to provide a simple, hands free, face-based login. There are obvious weaknesses with such a system that might not make it suitable in, for example, a public library setting. It might, however, be very useful in a 24 x 7 professional or research library setting.

Consent: The use of the face recognition login should not be activated automatically. In this case it was triggered by the user, should s/he wish to use this method for authentication. Traditional password authentication was enabled during the proof of concept to allow flexible opt in/opt out for the new authentication path.

Concluding the Proof of Concept and Moving to Production

The purpose of the exploration described in this case study was to determine the feasibility and complexity of integrating an image recognition toolkit with the well-known open-source library system Koha. The journey demonstrated that such a toolkit could be constructed using a range of components and methodologies with minimal infrastructure costs, indeed on a budget of $5 per day.

The next stage of the journey is a lengthy process. Moving from proof of concept to production and implementation requires considerably more testing, an evaluation of scalability and a review of security and ethical issues. The toolkit chosen and others should be tested against the same methodology to evaluate the most effective method for achieving the desired outcomes. The same kind of agile proof of concept can help to quickly determine the viability of the approach and which of the possible solutions might represent an appropriate path forward.

Following further testing of the methods used, the considerations for production implementation include:

- Testing across different devices and environments
- Establishing scalability of the solution – what happens when 1000 people are using it?
- Testing across different facial profiles, population, and gender sets
- Conducting a security review of the solution. How safe are all the components used? What vulnerabilities apply, and can they be mitigated? and
- Running a project ethical review. What are the implications for use in specific contexts?

The purpose of this exercise was to demonstrate the facility with which an agile process with open-source software components can be used to develop and test an AI application with very low cost. The project explored the use of AI integration methodologies with an existing open-source library management system. The many open-source AI toolkits available, and API extensions of commercial systems such as ChatGPT mean that system integration tasks with AI systems are not intrinsically technically complex to undertake.

References

Balnaves, Edmund. 2008. "Open Source Library Management Systems: A Multidimensional Evaluation." *Australian Academic and Research Libraries* 39, no. 1: 1–13. https://doi.org/10.1080/00 048623.2008.10721320.

Caffe. n.d. "Deep Learning Framework by BAIR." https://caffe.berkeleyvisiGeiscilit.org.

CodeProject. 2024a. "CodeProject: A Guide: What is CodeProject?" https://www.codeproject.com/info/guide.aspx.

CodeProject. 2024b. "CodeProject.AI Server: AI the Easy Way." February 29, 2024. https://www.codeproject.com/Articles/5322557/CodeProject-AI-Server-AI-the-easy-way.

Dlib C++ Library. 2022. http://dlib.net/.

Geitgey, Adam. 2021. "Face_recognition." v1.2.2 latest April 3, 2018. https://github.com/ageitgey/face_recognition.

Inmotion Hosting Support Center. 2023. "How to Install Let's Encrypt SSL on Ubuntu with Certbot." Updated December 1, 2023. https://www.inmotionhosting.com/support/website/ssl/lets-encrypt-ssl-ubuntu-with-certbot/.

Keras. n.d. https://keras.io/.

Koha. 2024. "Koha on Debian." Last modified March 18, 2024. https://wiki.koha-community.org/wiki/Koha_on_Debian.

Kundu, Rohit. 2023. " YOLO: Algorithm for Object Detection Explained [+Examples]". *V7Labs: Blog.* January 17, 2023. https://www.v7labs.com/blog/yolo-object-detection.

Maunder, Chris. 2024. "CodeProject.AI Module Creation: A Full Walkthrough in Python." February 15, 2024. https://www.codeproject.com/Articles/5377531/CodeProject-AI-Module-creation-A-full-walkthrough.

Mxnet. 2022. "Apache Mxnet: A Flexible and Efficient Library for Deep Learning." https://mxnet.apache.org/versions/1.9.1/.

OpenCV. 2024. "Open CV University." https://opencv.org.

Pandeyer, Yash. 2024. "YashNita /FaceNet-Object-Detection-Net-." https://github.com/YashNita/FaceNet-Object-Detection-Net-?tab=readme-ov-file#readme.

PyTorch. 2024. https://pytorch.org/.

Scikit-learn. 2024. "Machine Learning in Python." https://scikit-learn.org/stable/index.html.

Stratis, Kyle. 2023. "Build Your Own Face Recognition Tool with Python." *Real Python.* April 24, 2023. https://realpython.com/face-recognition-with-python/

Tensorflow. n.d. "An End-to-end Platform for Machine Learning. TF2.16 Released." https://www.tensorflow.org/.

Glossary

Note: this glossary has been compiled with the assistance of GPT4. It is by no means complete and other terms are used throughout the book.

Algorithm: A set of rules or instructions given to an AI, or a machine that it uses to solve problems or make decisions.

Artificial Intelligence (AI): The simulation of human intelligence processes by machines, especially computer systems. The processes include learning, reasoning, problem-solving, perception, and language understanding.

AutoML (Automated Machine Learning): The process of automating the end-to-end process of applying machine learning to real-world problems. AutoML makes it feasible for non-experts to effectively use machine learning models and techniques.

Autonomous Agents: In artificial intelligence, autonomous agents are systems capable of independent decision-making and action-execution based on the environment they are in, without continuous human guidance. For libraries, this could manifest in several ways, such as virtual assistants that help patrons navigate the digital library resources, autonomous robots that assist with book sorting or shelving, or intelligent systems managing queries and administrative tasks.

BERT (Bidirectional Encoder Representations from Transformers): A Transformer-based machine learning technique for natural language processing tasks. Developed by Google, BERT is designed to understand the context of a word in search queries, thereby helping data retrieval systems grasp the intent behind a user's query.

Bias in AI: Prejudice or unintended favoritism in AI decision-making. This bias occurs due to the data used to train the AI and can lead to unfair outcomes.

Big Data: Extremely large data sets that may be analyzed computationally to reveal patterns, trends, and associations, especially relating to human behavior and interactions.

Chatbot, aka Conversational Agent: A computer program that simulates and processes human conversation (either written or spoken), allowing humans to interact with digital devices as if they were communicating with a real person.

Collections-as-data: The implications of seeing GLAM collections as data.

Data Lake: A storage repository that holds a vast amount of raw data in its native format until needed. Libraries dealing with large sets of unstructured data can use data lakes for storage, which can then be processed by AI models for various tasks.

Data Mining: The process of discovering patterns and knowledge from large amounts of data. The data sources can include databases, data warehouses, the internet, and other information repositories.

Deepfakes: Use of generative AI techniques to create hard to detect false images or other content.

Deep Learning: A subset of machine learning where neural networks with many layers (hence "deep") learn from large amounts of data. Deep learning methods are highly effective in discerning patterns and representations of data.

Digital Assistant (or Virtual Assistant): An application programme that understands natural language voice commands and completes tasks for the user.

Facial Recognition: A category of biometric software that maps an individual's facial features mathematically and stores the data as a faceprint. It is used to identify individuals in photos, video, or real-time.

Federated Learning: A machine learning approach where the model is trained across multiple decentralised devices (or servers) holding local data samples and without exchanging them. This approach is useful in privacy-preserving and efficient decentralized systems.

Fine-Tuning: In the context of AI, fine-tuning refers to the process of making minor adjustments to a pre-trained model so that it can perform well on a new task. This process is essential when applying large language models to specific tasks or industries, including library science.

General AI: Also known as Strong AI. AI that works across multiple contexts, as opposed to narrow/weak AI.

Generative AI: AI that produces new content be that text, images or other media.

GPT (Generative Pre-trained Transformer): An advanced type of Transformer AI model used for natural language understanding and generation. GPT, developed by OpenAI, has had several versions, with GPT-3 being one of the most known for its large scale and versatility in handling various language tasks.

Hallucination: False information presented by AI, as in generative AI outputs.

Human-centred AI: An approach to AI development and use focused on benefiting humans.

Human in the Loop: The design of AI systems that retain a central role for human decision making, particularly in training and testing supervised machine learning.

Information Retrieval (IR): The activity of obtaining information resources relevant to an information need from a collection of information resources. Searches can be based on metadata or on full-text indexing.

Internet of Things (IoT): The network of physical objects – "things" – that are embedded with sensors, software, and other technologies for the purpose of connecting and exchanging data with other devices and systems over the internet.

Knowledge Graph: A form of knowledge base that uses a graph-structured model or network for semantic queries. It enhances search capabilities by understanding the context and relationships between different pieces of information.

Latent Dirichlet Allocation (LDA): LDA is a specific type of topic modelling technique. It is an unsupervised machine learning method that helps systems understand and identify topic structures within a text body, based on a set of observations. In a library context, LDA can be instrumental in identifying patterns and topics across different documents, such as research papers, books, and articles, even when those topics are not explicitly stated. This process enhances metadata tagging, making the search and retrieval process more efficient and user-friendly.

Large Language Models (LLMs): These are types of artificial intelligence models trained on vast amounts of text data. They are designed to understand language and generate coherent, contextually relevant text based on the input they are given. LLMs can answer questions, summarize content, translate languages, and even create content.

Machine Learning (ML): A subset of AI that provides systems the ability to automatically learn and improve from experience without being explicitly programmed. It focuses on the development of computer programs that can access data and use it to learn for themselves.

Metadata: This term refers to data that provides information about other data. In the context of libraries, metadata is crucial for the organization, discovery, and management of information resources. It can include details about the content, format, author, and creation date among other attributes of resources.

MLOps (Machine Learning Operations): A set of practices that combines machine learning, DevOps, and data engineering, which aims to automate and enhance the end-to-end lifecycle of ML models.

Multimodal AI: Multimodal AI refers to systems that can engage and integrate multiple types of data input or output, such as text, audio, visual, and sensory data, to make decisions or provide responses. In the context of libraries, multimodal AI can revolutionize user interactions by enabling more dynamic engagement. For instance, a system that understands speech, text, images, and gestures could provide more accessible services catering to diverse user needs, including those with disabilities. It could allow patrons to search for books through voice commands, receive information through interactive displays, or even direct them using augmented reality through their smartphones, creating an inclusive and interactive environment.

Narrow AI: Also known as weak AI. AI that solves a specific problem, as opposed to general/strong AI which could operate across multiple contexts.

Natural Language Processing (NLP): A field of AI that focuses on the interaction between computers and humans through language. It allows machines to read, decipher, understand, and make sense of human languages in a valuable way.

Opacity: A lack of transparency and explainability in AI decision making and outputs.

Optical Character Recognition (OCR): The electronic or mechanical conversion of images of typed, handwritten, or printed text into machine-encoded text, whether from a scanned document, a photo of a document, or text superimposed on an image.

Predictive Analysis: The use of data, statistical algorithms, and machine learning techniques to identify the likelihood of future outcomes based on historical data.

Prompt Engineering: The crafting of requests in natural language to shape the outputs from generative AI in desired directions.

Recommender System: A subclass of information filtering systems that seek to predict the "rating" or "preference" a user would give to an item. In libraries, this could be used to suggest books, articles, and other resources.

Reinforcement Learning (RL): A type of machine learning where an agent learns to behave in an environment by performing actions and receiving rewards for them. It is about taking suitable action to maximize reward in a particular situation, used in various sectors, including information retrieval and organization systems.

Reinforcement Learning with Human Feedback (RLHF): This is an approach combining reinforcement learning with human feedback to train models more efficiently or towards objectives that are hard to define formally using rewards alone. It's particularly relevant in interactive systems where human preferences or quality assessments guide the AI.

Responsible AI: A label applied to AI development which is ethical and trustworthy.

Robotics Process Automation (RPA): Technology that allows anyone to configure computer software, or a "robot," to emulate and integrate the actions of a human interacting within digital systems to execute a business process.

Semantic Analysis: The study of meaning in language, covering the understanding of meaning in text or speech. In AI, this refers to machines understanding the meaning and nuances of human language.

Sentiment Analysis: Also known as opinion mining, it involves the use of NLP, text analysis, and computational linguistics to identify and extract subjective information from resources.

Strong AI: See General AI/

Synthetic Data: Data created artificially rather than from real world events. Sometimes used as training data.

TF-IDF (Term Frequency-Inverse Document Frequency): A numerical statistic that reflects how important a word is to a document within a collection or corpus. It's often used in information retrieval and text mining to evaluate and rank documents in relation to user queries.

Topic Modelling: In the context of AI, topic modelling is a type of statistical model used to uncover abstract topics within a large volume of text. For librarians, this is particularly useful in categorising and clustering large collections of documents or books based on their themes, significantly improving information retrieval processes. It allows for more intuitive searching capabilities, where users can search by topic or theme, rather than specific or exact keywords.

Transformer Models: A type of neural network architecture used in natural language processing. Unlike previous sequential models, Transformer models process words in relation to all other words in a sentence, making them more effective for understanding context within language.

Trustworthy AI: The European Union's key term to describe responsible, ethical AI.

Turing Test: A test of a machine's ability to exhibit intelligent behavior equivalent to, or indistinguishable from, that of a human.

Uncanny Valley: The negative emotional response of unease or disgusts when AI appears too human.

Weak AI: See Narrow AI.

Zero-shot Learning: A machine learning approach where the model can correctly make predictions about data it has not been explicitly trained on. This approach allows for more flexible and expansive applications of AI, as it requires less data-specific training.

Resources

International Federation of Library Associations and Institutions (IFLA). Artificial Intelligence Special Interest Group (AI SIG)

Resources to Get Up to Speed on Artificial Intelligence

Selected by the IFLA Artificial Intelligence Special Interest Group

Artificial intelligence is said to be having a dramatic, even transformative effect on many aspects of society. It will affect libraries in multiple ways, through its use in library services but also through changing the search landscape, and so information literacy. In December 2023 the IFLA AI SIG selected 23 resources to help any information professional get up to speed on this complex topic. We have made a couple of small updates to this to reflect developments, setting aside generative AI which is covered by our second guide.

1. Starting Point: What is Artificial Intelligence?

1. Elements of AI. 2023. "A Free Online Course Explaining the Basics of AI Technologies." https://www.elementsofai.com/.
    It is translated into several European languages. There is also an Ethics of AI course created by the University of Helsinki: https://ethics-of-ai.mooc.fi/.

2. DeepLearning.AI. n.d. "AI for Everyone: Course." https://www.deeplearning.ai/courses/ai-for-everyone/.
    Includes learning materials that can be reused.

3. FUN France Université Numérique. 2023. "ChatGPT et IA : mode d'emploi pour managers et RH." MOOC. L'intelligence artificielle pour tous! https://www.fun-mooc.fr/fr/cours/lintelligence-artificielle-pour-tous/.
    A French language MOOC from FUN: France Université Numérique.

2. Applying Artificial Intelligence to Library Work

2.1. General

4. CILIP. 2023. "Research Report: The Impact of AI, Machine Learning, Automation and Robotics on the Information Professions: A Report for CILIP." https://cdn. ymaws.com/www.cilip.org.uk/resource/resmgr/cilip/research/tech_review/ cilip_%e2%80%93_ai_report_-_final_lo.pdf. *A review of the potential impact of AI on the information profession.*

5. Upshall, Michael. 2022. "An AI toolkit for libraries." *Insights: The UKSG Journal* 35: 18. https://doi.org/10.1629/uksg.592.
    An overview of AI illustrated with examples of AI applications and a tool-kit for evaluating AI tools.

2.2. Machine Learning and Library Collections

6. Cordell, Ryan C. 2020. *Machine Learning + Libraries: A Report on the State of the Field.* Washington, DC: LC Labs, Library of Congress. https://labs.loc.gov/static/ labs/work/reports/Cordell-LOC-ML-report.pdf.
    An authoritative analysis of the issues around the application of machine learning to knowledge discovery in libraries.

7. Europeana Pro. 2023. "AI in Relation to Glams." Task Force December 1, 2019 to August 31, 2021. https://pro.europeana.eu/project/ai-in-relation-to-glams.
    The Task Force investigated the role and impact of artificial intelligence in the digital cultural heritage domain, especially with regards to collections analysis and improvement and issued interim and final reports in 2023.

8. AI4LAM: Artificial Intelligence for Libraries, Archives and Museums. n.d. https://sites.google.com/view/ai4lam.
    AI4LAM is an international, participatory community focused on advancing the use of artificial intelligence in, for and by libraries, archives and museums.

9. Padilla, Thomas, Hannah Scates Kettler, Stewart Varner, and Yasmeen Shorish. 2023. *Vancouver Statement on Collections as Data.* Zenodo. https://doi.org/10.5281/ zenodo.8341519.
    A collective statement of principles to govern how to share collections as data.

10. Lee, Benjamin Charles Germain. 2023. "The 'Collections as ML Data' Checklist for Machine Learning and Cultural Heritage." *Journal of the Association for Information Science and Technology*. Early view. First published May 2, 2023. https://doi.org/10.1002/asi.24765.
Develops a checklist for the whole cycle of using machine learning with heritage material.

2.3. Chatbots

11. San Jose State University. Dr Martin Luther King Jr. Library. 2023. "What are Chatbots?" Last updated October 11, 2023. https://libguides.sjsu.edu/library-chatbot.
A library guide providing an explanation of what a chatbot is, how it can be developed for a library setting and with a link to a local example.

12. Ehrenpreis, Michelle, and Jennifer DeLooper. 2022. "Implementing a Chatbot on a Library Website." *Journal of Web Librarianship* 16, no. 2: 120–142. https://doi.org/10.1080/19322909.2022.2060893. Available at https://academicworks.cuny.edu/cgi/viewcontent.cgi?article=1400&context=le_pubs.
A case study of developing a library chatbot.

2.4. Living Systematic Reviews

13. Cochrane Community. 2024. "Living Systematic Reviews." https://community.cochrane.org/review-development/resources/living-systematic-reviews.
AI tools can assist in updating systematic reviews as new evidence becomes available: this could be referred to as a living systematic review.

3. Hands on with the Technologies

14. JISC. n.d. "The Home of AI Demos: A Collection of AI Demos to Discover and Explore." https://exploreai.jisc.ac.uk/.
A website containing demos of different types of AI. Playing around with these tools gives you a good sense of the kind of thing that might be possible.

15. The Carpentries. n.d. https://carpentries.org/.
    AI is premised on data. Data Carpentries teaches foundational coding and data science skills to researchers worldwide. They have an incubator and lab and there are some machine learning introductions for GLAM under development. https://carpentries.org/community-lessons/. *An introductory course for GLAM is being piloted* https://carpentries-incubator.github.io/machine-learning-librarians-archivists/aio/index.html.

4. Artificial Intelligence and Data Literacy Training

16. Ridley, Michael, and Danica Pawlick-Potts. 2021. "Algorithmic Literacy and the Role for Libraries." *Information Technology and Libraries* 40, no. 2. https://doi.org/10.6017/ital.v40i2.12963.
    Explains two ways that libraries can contribute to understanding of AI: through including it in IL training and through helping to produce explainable AI.

5. Responsible Artificial Intelligence and its Ethics

17. International Federation of Library Associations and Institutions (IFLA). 2020. "IFLA Statement on Libraries and Artificial Intelligence." https://www.ifla.org/wp-content/uploads/2019/05/assets/faife/ifla_statement_on_libraries_and_artificial_intelligence.pdf.

18. Padilla, Thomas. 2019. Responsible Operations: Data Science, Machine Learning, and AI in Libraries Dublin, OH: OCLC Research. https://doi.org/10.25333/xk7z-9g97.
    An influential report on how to do AI responsibly.

19. Data Ethics. 2020. "Practical Data Ethics." https://ethics.fast.ai/.
    An online course explaining data ethics.

6. Strategic Context

20. Collett, Clementine, Gina Neff, and Livia Gouvea Gomes. 2022. *The Effects of AI on the Working Lives of Women."* Paris: UNESCO, OECD and IDB. https://unesdoc.unesco.org/ark:/48223/pf0000380861.
An important report pointing out ways to influence the inclusivity of developments around AI.

21. OECD AI. Policy Observatory. 2024. "Policies, Data and Analysis for Trustworthy Articial Intelligence." https://oecd.ai/en/.
Listing of international policies on AI. Available in multiple languages.

22. World Economic Forum. n.d. "Artificial Intelligence." Curation: Desautels Faculty of Management, McGill University. https://intelligence.weforum.org/topics/a1Gb0000000pTDREA2.
The World Economic Forum provides updates on many topics and also lists places to monitor for global news and analysis across the AI and robotics domain through its Agenda Articles on Emerging Technologies https://www.weforum.org/agenda/emerging-technologies-03402c4cf4/.

23. Stanford University. Human Centred Artificial Intelligence. 2022. "Artificial Intelligence Index Report 2022." Directors: Jack Clark and Ray Perrault. https://aiindex.stanford.edu/wp-content/uploads/2022/03/2022-AI-Index-Report_Master.pdf.
Fifth in series of annual reports on global AI developments.

This list is based on the list available on the IFLA SIG website, Version 2 December 17, 2023. AI4LAM maintains a curated "Awesome List" of resources, projects and tools in the libraries, archives and museums space.

For updates and to share your AI related news join the mailing list https://mail.iflalists.org/wws/info/ai-sig.

International Federation of Library Associations and Institutions
(IFLA). Artificial Intelligence Special Interest Group (AI SIG)

Generative Artificial Intelligence for Library and Information Professionals

Produced by the IFLA Artificial Intelligence Special Interest Group.

In compiling this resource, we are seeking to provide a useful non-technical
resource for information library and information professionals. We try to point to
authoritative sources which are open to all.

Introduction to Generative Artificial Intelligence

Generative artificial intelligence (AI) refers to systems that can produce new text,
images or other media. Generative AI can be differentiated from *descriptive AI*
which focuses on improving access to content such as text, images, audio and video
by identifying features in them to enhance search.

Resources

Miao, Fengchun, Wayne Holmes, Ronghuai Huang, and Hui Zhang. 2021. *AI and
    Education? Guidance for Policy-makers.* Paris, UNESCO. https://doi.org/10.54675/
    PCSP7350. Available in multiple languages.
Miao, Fengchun, and Wayne Holmes. 2023. *Guidance for Generative AI in Education
    and Research.* Paris: UNESCO, 2023. https://doi.org/10.54675/EWZM9535. Avail-
    able in multiple languages.
Ortiz, Sabrina. 2023. "What is Generative AI and Why Is It So Popular? Here's Every-
    thing You Need to Know." *ZDNet,* April 23, 2024. https://www.zdnet.com/article/
    what-is-generative-ai-and-why-is-it-so-popular-heres-everything-you-need-to-
    know/.
Sabzalieva, Emma, and Arianna Valentini. 2023. *ChatGPT and Artificial Intelligence
    in Higher Education: A Quick-start Guide."* ED/HE/IESALC/IP/2023/12. Paris:
    UNESCO and UNESCO International Institute for Higher Education in Latin
    America and the Caribbean (IESALC). https://www.iesalc.unesco.org/wp-con-
    tent/uploads/2023/04/ChatGPT-and-Artificial-Intelligence-in-higher-educa-
    tion-Quick-Start-guide_EN_FINAL.pdf.

1.1 Examples of Generative Artificial Intelligence

GPT has been around for some time. The launch of Chat GPT by OpenAI in November 2022 propelled this form of AI into the headlines probably because it made the use of GPT very user friendly through its chat interface.

– ChatGPT https://openai.com/blog/chatgpt
– The new Bing https://www.bing.com or Copilot https://copilot.microsoft.com/
– Gemini (initially known as BARD) https://gemini.google.com/, and
– HuggingChat https://huggingface.co/chat/.

Image generators:
– Dall-E2 https://openai.com/dall-e-2
– Midjourney https://www.midjourney.com/
– Niji Journey https://nijijourney.com/en/, and
– Stability.ai https://stability.ai/stablediffusion.

The wider proliferation of websites and apps with generative AI embedded can be tracked on websites such as:

– Hugging Face. "Models." https://huggingface.co/models
– Futurepedia. https://www.futurepedia.io/, and
– There's an AI for That https://theresanaiforthat.com/.

Within the research tool space, there are services like scholarlyAI, research buddy, and openread. They are being tracked by Ithaka S+R (Baytas and Ruediger 2024).

Resources

Baytas, Claire, and Dylan Ruediger. 2024." Generative AI in Higher Education: The Product Landscape." *Ithaka S+R. Issue Brief,* March 7, 2024. https://doi.org/10.18665/sr.320394.

1.2 How Generative Artificial Intelligence Works

An important example of generative AI are text generators like GPT. An excellent *Guardian* visual explainer listed in the resources below shows how the text generators work.

Resources

Clarke, Seán, Dan Milmo, and Garry. 2023. "How AI Chatbots Like ChatGPT or Bard Work: Visual Explainer." *The Guardian,* November 1, 2023. https://www.theguardian.com/technology/ng-interactive/2023/nov/01/how-ai-chatbots-like-chatgpt-or-bard-work-visual-explainer.

Colin, Eberhart. 2023. "A Guide to Generative AI Terminology." *Scott Logic [blog].* June 1, 2023. https://blog.scottlogic.com/2023/06/01/generative-terminology.html.

2. Ethical and Informational Issues

Generative AI such as ChatGPT has potential benefits with some uses mentioned below, but reflections on the ethics of AI should always be considered prior to use.

The following have been raised as issues with some versions of generative AI, such as ChatGPT. Details of the references are listed in the resources below:

- Makes biased statements because of biases in training data and how the training data was curated. For example, GPT has been shown to be biased about gender and race, amongst other factors (Webb 2023). Trained largely on open web data, GPT is bound to under-represent regions that are under-represented on the web, and areas which are under-represented in AI research (Komminoth 2023)
- "Hallucinates" information which is inaccurate, feeds the flow of misinformation, fails to acknowledge sources, often fabricates citations, and is in itself not citable because consistent answers are not currently generated
- Accelerates the content creation explosion leading to even more challenges of information overload
- Fails to be explainable because it is far from open about the basis of training data used or how it works (Burruss 2020)
- Risks invasion of privacy if data is shared, with many companies blocking use due to fear of loss of data. Students at many institutions are advised not to put personal data into such websites
- Appears to be violating intellectual property rights by using copyright information as training data without permission (Mahari, Fjeld, and Epstein 2023).
- Threatens jobs, for example, of journalists, editors and people in marketing. The German publisher Axel Springer has announced its use of AI and bots and potential replacement of some journalists
- Is available in more advanced forms to people with money to subscribe and creates inequities in access to information

- Was developed by exploiting very low paid Kenyan workers to detoxify content (Perrigo 2023)
- May not be environmentally sustainable: GPT models are known to use a lot of computing power (Ludvigsen 2022), and
- Reveals the disruptive power in the hands of the Big Tech companies.

The balance of importance of these factors may vary between contexts. In higher education and universities, the impact on academic integrity is central to the debate; in corporate research the inaccuracy of information is critical. In some contexts, it may be possible to ban some forms of generative AI or procure a localised system. For example, it is possible to run some open-source AI models locally via Python or R without uploading private documents to the cloud. Retrieval Augmented Generation (RAG) is a promising technology that seeks to combine text generation with information quality assurance through trusted sources.

Fundamentally, although generative artificial intelligence has enormous potential for innovation and undeniably has significantly more knowledge than any individual human, it lacks the ability to reason, consciousness and some of the most advanced human qualities.

Concerns raised by ChatGPT, among other factors, re-energised plans to regulate AI, with a notable achievement the European Union's *Artificial Intelligence Act (EU AI Act)*. It has been reported that:

> Generative AI, like ChatGPT …will have to comply with transparency requirements and EU copyright law:
> - Disclosing that the content was generated by AI
> - Designing the model to prevent it from generating illegal content
> - Publishing summaries of copyrighted data used for training (European Parliament 2023).

Bommasani et al. (2023) weigh up whether foundation model providers like OpenAI and Google comply with requirements in the draft *EU AI Act*.

Resources

AI, Algorithmic, and Automation Incidents and Controversies (AIAAIC). 2024. "ChatGPT Chatbot." *[AIAAIC Repository]*. https://www.aiaaic.org/aiaaic-repository/ai-algorithmic-and-automation-incidents/chatgpt-chatbot.

AI Incident Database (AIID). 2023. "Welcome to the AI Incident Database." https://incidentdatabase.ai/?lang=en.

Bender, Emily M., Timnit Gebru, Angelina McMillan-Major, and Shmargaret Shmitchell. 2021. "On the Dangers of Stochastic Parrots: Can Language Models

Be Too Big?" In *FAccT '21: Proceedings of the 2021 ACM Conference on Fairness, Accountability, and Transparency,* March 2021, 610–623. New York: Association for Computing Machinery. https://doi.org/10.1145/3442188.3445922.

Bommasani, Rishi, Kevin Klyman, Daniel Zhang, and Percy Liang. 2023? "Do Foundation Model Providers Comply with the Draft EU AI Act?" *Stanford University Center for Research on Foundation Models(CRFM) Human-Centered Artificial Intelligence.* https://crfm.stanford.edu/2023/06/15/eu-ai-act.html.

Burruss, Matthew. 2020. "The (Un)ethical Story of GPT-3: OpenAI's Million Dollar Model." [Blog], July 27, 2020. https://matthewpburruss.com/post/the-unethical-story-of-gpt-3-openais-million-dollar-model/.

European Parliament. 2024. "EU AI Act: First Regulation on Artificial Intelligence." *Topics,* June 8, 2023. Updated June 18, 2024. https://www.europarl.europa.eu/news/en/headlines/society/20230601STO93804/eu-ai-act-first-regulation-on-artificial-intelligence.

Floridi, Luciano. 2023. "AI as *Agency Without Intelligence*: On ChatGPT, Large Language Models, and Other Generative Models: Editorial." *Philosophy and Technology* 36, art.no.15. https://doi.org/10.1007/s13347-023-00621-y. Available at http://dx.doi.org/10.2139/ssrn.4358789.

Komminoth, Leo. 2023. "Chat GTP and the Future of African AI." *African Busines,* January 27, 2023. https://african.business/2023/01/technology-information/chat-gtp-and-the-future-of-african-ai.

Ludvigsen, Kasper Groes Albin. 2022. "The Carbon Footprint of Chat GPT." *Medium,* December 22, 2022. Updated March 20, 2023. Published in *Towards Data Science*. https://towardsdatascience.com/the-carbon-footprint-of-chatgpt-66932314627d.

Mahari, Robert, Jessica Fjeld, and Ziv Epstein. 2023. "Generative AI is a Minefield for Copyright Law." *The Conversation,* June 26, 2023. https://theconversation.com/generative-ai-is-a-minefield-for-copyright-law-207473.

Perrigo, Billy. 2023. "Exclusive: OpenAI Used Kenyan Workers on Less Than $2 Per Hour to Make ChatGPT Less Toxic." *Time,* January 18, 2023. https://time.com/6247678/openai-chatgpt-kenya-workers/.

Webb, Michael. 2023. "Exploring the Potential for Bias in Chat GPT." *JISC Artificial Intelligence,* January 26, 2023. https://nationalcentreforai.jiscinvolve.org/wp/2023/01/26/exploring-the-potential-for-bias-in-chatgpt/.

3. Uses

3.1 Uses for Information Professionals

Large language models (LLMs) have immense potential for information work. Many of the problems of specific services such as ChatGPT are more about how it has been implemented than about the underlying technology.

Text-based generative AI can be used in one of its current versions for:

- Summarisation of texts, for example lay summaries of academic papers
- Generating draft metadata to describe material, and
- General uses such as drafting documents and communications, for example policy documents, and targeted marketing.

3.2 Guiding Users to Safe Uses

This section summarises how an information literate user should be trained to approach generative AI tools to evaluate how to use them effectively and to understand critically the wider context of how platforms work to shape information experiences and is presented as a set of prompts.

1. Learn how to use generative AI effectively, by experiment and reading reviews:
   a. How should the tool be conceived? A clever writing assistant or a single point of truth?
   b. For what tasks might it be helpful? Brainstorming, drafting, editing, writing in different styles, summarisation?
   c. Is it trustworthy as a source of information? Is the information supplied accurate and are sources given?
   d. Are there systematic inaccuracies in the material produced? Any biases?
   e. How can questions be formulated to get the best answer? (Sometimes referred to as prompt engineering)
      i. Define style and/or audience
      ii. Repeat the request and synthesise answers
      iii. Ask for sources that can be checked
   f. Are there alternatives that might be better for certain tasks?
   g. Keep on learning: the tools are evolving rapidly
2. Use generative AI to improve how you learn and be reflective about the type of use:
   a. Is it helping to improve your learning or just making things too easy?
   b. How does using the tool make you feel?

c. Is it making you feel less connected to people?
3. Protect your own privacy:
   a. What type of information is it safe to share?
4. Ask who owns, develops and profits from it and the wider related system of information discovery on the platforms you use:
   a. Is it owned by commercially driven corporations so that use feeds their power and control?
      i. Is the system open about how it works? Is recommendation narrowing access to information as a form of filter bubble?
   b. Was it created exploitatively by using low paid labour or by mining information without permission?
   c. Does it have a negative environmental impact?
   d. Does everyone have equal access or is using it give some an unfair advantage?
5. Use it ethically, acknowledging the use:
   a. What are appropriate uses in any particular context? Such as for assessment tasks in learning or in an organisational setting.
   b. Acknowledge use appropriately for the context. There are citation guides https://apastyle.apa.org/blog/how-to-cite-chatgpt.

A model of generative AI literacy has been published by Zhao, Cox, and Cai (2024).

Resources

Zhao, Xin, Andrew Cox, and Liang Cai. 2024. "ChatGPT and the Digitisation of Writing." *Humanities and Social Sciences Communications* 11, article no. 482. https://doi.org/10.1057/s41599-024-02904-x.

3.3 Guiding Researchers

It remains unclear what uses of generative AI will be determined to be legitimate. There are many open questions about how Generative AI might be used in science (Birhane et al. 2023).

Questions important to researchers include:
– What uses of AI in the research process are permitted? Transcription, simulation of data or writing papers?
– Which journals or publishers allow which types of use?

Resources

Birhane, Abebe, Atoosa Kasirzadeh, David Leslie, and Sandra Wachter. 2023. "Science in the Age of Large Language Models." *Nature Reviews Physics* 5, 277–280. https://doi.org/10.1038/s42254-023-00581-4.

This list is based on the list available on the IFLA SIG website, Version 04 01 2024.

Contributors

Akça, Sümeyye

Assistant Professor, Department of Information and Records Management, Marmara University, Istanbul, Türkiye, and a Board Member of the University's Digital Humanities Application and Research Centre. Sümeyye completed in 2017 at Hacettepe University her PhD thesis entitled "Increasing the Visibility and Usage of Cultural Heritage Objects with the Digital Humanities Approach: A Proposal of a Conceptual Model for Turkey". Her research interests include digital humanities, information science, cultural heritage, digital history, network analysis, Ottoman history and manuscripts. She has been a reviewer at the annual conferences of the Alliance of Digital Humanities Organizations (ADHO) since 2016, a member of the Association for Information Science and Technology (ASIS&T) and country representative of the European Chapter of ASIS&T. She has various publications on information science, librarianship, biblio-metrics, social network analysis, and digital humanities. Sümeyye has won various awards and scholarships from organisations including the European Association for Digital Humanities (EADH) and the University of Victoria, British Columbia, Canada.

Balnaves, Edmund

CEO, Prosentient Systems (Australia) and an active technologist in the library field. Edmund holds a a PhD from the University of Sydney, an MBA from Charles Darwin University, and a BA in computer science and librarianship from the University of Canberra. His doctoral research was in the area of systematic content reuse and metadata. Edmund is Chair, Division G of the International Federation of Library Associations and Institutions (IFLA) and has been heavily involved in IFLA's Information Technology Section and Artificial Intelligence Special Interest Group (AI SIG). Edmund is actively engaged in the software development of open-source systems, and AI and discovery for libraries. His business provides hosted open-source library services, AI-enabled discovery and multi-network library resource sharing systems. His Inter-Search™ hosted services are used by over 500 libraries in Australia and the Asia Pacific region.

Börjeson, Love

Head, KBLab, National Library of Sweden and Senior Researcher at the Stockholm School of Economics. Love has a PhD in organizational economics from Mälardalen University, Vasteras, Sweden, and an MSc from the Stockholm School of Economics. His background includes research in applied language technology at Stanford University Computational Social Science Laboratory. Among his publications are articles on human relations, research policy, and governance. His awards include best paper from the Academy of Management conference.

Bradley, Fiona

Director, Research & Infrastructure, University of New South Wales (UNSW) Library, Sydney. Fiona is a PhD candidate in political science and international relations at the University of Western Australia (UWA) and holds a BA from UWA, and MA and MIM degrees from Curtin University in Perth, Western Australia. She leads the UNSW Library's scholarly communications and repositories, digital and physical infrastructure, and corporate services. She has previously held roles with the International Federation of Library Associations and Institutions (IFLA) and Research Libraries UK representing libraries and their users at global and national levels. Among other appointments Fiona is currently a member of the IFLA AI SIG, has led IFLA's open access working party, chairs the Global Sustainability Coalition for Open Science Services (SCOSS) Advisory Committee supporting investment in open science infrastructure, and is a member of the Executive Committee of Open Access Australasia. She has published and presented on AI regulation and the role of advocacy networks in access to information.

Bultrini, Leda

Leda holds various degrees and qualifications from the University of Rome Tor Vergata and the Sapienza Università di Roma. She has been involved in leading digital transition at the Lazio Regional Environmental Protection Agency in Rome (ARPA) and previously held the position of Director of the Operating Systems and Knowledge Management Division, as well as Director of the Planning, Development, and Internal Control Division and the Education Center at the same agency. She has presided over independent assessment bodies for various public institutions and has been a member of the Board of Directors at the Università degli Studi dell'Aquila in Central Italy. Throughout her career, Leda has been an active member of the Italian Library Association, notably as a long-standing member of the Research Group on Subject Indexing. She has served on several Standing Committees (SC) within IFLA, including the SC on Classification and Indexing, the SC on Knowledge Management with a role as Chair, and the SC on Information Technology.

Chakarova, Juja

Librarian/Information Specialist at the International Atomic Energy Agency (IAEA), Vienna. Juja holds an MSc in electronic information management from Robert Gordon University, Aberdeen, Scotland, an MSc from the Technical University of Sofia, and a BA in library and information science from the State Institute of Librarianship in Bulgaria. Previous positions include the Head of Library at the Max Planck Institute (MPI) Luxembourg for Procedural Law which she established in late 2012. Passionate about innovation, Juja actively promotes the use of robots and AI in libraries. In 2016 she launched LIKE (Lab for Innovation, Knowledge and Exchange at MPI) to test and implement innovative ideas, including robots. She created the library of the Special Tribunal for Lebanon in The Hague, and worked for the Library of the International Criminal Tribunal for Rwanda (ICTR) in Arusha, Tanzania. Her background as librarian, software

engineer and electronic information manager has led to involvement in many library automation projects. Juja has also contributed to innovative projects in energy efficiency, wind energy and ultrafiltration in Stara Zagora, Bulgaria.

Chan, Alex Hok Lam

Library Assistant, Hong Kong Sheng Kung Hu (HKSKH) Ming Hua Theological College Library. Alex is a graduate of the University of Hong Kong and majored in electrical engineering. During his undergraduate studies, he studied computer programming in Python and R, and AI algorithms, such as regression models and neural networks, during his exchange programme at the University of Salzburg, Austria. His research interests are machine learning and deep learning, especially in the application of image analysis and natural language processing. He has assisted in various digital humanities and library user education projects, using computer programming and AI technology. Examples include image classification of seal script using App Inventor and emotion analysis using mBlock. He is passionate about international library collaboration projects, which can promote information technology, cultural heritage and access to knowledge for different types of library users.

Cher. Patrick
Senior Project Manager, Digital and Library Services Group, National Library Board (NLB) Singapore. Patrick has studied information systems management and computing at Singapore Management University and Ngee

Ann Polytechnic. At NLB, he has successfully delivered numerous omni-channel services, focusing on content discovery, search capabilities, and machine learning integration. He collaborates closely with senior management to craft and execute a long-term digital strategy, reshaping the online content and services landscape. An advocate for users, Patrick is dedicated to facilitating the discovery of Singapore's rich cultural heritage and has led the development of OneSearch, which provides access to resources in galleries, libraries, archives, and museums in Singapore. He has also spearheaded open-source geographical information systems (GIS) to enhance researchers' access to high-resolution digitised maps, reducing physical map requests and allowing seamless integration of geo-referenced maps into digital scholarship projects. Patrick has been involved in expanding the NLB mobile app into a compre-hensive learning superstore that leverages data and machine learning to facilitate multimodal content discovery, provide personalised title recommendations, and create learning pathways for lifelong learners. Patrick serves as the Convenor of the Committee of the IFLA Big Data Special Interest Group.

Cheung, Helen Sau Ching
College Librarian, Hong Kong Sheng Kung Hu (HKSKH) Ming Hua Theological College, Adjunct Researcher, Charles Sturt University,

Australia, and affiliated faculty member Virginia Theological Seminary, US. Helen gained a PhD in information and technology studies from the University of Hong Kong and an MLIS from the University of Pittsburgh. Her research interests are digital humanities and technology in education. She enjoys being a librarian and a researcher as her lifelong professional career and has developed several international library projects combining library user education, library collections, technology and partnerships both locally and with overseas countries, such as Japan and Australia. The projects operate across the world and provide the participants with enhanced opportunities for their learning, teaching, and research. Helen's publications include books, journal articles and conference papers covering digital literacy, digital humanities, and the use of AI in education and libraries.

Cox, Andrew

Senior Lecturer, Information School, University of Sheffield, UK. Andrew's PhD from Loughborough University focused on knowledge sharing among web managers in the UK. Much of his current research relates to the information professions and their response to contemporary trends such as AI, datafication and managerialism. He is currently the convenor of the Committee of the IFLA AI Special Interest Group. He is also Chair of the Association for Information Science and Technology (ASIS&T)'s Special Interest Group on AI, SIG-AI. In 2021 he wrote an influential report for the UK library and information association, CILIP: *The Impact of AI, Machine Learning, Automation and Robotics on the Information Professions*.

Elstein, Rael

Senior Product Manager, Ex Libris Group,, part of Clarivate. Rael holds an MBA from the Hebrew University of Jerusalem and a BSc in industrial and management engineering from the Jerusalem College of Engineering. She has extensive experience in product and project management and seeks to negotiate the best fit and best results for the customer community and to ensure customer satisfaction with the company and its values. Rael has been involved in the end-to-end content ingestion lifecycle, product management, project management, and the marketing of Ex Libris products.

Fano, Elena

Knowledge Solution Analyst, Expert.ai, Italy. Elena holds a Master's degree in computational linguistics from Uppsala University and a Master's degree in cognitive science and linguistics from the Università di Siena. She

was formerly on the staff of KBLab at the National Library of Sweden. Elena works with expert systems and large language models and specialises in natural language processing.

Haffenden. Chris

Research Coordinator, KBLab, National Library of Sweden (KB) and Researcher, Department of History of Science and Ideas at Uppsala University. Chris has an MPhil in political thought and intellectual history from Cambridge University and a PhD in the history of science and ideas from Uppsala University. His role at the National Library of Sweden includes supporting research collaboration at KBLab, running workshops on digital methodology, and scientific and popular communication about the use of AI at the library. He is currently also completing a research project on the emergence of self-erasure in the nineteenth century and the longer history of the right to be forgotten. His research interests include memory studies, the history of celebrity, and digital research infrastructure. Recent publications have explored the notion of erasure studies, the emergence of celebrity culture in the Romantic period, and the possibilities of using AI in research libraries and include open access articles in the journals *Memory, Mind & Media* and *College & Research Libraries.*

Hirose, Yoko

President of RapidsWide, and Lecturer part-time in the library science programmes at Tokyo University of Agriculture and Showa University of Music. Yoko holds a BA in library and information science from Keio University and a Master's degree from the University of Pittsburgh. Her current portfolio includes the organisation and facilitation of library tours and the execution of comprehensive marketing research in the domains of public and university libraries. Additionally, she is the author of a book dedicated to enhancing the styling and branding of library professionals. Yoko is actively engaged in delivering lectures that explore various facets of personal style and effective communication strategies within the realm of library professionals.

Kasprzik, Anna
Head, Automation Subject Indexing, Leibniz Information Centre for Science and Technology (ZBW). Anna's PhD was in theoretical computer science from the University of Trier and other studies included linguistics and cognitive psychology at the University of Tübingen. Anna entered the library world via additional

qualifications as a subject librarian through the University Library of Constance and the Bavarian Library Academy and previous employment included the Bavarian State Library and in the Department of Research and Development at the German National Library for Science and Technology (TIB) before commencing at ZBW as the coordinator for the automatisation of subject indexing via machine learning methods. Research interests include both symbolic approaches, such as ontologies, knowledge graphs, and the semantic web, and sub-symbolic approaches from the realm of AI intelligence, and the question of how they might be intertwined in a more fruitful way.

Khamis, Iman

Library Director, Northwestern University in Qatar. Iman is currently enrolled in the EdD programme at Johns Hopkins University and she has a Master's degree in data science from Northwestern University, an MLIS from University College London, and a BEd from Alexandria University. Prior to joining

Northwestern in Qatar, she worked at the Bibliotheca Alexandrina for ten years. Iman's research interests include machine learning and AI in libraries. She is the author of two chapters on the concepts used by data scientists to build chatbots and book recommender systems in the *Handbook of Research on Advancements of Contactless Technology and Service Innovation in Library and Information Science* by Barbara Holland (Hershey Penn.: IGI Global, 2023). Iman is a member of the Committee of the IFLA AI Special Interest Group.

Kim, Bohyun

Associate University Librarian, Library Information Technology, University of Michigan, US. Bohyun holds an MA from Harvard University, an MS(LIS) from Simmons College in Boston, and an MA and BA from Seoul National University, Korea. Previous experience includes Chief Technology Officer and Professor, University of Rhode Island and Associate Director for Library Applications and Knowledge Systems at the University of Maryland. Her research interests lie in emerging technologies and their application in the library context, including AI and machine learning. She has published widely, including "Moving Forward with Digital Disruption: What Big Data, IoT, Synthetic Biology, AI, Blockchain, and Platform Businesses Mean to Libraries"(*Library Technology Reports* 56 no. 2: February/March 2020); "Understanding Gamification" (*Library Technology Reports* 51, no. 2: February/March 2015); "The Library Mobile

Experience: Practices and User Expectations" (*Library Technology Reports* 49, no. 6: August/ September 2013); and many articles. She is a frequent speaker at international and national conferences; a former President of the Library and Information Technology Association (LITA), a division of the American Library Association (ALA); and a member of the Standing Committee of the IFLA Information Technology Section.

Klingwall, Fredrik

Metadata Strategist, National Library of Sweden. Fredrik has a background as a developer and data curator working in the linked data area, primarily with Libris, the Swedish national union catalogue which is natively published in Resource Description Framework (RDF). He works part-time with the KBLab team at the National Library of Sweden in its mission to explore new ways of extracting knowledge from digital collections. Fredrik represents the National Library of Sweden on the Dublin Core™ Metadata Initiative (DCMI) Governing Board.

Korošec, Mojca Rupar
Head, Library Research Department, National and University Library Ljubljana, Slovenia (NUK) and Research Assistant, Liber Europe Data Management Working Group. Mojca holds a PhD from the Faculty of Arts at the University of Ljubljana. Her current research interests are in the area of ethical values of data handling in the information community. She is the author of a chapter reviewing global trends concerning the

ethical approach to data handling in libraries published in the *Handbook of Research on Knowledge and Organization Systems in Library and Information Science* by Barbara Holland (Hershey Penn.: IGI Global, 2021). Mojca is the representative from Slovenia on the European Resource Description & Access (RDA) Interest Group (EURIG) which is the organising body for European representation to the RDA Steering Committee (RSC). Mojca is a member of the Committee of the IFLA AI Special Interest Group.

Kurtz, Robin

Senior Data Scientist, KBLab, National Library of Sweden. Robin's doctoral studies at Linköping University on semantic dependency parsing combined research from theoretical computer science, machine learning and natural language processing. He has co-authored multiple papers in natural language processing journals and conference proceedings and is engaged in developing models on the library's data resources using machine learning, to make them accessible for researchers in the humanities and language technology.

Kwan, Kenny Ka Lam
Formerly part-time Library Assistant at Hong Kong Sheng Kung Hu (HKSKH) Ming Hua Theological College Library (MH Library) before taking up an appointment as a full-time structural engineer. Kenny obtained his Bachelor's and Master's degrees in civil engineering at the Hong Kong University of Science and Technology. During his studies, he gained valuable research experience in the

application of AI to enhancing construction safety. His academic background and hands-on experience at the MH Library in developing mini-AI games have enabled him to widen his outlook on the use of AI in areas such as promoting digital humanities and innovation in studying. He hopes that the mini-AI games might serve as a preliminary study on the use of AI tools in gamification for digital humanities and library user education and also to develop AI games to benefit a broad range of users.

Le Provost, Aline
Librarian, Agence Bibliographique de l'Enseignement Supérieur/Bibliographic Agency for Higher Education (Abes), Montpellier, France. Aline completed a Master of Information and Documentation at the University of Lille in France and also studied at the University of Rennes. She is a metadata specialist and works primarily

on the automatic generation and assessment of links between bibliographic data and authority data. She was part of a team which developed a research project IdRef, Paprika and Qualinka which has been implemented as a toolbox for authority data quality and interoperability and released as open source software.

Lindström, Niklas

Senior Systems and Data Developer, National Library of Sweden, with responsibility for the data modelling and semantic interoperability of the Swedish national union cataloguing system (Libris). He specialises in web and linked data technology to establish wider interoperability, and has been active in the Resource Description Framework (RDF) community since the early 2000s, working on tools and standards such as JavaScript Object Notation for Linked Data (JSON-LD) and RDFa. He is Co-chair of the Dublin Core™ Metadata Initiative (DCMI) Usage Board.

Lundborg, Viktoria
Librarian, National Library of Sweden, and Editor of the thesaurus Swedish Subject Headings (SAO). Viktoria holds a Master's degree in library and information science. She has a background in cataloguing and authority work and is the National Library of Sweden's representative on European and international committees in matters concerning subject headings and genre/form terms.

Malmsten, Martin
Head Data Scientist, KBLab, National Library of Sweden and IT-architect, National Library of Sweden. Martin's background is in computer science and software development. Having

implemented and worked closely with numerous metadata standards and systems, he is a strong supporter of linked open data as a paradigm and a way to connect information. He has worked extensively with, and advocated for, linked data for cultural heritage. His focus for the last couple of years has been on training large language and acoustic models and their application in a library setting. He also works on infrastructure design for machine learning and prototyping.

Nicolas, Yann
Head, Le labo, Agence bibliographique de l'enseignement supérieur (Abes)/Bibliographic Agency for Higher Education, Montpellier, France. Yann holds an MPhil from the University

of Nantes and after studying and teaching philosophy became a metadata librarian at Abes in 2003. He has applied the most recent technologies to university bibliographic data to integrate, enrich and disseminate the data, and facilitate the design and creation of services to meet users' needs. He has striven to maintain the link between innovative technical solutions and strategic thinking and led and contributed to many applications and projects developed by Abes with a strong focus on authority data and a semantic web approach. As head of the Abes lab, Yann now gives priority to efforts to enhance Abes data and services with AI.

Potter, Abigail

Senior Innovation Specialist, and founding member of LCLabs, Library of Congress, Washington DC. Abigail has an MSI from the University of Michigan School of Information in digital preservation and human-computer interactions, and a BA from Western Michigan University. LCLabs is a digital innovation team in

the Office of the Chief Information Officer at the Library of Congress. Abigail has a background in digitisation, publishing, digital preservation and international network building and has been with the Library of Congress since 2006. Prior to that she worked at National Public Radio, the University of Michigan Library and the Bulletin of the Atomic Scientists.

Prabhakar, Annu
Professor, School of Information Technology, University of Cincinnati. Annu holds a PhD in human computer interaction and design, and health informatics, and a Master's degree in informatics, from Indiana University, Bloomington, and an MS from Mississippi State University. Her research intersects interaction design, health informatics, diversity, equity,

and inclusion (DEI), and AI. Her scholarly work has been presented at both national and international conferences sponsored by leading organisations including the Special Interest Group on Computer–Human Interaction of the Association for Computing Machinery (ACM SIGCHI), the Institute of Electrical and Electronics Engineers Connected Health: Applications, Systems and Engineering Technologies (IEEE CHASE), and Pervasive Health, and she has garnered multiple awards.

Rekathati, Faton
Data scientist, KBLab, National Library of Sweden. Faton holds a Master of Science in Statistics from Linköping University. He works at the National Library of Sweden on improving

searchability and accessibility of the library's collections.

Riep, Josette

Assistant Vice President, Integrated Data, Engineering and Applications, University of Cincinnati, US. Josette holds an MS(IT) from the University and is a PhD Student in the School

of Information Technology where her research focuses on the use of AI and machine learning to create bias-free services and structures specifically in the area of Science, Technology, Engineering and Medicine (STEM) education. At the University, Josette is responsible for the development of information technology innovations and partnerships. She is committed to creating a more inclusive environment within STEM through the discovery of AI driven pathways for success and to creating an environment that does not tolerate but embraces difference and empowers individuals and organisations to excel.

Saccucci, Caroline

Chief, US Programs, Law, and Literature Division, Library of Congress, US. Caroline holds an MS(LIS)

from Simmons University in Boston, and a BA in history from Longwood University. She is responsible for managing the operations of four key programmes at the Library of Congress: Cataloging in Publication (CIP), Dewey Decimal Classification (DDC), International Standard Serial Number (ISSN), and Children's and Young Adults' Cataloging (CYAC). She is the US representative to the ISSN Governing Board, Chair of the Standing Committee of the IFLA Subject Analysis and Access Section (SAA), and Convenor of the Automated Indexing Working Group of SAA. Caroline has written or coauthored articles published in *Cataloging & Classification Quarterly, Library Resources & Technical Services*, and *JLIS.it: Italian Journal of Library, Archives and Information Science*.

Tshabalala, Neli

Director, Shared Library and Information Services, North-West (NWU) University, Potchefstroom, South Africa. Neli holds an MS (LIS) from Clark Atlanta University, Atlanta, Ga. US, a BEd from the University of Zululand, honours in library and information science from the University of KwaZulu-Natal, and project management qualifications from the University of South Africa. Her background is in library resource management, systems and operations involving administration services, fiscal management, and special projects management. Previous positions include the Senior Manager at the National Library for the Blind in South Africa, and the Director, Operations and Collection Management at the University of Johannesburg. Neli has been heavily involved in IFLA activities including the third IFLA Artificial Intelligence Symposium which was hosted by NWU, and the IFLA IT Section. She has served as a member of the Standing Committee of the IFLA Libraries Serving People with Print Disabilities Section and is currently a member of the Committee of the IFLA Big Data Special Interest Group.

Uzwyshyn, Raymond

Director of Research Services, University of California, Riverside. Raymond holds a PhD in media studies from New York University, an MBA in information technology management from the American Public University, and an MLIS from the University of Western Ontario. Previously he served as Director of Collections and Digital Services, Texas State University Libraries, other related roles at Mississippi State and Texas State University, and the American Public University System, University of West Florida Libraries and the University of Miami. Raymond has chaired the Association of Information Science & Technology (ASIS&T) Special Interest Group for Visualization, Images and Sound (SIG-VIS),

served as a reviewer for the Bill & Melinda Gates Foundation, currently serves on the IFLA Information Technology Section Standing Committee and is editor of the Section's newsletter, *Trends and Issues in Library Technology (TILT)*. Raymond's interests include artificial intelligence, research data repositories, digital scholarly research ecosystems, online education, multimedia digital libraries, learning commons and new IT infrastructure implementation.

Veltzman, Itai
Director, Product Management, Ex Libris Group, part of Clarivate. Itai leads the cross products and innovation group in the Library Solutions business unit at Ex Libris. His main responsibilities are to promote new services and infrastructure in the areas of analytics and AI, linked open data, user experience, openness, security and privacy. Itai's previous experience was with the Alma system. He strongly

believes in true user-centric collaboration and partnership with the customers community. It is all about the data, how it is managed and how it is presented. He is seeking to increase and develop his expertise in library management systems, especially linked open data.

Zaragoza, Thomas

Intern, le labo, Agence bibliographique de l'enseignement supérieur (Abes)/Bibliographic Agency for Higher Education, Montpellier, France. Thomas holds a BUT degree in computing science and a Master's degree specialising in the field of data science from

the University of Montpellier. His work has focused on the application of machine learning approaches to data quality issues of a bibliographical nature. Thomas is currently enrolled as a doctoral student at the Laboratoire Informatique de l'Université de Pau et des Pays de l'Adour (LIUPPA) focusing on green IT in reducing software energy consumption through behavioural change.+